DATE DUE			

COUNT WITTE

and the Tsarist Government

in the 1905 Revolution

INDIANA UNIVERSITY

INTERNATIONAL STUDIES

COUNT WITTE

and the Tsarist Government

in the 1905 Revolution

HOWARD D. MEHLINGER

A N D

JOHN M. THOMPSON

Indiana University Press

Bloomington / London

Published in Canada by Fitzhenry & Whiteside Limited,
Don Mills, Ontario

Library of Congress catalog card number: 77–165048

ISBN: 0–253–31470–4

Manufactured in the United States of America

Contents

[v

Contents

Preface

THE ORIGINS AND MOTIVES OF A SCHOLARLY STUDY are not always pertinent to its concept and theme, but in this case they are. Moreover, a joint study is quite rare in American historical scholarship, and a word explaining how our collaboration came about is needed.

In the course of teaching a seminar on modern Russia from 1894 to 1921 at Indiana University during the early 1960's co-author Thompson became interested in two comparative aspects of the revolutions of 1905 and 1917: the differing roles of the rank-and-file members of the armed forces (basically loyal and revolutionary, respectively) and the difficulties faced by the tsarist government in 1905 and the Provisional Government in 1917. As a beginning, therefore, to what was originally planned as a brief comparative interpretation of the two revolutions (within the framework of the comparative study of modern social revolutions in general) Thompson began in 1961–62 to investigate the roles of the army and navy and of the government as a whole in the Russian revolution of 1905. It soon turned out, however, that little basic research on these topics had been done by Western scholars. As a consequence, Thompson was led into thorough study of these questions based on primary sources and on what little work on them Russian and Soviet scholars had completed. In the spring of 1964 Thompson spent six months in the Soviet Union as a research scholar in the academic exchange between the American Council of Learned Societies and the U.S.S.R. Academy of Science (Institute of History), and was able to gather material from the Soviet archives with almost complete cooperation from the Soviet side.

He soon discovered that the answer to the first question that had interested him—the role of the armed forces—was comparatively simple. Despite some minor and occasionally troublesome mutinies in the army and navy, well publicized because they were dramatic and later overemphasized to reinforce Soviet revolutionary mythology, the bulk of the armed forces was generally not politicized in the revolution of 1905 and remained loyal to the government (see chaps. 3 and 4). Since the mutineers' complaints stemmed most often from local grievances, conditions of service, and a generalized desire to be demobilized, the soldiers and sailors as a whole never became a truly revolutionary force (though their superiors had some qualms on this score), and they proved a reliable instrument for suppressing the revolution in the winter of 1905–06 (see chap. 5). Moreover, Thompson discovered that a Soviet scholar, V. A. Petrov, with whom he met in Leningrad, was just completing a detailed monograph on the subject, using in part military archives not accessible to Thompson. Therefore, Thompson dropped that line of investigation and concentrated on government policy, primarily in the period of the prime ministership of Count Sergei Witte, from October 1905 to April 1906—that is, from the October Manifesto to the opening of the First Duma—and on the elections to the First Duma, which had not been studied in the West.

During that same year, and unbeknownst to each other, Mehlinger was completing a doctoral dissertation at the University of Kansas, utilizing the extensive documents published by Soviet scholars in the 1920's and 1950's. The dissertation was entitled "Count Sergei Iu. Witte and the Problems of Constitutionalism in Russia in 1905–1906." Mehlinger's interest in the topic had grown out of an earlier investigation of the 1905 pogroms and their relationship to the revolutionary events of the period. The difficulty he encountered in sorting out and in validating many charges and countercharges leveled against the government with regard to the pogroms led him to a more general inquiry into the seriousness with which the government sought to carry through the reforms promised by the October 17 Manifesto. In particular, he became interested in Count Witte, especially in his effort to undertake political reform while striving to reestablish order.

In 1965 Mehlinger moved to Indiana University and our mutual interest was at once discovered. We decided to pool our research to produce in collaboration a major study of government policy in the revolution of 1905, but because of other commitments on both our parts we were unable to begin work on the manuscript until 1968.

We believe such a study is justified for two reasons: First, the great majority of both Soviet and Western writing on the revolution of 1905 has treated the events of that period from the viewpoint of the revolutionary and oppositionist movements, which have been studied, documented, and analyzed in some detail. (See, for example, in our bibliography secondary works by Anweiler, Erman, Fischer, Iakovlev, Keep, Schapiro, Schwarz, Spiridonov, Treadgold, and Wolfe.) The revolution has never been viewed in depth from the vantage point of the government: how did it react, what did it do, what was it hoping to achieve, how sincere were its reform efforts, in what ways did it succeed and fail? We believe that this is an important and instructive part of the story, in terms of the 1905 revolution itself and its effects on subsequent Russian history, as well as in the context of a clearer understanding of the general nature and process of modern social revolutions, particularly in developing countries. Second, despite an excellent brief article by von Laue published in 1958, no full-scale attempt has been made to analyze the leading role of Count Witte during the crisis of the revolution. Much of the interpretation of Witte's policies in this period has come from the pens of his enemies or from the writings of radical and liberal memoirists and historians, most of whom have naturally been very critical.[1] We have deliberately tried to avoid "rehabilitating" Witte, but we hope, on the other hand, that our study presents a more balanced interpretation of his role, one which takes due account of the overwhelming difficulties he faced, the major and often enlightened effort he made, and the reasons for his ultimate failure.

Moreover, as our collaboration progressed in discussion and writing, we became convinced that beyond the fascinating questions connected with Witte's enigmatic actions and character and with the personal and political tragedy of his rule, the study has broader implications concerning the difficulties of "reform from above" in a revolutionary situation. The moderate reformer is caught in a revolutionary crisis between the millstones of the popular desire for radical change and the conservative demand for the preservation of order and for retention of the best of the old system. The dilemma posed seems particularly crucial, and perhaps insoluble, when the society is a developing one undergoing profound and rapid political, economic, social, and cultural change, as Russia was in 1905 and as many nations of Asia, Africa, and Latin

America are today. We hope our study throws some light on the problems of modernization and revolution, at least from the standpoint of the government's role.

In 1965 our research was stimulated when the Witte papers held at the Archive of Russian and East European History and Culture at Columbia University were opened to scholars. For our period the papers added relatively little new and unpublished material, although a few interesting letters and memoranda were found. Most of the documents on 1905 and 1906 in the Witte papers are included in Witte's memoirs (Witte obviously used the papers in composing his memoirs), or have been published in various Soviet collections. The manuscript versions of his memoirs (one written in St. Petersburg, one in France) are among the papers, but for our period no significant differences with the published Russian version were found (see the introduction by A. L. Sidorov to the 1960 Soviet reprinting of Witte's memoirs for an account of how they were compiled and for the history of their printing).

Throughout the study dates are given in the Old Style, or Julian, calendar, which was used in Russia until February 1918, and which in the twentieth century was thirteen days behind the New Style, or Gregorian, calendar used in the West. Thus the October Manifesto was dated October 17 in Old Style, October 30 in New Style.

Transliteration from Cyrillic to Roman characters is based on a modified Library of Congress system (without diacritic marks, with "v" for "g" in certain masculine and neuter genitive singular adjectival endings). Proper names have been transliterated according to popular usage, e.g., Witte instead of Vitte.

In every respect this study is a joint effort. Although Mehlinger originally drafted the majority of the chapters, they were then expanded and revised on the basis of Thompson's research. Chapters one and two are primarily Mehlinger's four and eight primarily Thompson's, but throughout, each chapter has been revised and rewritten at various times by both authors. All the main ideas and conclusions have been discussed and agreed upon by both. Based on our experience, we find joint authorship a stimulating and efficient way to work, which should probably be used more often in American scholarly writing.

Acknowledgments

B OTH AUTHORS WISH TO EXPRESS THEIR DEEP APPRECIATION to the following individuals whose generous assistance helped make this study possible: Professor Philip E. Mosely for permission to use the Witte Papers and other materials in the Archive of Russian and East European History and Culture at Columbia University; Mr. Lev Magerovsky, curator of that Archive, for cheerful and valuable counsel and help in using it; the librarians of Indiana and Columbia Universities; Mr. Eugene Michaels for useful bibliographic searching in post-1960 materials; and, above all, Carolee Mehlinger for faultless and uncomplaining typing of the whole manuscript.

We are also grateful to Indiana University for a research grant-in-aid during 1967–68, which enabled us to review recent materials and to travel to libraries on the East Coast.

Mehlinger wishes to thank the University of Chicago for permission to examine relevant materials in the Samuel N. Harper Archive and librarians at Carnegie-Mellon University and at the universities of Kansas and Pittsburgh.

Mehlinger owes a special debt to Professor Oswald P. Backus III of the University of Kansas. Professor Backus introduced him to Count Witte and the 1905 Russian revolution, counseled him throughout his graduate work, supervised his dissertation, "Count Sergei Iu. Witte and the Problems of Constitutionalism in Russia 1905–1906," and encouraged him to continue his research on Witte in order to complete this book.

Thompson acknowledges with gratitude research fellowships from the Committee on International Studies of Indiana University in 1963–64, when his study of this subject was launched, from the American Council of Learned Societies and the U.S.S.R. Academy of Sciences in the spring of 1964, which permitted his participation in the exchange of scholars between the United States and the Soviet Union and the gathering of materials for this book in Soviet libraries and archives, and from the Guggenheim Memorial Foundation in 1968–69, when a final revision of the book was completed.

Thompson wishes also to thank the librarians at the American Academy in Rome, the University of Helsinki, the Fundamental Library of the Social Sciences of the U.S.S.R. Academy of Sciences, and the State Public Historical Library of the U.S.S.R., as well as archivists at the Central State Historical Archive in Leningrad and the Central State Archive of the October Revolution in Moscow —all for generous and pleasant assistance which often went well beyond that normally required by their position.

In addition, Thompson is especially indebted to the following individuals: Professor Philip E. Mosely, in whose seminar at the Russian Institute of Columbia University in 1950 Thompson first became interested in the revolution of 1905 and who consistently encouraged him to develop and carry forward this study; A. Ia. Avrekh of the Institute of History of the U.S.S.R. Academy of Sciences, who in the spring of 1964 facilitated Thompson's research arrangements in the Soviet Union, including access to archives, and who provided friendly but sharp criticism of many of the major approaches and conclusions of this study; Soviet scholars, B. V. Anan'ich, R. Sh. Ganelin, A. L. Gukovskii, V. A. Petrov, and M. N. Simonova, all of whom were friendly and helpful in consultations and interviews; J. H. L. Keep of the University of London and Geoffrey Hosking of the University of Essex, with whom the study was discussed at some length on various occasions; Ned Bayne and Joan Curtis of the Center for Mediterranean Studies in Rome, who provided pleasant quarters and necessary encouragement during final revision of the manuscript; and Father Gustav Wetter of the Russicum of the Oriental Institute in Rome, who generously opened his library for some last-minute checking of sources and footnotes.

COUNT WITTE

and the Tsarist Government

in the 1905 Revolution

I

INTRODUCTION

For if we will think of it, no time need have gone to ruin, could it have found a man great enough, a man wise and good enough; wisdom to discern truly what the time wanted, valor to lead it on the right road thither; these are the salvation of any time.

—Thomas Carlyle
Heroes, Hero-Worship

The Time

To the casual observer Russia in 1900 resembled the Russia of a century before. As in the past, society was divided legally and socially into three broad groups: nobility, burghers, and peasants. Each member of these estates registered with the appropriate local body or institution. Each estate enjoyed separate and unequal privileges. Over them all ruled the Russian autocracy that had remained remarkably unaffected by Western liberal theories. A. A. Mossolov, head of the Court Chancellery to Nicholas II and an ardent admirer of the autocratic idea, defined Russian autocracy in the first decade of the twentieth century in the same way as his predecessors had generations before.

At the head of all stands the Sovereign, the autocrat. Below him, teeming and inchoate, is the struggling mass of his subjects. In order that Russia may live in entire tranquillity and content, all that is necessary is that there shall be direct relations between the Sovereign and his subjects.

The Tsar can do no wrong; he stands above classes, party politics, and personal rivalries. He desires the good of his people, and has

[3

practically unlimited means for achieving it. He seeks nothing for himself; he has a profound love of all those whom God has confined to his supreme care. There is no reason why he should not be the benefactor of each and all. All that is wanted is that he should know exactly what his people need.

The subjects love the Tsar, for he is the source of all their well-being. They cannot fail to love the Sovereign, for no other feeling is possible toward Beneficence personified.[1]

Such a conception of the state could include no provision for political parties, constitutions, and parliaments. These could only disturb the unique relationship between the tsar and his subjects. Russian autocracy was a political system based on trust and confidence. The subjects maintained faith in the essential goodness of the tsar; the tsar relied upon the loyalty of his subjects. The tsar ruled in the interests of all; his subjects toiled to provide the means to support the state. Moreover, Russian autocracy was absolute. In theory, all initiative and responsibility rested with the tsar; in practice, no tsar was able to coordinate all the activities of government, thereby leaving considerable opportunity for government advisers, ministers, and civil servants to maneuver and to pursue independent policies. The legion of bureaucrats that extended the power and authority of the central government into every village of the empire was known for its corruption, arrogance, and incompetence. Many regarded the *chinovnik* ("bureaucrat") as the chief obstacle to progress and reform, the Slavophiles and peasants seeing him as someone who stood between the tsar and the people and who prevented the Little Father from understanding the problems of the people and from acting to resolve them, the liberals viewing him as the usurper of functions that should rightfully belong to elected representatives of the people.

Within the government itself there was no institution comparable to the cabinet system that had evolved in Western Europe. The tsar was his own prime minister. The ministers, who met together infrequently as an advisory body in the Committee of Ministers, were, however, individually responsible directly to the tsar. There was also a Council of Ministers that met at the call of the tsar and was presided over by him, but it provided only a forum for the exchange of views and did not serve to formulate or execute policy jointly. The State Council and the Senate were the two other major organs of the central government. The State Council, composed of an unlimited number of members appointed by the tsar, met periodically to advise him on legislation and to confirm laws and decrees, but it had no independent legislative or executive role. The Senate, first established by Peter the Great in 1711 and the oldest of the several organs of the central government, had largely judicial responsibilities.

For purposes of administration, Russia was divided into forty-nine gubernias or provinces plus some special regions, each in turn usually divided into uezds or districts and these into volosts or cantons. The representative of the central government in each gubernia was a governor, or governor-general, appointed by the tsar and immediately responsible to the Ministry of Internal Affairs. The governors maintained order and reported unusual problems to the minister of Interior to be ultimately brought to the attention of the tsar. Except for certain activities that were the direct responsibility of a central ministry and certain local activities reserved for local units of government, each governor was the authority in his province. In thirty-four gubernias certain aspects of administration at the provincial and district levels were in the hands of the zemstvo, an organ of elected self-government created in 1864 as one of the "great reforms" of Alexander II. Through the years a suspicious central government had periodically encroached on the zemstvo's authority. However, the concerns of the zemstvo remained basically the same—roadbuilding, hospital and medical care, education, and famine relief. To pay for these activities zemstvos were permitted to collect local taxes on real estate and business establishments. In many cities there were also municipal dumas, elected assemblies concerned with local affairs.

Over this governmental system presided, at the beginning of the twentieth century, Tsar Nicholas II, last of the Romanov dynasty, who ruled Russia from 1894 to his abdication in 1917. Nicholas II is a tragic figure in Russian history.[2] He had many qualities one could admire in a man—a deep sense of responsibility to his position, a genuine concern for the welfare of his country and people, loyalty to his friends, and a profound affection for his family. Yet he lacked many of the traits required for bold and forthright leadership. He had little ability to analyze problems and to synthesize policy.[3] He lacked decisiveness and feared controversy, often appearing to agree with a minister and then later discharging him in writing.[4] He distrusted intellectuals and independent thinkers, preferring to surround himself with people of intelligence no greater than his own, which was average.[5] He was withdrawn and impersonal, almost aloof, outside his family. He was a poor judge of people and often relied upon courtiers and mystics who were pursuing only personal advantage. He shied away from cold calculation and reasoned choices, preferring to rely on instinct and intuition to guide him to fulfill his duty and destiny before God and his Romanov predecessors. Finally, he was often stubborn and irrational when a problem called for compromise and calm judgment. When most in doubt over a decision he tended to fall back on the slogan, "I am absolute and I answer only to God."[6]

In political and social outlook Nicholas II was more intent on looking backward than forward. He was obsessed with the autocratic idea as it was left by his domineering father.[7] Such a man, committed as he was to the past, was not the one to encourage Russia's break with tradition; Nicholas was "anti-capitalist, anti-modern and inwardly resentful of the changes in Russian life he could not grasp."[8] The political, social, and economic changes that affected many facets of Russian society during his reign also undermined absolutism. He was not a ruler who could easily accept or cope with such changes.

Despite Nicholas' disapproval, by the close of the nineteenth century Russia was in the throes of rapid economic and social development that amounted to revolution and that ultimately was to have far-reaching implications for the entire fabric of Russian society and life.[9] In her desire to be like the West industrially, Russia was forced to become more like the West in other ways. Industrialization required new forms of social organization. And as the pace of economic and social change grew, from Western Europe came new doctrines—pragmatism, liberalism, and Marxism —that were to clash with tsarism's creed of Orthodoxy, autocracy, and nationalism. Under the stimulus of this interplay and hastened by the pressure of new socio-economic demands, political consciousness and activity blossomed forth at the turn of the century. To be sure, although Russian autocracy did not tolerate the existence of political parties, there had been no lack of political thought and debate in nineteenth-century Russia. Political consciousness, however, was the monopoly of the educated few; the great mass of the Russian population went about its daily tasks unaware of the intellectual debate going on in the parlors of its social superiors. Not all well-educated Russians, of course, were caught up in the intellectual maelstrom. Some served the court loyally and faithfully, tended to their estates, or pursued their professions without becoming involved in the great debates. Yet, it was difficult for an educated Russian to compare his semifeudal country with the rapidly advancing states of Western Europe without becoming deeply concerned.

By 1900 this concern, in conditions of rapid economic change and marked social upheaval and of growing communication and education, had begun to affect broader segments of Russian society than the intelligentsia. Moreover, the situation of the newly industrialized workers and of the semiemancipated but fecund and land-hungry peasants was becoming desperate. Thus, the moment was ripe for a new and more effective outburst of political debate and action. Most of the political theories current in nineteenth-century Russia had proven ineffectual. The populists, who favored a moral regeneration of society through education and agrarian socialism, had been the dominant influence in the 1870's but the resort of some of their adherents to terror, culminating in the assassination of Alexander II in 1881, had led to severe repression and the partial discrediting of populist ideas. Thus, in the early twentieth century the three chief ideological competitors in the political arena were Marxism, a regenerated and reformed populism, and liberalism of the Western stamp. Surprisingly, both the ideals and the force of Russian conservatism were poorly represented in political action at this time, though a minor effort was launched in 1905, centered on the Union of Russian People, and though conservative views were widespread among leaders of the central government and throughout the bureaucracy.

In March 1898, the Russian Marxists attempted to unify their efforts by establishing the Russian Social Democratic Labor party. This effort was more formal than real as eight of the nine delegates were arrested shortly after this First Congress. At the Second Congress, held July–August 1903 in Brussels and London, the party first divided into its two factions: the Bolsheviks led by Lenin and the Mensheviks. Although both Lenin and the Mensheviks agreed that Russia was a backward state, in which a bourgeois revolution, spearheaded by the "vanguard" of the proletariat, should take place, on other issues their differences were acute. Each looked for allies; the Mensheviks found theirs in the bourgeois liberals;

Lenin distrusted the liberals and relied principally upon landless peasants to support the proletariat. The Mensheviks hoped to attract broad masses to the party. Lenin wanted an elite party consisting of only the most disciplined and dedicated revolutionaries. After the Second Congress a struggle for control of the party took place, and by 1905 the Bolsheviks dominated party committees in St. Petersburg, Moscow, Riga, and Odessa, while the Mensheviks controlled those in Kiev, Kharkov, Rostov, and Ekaterinoslav. Each tried to organize separate committees in the other's strongholds.[10]

Another radical party which appeared in the last decade of the nineteenth century was the Socialist-Revolutionary party, which traced its origins to and carried forward the tradition of the populist movement of the *Narodniki* and of the *Narodnaia voila* of the 1870's. In the 1880's and 1890's populism was in decline while Marxism was gaining in influence. Near the turn of the century, however, some of the former populists began to meet in small groups and to refer to themselves as Socialist Revolutionaries to distinguish themselves from the Social Democrats. Although the Socialist Revolutionaries did not hold their first party congress until December 1905, in 1901 the most important Socialist-Revolutionary groups merged to form the Socialist-Revolutionary party, and a party journal, *Revoliutsionnaia rossiia* [Revolutionary Russia], was published abroad. In view of the populist origin of most of its leaders, it is understandable that the party placed its hopes on the class of society it knew best—the peasants. The party was committed to socialism and mass revolution but not through capitalism. For the Socialist Revolutionaries the basis for Russian socialism was to be the peasant commune. Although they ignored neither the urban proletariat nor students, they were more interested in the villages than in the cities.

Like the Social Democrats the Socialist Revolutionaries expected and prepared for a mass revolution. But unlike the Social Democrats, who at that time considered political assassinations to be "unscientific," the Socialist Revolutionaries accepted terror as a tactic that helped pave the way for popular insurrection. The *Boevaia organizatsiia*, the "combat brigade," was founded as an autonomous part of the Socialist-Revolutionary party in 1901. Some members of the brigade engaged in terror to further the goals of the party; others were in reality anarchists who believed in terror for its own sake. From 1902 until 1907 the terrorist brigade was active, and was directly responsible for the assassinations of V. K. von Plehve, minister of Interior, on July 15, 1904, and of the tsar's uncle, Grand Duke Sergei Aleksandrovich, on February 4, 1905.[11]

In addition to the radical political groups that emerged in the last decade of the nineteenth century, a liberal movement developed that may be traced from the establishment of the zemstvos in 1864. Russian liberals were quite unlike the middle-class liberals of Western Europe since liberalism in Russia was at first confined almost entirely to the gentry class. Gentry liberals were men in financially and socially secure positions of Russian society.[12] Consequently, they tended to be reformist and philanthropic; rather than advocating *laissez faire* doctrines, they called for government interference to correct social injustice.

Liberalism developed as a political philosophy among the members of the zemstvo for two main reasons. First, the zemstvo was the chief participatory political institution tolerated in Russia. Even then, the zemstvoists were supposed to refrain from engaging in political discussions beyond the concerns of their local area. Second, despite this restriction, members of the gentry active in government at the local level became anxious to discuss, and participate in the solution of, national problems. The zemstvos, therefore, posed a potential threat to the autocratic government, a threat that was difficult to meet. If the zemstvos were abolished, the central government would have to assume the zemstvo functions at the local level. If they were permitted to continue, the experience in local self-government would lead to a desire for self-government at the national level.[13]

The zemstvo was important not only for the many members of the gentry who became interested in social and political reform. Attached to each zemstvo were numerous professionals—doctors, lawyers, teachers, agronomists, and statisticians, who were in constant contact with the masses and appreciated their problems.[14] This so-called third element—the other two being elected zemstvo officials and government bureaucrats—was more open to appeals from radical groups and tended to pull the zemstvos leftward. This gradual lean to the left was to change the nature of the liberal drive in Russia from an interest in a consultative assembly to a demand for a legislative assembly, from a desire to strengthen the zemstvos and to form equivalents at the national level to a call for

[9

a national Duma, and from avowals of loyalty to the monarchy to an active flirtation with radical parties.

The zemstvos' political activity peaked from November 6–9, 1904, when the First Zemstvo Congress met in Moscow. This was a period of a momentary lull in the government's repression of opposition groups, and although it did not sanction the congress, it agreed not to interfere. More than one hundred delegates from thirty-three of the thirty-four gubernias having zemstvos met in private homes to discuss common problems. At the end of the congress an eleven-point call for reform was agreed upon. Most of the points called for an extension of civil rights; the tenth point asked for popular participation in an elected, legislative institution; and the eleventh point appealed to the tsar to call "together freely elected representatives of the people to lead the fatherland . . . on a new path of state development."[15] A minority, led by D. N. Shipov, preferred a consultative assembly, but those favoring a legislative assembly carried the day and also contributed to a future split in the liberal movement.

Another impulse to the liberal movement came from the "banquet campaign" in November 1904, planned ostensibly to commemorate the fortieth anniversary of the "great reforms." In major Russian cities various professionals—lawyers, journalists, professors, members of the "third element"—held banquets. The series of banquets extended over a two-week period beginning November 21, and each banquet concluded by passing a resolution demanding a constitution.[16] Members of the various professions also formed professional unions that were joined together in a Union of Unions on May 8, 1905, under the leadership of Paul Miliukov, an historian and future leader of the liberal Kadet party.[17]

The rise of political organizations and activity, both liberal and radical, could not have offered a serious threat to the government, however, had it not coincided with growing distress among the masses of the population in both the cities and the peasant villages. The industrialization of Russia brought more and more workers from the village to the city to work in factories. Wages were low, and living and working conditions abominable. A composite picture of the average factory worker in 1897 showed him to be a male worker, either single or living apart from his family because he could not afford to bring them to the city, who in most cases held some land in the village of his origin and who was still liable for assessments in his commune. His ties to the village were thus strong, and the commune continued to provide both security and companionship for him.[18] Both strikes and unions were prohibited by law. In 1902 workers' associations were organized by the police under the direction of Sergei V. Zubatov in an attempt to wean workers away from revolutionary organizations, but these were eventually abandoned as being too dangerous; in addition, the industrialists were violently opposed to them.

Much of the difficulty with labor was a result of the ambivalence of government attitudes on this question. In the Ministry of Finance two concurrent policies conflicted with each other. One was aimed at the rapid industrialization of Russia, which required providing industry with cheap labor. The second policy reflected the desire of Minister of Finance Sergei Iu. Witte to transform the peasant from a communal-bound individual to a free agent able to enter into labor contracts and to join with his fellow employees in mutual association to press his demands. The second policy inevitably clashed with the first, which soon won out. In the Ministry of Interior there was also a conflict in attitudes. On the one hand the minister of Interior asked for and received more police to quell labor disturbances. On the other hand there was an evident concern for the plight of workers and a desire to help them, as the Zubatov idea showed.[19] The inability of the government to develop a consistent and effective policy toward labor helped open the way to the successful spread among workers of propaganda of the revolutionary parties. Strikes, which in Russia were relatively unknown as well as illegal, grew in number from 68 affecting 31,195 workers in 1895 to 13,995 affecting 2,886,173 workers in 1905. Thus in 1905 ninety-three percent of Russian factories were affected by strikes.[20]

Despite the growing importance of the urban proletariat, the vast majority of the Russian population at the turn of the century remained peasants. Agriculture was still the main basis of the Russian economy: more than four-fifths of the population was employed in it; agricultural products were the principal export and source of foreign exchange; and two-thirds of all work in factories and mills was devoted the refinement of agricultural goods.[21]

However, the last years of the nineteenth and the opening years of the twentieth century saw important changes taking place in the countryside. By 1905, although Russian agriculture in general had prospered since 1861, certain regions were undergoing steady impoverishment. Taken as a whole, the Russian Empire could hardly be said to have been overpopulated; but population growth did tend to undermine the vitality of some provinces. The rapid increase in peasant population caused the average size of land holdings per peasant household to fall from 13.2 desiatins (one desiatin equals 2.70 acres) in 1877 to 10.4 desiatins in 1905. Consequently, in those regions where population growth was rapid and industry was relatively undeveloped, a serious depression and occasional famine began to be felt in the countryside.[22] Especially hard hit were certain provinces in the central black-soil region.

Besides a shortage of land for the peasants, the low level of rural technology and the social organization of the peasantry in the commune contributed importantly to rural poverty and to the growing agricultural crisis around 1900. The Emancipation Act of 1861 had freed the serf from the landlord, but the peasant continued to be shackled to the commune, the traditional administrative and fiscal organization of village life, which by 1905 had become a drag on the agricultural economy. Periodic redistribution of land, practiced in so-called repartitional communes, contributed to overpopulation as the large families seemed to gain an unfair advantage from redistribution. Furthermore, the peasant had little incentive to improve his land when redistribution might force him to turn it over to another. It was difficult to introduce new techniques and new technology for to do so required the assent of the majority of the commune, who usually preferred traditional and primitive methods. Customary practices also interfered with efficient farming. Common grazing privileges were destructive to fields and meadows. Scattered strip farming was wasteful as it forced farmers to cultivate in the same way, using the same pattern of rotation. The strips were often so narrow that it made the use of machinery impracticable and it required plowing in ways that contributed to soil erosion. Remote strips could not be manured; land set aside for boundaries could not be cultivated; and peasants wasted time going from one field to another.[23]

All attempts by the government to solve rural problems ultimately faced the same two dilemmas. The principal grievance of the peasants was economic, but it also had social overtones. Thus, one possible remedy was abolition of the commune and transformation of the peasants into small, private landholders, who would presumably farm the land more efficiently. But such a solution required destruction of a traditional institution beloved of the Slavophiles, and regarded by conservatives as an important bulwark of political and social order. A second fundamental approach was to provide much more land to the peasants that they might till in traditional ways. Yet to do this involved confiscation of the larger and often more productive estates, thereby threatening agricultural production itself not to mention the destruction of the rural noble class. A government that derived its most reliable support from the landowning nobility found it difficult to contemplate such a drastic action.

On February 6, in the village of Kholzovki in Kursk province, the first major agrarian disturbances of 1905 took place, though there had been periodic uprisings throughout the nineteenth century and serious disorders in 1902–03. From there rural rebellion spread to other provinces. In most places it involved illegal timber cutting and pasturing, and sometimes rent and labor strikes. There was very little general pillaging or outright seizure of land during the first eight months of the year. The most notable exceptions were in Poland and the Baltic provinces, where nationalism was mixed with economic grievances and where some burning of manorial estates took place. In the summer of 1905 a rudimentary national organization of rebellious peasant intellectuals came into being at the First Congress of the All-Russian Peasants' Union. The congress did not demand the overthrow of the monarchy, but it called for the abolition of private property. Under the influence of the Socialist-Revolutionary party the Peasants' Union became increasingly radical during 1905. Its efforts to mobilize and direct peasant discontent against the government met with mixed success in a rural rebellion that was largely economically motivated and basically anarchic and disorganized, but it undoubtedly reflected the desperation and hostility toward society many peasants felt.[24]

Another less widespread but nonetheless significant factor contributing to the rapid development of a revolutionary situation in 1904 and 1905 was the growth of nationalist sentiment and anti-government agitation among the non-Russian peoples of the empire, particularly in Poland, Finland, and the Baltic provinces, but to some extent also among the Ukrainians, Caucasians, and Islamic groups in various parts of the tsardom. Usually beginning as a movement for cultural autonomy in opposition to traditional tsarist policies of Russification and religious intolerance, nationalistic activity began to acquire after 1900 social and political goals, often liberal, sometimes radical, but almost always united in struggle against Russian centralized rule from St. Petersburg and against tsarist political oppression. By 1904 unrest among non-Russian national minorities was rapidly increasing and soon posed a serious threat to the government.

Finally, in early 1904 an adventurous and imperialist foreign policy in the Far East helped lead Russia into a war with Japan for which neither the Russian government nor the people were prepared. Some may have thought wishfully that the war would rally the people and help avert imminent revolution, but the Russian population as a whole had little knowledge about or understanding of the causes and aims of the war. Although there were initial patriotic demonstrations and some liberals argued that it was disloyal to oppose the government in time of national emergency, the war stimulated rather than hindered the revolutionary movement. Russian forces proved to be inept against the Japanese army and navy. The fall of Port Arthur on December 20, 1904, and the destruction of the Baltic fleet off Tsushima on May 14, 1905, damaged the government's prestige at home and abroad. Moreover, the war sapped the financial resources of the nation, and discontent and opposition grew apace. As we saw, the liberals stepped up their activity at the end of 1904, and in January 1905, 400,000 strikers left their jobs, a figure equal to that of the previous ten years combined. Thus the government faced war on two fronts: foreign and domestic. With its army and navy being humiliated in the Far East, with declining morale and even occasional mutinies in the armed forces, and with relatively few soldiers remaining in European Russia to keep order, the autocracy was in no position to win either struggle.

The government's policy toward the growing discontent in the nation was hesitant, clumsy, and inconsistent. For a time it followed a policy of severe repression, then failing to see progress in that, it began to consider a policy of limited concessions. It granted reforms when forced to, but at the same time it insisted on the maintenance of order and the autocracy. Moreover, reforms always seemed to come too late; and giving ground a little appeared merely to whet the appetite of the revolutionaries for genuine reforms. Ministers gave way one after another when unable to solve the growing crisis.

Following the assassination by revolutionary terrorists of Minister of Interior von Plehve in July 1904, Tsar Nicholas made his first attempt to win public confidence in the government and to restore order by adopting a more conciliatory position; he appointed Prince Sviatopolk-Mirsky, who was known to favor a more liberal domestic policy, as the new minister of Interior. A short time later, in November 1904, the First Zemstvo Congress met, without either Mirsky's approval or his interference. Afterwards Mirsky urged the tsar to accept the eleven-point resolution proclaimed by the congress and to make it the subject of an imperial ukase. As a result of governmental meetings presided over by Nicholas, on December 12, 1904, an imperial ukase was proclaimed that included four of the eleven points contained in the zemstvoists' resolution.

Mirsky had also recommended adding elected zemstvo representatives to the State Council for purposes of legislative consultation. The day before the ukase was published, however, Nicholas sought Witte's advice on the Mirsky proposal. Since his dismissal in 1903 as minister of Finance, Witte had had little influence on government policy, but as chairman of the largely formalistic Committee of Ministers he was still officially a member of the government and an adviser to the tsar. He favored granting reforms and, in fact, had helped draft the December 12 ukase, but on two grounds he opposed inviting representatives from the zemstvos to consult with the government. First, he feared this half-measure would not satisfy but rather would inflame liberal opinion, which would demand full representative government. Second, if the reform were to open the way toward a constitution, as Witte feared it would, he believed this would be dangerous and premature since the mass of the Russian people were too uneducated and unenlightened for such a system and since Tsar Nicholas bitterly opposed a constitution, convinced he had a religious duty to preserve the autocracy.[25] Thus, when Witte told Nicholas that Mirsky's recommendation would be but the first step on an irrevocable road leading toward representative government and a constitution, Nicholas deleted that section from the ukase.[26] Mirsky immediately asked to resign, recommending Witte as his successor, but the tsar said he did not trust Witte, even "suspecting that he was a Mason," and Nicholas refused to accept Mirsky's resignation.[27]

The ukase of December 12, 1904, entitled "Concerning Plans for the Improvement of the Social Order," promised measures that would ease restrictions on the press, provide state insurance for factory workers, allow greater religious toleration, define the scope of local self-government, reduce certain disabilities on national minorities, limit the application of exceptional laws, and improve the lot of the peasants.[28] At the same time, in a pattern that was to become familiar in succeeding months, Nicholas accompanied his pledge of reform with a sharply worded official statement calling for a return to order, prohibiting illegal meetings in the future, and demanding that zemstvos, city dumas, and other bodies stop meddling in matters outside their jurisdiction and stick to their own affairs.[29] For Nicholas, it was clear; reform was to be granted only grudgingly and under pressure, and its purpose was the restoration of order and harmony in the state, which should continue to be governed through a benevolent autocratic system, one that remained fundamentally unchanged from that of the past. But, for the opposition—again in a pattern that was to become familiar— the tsar's promises were too little, too late, serving primarily to stimulate renewed efforts for greater change. The lesson that agitation produced reform was not lost on the liberals. Moreover, the omission from the December 12 ukase of Mirsky's proposal for a consultative voice for zemstvo representatives and the long delay that could be expected in implementing the tsar's program certainly blunted the efficacy of the ukase in quieting the opposition; but in any case by December the liberals had moved considerably beyond their position of a month or two earlier and now wanted more extensive reforms, including full civil liberties and, according to some spokesmen, a national legislative assembly.

Thus, although a momentary lull followed promulgation of the December 12 ukase, opposition leaders were by no means satisfied, and within a few weeks a tragic and foolish act, the "Bloody-Sunday" incident of January 9, 1905, inflamed opinion in all strata of Russian society and helped evoke a genuine, though still inchoate, revolutionary movement throughout the country. On that day Father George Gapon, a young priest interested in the plight of the workers whom the police had encouraged to develop an organization among the proletariat of St. Petersburg, arranged and led a march of protest by workers and their families, as culmination of a major strike in the capital, with the aim of presenting a petition of grievances to Tsar Nicholas. At various points in the city army and police units met the marchers and opened fire on them, killing hundreds and perhaps thousands.[30] The government had been forewarned of the demonstration, but because of weak and ineffective leadership (Nicholas himself was not even in the city), it was decided to prevent the march rather than to prepare to receive the petition and then to disperse the crowd peacefully.

The consequent tragedy shocked society and contributed significantly to the distrust, bitterness, and alienation that increasingly marked relations between the government and the opposition movement. "Bloody Sunday" also badly tarnished, perhaps for good, the image of the benevolent tsar as Little Father to his people; individuals in all walks of life came to see Nicholas and his government as inherently evil, violent, and expendable. Yet within the government the only immediate results were that General Trepov was made a special governor-general to restore order in St. Petersburg, Mirsky was forced to give way to Aleksandr G. Bulygin, and on January 19 the tsar received a hand-picked group of thirty-four workers and treated them to tea and cookies as if somehow this would make amends for the more violent reception their colleagues had received ten days before.

Nevertheless, certain ministers and advisers recognized the necessity of taking definite steps to attempt to conciliate society, and Nicholas himself was amenable to such a course of action. At the same time the tsar, particularly after the assassination of his uncle, Grand Duke Sergei, on February 4, remained convinced that order must precede reform and that reform should not go too far. Thus, he issued three separate and somewhat contradictory announcements on February 18, 1905. One, a manifesto, lashed out at the revolutionaries and called on all loyal Russians to rally around the throne. The second, a decree to the Senate, affirmed the right of every subject in the empire to be heard by the throne and invited suggestions from both individuals and institutions to further the welfare of the public. The third, a rescript to Bulygin, proclaimed on the one hand the immutability of autocracy and on the other the tsar's decision to "permit elected representatives of the people to take part in preliminary discussion of legislation."[31]

These three announcements seemed to cancel each other, but they did encourage continued discussion and agitation as the citizenry was now free to petition the throne for change. Additional minor reforms followed: an ukase of April 17, 1905, that abolished discriminatory regulations against Old Believers, and measures in

May and June that curtailed some restrictions on nationality groups and relaxed censorship codes on newspapers.[32] But these were all too insignificant and too late to stop those members of society who thought they had autocracy on the run and were looking for an opportunity to deliver the final blow. Moreover, the war continued to go badly and the liberal opposition was now joined by restive national minorities, rebellious peasants, striking workers, and a few mutinous soldiers and sailors. In short, government actions produced neither order nor genuine reform, and the revolutionary movement grew apace.

Finally, on August 6, 1905, the government announced its scheme for the State Duma, or national representative body, which had been promised in the rescript to Bulygin on February 18. The Bulygin Duma, as it was called, was to be a consultative rather than a legislative assembly; it was to give advice rather than make laws. Moreover, though it was to be the first national assembly in modern Russian history, it was to be elected by indirect and unequal suffrage, and the franchise was heavily weighted in favor of large property holders and peasants. Most town dwellers were denied the vote, as they could not meet the property qualifications. The government placed its faith in rural Russia to elect deputies loyal to the tsar. Workers were entirely excluded, while many liberals and professionals were disenfranchised.[33]

Witte criticized the plan, charging that those in the government who were proposing the Duma wanted to provide the form of a Western European parliament but none of the power. These men were saying in effect, "We will listen to your opinions, and then do as we please." Witte said he opposed such a scheme because it would either fail after a few months or lead to an actual parliament. Witte argued, as he had previously regarding the zemstvos, that the government could not continue to create forms without this either leading toward a real constitution or stirring up more unrest.[34] Although a few liberals accepted the plan, most considered it inadequate. The radical groups repected it and proposed to boycott the elections to the Bulygin Duma. Again, the government's gesture was tardy and insufficient. But, for the moment, the tsar had gone as far as he would go. He had already granted far more than he would have believed it possible for him to do a year before. Nothing other than a direct and total threat to the throne could force him to make further concessions. Such a threat was only two months away.

The Man

THE MAN to whom Nicholas II ultimately assigned the responsibility for rescuing Russia from its declining state of affairs was Sergei Iulevich Witte. Witte, born in Tiflis in 1849, was the son of Julius Witte, head of the agricultural department in the office of the governor-general of the Caucasus. His father's ancestors were Baltic Germans; his maternal grandmother was a member of the Dolgoruky family.[35] Therefore, Witte came from a respected segment of Russian society, although his mother's family outranked his father's.

Witte received his early education in Tiflis, then attended Novorossiisk University in Odessa, where he specialized in mathematics. After graduation he chose a career in railway administration. From 1871 to 1874 he served first in the office of the governor-general of Odessa and Bessarabia and later in the Odessa office of the Ministry of Communications, concentrating on problems of railway management. Since some state railways were transferred to private ownership in 1877, Witte left government service and soon, by diligence and effort, advanced to the position of executive director of one of the largest of the southwestern railways.

This period of Witte's life was very important in the formation of his personality. His contemporaries later evaluated him in terms that suggest his identification with bourgeois values. They described him as a "self-made man"; one "who turns dreams into facts, ambitious, emotional, and determined"; one to whom "no obstacles were great enough to deter him when once he visualized his goal"; one who was "first and foremost a practical man"; one to whom "not words, nor thought, nor articles, but deeds, deeds, and deeds . . . was the one thing that was important."[36] Perhaps the most revealing statement of all is from Witte himself, who offered one reason why Alexander III was a great autocrat: "I have not met anyone either in the Imperial family nor among the nobility who better appreciated the value of a ruble or a kopeck than did Emperor Alexander III."[37]

This *kupets* ("merchant"), as he was slightingly but revealingly named by the more gentle segments of society, was in many ways a rough stone in a society accustomed to polished gems. He did not have a broad education. His training was specialized—Russian, business, and technical. Forced to move among those who prided themselves on their level of culture, Witte appeared to be brusque and even uncouth.[38] His French was barely adequate, and he knew neither German nor English.[39] His second marriage in 1892, which followed by only a few years the death of his first wife and which tied him to a commoner, a divorcee, and a woman with a questionable moral reputation, revealed both his impetuosity and his contempt for the standards of polite society. This marriage proved to be a serious obstacle to social life in the capital and was a severe handicap to his professional career.

In 1889 Witte left private business for a post in the Ministry of Finance; he was charged with establishing the railroad department within that ministry. Conspicuous success in this assignment earned him appointment as minister of Communications in 1892, with the chief responsibility of building the Trans-Siberian railroad. Later in the same year Alexander III picked him to be the new minister of Finance.

It was as minister of Finance from 1892 to 1903 that Witte was best known and most clearly left his stamp on Russian life.[40] By 1892 Witte had accepted as the core of his basic economic philosophy the theories of Friedrich List. He borrowed from List his ideas of a national economy, especially the need to build national industries. List stressed that industrialization creates its own markets. One should build heavy industry first and luxury industry last. This meant that present advantages in terms of a higher standard of living must be sacrificed for future benefits. List also favored protectionism, that is high tariffs which would permit national industries to grow and to flourish.

There were, however, elements in List's philosophy which Witte did not embrace. List, who used England as his ideal nation, stressed the importance of liberty and constitutional government. To List, religious toleration, empire, a parliamentary system, and industrialization were the basic ingredients of an advanced civilization.[41] Witte sought to gain the social, cultural, and economic advantages of industrialization through a progressive autocracy. He once confided to the British journalist, E. J. Dillon, "with vision, enterprise, and resource, it [autocracy] can be made as productive of good as a parliamentary government, especially in a backward country like ours."[42]

The "Witte system," as his financial and economic policies were termed, was in substance an experiment in state capitalism. By a policy of public works, especially railroad building, the government stimulated individual enterprise to exploit the vast natural wealth of Russia. There was no great plan; each problem was met pragmatically as it arose; only the direction was clear. According to Witte's theory, railroad construction stimulated the light industries. Growth in these stimulated rural production and prosperity. From an initial effort by the government in railroads and through protective tariffs would ultimately flourish the well-being of all.[43]

With this base in mind, the rationale behind a great number of Witte's specific policies becomes clear. First and foremost Witte favored the business community over all other sections of the economy. By protective tariffs, by encouraging the formation of monopolies, by reorganizing the State Bank in order to permit issuance of industrial loans, by establishing savings banks throughout Russia to encourage public saving, and by subsidies and favorable patent laws, Witte tried to blunt the risks of business enterprise and to encourage private investment.[44] Witte favored public education and established a liquor monopoly for the government, the first because literacy was necessary in order to have a well-trained work force, the latter because the sale of vodka proved to be a vast source of new income for the government.[45] In 1897 Russia converted to the gold standard. This strengthened her credit position abroad, making it easier to obtain the foreign loans required to meet investment needs. Witte established close contact with banking houses in Germany and England, but his closest ties were with Crédit Lyonnais in France. Witte maintained an agent, Arthur Rafalovich, in Paris to keep him abreast of developments there. Witte also learned to bribe French newspapers in order to gain a favorable press.[46]

To ensure the success of his policies Witte set out to establish his own empire-within-the-Empire. He gained immense power over the other ministries not only because of his energy and ambition but because Alexander III placed full confidence in him and refused to grant any credit that Witte did not sanction. In the beginning of his reign Nicholas II was equally under Witte's discipline.

In 1895, when Nicholas' mother tried to induce her son to intercede to secure a loan for a mutual friend with doubtful credit reliability, Nicholas refused, saying, "It would be a fine state of affairs indeed at the Treasury if, in Witte's absence (he is at present on a holiday), I were to give a million to one, two millions to another, etc."[47] Unfortunately, for Witte and for Russia, Nicholas did not maintain such a scrupulous point of view in later years of his reign. To strengthen his position, Witte placed his own agents in the Ministries of War, Navy, Justice, Education, Communications, in the diplomatic service, and at the court. To some extent he had both an army and a navy at his disposal, as well as a railway.[48] This insistent promotion of his own power and policies inevitably aroused resentment against him in other ministries and at the court as well.

As a result, from 1899 until his dismissal in 1903, Witte was in a constant struggle to preserve his position and his policies. Under the "Witte system" taxes had risen sharply and were especially oppressive on rural and town populations as compared to industrial and commercial groups. Many were distressed at the size of the foreign debts. Others disliked the obvious favoritism toward industry, particularly industry in the hands of foreigners. Many of the peasants were in a serious plight. By 1899 the arrears in redemption dues were greater by 16 million rubles than the dues collected that year.[49] Witte's policies also affected the nobility, the pillar upon which autocracy rested. Since the emancipation of the serfs in 1861, there had been a steady retreat from the countryside, and from 1877 to 1905, landownership by the nobility declined by one-third.[50] Witte's policy of industrialization with its extreme protectionism hurt the gentry. Yet this was only a part of their problem. Russian agriculture was grossly inefficient when compared to agriculture in Western Europe and North America, and Russian grain found it ever more difficult to compete in the international market place. In addition, many of the nobles proved to be poor managers when they were no longer able to rely upon serf labor. The result was that many of those who still owned estates were deeply in debt, and while still loyal and in many cases influential in the government, there was a growing discontent among this most privileged Russian class.[51]

Witte was not unaware of these problems and sought ways to remedy the situation. In 1898 he drafted a long note to Nicholas urging peasant reform but had little response from the tsar. In January 1902, he succeeded in organizing a group representing bureaucrats and gentry to study the rural problem. Known as the Special Commission on the Needs of Agricultural Industry, it met from January 22, 1902, to March 30, 1905. The conference gathered a mass of data, but Nicholas dissolved it abruptly without accepting its recommendations for reform of the peasant commune.[52] Yet Witte's acknowledgment of the problems created by his financial policies did not in any sense cause him to retreat from them. In a secret memo to Nicholas he admitted that serious problems had arisen, but such was the penalty of backwardness. Only by forced industrialization could Russia ever hope to take her rightful place beside the industrialized nations of Europe. He acknowledged that other policies might have been followed, but once a policy had been agreed upon, it should be pursued to its ultimate conclusion.[53]

On August 17, 1903, Nicholas decided differently. On that day he "promoted" Witte to the largely honorary position of chairman of the Committee of Ministers, thus stripping him of his powerful post as minister of Finance. For the next two years Witte was in a state of limbo. He did not receive another important assignment from Nicholas until August 1905, when he led the Russian delegation to Portsmouth, New Hampshire, to negotiate the peace settlement ending the Russo-Japanese war.

In order properly to judge Witte's actions as chairman of the Council of Ministers and sponsor of the October 17 Manifesto later in 1905, it is important to examine his views about constitutions and autocracy before October 1905, when he returned to power. Witte's preference for autocratic as opposed to constitutional regimes was both emotional and practical. As a young man reacting from the grief that followed the assassination of Alexander II, Witte suggested the founding of a secret society that would seek out the revolutionists and retaliate in kind to each of their terroristic acts. A society, known as the "Holy Brotherhood," was indeed established, and Witte was initiated into membership. Very shortly thereafter, he was sent to Paris to supervise the assassination of a revolutionist. The plot collapsed and Witte, sickened by the whole affair, resigned his membership.[54]

Aside from the emotional attachment to autocracy reflected in this incident, Witte believed in autocracy for practical reasons. He knew all too well that his financial policies were not popular and would never be approved if submitted to a democratic referendum.[55] He was not interested in courting public opinion nor in wooing the press, although he was perfectly capable of doing so in a rather Machiavellian fashion. During the Portsmouth peace conference in August 1905, he deliberately manipulated the American press, and in France it was his regular policy to bribe the press whenever Russian loans or credits were at stake.[56] What Witte liked most about autocracy was that under its shelter a man could do what he did best. An official of the tsarist government did not have to worry about pleasing a fickle, democratic populace each election year. One could work consistently toward long-range goals.[57] This was the practical basis for his opposition to the zemstvos. The zemstvoists impeded rather than furthered Witte's plans, as they were always suggesting ideas which would only sidetrack the national effort as he envisioned it.

Witte saw nothing inconsistent in championing both reform and autocracy. To Witte, reform should come from the tsar and not be forced from him either by a rebellious nation or by a quarrelsome parliament. His ideal was a tsar cut from the pattern of Alexander II and Alexander III. The former took the initiative in granting the "great reforms" of the mid-nineteenth century; the latter permitted himself to be guided by his ministers. Witte once confided to E. J. Dillon that "you must first find a monarch with wisdom, enterprise and resource, or with discrimination and modesty enough to select a statesman who possesses them and to maintain him in office. Alexander III was such a monarch, and I shall never cease to lament his death."[58]

Witte did not favor absolutism; the tsar must be guided and controlled by law just as his subjects should be.[59] The autocrat should not operate by fit and by fancy. Once he has appointed his ministers and has agreed upon a course of action, he should accept their advice. If he disagrees with them, then he may replace them; but as long as they are his ministers, he should support their policies.[60] What Witte conceived was something on the order of the German state under Bismarck, with a strong monarchy, an effective bureaucracy, and guarantees of civil rights—a system within which people could live peaceful and orderly lives. If revolution came, it was the fault of the government for having lost touch with society and for having failed properly to direct its engeries.[61]

Although Witte was a champion of autocracy, he was not an

admirer of Nicholas II. The friction between them was well known in ruling circles.[62] Nicholas' lack of will power, his perverse tendency to reject the advice of his ministers in favor of that of mystics or courtiers, his capacity to waver and to vacillate when conditions became difficult, his stubbornness when his views were challenged, all this thoroughly exasperated Witte, who in anger and frustration wrote: "I was born a monarchist and I hope to die one, but I hope there will never again be such a tsar as Nicholas II, one who wavered so much on his principles. God grant that I do not see this. . . ."[63] Witte's hopes were fulfilled, though hardly as he would have wished; never again was there such a tsar—or any tsar.

The Crisis

THE UNCOORDINATED and sporadic instances of strikes, peasant uprisings, and mutinies which swept across Russia during the first eight months of 1905 grew to such a climax by September, despite conclusion of the war with Japan, that they were a major threat to the autocracy. The government unwittingly added to its difficulties by granting the universities autonomy on August 27, thereby restoring the privilege of self-government which the universities had lost in 1884. Since "Bloody Sunday" the universities had been closed as many of them were centers for antigovernment activity. According to Alexander Kerensky, "There were no arguments among the students whether autocracy was to be fought or not. This was self-understood. The only argument was where the real truth was to be found, with the Marxists or the *Narodniki*."[64]

From the first of September—two weeks before classes were scheduled to begin—university students gathered in classrooms and auditoriums to listen to political oratory and to pass condemnatory resolutions against the government.[65] Moscow University was controlled by its students, and they, in turn, were controlled by the most radical in their midst. After the session began on September 15 students attended classes during the day and revolutionary meetings in the same rooms at night. They boycotted unpopular professors and, in at least one case, refused to let a professor teach by demonstrating in his classroom.[66] At St. Petersburg University students tried to purge certain "reactionary" members of the faculty. The faculty resisted, however, and a compromise was reached. The faculty handled academic affairs; the students took charge of planning the revolution. Students and certain radical faculty members conducted courses in political and economic indoctrination for workers. At first the government did nothing to break up these meetings—at least in the large cities. In the provinces armed bands led by police agents sometimes raided schools.[67]

In reality neither the students nor the professional revolutionaries created the revolution, though the universities served as a convenient base of operations. What drove the revolution forward was the general feeling of discontent that had developed within all segments of Russian society and that led to a collective assault against the government. Each class or group had its own ideas about what should be achieved, but, for the moment at least, all were moving together in more or less parallel paths. Even the liberal gentry were no longer satisfied with half-measures and supported a thoroughgoing reform of the old order. Moreover, the industrialists, demonstrating political consciousness for the first time, urged political changes as a means of appeasing the dissatisfaction of the workers and diverting their economic demands, as well as a way of obtaining more social recognition and some voice in the affairs of state for their own class. The bourgeoisie also hoped reform would lead to a restoration of order and normal business activity. Typical was an appeal of the Moscow industrialists of October 14:

> ... violence must be met by violence, and military measures must be taken with the fullest concern for the protection of individuals as well as of the property of citizens ... [but] such measures will not achieve their purpose if together with them reforms are not given, if there remains unsatisfied the striving of the suppressed majority of society for improvement in its life in ways which fully guarantee against any possibility of returning to the old system which has led Russia to its present ruin.[68]

General discontent, fueled by the university meetings, now began to take active form in a wave of strikes. On September 23, the Moscow printers walked off their jobs to begin what was intended to be a four-day strike. They were followed the next day by the bakers and some factory workers in Moscow.[69] Soon thereafter a convention of railway employees met in Moscow at the request of the Ministry of Communications to discuss an old-age pension plan. The content of the talks gradually shifted from the pension plan to demands for civil rights, for the right to collective bargaining, and for a general amnesty for those in prison for political and religious crimes. The press became interested and provided news coverage. The government, now thoroughly alarmed, threatened to dissolve the meeting.[70] Rumors spread in Moscow that the representatives of the railroad workers had been arrested. Despite government denials workers on the Moscow-Kazan railroad left their jobs in protest on October 6.[71] The strike quickly spread to other railroads and other cities as each of the succeeding days found trains coming to a halt, deserted by their crews. On October 9 the telegraph workers walked out. Moscow, St. Petersburg, and other major cities were cut off except by road or by boat.[72]

At this point the revolutionaries ceased to be the leaders of the workers. In September the Social Democrats had urged strikes and demonstrations by workers to keep pressure on the government. Now the strikes were out of control. Some revolutionaries who feared the repression that would surely follow an armed rising tried to prevent the movement from going too far. On October 11 workers gathered at St. Petersburg University and called for a general strike. Representatives of the revolutionary parties at first spoke *against* it, but the workers ignored their objections and voted to begin a general strike the next day, October 12.[73]

Up to this point the government had made little overt response to the growing crisis. For one thing, it had survived difficulties of this sort, though not as widespread, before; for another, over one-third of the territory of the empire was under martial law or in a state of "strengthened security," and some in the government felt the situation could be controlled. Nevertheless, behind the scenes discussions were going on that would take Russia in an entirely new political direction, but these discussions were not known to the general public. When the strike became total on October 12, Nicholas II ordered General D. F. Trepov, military governor of St. Petersburg and assistant minister of Interior, to adopt more aggressive measures.[74] Trepov ordered commanders of military garrisons throughout Russia to use whatever force was necessary to protect property and to end the disturbances. On Ocobter 14 he told his troops not to permit crowds to form and gave the command, which might have made him famous had it not been directed against Russian citizens, "Should the people resist, do not use blank cartridges and do not spare your ammunition."[75]

During the peak of the strike major cities were without newspapers, water, electricity, or heat. Many civil servants also joined the strike, and when on October 17 Minister of Finance Kokovtsov, personally appealing to the striking workers of the State Bank to return to their jobs, declared, "What will you say to your children when they will ask you if you were not on the side of order during these tumultuous times?" an employee cried, "And what will we say to our children when they ask us if we were not on the side of freedom now?"[76] Most of the stores were closed with the exception of food stores, which were permitted to open a few hours each morning. Crowds of workers roamed the streets, but there was little fighting between police and crowds. Trepov tried to put the electric plants into operation, but workers had damaged the controls. At night soldiers lit bonfires on street corners in order to provide some illumination. On October 15 troops surrounded a building at St. Petersburg University and broke up a revolutionary meeting without firing a shot. At this point the strike seemed to have reached an impasse. Although many of the workers preferred to fight rather than to surrender, they were so poorly armed that the students among the Social Democrats discouraged them. The government gave every indication of being prepared and able to maintain order and to wait out the strike. Disillusionment and despair grew among the revolutionaries.

On the night of October 17 a representative of the Central Committee of the Social Democratic Labor party told students and workers in St. Petersburg that the strike was lost. Mass arrests would begin the following day with prominent leaders being rounded up first. It was suggested that party leaders prepare to flee to the provinces and to change their identities in order to escape arrest.[77] That night, just as the leaders of the revolution were acknowledging defeat, the government capitulated. It was an odd twist of fate that Nicholas II signed the October 17 Manifesto—a document he came to despise—and turned over the government to Count Witte —a man he did not really trust—at the very moment when his opposition was about to retire from the field.

II

OCTOBER 17 MANIFESTO

There was no other way out than to cross oneself and give what everyone was asking for.

—Nicholas II
The Secret Letters of the Last Tsar

T HE SIGNIFICANCE of the Imperial Manifesto of October 17 and of Witte's accompanying report, which was sanctioned by the tsar and published together with the Manifesto, is that these two documents set forth the framework on which Witte hoped to erect a new order designed to end the revolution and to adapt Russian society to the modern world.[1] Many liberals also viewed these promises as the first step toward establishment of a constitutional order in Russia. Not that the Manifesto was a constitution, although some including the tsar momentarily confused it with a constitution,[2] but the Manifesto did change the essence of Russian autocracy. It confirmed civil freedom and announced that in the future no law would become binding without the consent of freely elected representatives of the citizenry. From its publication on October 17, the government was judged according to how it fulfilled its own proclamation.

Yet, the October 17 Manifesto arrived as an unwanted child. Conceived in haste and desperation, it was prompted not by far-sighted concern for the welfare of the people but by the need to act quickly in the face of the October general strike and the growing revolutionary movement in the country. Witte, who had to assume responsibility for it, had opposed it, favoring something less dramatic and less difficult to fulfill. Alexei Obolensky, its principal author, soon repudiated it, calling it "the greatest sin of his life."[3] Nicholas II gave it a home because he had no other choice, but he despised it and ultimately treated it as an orphan. It received a mixed reaction from society. Peasants believed that terms relating to distribution of the land were being withheld; monarchists viewed it as an act of treachery; revolutionaries judged it as nothing more than an empty promise designed to deceive the people and to permit the autocracy to recapture power. Only moderate liberals rejoiced over it.

Properly to judge Witte's government from October 1905 to April 1906, it is important to understand how the Manifesto originated. The actions of the government during Witte's six-month premiership acquire greater meaning when set in the context of the hopes, frustrations, and fears of those responsible for publication of the Manifesto.

Witte returned to Russia in mid-September from his diplomatic triumph at the Portsmouth conference. To reward him for successful completion of the peace treaty, Nicholas made him a count, an honor that deeply touched Witte.[4] Witte's arrival coincided with the growing assault on the government by both liberal and revolutionary groups. The peace with Japan seemed to inflame rather than to pacify the Russian public. There is no evidence to indicate that Witte expected that one month after his return he would be responsible for leading the Russian government on the path of political experimentation. He had no delusions about his support at the court and knew that even his most recent recognition by the tsar would probably not have been conferred had he not been so well received in Berlin, where he stopped en route home from the United States. Witte hoped to rest after the Portsmouth conference and expected to vacation in Sicily. However, his diplomatic success convinced some that he was the one man who could save Russia from revolution. Writing to D. A. Miliutin on September 16, A. A. Saburov, a member of the State Council, declared: "A splendid new task is being readied for Witte: to bridle the revolutionary movement in Russia. Put forth as the guardian of the autocracy and at the same time possessing numerous admirers in the opposition camp, he more than anyone else will be in a position to guide the ship of state in these stormy times."[5] Count Dmitri M. Sol'sky, chairman of the State Council and one who had confidence in the former minister of Finance, told Witte that if he went away Russia was lost.[6]

In his memoirs Vladimir I. Gurko, an official in the Ministry of Interior, has questioned whether Witte was in fact planning to leave Russia. Gurko maintains that Witte saw the crisis in Russia as an opportunity to regain power—more power than he had enjoyed as minister of Finance. According to Gurko, Witte played a very clever game in late September and early October. He was careful to alienate neither the public nor the court. He boldly announced that he could save Russia and devised a plan which would concentrate power in his own hands, while offering the tsar only alternatives which somehow seemed less desirable than his own plan.[7]

Witte spent the first few days after his return talking to leaders within and outside the government. He received conflicting opinions and advice but most—including certain well-known reactionaries—favored the granting of a constitution.[8] Although Witte in his outlook and behavior seemed to be hesitant and even ambivalent about what should be done, he sensed that some form of constitutional government should be established in Russia. In his memoirs he wrote that although the steps leading to the October 17 Manifesto should have been taken with greater care, eventually something similar to the Manifesto was destined to become a reality; "it was an inevitable event of history."[9]

Witte's first direct involvement in governmental activity and planning to meet the growing crisis took place shortly after his return to Russia; the outcome foreshadowed the kind of difficulties he would encounter after October 17 and the sort of compromise which was to characterize his whole effort to reform and thereby to "save" the Russian government. After publication of the Manifesto of August 6 calling for a consultative Duma, there had been considerable discussion in both liberal and bureaucratic circles concerning the need to strengthen central control and direction of the government as it moved into an era in which the voice of the people would be heard, however faintly. From this emerged a proposal radically to alter the nature and role of the existing Committee of Ministers, a formal but essentially powerless council of heads of ministries and departments, to make it much more like a true cabinet or executive committee coordinating and supervising the policies and operations of the whole bureaucracy.[10] On August 27 the tsar referred to the Special Conference under Count Sol'sky which was charged with implementing the August 6 Manifesto a note suggesting unification and streamlining of the central direction of the government. Arguing that the new Duma would be a focus of dissatisfaction and would try to reform the existing order, the proposal urged creation of a new Council of Ministers, which would coordinate and consolidate both the opinion and action of the ministries, in order to ensure a "strong" government that could keep necessary concessions within the bounds originally set forth in the tsar's ukase of February 18. It was suggested that the chairman of the Council nominate to the tsar candidates for ministerial posts, except for those of War, the Navy, Foreign Affairs, State Controller, and the Imperial Court and Lands. In transmitting the note Nicholas commented that he found in it "a great deal that was true and useful," and he asked Sol'sky's conference to review the plan and recommend action on it.[11]

Selected ministers, State Council members, and senior officials, including Witte, discussed this proposal in private meetings at Count Sol'sky's house on September 21 and 28. A draft memoir was then drawn up, which Sol'sky's Special Conference examined on October 3–4 and 11–12, meetings to which Witte apparently was specially invited.[12] Witte strongly supported the plan, arguing that it was essential to have "a strong government in order to combat anarchy" and that in the present threatening situation the revolutionaries were meeting "no organized opposition from the government." He maintained, undoubtedly with his own possible future role in mind, that the chairman of the new Council, while consulting closely with his colleagues, should have the authority to act for the government as a whole. Witte even insisted that if a minister did not agree with the views or actions of the chairman, he should resign rather than try to operate independently. This was a bold concept, but later, as we shall see, Witte's own hand-picked minister of the Interior, P. N. Durnovo, would act quite outside the control of the Council and its chairman. Most of the members of the Special Conference, while agreeing that a strengthened ministerial committee was needed, opposed going as far as Witte wished, since they felt ministers should still be directly responsible to the tsar. A cabinet system such as Witte envisaged might work under a constitutional monarchy, but it would destroy the essence of the autocratic authority if applied in Russia. Witte replied that under the concept espoused by the majority the chairman of the new Council of Ministers would not be given the powers he ought to have; consequently, "one could not expect from the unified Council a complete reform in conducting the affairs of government but only the improvement of chancellery business." Then Witte announced that the others could do as they wished but, should he be asked to become chairman of the future Council of Ministers, he would organize the Council according to his own concept. At last, in a typically bureaucratic and equivocal fashion, the Special Conference recommended to the tsar that since all ministers and heads of departments should have similar views and follow a concerted policy, the chairman should indeed have the right "to propose to Your Imperial Majesty candidates to head ministries and departments exclusive, however, of those of War, the Navy, and the Imperial Court and Lands," but that this provision, because it might be misinterpreted, should not be included in the act or ukase that created the new Council of Ministers. As we shall see shortly, Nicholas, even before his reluctant decision to approve the October Manifesto—and perhaps as a way of trying to postpone or avoid that decision—did act to put into effect this reform of the central government, and shortly after October 17 he confirmed the new organization of the Council of Ministers in an imperial ukase of October 19. Later, however, in the Fundamental Laws adopted in April 1906, the responsibility of the Council of Ministers to the tsar was clearly spelled out (see chap. 9).

It is significant that Witte's earliest advice in the mounting crisis in the fall of 1905 was to reform Russia's government, beginning with the central authority. Yet there was doubt at work in Witte. On October 1 Witte confided to A. A. Polovtsev, a senior member of the State Council, that he believed only a dictator could save Russia but that he had no idea where such a man could be found.[13] This ambivalence—a sincere desire to modernize governmental practices and institutions yet a gnawing fear that what was needed was force—continued to influence Witte's thinking up to the signing of the Manifesto itself, as well as afterwards. In October Witte's own prescription to the tsar was for reform, but he was always careful to point out he might be wrong and the tsar should consult with others who believed a dictatorship was the best answer.

On the urging of Count Sol'sky, Witte sent a note to Nicholas on October 6 requesting an audience in the near future to discuss the dangerous domestic situation. On October 8 Nicholas replied, indicating that he too was anxious to review the situation with Witte and would receive him at 6:00 P.M. the following day.[14]

In preparation for his audience with the tsar, Witte drew up a rather long memorandum evaluating the present crisis and proposing a set of principles to guide the government in the future. It was neither a manifesto nor a detailed plan of action, but a pragmatic statement of political outlook—an outlook which combined elements of enlightened absolutism with principles of Western political liberalism. The memorandum was largely based on, or may even have been a revised version of, a statement written by a leading zemstvo liberal, V. D. Kuz'min-Karavaev, who was later to be an intelligent and articulate deputy to the Second Duma representing the splinter liberal Party of Democratic Reform.[15] Nevertheless, it seems clear that Witte's presentation to the tsar in most respects accurately reflected his political views in 1905 and that much of what he proposed formed the basis of his later actions as chairman of the Council of Ministers.

In the memorandum Witte stated that autocracy could not survive if it continued to rule as if it were all of society or as if society existed for its pleasure.[16] The government should have a goal when it ruled in behalf of others. Witte declared, "This goal is founded in the maintenance of a good life, both moral and real." Pursuing the good life in moral terms involved the progressive development of freedom in man. The good life in "real" terms was the sum total of the economic progress of society. According to Witte, the duty of government was to advance man's spiritual and material condition.

Witte acknowledged that power and authority must be restored to the government, as the government could not advance the well-being of its citizens unless it had power concentrated in its own hands. Yet, power should not exist for its own sake. The government's monopoly of force should be used only to achieve and maintain civil freedom. Since men naturally strove for freedom, freedom should be the goal and policy underlying the conduct of public life. There was no other way to salvage the government in this crisis. If freedom did not come by reform, it would come by revolution. Witte went on to point out that revolution would smash everything, it would be a senseless and merciless riot; socialism, which could not succeed, would only result in the destruction of the family, religion, property, and law. Thus, the government really had no choice but to lead the nation on the path of freedom. To be sure, this would mean a break with the past, but change was an inevitable part of the historical process.

Witte regretted that the type of enlightened leadership which characterized Russian government in 1861 and which led to the Great Reforms had not continued. Since that time the government had retreated from reform and found refuge in reaction. Accordingly, the government no longer provided leadership for society but seemed to be constantly trying to catch up. Whereas only a year before, the idea of a constitution for Russia had been espoused by only the most radical elements of the population, now there was hardly a party or newspaper that did not subscribe to the idea.

Witte wanted the government to recapture the leadership of Russian society rather than to attempt to swim against the current. To control the liberation movement, the government must be in a position to channel its force rather than to attempt to dam its energy. Thus, Witte wrote, the word "constitution" must not frighten the government nor should the government attempt to suppress the idea. "The government must be ready to move along the path of constitutionalism," Witte noted. "The authority of government must strive for good government and not for the preservation of any particular structure."

Thus, Witte was not very specific concerning what reform program the government should undertake. He suggested an end to illegality and arbitrariness, the guaranteeing of civil freedoms and of equality before the law, and reorganizing the State Council so that it would become partly elective and could serve both as a link between the government and the Duma and as a buffer between the tsar and Duma. Yet he insisted that under the new governmental structure the tsar should retain an absolute veto over the decisions of the people's representatives. He urged broadening of the restricted franchise envisaged under the decree of August 6 and warned the government must not interfere in free elections. For the workers Witte proposed temporary measures of relief: setting limits on the length of the workday, providing state insurance, and establishing mediation boards; for the peasants Witte argued immediate steps to lessen their land hunger must be taken, including distribution of some state lands and of some held by the Peasants' Bank, as well as redemption of some private lands; for the national minorities Witte recommended introduction of some local autonomy in regard to elementary and secondary education, lower courts and police, and taxation for local needs.

In this note Witte revealed a pragmatic and eclectic attitude toward the problems which faced Russia. He was no ideologue; he neither defended the autocratic ideal nor championed a democratic creed. Rather than a formula, he suggested a direction in which the government should move. Nicholas, who was perhaps more accustomed to panaceas and patriotic defenses of autocracy, later confessed to having found the report to be guarded and confusing.[17]

At his meeting with the tsar on October 9, Witte read the memorandum to him and then told Nicholas that he could imagine only two possible courses of action open to the government. One solution would be to adopt a program based on the ideas contained in Witte's memorandum; the second alternative would be to appoint a dictator—preferably a strong, military man—and to attempt to dam the revolution by subduing the country with military force. Witte made it clear that he preferred the former course but acknowledged that he could be wrong. He, therefore, suggested that the tsar consult with others before rejecting the latter alternative.[18]

Gurko subsequently charged that this was part of Witte's scheme. By offering the tsar a choice, Witte appeared not to be pressing his own candidacy as head of the government. In reality, according to Gurko, Witte knew that the tsar would not choose a dictator and initiate a blood-bath.[19] Therefore, Witte's suggestion of alternatives was meaningless. Gurko's opinion is both cynical and prejudicial. Witte was not positive that his was the best approach, as has already been indicated. It was quite proper for Witte to advise the tsar of the course of action he believed to be best, and then to suggest the tsar consider other alternatives before making a final decision. Furthermore, as will be described later, the tsar very nearly *did* appoint a dictator and only accepted Witte's program at the last instant.

Later in the evening following his return to St. Petersburg, Witte reviewed his memorandum with N. I. Vuich, then temporary chairman of the Committee of Ministers. Together they made several additions and clarifications, including an explicit presentation of the second alternative open to the tsar, that is, the appointment of a dictator.[20] On the following day, October 10, Witte returned to Peterhof to explain his ideas once again. This time he described his program to the tsarina as well as to the tsar. Again Witte presented two alternatives—reform or dictatorship. At this conference Witte stressed that the tsar's choice of a man to lead Russia should be dependent upon the policy ultimately agreed upon. If the tsar wished to adopt a policy of force, then he should choose a man who believed in dictatorial methods. If the tsar wished to support reform and to appoint Witte as prime minister, then Nicholas should assent to Witte's program and give him a free hand in carrying it out. With the exception of a suggestion from Nicholas that Witte prepare an abstract of the memorandum in the event it was necessary to publish it as a manifesto, the tsar and tsarina had no comments to make on Witte's report.[21]

During October 11 and 12, Witte received no information from Peterhof. He used these days to confer with government officials and military officers. In a meeting of government officials on October 11, Witte raised again the idea contained in his memorandum of October 9 that one way to widen public participation in the government might be to change the State Council so that in the future one-half of its members would be appointed by the tsar —as the entire Council was at that time—and one-half elected as representatives of the public. The idea was rejected.[22] The next day he participated in a meeting which included the ministers of War, Finance, Internal Affairs, Justice, and the governor-general of St. Petersburg. The consensus of this group was that first, the work of the various ministries should be coordinated so that the government pursued a common program. Second, they recommended increased reliance on military force in order to subdue the rebellion, beginning with the use of soldiers to terminate the railroad strike. Although the recommendation to use force was contrary to Witte's ideas as expressed in his memorandum of October 9, he reported the results of this meeting to the tsar and urged him to give this viewpoint careful consideration.[23]

The next day, October 13, Witte received the following telegram from Nicholas:

Until confirmation of a law on the Cabinet of Ministers, I direct you to coordinate the activities of the ministers, with the primary aim of restoring order at once. Only through the calm conduct of the

Empire's life will it be possible for the Government to cooperate in constructive work with the representatives of my people who are to be freely elected.[24]

In this telegram Nicholas revealed either his lack of understanding of Witte's position or his contempt for it. Witte had, it is true, recommended that the ministers be brought under the control of a prime minister or a chairman. To this extent the telegram endorsed Witte's conception, but on the more important issue it violated Witte's advice of October 10. On that occasion Witte had argued that choice of a leader was dependent upon the nature of the policy selected. Although in his telegram Nicholas wanted to give the return to order first priority, thereby implicitly rejecting Witte's policy of reform as the key to stability, the tsar nevertheless asked Witte to take charge of the government, the very situation Witte had tried to prevent.

The following morning, October 14, Witte went to Peterhof to meet with the tsar. He told Nicholas that merely coordinating the ministers was not sufficient. To put an end to the unrest, the tsar must choose one policy or another and pursue it diligently. If he desired a policy of repression, he should select a dictator. Witte would not accept that post. If he wished to pursue a program of reform based on the principles indicated in Witte's memorandum, Witte would be willing to lead the government.[25] Since the tsar had asked Witte to prepare an abstract of his memorandum in the event it was needed as a manifesto, Witte gave it to him during this meeting.[26] This abstract, which formed the basis for the report that was later issued with the October Manifesto, contained most of the basic ideas of the memorandum of October 9 but in a somewhat softened and more imprecise form. For example, the term "constitution" was replaced by the more abstract formulation, "legal order," and the brief list of specific social reforms disappeared in favor of the pious hope that "the economic policy of the government should be directed toward improving the welfare of the popular masses," but, "of course, within the limits of those property and civil rights recognized in all cultured countries."[27]

While making minor modifications in his recommended program Witte nevertheless told the tsar that for two reasons he opposed publication in the form of an imperial manifesto of the basic promises he hoped the tsar would make. First, imperial manifestoes were traditionally read in the churches and were generally looked upon as gifts from the emperor. If the program set forth in a manifesto did not succeed, such a failure would be attributed directly to the tsar. If, on the other hand, the tsar merely sanctioned the report of a minister, then it was the minister's responsibility to bring the program to a successful completion. Failure would be blamed on the minister rather than on the tsar. Second, a manifesto would raise hopes that the reforms were to be introduced immediately when, to be practical, some delay would probably be unavoidable. If, however, Nicholas merely endorsed Witte's report, he would have indicated only that he wished Russia to follow the path of reform outlined in it and that these reforms were to be achieved as rapidly as the government could put them into effect.[28]

It is difficult to be certain of the real reasons for Witte's opposition to publication of the manifesto. Witte's arguments that publication of a manifesto was unnecessary, that it could stimulate fresh disturbances,[29] and that it could possibly bind the tsar to an unsuccessful policy were doubted by his political opponents. They believed that Witte wanted to use his report to strengthen his own prestige with the public. If there were no manifesto but only Witte's recommendations, then reform would be associated with Witte, not Nicholas. Witte's foes argued that the tsar should offer reform as an imperial gift by manifesto in order that the credit would accrue to the throne. Witte's opponents whispered that he was trying to maneuver into a position as president of a Russian republic.[30] It seems more likely that Witte was not nearly as concerned with saving the tsar embarrassment or initiating a personal power play as he was with fighting for freedom in which to operate. It was important to have the tsar's endorsement and commitment, but to have the throne bound to specific reforms and measures at the outset could only be restrictive. Witte wanted exactly what he had indicated in his report—a pledge which committed Russia in the direction of reform but which provided sufficient flexibility to permit initiation of specific reforms at a pace and in a form that seemed possible and desirable as circumstances dictated.

Following his audience with the tsar, Witte returned to St. Petersburg, where at his own home he met with General A. F. Rediger, minister of War; General D. F. Trepov, assistant minister of Interior and governor-general of St. Petersburg; and Prince M. I.

Khilkov, minister of Communications, to ascertain if the military force available was sufficient to restore rail service. Both Trepov and Rediger said it was not.[31]

During the evening Prince V. N. Orlov called Witte to say that the tsar wanted him to attend a conference at Peterhof the following morning. He was to bring a draft of a manifesto which could be published.[32] Although Witte still preferred imperial sanction of his own report to an imperial manifesto, he laid plans to have a manifesto ready if the tsar should insist on its publication. Presumably, if a manifesto were to be issued, Witte wanted it to be based on his report.

The initial writing of the manifesto, which is often attributed to Witte, was in fact the work of Alexei Obolensky, then a member of the State Council and later procurator of the Holy Synod in Witte's cabinet. According to Witte's memoirs, on the night of October 14 Obolensky was his house guest when he received the call from Orlov. Since he was not feeling well, before retiring Witte asked Obolensky if he would compose a manifesto, presumably based on their discussions of Witte's report.[33]

The following morning, October 15, Witte, Vuich, and Obolensky boarded the steamer for Peterhof. Baron Vladimir B. Fredericks, minister of the Imperial Court, joined them on the boat. Vuich recalled that shortly after the trip began Obolensky produced a rough draft of a manifesto, which Witte had not seen.[34] During the trip to Peterhof the three men—Vuich, Obolensky, and Witte —discussed, amended, and revised Obolensky's draft. Discussion centered on three points which Obolensky had included in his manifesto. The first point related to extending civil freedom. Witte approved of this point and suggested it be retained essentially as Obolensky had originally formulated it. For a time they considered linking it somehow to the ukase of December 12, 1904, but as the boat was approaching Peterhof, they decided there was insufficient time to work in this detail. The second provision dealt with widening the franchise to include classes not eligible to vote under the electoral laws proposed for the Bulygin Duma. Brief discussion led to agreement on this point. Finally, Obolensky's conception of the Duma was revised in favor of Witte's formulation which transformed it into a legislative body.[35]

When the boat arrived at Peterhof, Witte asked Obolensky and Vuich to continue working on the manifesto in order to put it in final form while he went to the court with Baron Fredericks. Fredericks and Witte were met by General O. B. Richter and Grand Duke Nikolai Nikolaevich, and at 11:00 A.M. they were ushered into the room where the tsar awaited them. Nicholas directed Witte to read the report which he had presented the day before in order that those attending the meeting could discuss it. As Witte read his report, he was frequently interrupted by questions, especially from the grand duke. Witte answered these questions and then once again declared that in his view the tsar had only two alternatives. Either he could move along a path of reform or he must choose a dictator and try to end the civil unrest by forceful repression. After Witte finished, the tsar asked if he had prepared a manifesto. Witte replied that one was being drafted, but he still preferred that the tsar merely sanction his report rather than publish a manifesto. The meeting was adjourned at 1:00 P.M. to be reconvened at 3:00 P.M., by which time Nicholas instructed Witte to have available a copy of a manifesto in order that it could be discussed.[36]

After the meeting with the tsar Witte once again met with Obolensky and Vuich to discuss the manifesto. Witte told them what had taken place at court, but he said that he could stall for a day or two on the manifesto. Obolensky became very excited and demanded that Witte introduce the manifesto that afternoon.[37] Witte agreed to do so, and they began to put the manifesto into final order. Witte said that the first point they had discussed that morning could remain since the tsar was ready to extend civil freedom. Witte was skeptical about the second point, which widened the franchise. However, he finally consented to a wording of the manifesto which promised that new classes would be enrolled as voters as rapidly as possible but without delaying elections to the first Duma. Witte regretted that there was insufficient time to clarify point three on the role of the Duma, but he hoped that this might be remedied through publication of his own report simultaneously with the manifesto.[38]

When Fredericks, Witte, Richter, and the grand duke reassembled with the tsar at 3:00 P.M., Witte read the manifesto; and according to Witte, no one raised objections. Vuich wrote that Grand Duke Nikolai Nikolaevich, who at the beginning of the session had favored strong measures to suppress the rebellion, ended by supporting Witte, as did General Richter. Baron Fredericks opposed Witte's plan.[39]

Following the meeting, Nicholas ordered Fredericks to send Witte's manifesto and report to General Trepov for his "frank opinion and advice." In the note to Trepov Nicholas asked him to estimate how long he could continue to maintain control in St. Petersburg and whether it would be possible to pacify the country without excessive bloodshed. Trepov was asked to respond quickly as the tsar hoped to reach a final decision on the following day.[40]

On the morning of October 16 Trepov replied to the tsar's letter.[41] He approved the guarantees of various civil freedoms contained in the manifesto and in Witte's report but insisted that they should be extended under strict legal safeguards, and he opposed equal rights for the Jews. Trepov further stated that the tsar should not be afraid of a constitution in principle as Prussian experience revealed that a constitution could be most useful. On the question of using force to subdue the rebellion, Trepov asserted that he could not assure the absence of bloodshed either at the moment or in the future. However, he declared that whatever course of action was finally adopted, the tsar should retain control of the military. If the tsar had been hoping to get support for the alternative of a dictatorship from Trepov, he was disappointed.

Unknown to Witte the tsar had been conducting separate negotiations with Ivan L. Goremykin and Baron Aleksandr A. Budberg, both members of the State Council. (Goremykin was destined to succeed Witte as chairman of the Council of Ministers in April 1906.) On October 13 the tsar met with Budberg and Goremykin to consider their views. On October 16 he and Fredericks met with them again, this time not only to consider the Goremykin-Budberg plan but Witte's manifesto as well.[42] The result of this conference was two manifestoes—one, a final version of the Goremykin-Budberg recommendations, which did not give the Duma a decisive voice in legislation and retained a restricted franchise; the other, a revised version of the manifesto drafted by Obolensky and Vuich under Witte's direction.[43]

Witte learned of these consultations during the course of October 16 and telephoned Fredericks to protest against the secret negotiations taking place behind his back. Witte declared that while he could not object to the tsar revising his plan, the tsar should know that it would be impossible for him to head the government except on the principles of his own program. Fredericks assured Witte that only editorial changes had been made and that he would show him the final draft of the manifesto late that evening.[44]

Shortly after midnight on the morning of October 17, Fredericks arrived at Witte's home, accompanied by A. A. Mossolov, head of the Court Chancellery, and bearing copies of two separate manifestoes.[45] One was the Goremykin-Budberg manifesto; the other was a revised version of Witte's own plan. Before examining the documents Witte asked if Trepov had approved of them. Fredericks answered that they had just left Trepov and that he had agreed to the contents of both manifestoes. After examining both documents, Witte announced that he did not approve of either manifesto; each was out of harmony with the ideas contained in his report. Since the conflict was apparent, the public would rightfully question the sincerity of the government in publishing contradictory documents. Then Witte repeated that he was opposed to publication of a manifesto and preferred instead that the tsar sanction and publish his report. Fredericks retorted that this was a closed issue. Nicholas had decided to publish a manifesto; the only question remaining was which one it would be. Hearing this, Witte directed Fredericks to inform the tsar that it was Witte's opinion that the tsar should appoint one of the authors of the Goremykin-Budberg manifesto to head the government since it had become clear that he, Witte, did not enjoy the confidence of the tsar. Witte declared that he could not assume control of affairs under terms of a policy he opposed. Witte said he would accept a secondary role in the new government if the tsar wished this.

Nicholas was now left with three possible courses of action. He could adopt one of the two manifestoes that had been prepared and select someone other than Witte to head the government; he could accept Witte and his report; or he could appoint a dictator. At this point Witte's candidacy received help from an unexpected direction, from Grand Duke Nikolai Nikolaevich, who was one of the few in the royal family who exerted an influence on the tsar.[46] As the grand duke was widely believed to be a reactionary and a staunch opponent of constitutions, Fredericks apparently hoped at this time that Nikolai Nikolaevich might be persuaded to become a dictator, thereby making Witte's appointment unneccessary.[47]

On the morning of October 17 Fredericks related to the tsar the details of his session with Witte a few hours earlier. According to Fredericks, the tsar listened without comment. It was evident that he was awaiting a visit from Grand Duke Nikolai Nikolaevich. After Fredericks left the tsar and returned to his own rooms, the grand duke came to see him. Fredericks described what had happened, that Witte was not available to lead the government on the tsar's terms, that it would now be necessary to establish a dictatorship, and that the grand duke was the one to assume the role of dictator. Upon hearing this, the grand duke pulled a revolver from his pocket and exclaimed, "Do you see this revolver? I am now going to the tsar and will ask him to sign Count Witte's program and manifesto. Either he will do this or I shall shoot myself in the head."[48] The grand duke turned and strode away to find the tsar. Soon he returned with directions for Fredericks to prepare fresh copies of Witte's report and the Witte-Obolensky manifesto in order that the tsar might sign them when Witte arrived.

The grand duke's excited reaction was prompted in part by a visit he had had with a labor leader named M. A. Ushakov on October 14 or 15. According to Ushakov, the grand duke asked him what the workers wanted.[49] Ushakov answered that while the workers remained basically loyal to Russia, they desired a constitution and a greater share in the public life of the country. The grand duke replied that this was easier to discuss than to accomplish. Ushakov responded that there was only one man capable of doing the task properly and that man was Count Witte. He alone could save Russia. Witte has been accused of sending Ushakov to confer with the grand duke in order to persuade the latter to accept Witte's plan and to reject the idea of a dictatorship. Ushakov denied such an arrangement, noting that Witte had direct ties with neither the revolutionaries nor the workers. Although Witte admitted to knowing Ushakov, he did not accept responsibility for Ushakov's contact with the grand duke.[50]

Following the grand duke's emotional outburst, the tsar decided to accept Witte and his program. Witte was summoned to Peterhof and, upon his arrival, was informed by Fredericks that the tsar had agreed to publish both his report and his manifesto and wished him to assume the post of chairman of the Council of Ministers. Later Witte met with the tsar. During this conference he tried to convey how important it was for the tsar to maintain faith in his ministers as they began an experiment filled with hazards. Witte compared the situation to a man who must cross a dangerous sea. Several boats and routes were available to Nicholas; each offered certain risks. Nicholas must decide for himself which boat he would take. If he chose to ride with Witte, he must be prepared for storm, rolling waves, and perhaps even some damage to the ship. Critics would undoubtedly say that the trip would not have been so bad had Nicholas chosen another ship and another route.[51] Nicholas answered that he had faith in Witte and would give him full support. At 5:00 P.M. Nicholas signed the manifesto and sanctioned Witte's report.[52] Nicholas noted in his dairy: "After such a day my head began to hurt and my thoughts were confused. God help us and comfort Russia."[53]

It is not surprising that Nicholas' head hurt, for absolute monarchs do not abolish absolutism casually. By signing the Manifesto Nicholas granted to all Russians basic civil liberties, including freedom of conscience, speech, assembly, and association. Furthermore, despite the short time remaining before the Duma elections, he agreed to grant the franchise to additional groups of people who were denied the right to vote by the August 6 law. Moreover, he implied that he would not raise objections if the Duma were to support legislation tending toward universal suffrage. Finally, he established an "unbreakable rule" that no law would be valid in the future without the approval of the Duma. Witte's report, sanctioned by the tsar and published at the same time as the Manifesto, was more bland and less forceful, but wholly consistent with the spirit of the Manifesto. Taken together, they promised a new, more liberal political order.

Still to be answered is why Nicholas finally agreed to accept Witte and his program. The tsar had received advice both favoring and opposing Witte's appointment. One who recommended Witte's selection was the dowager empress, Maria Feodorovna, who wrote to her son on October 16: "I am sure that the only man who can help you now and be useful is Witte . . . he certainly is a man of genius, energetic, and clearsighted."[54] The influence of Grand Duke Nikolai Nikolaevich has already been described. Yet, as has been shown, there were others close to Nicholas who distrusted Witte and who conveyed their suspicions to the tsar.

At the same time there seems little doubt that Nicholas genuinely wished to avert violence and bloodshed, if at all possible; consequently, Trepov's inability on October 16 to reassure the tsar on this score clearly influenced Nicholas' decision. On October 16 the tsar replied to Trepov's comments on the Witte program, saying that Trepov's judgment that bloodshed was inevitable if force were used "significantly lightened the burden of making a final decision on the question of undertaking the broadest reforms."[55]

Perhaps the explanation Nicholas gave to his mother in a letter dated October 19 throws the clearest light on his reasoning. The tsar wrote that there were only two paths open to him—either to find a dictator to crush the rebellion, or to "give to the people their civil rights, freedom of speech and press, also to have all laws confirmed by a State Duma . . . [which] would be a constitution."[56] If he had chosen the first course, it would have provided "time to breathe," but force would have been required a few months later, and "that would mean rivers of blood, and in the end we should be where we had started." Such a course of action would have done no more than prove that the government still had force behind it; it could not have provided a "positive result." Only the second path, that of reform, held out any hope of real success. Nicholas noted: "From all over Russia they cried for it, they begged for it, and around me many—very many—held the same views. . . . There was no other way out than to cross oneself and give what everyone was asking for." Nicholas consoled himself with the belief that this must be the will of God and that his agonizing decision would somehow rescue Russia from her crisis.

There is no doubt that Nicholas was aware of the implications of his decision. Although the Manifesto was not a constitution, Nicholas himself used that term in describing the results which would follow from its publication. This document, which violated the political and moral principles he held dear and which caused him such agony, was concluded only when he decided there was no other choice.

III

ORDER AND REFORM: THE FIRST

WEEKS OF WITTE'S PREMIERSHIP

The government ought to be given time to carry out its program [of reform], and the prime requisite for its success in this effort is the reestablishment of order.

—Government statement of October 20

The Dilemma of Ends and Means

WITTE ASSUMED control of a government enmeshed in a dilemma over ends and means. It is clear that Tsar Nicholas II was in principle no champion of constitutions or of reform. He toyed momentarily with the idea of a dictatorship to end the general strike and to subdue the countryside, and he retreated from this plan only when his advisors insisted that this would lead to increased violence and bloodshed and that in any case there was not sufficient military force to ensure the success of such a policy. He accepted Witte's program on the basis that a promise to introduce civil freedom, reform, and public participation in the government would pacify the populace and thereby help to restore order. For Nicholas, a program of reform was simply a means to an end—the safest route on the return to order.

Nor was Nicholas very patient with his prime minister in the latter's efforts to establish order. On October 27, just ten days after publication of the Manifesto and with Witte still involved in selecting a cabinet, Nicholas wrote to his mother with more than a trace of sarcasm, "It is strange that such a clever man should be wrong in his forecast of an early pacification." Maria responded she sympathized with Witte and Nicholas must demonstrate confidence and patience toward him.[1] Nicholas answered her on November 10, complaining that despite all his efforts, "everybody is afraid of taking courageous action." He noted that he was trying to maintain confidence in Witte but that he was disappointed in what Witte had accomplished toward the restoration of order.[2] For Nicholas, it is clear, the test of Witte's government was how quickly and efficiently order was reestablished.

Before October 17 the public as a whole had obviously been willing to sacrifice order to achieve the long-sought goal of reform. It was unlikely that the majority of the Russian people would welcome a return to order after October 17 until they perceived tangible evidence that their assault on the government, which appeared on the surface to have forced its surrender, had actually been successful. Yet, it is easier to generalize about Russian society before the Manifesto than it is about that same society after the Manifesto's publication. As was indicated in the first chapter, the revolution made for strange bedfellows. Those attacking the government ranged from Leninists to landowners—the former seeking among other things to seize land for the peasants, the latter hoping through government reform to save their land from the peasants. Each discontented group assigned responsibility for its discomfiture to the government, although many of these groups had quite different and even incompatible remedies in mind.

The October 17 Manifesto fractured this informal coalition. The groups which had earlier cooperated in a struggle against the government now divided to pursue their own individual goals. Some wished to push forward to the final overthrow of the government; others sought to extract further concessions from the government but to oppose revolution; still others, now thoroughly frightened by the threat of anarchy, rallied to one degree or another behind the government. The result was that whereas on October 16 the government seemed to be standing alone against the combined force of Russian society, this opposition now lost its cohesion, thus facilitating the ultimate restoration of government authority.

This splintering of the opposition is more real to the historian than it must have been to Witte and others in the government in October and November 1905. The clamor for reform was still being heard, and the government hesitated to ignore it. From many quarters came demands for immediate fulfillment of the promises that had been made and for instant improvement in the lot of the Russian people. Yet others, including a number of moderate groups and individuals, satisfied with what had been wrung from a reluctant autocracy and appalled at the continuing chaos, urged a prompt reestablishment of law and order. Witte soon found himself caught between these two imperatives. He too wished, quite apart from the goadings of the tsar, to see order restored, for the sake of the country and because he believed in it. On the other hand he was genuinely anxious to initiate the reform platform on which he had come to power. But it was difficult to begin needed changes and launch organic reforms when violent attacks against the whole structure of government and society continued and when he faced a largely hostile and demanding public and a mistrustful and uncooperative court. Witte fully and cruelly experienced the fate of the non-fanatic, of the man-in-the-middle, in a revolutionary situation.

In these circumstances Witte has been accused of lack of purpose, inconsistency, pusillanimity, and duplicity. As the French ambassador in St. Petersburg concluded:

> His [Witte's] most serious deficiency, in a political vein, was in never being able to trace a determined line of conduct and thus, pursuing fragmentary ends that he took up each in turn, under the pressure of circumstances, he dissipated his actions in directions that were often divergent. He had no program; it is impossible to discern where he wanted to go. . . . Self-taught as he was, he was a rebel to general ideas and clung in all things to the purest empiricism.[3]

That Witte was an empiricist none can doubt. The program with which he embarked on the stormy seas of the 1905 revolution was essentially eclectic and pragmatic. Witte had no overriding political creed to guide him, except his sincere devotion to the welfare of Russia. He wanted to see an end to disorder and anarchy; he also earnestly desired a more modern and rational state system in Russia. He fervently, if not always tactfully or skillfully, pursued both objectives. The difficulty was that they often seemed (and sometimes were) incompatible, and at times Witte himself felt that the first was a prerequisite to the second. Nevertheless, although, as we shall see in the next chapter, Witte unquestionably experienced a crisis of nerves in early December which led to a significant harden-

ing of his opposition to the revolutionary movement, he never lost
sight of his dual aims and he pursued them forlornly to the end of
his premiership, in the face of growing isolation and loss of autocratic and public support. Thus Witte the reformer and Witte the
policeman cannot be separated, and in the crucial first weeks after
he came to power, both strands of his policy must be followed if
the confusing and often futile results of his efforts are to be accurately and effectively delineated.

Moreover, in the early days of his stewardship of Russia's
destiny, Witte was faced with problems that would have taxed a
government far more stable than his, weakened as it was by its
lack of any base of political support and by its need to devise new
methods and blaze new trails. Witte was forced to cope with revolutionary parties and institutions, further strikes, mutiny in the
army, pogroms, peasant riots, nationalist revolts in the provinces,
and imminent financial collapse.[4] Despite these problems he had to
choose a cabinet which would win the confidence of both the public
and the tsar, to compose new election laws for the selection of the
first Duma, to bring the army back from the Far East, to solve the
agricultural problem, to revive the Russian economy, and to re-
order the state structure of Russia. And above all, while meeting
each of these formidable tasks, Witte somehow had to try to please
a distrustful tsar and a doubting public. Thus, it is hardly surprising
that Witte attempted to feel his way cautiously as he moved in the
direction of reform, alternating between displays of force to restore
order and measures of concession to win support. As he maneuvered
from left to right and back again, he alienated one group after
another. Despite his efforts, he seemed unable to gain the needed
support of any important segment of society. Conservatives suspected him of constitutionalism, radicals of placing order before
reform. To a degree both were right.

There was not one response to the Manifesto but many re-
sponses. In some cases these responses reflected individual feelings;
in other cases the response was conditioned by the group to which
one belonged. There were such personal reactions as that of the
Grand Duke Nikolai Nikolaevich, who, in the steamer returning to
St. Petersburg following the signing of the Manifesto, turned to
Witte and said, "Today October 17 . . . the dynasty was saved."[5]
Or that of Princess Sviatopolk-Mirsky, wife of a liberal landowner

who had been minister of Interior in 1904—she wrote in her diary on hearing the news: "In a word [it means] everything we strove for so long and stubbornly, and in the first minute I was more stunned than happy. . . . Finally, Russia is a free country. But I fear that the revolutionaries will go farther."[6] Others, especially police and government officials, felt betrayed by the Manifesto, and some reacted as Yaroslav Governor-General A. P. Rogovich, who first confiscated the newspapers which published the Manifesto, and then, learning it was true, resigned.[7] Those at the court who had opposed Witte and his program from the beginning lost no time in trying to undermine Witte's government and to convince the tsar that he should renounce the Manifesto.[8] Some charged that the Manifesto contributed to the growth of moral decay in society. Gurko was shocked to learn that under the new spirit of freedom "menservants drank freely of the master's wine [and] the maids used the perfume and wore the underwear of their mistresses."[9]

The most common type of reaction to the Manifesto was mass demonstrations which took place in all the major cities of Russia. Witte had anticipated these demonstrations and gave orders on October 17 to police officials not to interfere with peaceful demonstrations but to suppress all those aimed at creating unrest.[10] The demonstrations were of two kinds. One type consisted primarily of students and workers led by representatives of the various radical parties. They marched through the streets singing revolutionary songs, including the "Marseillaise," while carrying red flags. They listened to speeches denouncing the government, the Manifesto, and the tsar, and sometimes marched to the jails, demanding that all prisoners be released.[11] Another group of demonstrators supported the monarchy and walked through the streets carrying icons and portraits of the tsar while singing hymns and the national anthem. Clashes inevitably occurred between the two groups of demonstrators, and in many cases these clashes spiraled into pogroms.[12] In several cities "patriotic" crowds set fire to buildings in which striking workers were meeting.

Perhaps the largest demonstration occurred on October 20 in Moscow. The demonstration was prompted by the burial of N. E. Bauman, a member of the Moscow committee of the Social-Democratic party, who was killed during a clash between radical and monarchist groups on October 18.[13] The socialists used his funeral to stage a large parade through Moscow. It was estimated that 10,000 to 15,000 people marched in this parade while another 100,000 to 200,000 looked on.[14]

The response of the Social-Democratic party to the October 17 Manifesto was to refuse to respect it and to continue to oppose the government. Lenin, representing the Bolshevik faction of the Social Democrats, wrote on the day the Manifesto was signed but before he had become aware of it that any constitution which would be given would be a "deception of the people" as the government would never permit complete and free elections so long as the tsarist regime and not a revolutionary government was in charge of the elections.[15] The position of both the Mensheviks and Bolsheviks was represented by the *Bulletin of the Soviet of Workers' Deputies* for October 20, 1905:

> And now we have been granted a constitution.
> We have been granted freedom of meetings, yet meetings are being surrounded by soldiers.
> We have been granted freedom of speech, yet the censorship remains unshaken.
> We have been granted freedom of knowledge, yet the universities are occupied by military force.
> We have been granted personal inviolability, yet the jails are full of prisoners.
> We have been granted a constitution, yet autocracy remains.
> We have been granted everything, and we have been granted nothing.[16]

A popular socialist refrain of the time ran:

> Tsar' ispugalsiia, izdal manifest
> Mertvym svoboda! Zhivykh pod arrest!
> ("The tsar became afraid, issued a manifest[o]
> For the dead there is freedom! The living are under arrest!")[17]

The Social Democrats, believing that autocracy was on the run, wished to chase it to its final destruction. They demanded removal of troops from the cities, the arming of citizen militias, immediate convocation of a constituent assembly, abolition of class differences, full amnesty for all political prisoners, and an eight-hour day for all workers.[18] Without these guarantees—which they knew full well would not be forthcoming—the struggle would be continued.

Among the Socialist Revolutionaries, attitudes were divided over the Manifesto. Some thought they could use the Manifesto to their advantage and should therefore come to the aid of Witte—to "surround him"—in order that the government would not violate its pledges. The majority distrusted the Manifesto and Witte but agreed to take advantage of the new freedom to begin more active work in the cities and villages. Many political émigrés returned to Russia to carry the message of the Socialist-Revolutionary party to the villages.[19]

The Manifesto did more to affect the activities of the Socialist-Revolutionary Combat Brigade than had earlier persecution by the government, because it provoked a split between the Brigade and the Central Committee of the Socialist-Revolutionary party.[20] The majority of the Brigade wished to continue the use of terror, believing that the sole guarantee of the civil liberties promised by the Manifesto was in the pressure brought to bear on the government by active terror. The Central Committee, on the other hand, believed that terrorism could be justified only as an extreme measure in unconstitutional countries where there was no freedom of speech or press. Now that Russia had these freedoms, the Central Committee argued that terror should be suspended. Terrorist leaders held that the Brigade's discipline would crack in the face of inaction and, early in November, they declared the Brigade dissolved. Acts by individual terrorists nevertheless continued during November and December, and then in January 1906, as a result of increased repression by the government, the Combat Brigade once again resumed operations.[21]

The position of the liberal camp *vis-à-vis* the government was quite different from that of the radical parties. Witte had no intention of seeking the cooperation of the revolutionaries, but he had counted upon the support of moderates and made a sincere attempt in the first days after the Manifesto's publication to attract liberals to his cabinet. As will be discussed later in this chapter, Witte was unable to do this and had ultimately to fall back on bureaucrats as ministers. The Manifesto placed the liberals in an embarrassing and frustrating position. Before October 17 they had led the opposition to the government in the attempt to secure constitutional reforms. Now a kind of constitution seemed to be offered, but they were unsure of just what it meant and how it would be implemented. Moreover, they were unwilling to yield the critic's security for the responsibility and vulnerability of participation in the government. And at heart they mistrusted the tsar and his bureaucratic system.

The Manifesto affected the liberal camp in still another way; it completed the split which had been gradually widening between the zemstvoists and the intelligentsia. Publication of the Manifesto coincided with the First Congress of the Constitutional Democratic party (Kadets) held in Moscow from October 12–18, 1905. It proved to be a party based primarily on intellectuals and professional men. The Congress was dominated by the personality of Paul Miliukov and ultimately adopted his position toward the Manifesto. Upon learning of the tsar's proclamation, Miliukov reputedly said, "We have gained a victory, but essentially nothing has been changed; our struggle and our political direction must remain as before."[22] The Kadet leaders had already agreed to use the Bulygin Duma to oppose the government; therefore, they merely approved the same tactics toward the new Duma promised by the Manifesto. P. B. Struve, an exponent of "legal Marxism" in the 1890's and a member of the Kadet party in 1905, opposed Miliukov and suggested that liberals should close ranks and seek by open and legal means to aid the government in reform. Struve was joined by N. N. L'vov and V. A. Maklakov, who saw in the Manifesto a constitutional monarchy which met the liberals' "minimum demands."[23] Despite this disagreement these men remained within the Kadet party, becoming leaders of its right wing.

Confronted by the Manifesto, the leftist elements of the zemstvo movement split with their more conservative colleagues, some of them joining the Kadets. Others led by D. N. Shipov wished to support the government but refused to join it when asked to do so. Nevertheless, by the end of October Shipov and his right zemstvoist followers had joined forces with A. I. Guchkov, other liberal industrialists, and representatives of the city dumas and the moderate bureaucracy to form the Union of October 17 (Octobrist party), which was pledged to support the program of the October 17 Manifesto and not to go beyond that. Although the Sixth Congress of Zemstvo and City Duma Representatives, held November 6–13, 1905, declined, after much debate, to back Witte, the united oppositional front of moderates which had confronted the government earlier in 1905 was broken.

Moreover, major industrial and financial groups, which had vigorously attacked the government in the summer and early fall and which, in many cases, had supported the workers in the October general strike, blaming the unrest on the failure of the autocracy to grant adequate political reforms, now gradually swung behind the Witte ministry, fearing that continued unrest would threaten their own interests. Moreover, they were largely satisfied with the promises made.[24] Typical of many telegrams and petitions from liberal and bourgeois organizations which congratulated Witte and euphorically welcomed the dawn of a new day were those from Moscow. On hearing of the Manifesto the Moscow City Duma wired:

> The Moscow city duma, having with a sense of profound gratification examined the Manifesto of October 17—by which the whole population of Russia, regardless of nationality and religion, received the right of civil and political freedom, a law and order built on stable foundations, and an active part in the state system and government—perceives this great act as a guarantee of the utmost free development and full renewal of the life of all the people, and conveys feelings of gratitude to the Monarch in the name of the henceforth free population of the city of Moscow.[25]

In less florid terms the Moscow Bourse Committee added its gratuitous advice to Witte: "Take heart, carry the affair through to the end, to the calling of the State Duma on the principles of October 17. Any changes of personnel or direction can only cause harm. You must not heed any of the cries and demands of the extreme parties."[26] Taking advantage of their newly bestowed freedoms, the industrialists, besides helping found the Octobrist party, established a half-dozen or more smaller "business" parties to contest the elections to the forthcoming Duma.[27] In addition, when the strike movement revived in November and December, the bourgeoisie strongly urged the government to take stern measures to suppress it, while they themselves used such tactics as lockouts and strikebreakers to resist demands for an eight-hour day and other economic claims of the workers.

Other groups reacted to the Manifesto as well. Those workers who were active members of one of the revolutionary parties continued to favor struggle against the government, but many workers viewed the Manifesto as a victory and were anxious to return to work.[28] The majority of landowners, thoroughly frightened by the danger of a new *Pugachevshchina*, hastened either to express their support for the new order or to call for a return to the gentry-dominated system of the past. The peasants, sullen and silent, responded by deeds as much as words, except for widespread rumors that the Manifesto contained secret, unpublished provisions for a "black repartition" (division of all the land to the peasants) and for the continuing radical, antigovernmental appeals of the All-Russian Peasants' Union. Peasant disorders in central European Russia and in some of the borderlands reached new heights in mid-fall 1905, probably as much a result of the completion of the harvest as of any real understanding of or serious doubts about the October Manifesto.[29]

The impact on the army and navy of the October 17 promises was mixed. In many military units the Manifesto was interpreted as a sign of the reestablishment of peacetime conditions and as an augur of the imminent demobilization of reserves and conscripts, who were chafing to return home following their service in the Russo-Japanese war. When these hopes were disappointed, insubordination and mutinies often resulted. Many enlisted men and officers assumed that the guarantees of political and civil freedom applied equally to them (which was not true, as it turned out), and they began to participate in meetings, political activity, and demonstrations with a gusto.[30] Others decided that the Manifesto was an invitation to them to formulate and submit their protests and demands, sometimes orally, sometimes in writing, concerning a variety of military and political problems, in the expectation that their grievances would now be redressed peacefully. On one occasion a group of soldiers massed in front of unit headquarters and would not disperse until an officer had read them the Manifesto; when he had done so, they then drew up a detailed list of protests. On still other occasions, as in the mutinies in Vladivostok and in Sevastopol shortly after promulgation of the Manifesto, it acted as a spur to the forcible presentation of demands, whose rebuff led to insubordination and violence.[31]

The response to the Manifesto among the non-Russian nationalities of the empire was also varied. In Finland and to some extent in the Caucasus moderate nationalists tended to accept it as a portent of decreased Russification and greater local autonomy. In Finland, as we shall see below, these groups, their hand strengthened by concrete concessions from St. Petersburg, were able to stem the revolutionary tide and assist in the restoration of order.

But in the other areas the combined social and nationalist revolt swept on, and the government soon had to take extreme repressive measures to maintain its authority.[32]

Pogroms

THE MOST VIOLENT REACTION which followed publication of the Manifesto and the first major challenge to the stability of Witte's government was a wave of pogroms which swept across Russia in the fall of 1905. The pogroms were partly a result of the pattern of discrimination toward Jews which had continued for more than a century in Russia,[33] partly a result of the frustration of police and government officials who took advantage of the attacks on Jews to strike back at all those who had been active in the October strike, and last, but even more important, the result of violent reactions, whether spontaneous or inspired, on the part of counterrevolutionary, proto-fascist elements in the population—the "Black Hundreds"[34]—who under the guise of patriotism turned on Jews, intellectuals, and socialists in an attempt to "rescue the tsar" from the seditious Manifesto.

The growth of radical and liberal parties which desired to solve Russia's ills by importing Western political remedies in the late nineteenth and early twentieth centuries also stimulated the rise of opposing groups which wished to preserve the ancient virtues of Orthodoxy, autocracy, and nationalism and to resist the noxious Western medicines they believed would only poison Russian life. To these people, reforms based on non-Russian experiences were dangerous and subversive. Constitutionalism, they argued, would enslave Russia.[35]

The Union of Russian People (*Soiuz russkovo naroda*), founded November 8, 1905, in part to oppose the October Manifesto, was the best known of the reactionary parties representing this outlook, and it ultimately absorbed many of the smaller right-wing groups. It was headed by a St. Petersburg physician, Alexander I. Dubrovin, and its leaders were largely disenchanted professional men and civil servants. The rank and file were drawn primarily from the lower-middle class but also from some peasant and worker elements, and it aspired to represent all classes.[36] Dubrovin and the Union of Russian People were violently opposed to Witte and were

[57

behind the attempt on his life on January 30, 1907.[37] Although it is unlikely that Nicholas II was aware of all the activities of the Union, it is clear that he welcomed its support and on several occasions he received deputations of its leaders, accepting on December 23, 1905, badges of the Union for himself and his son.[38] Later, in 1906, the Union became one of only two parties (the other being the Octobrists) permitted legally to exist outside the Duma, and at that time, or perhaps earlier, the Union began to receive secret financial subsidies from the Ministry of Interior.[39] During 1905–06 there is no question that a number of government officials and civil servants, as well as many clergy, openly sympathized with the Union and on occasion participated in its activities, though neither the tsar nor the government ever openly endorsed it. The difficulty was that there was enough of a link to permit the opposition, with some credibility, to charge government complicity and to sow distrust among the public about the good faith of the government in regard to the Manifesto, but the support given was never sufficient to enable the Union to become a really effective and united conservative organization or party.

The Union and its sister organizations, though not always the chief instigators nor responsible for the worst excesses, undoubtedly played a significant role in many of the pogroms which engulfed Russia in the fall and winter of 1905–06. In October alone, it has been estimated, there were approximately 150 pogroms in various cities throughout the country.[40] Within a two to three week period some 4,000 died and 10,000 were injured as a direct result of the pogroms.[41] In most cases the pogroms were directed against Jews. However, others, either members of minority nationalities or members of radical parties, were also victims of the pogroms. For example, in the Caucasus "patriotic" Tatars, carrying portraits of the tsar, raided Armenian homes and shops.[42]

Of all the cities racked by pogroms, none suffered more than Odessa. From October 18–21 Odessa trembled from unrestrained murder and pillage. According to official figures more than 500 died, of whom 400 were Jews, and 289 were wounded, of whom 237 were Jews.[43] What happened in Odessa and why deserves closer attention both as a case study of pogroms themselves and as an illustration of the explosive and anarchistic forces just below the surface of Russian society in 1905 which greatly complicated Witte's efforts both to restore order and to initiate reforms.

Because Odessa lay in the Pale of Settlement within which Jews were forced to live in tsarist Russia and since it offered numerous commercial opportunities for Jews, in 1905 nearly one-third of its population was Jewish and Jews controlled a significant portion of the city's economic life.[44] Thus it is easy to see how many in Odessa were able to rationalize their economic and other difficulties by blaming them on the Jews. Yet because of the many legal, commercial, and educational restrictions imposed on the Jews under the tsardom, the early twentieth century witnessed a growing sense of discontent among the Jews in Odessa and elsewhere, particularly among the youth, who turned to political agitation and revolutionary activity in hopes of securing civil freedoms for all and of lessening or ending discriminatory laws and practices against themselves. Moreover, in 1905 Odessa experienced at least as much excitement and unrest as any other city in Russia, and perhaps more than most. For example, in mid-June, as a result of circumstances arising from a major strike in the city and the accidentally coincident famous mutiny on the battleship *Potemkin,* a wild and bloody riot swept the city, in which thousands were killed or injured.

By early October 1905, tension and agitation had once again reached a fever pitch in Odessa, stimulated in part by spirited political meetings held at Odessa University.[45] As a result the military garrison was reinforced by four battalions, and when on October 14 students walked out of the schools, joining striking railway workers in the streets, the Odessa town governor ordered out the troops to maintain peace. After a day of uneasy calm the students resumed their demonstration on October 16, shouting, "Down with the government!" and "Long live freedom!" and throwing up barricades, but they were finally dispersed by the army, with some casualties. The next day was quiet, and on the morning of October 18, in keeping with the spirit of the Manifesto, news of which had been received late the preceding night, Baron A. V. Kaul'bars, commander of the Odessa military district, decided to let the populace celebrate the Manifesto and to keep his troops off the streets. But the exuberant crowds, spurred on by radical and socialist orators, soon became unruly. Red flags appeared in a number of places, and slogans against the government and the tsar were proclaimed freely. Mobs, which, according to Kaul'bars, were led by Jewish students, gathered in front of several police stations, demanding the release of political prisoners. In some instances the authorities complied, and during the afternoon the police, now unable to control the situation, deserted their posts. Neidhardt, the city governor, then ordered the police off the streets and back to their stations. By late afternoon the city was without police protection.[46]

Neidhardt was harshly criticized for withdrawing the police. It has been charged that Neidhardt wished to punish Odessa citizens for their attacks on the police, that he deliberately opened the door to the reactionaries by removing the police, and that when police did finally appear on the scene, they directed the pillaging and murdering.[47] Neidhardt, on the other hand, testified that since the police were being attacked and disarmed by the mobs, it was necessary to hold the police in their stations and to send them out only in group patrols for their own protection. Altogether two policemen were killed and ten were injured during the four days of pogroms.[48]

When the police left the streets, two groups of volunteer defense brigades took their place. One was a student militia led by a Professor Shchepkin of Odessa University. The other was a Jewish self-defense force. Meanwhile, early in the evening of October 18, armed collisions took place in and around Odessa. One such incident occurred when a crowd carrying red flags met a group of Russian "patriots" and ordered them to take off their hats before the flags. The latter, who were armed, chased the crowd up a street where they were met by a Jewish self-defense force. Shots were exchanged, and four people were killed.[49] Thereafter fights which broke out in various parts of the city began to take on the appearance of a pogrom as Jews increasingly became the objects of attack. Jewish houses, apartments, and shops were destroyed. Finally at 8:00 P.M. a company of infantry was sent out and succeeded in restoring temporary order.

On October 19 a funeral procession was held, with the consent of Kaul'bars, to honor those killed in the clash three days earlier. Some "patriotic" groups, despite the efforts of Kaul'bars to dissuade them, decided to march through the city also, and, according to Kaul'bars, they proceeded in good order until they began to be fired on from roofs, balconies, and house windows and several bombs were thrown in their midst. Then the groups, embittered by what they believed to be the actions of Jews, began to seek revenge.[50] Shooting and bombings spread throughout the city. From the "Black-Hundred" marchers was heard the cry, "Kill the

Kikes, Death to the Jews." The demonstrators broke into Jewish stores and houses. Jewish property was destroyed, and that which remained accidentally untouched was plundered by the vagabonds and "hooligans" who accompanied the demonstrators as they roamed throughout the city, carrying their icons and singing patriotic anthems. Those Jews who were caught were killed and tortured with incredible savagery.[51]

Meanwhile the police were conspicuously absent. Almost without exception they remained in the police stations. Kaul'bars wrote that the police and military would have stopped the pogrom in its early stages but were prevented from doing so as they were constantly being fired upon.[52] Senator Kuzminsky, who investigated the affair for the government, insisted that had the Odessa police wanted to take positive action with the full force at their command, they could have ended the pogrom immediately. But when the police patrols did appear, according to most witnesses, they usually took no measures which would stop the excesses. Since the police saw in the Jews the source of all the political trouble and strikes which had plagued Odessa, according to Kuzminsky, rather than try to stop the pogrom, "in many cases the police forces directed crowds of hooligans to destruction and pillage of Jewish homes, apartments, and shops. They supplied hooligans with clubs of wood and together with them took part in these acts of violence, robbing and beating and leading the actions of the crowd."[53]

On October 20 the pogrom continued without letup. If anything, it increased in its savagery. Neidhardt wrote: "The army and police are busy trying to stop robbery. Shooting from windows prevents them from carrying out this task."[54] Kaul'bars also asserted that military patrols were once again fired upon and impeded in their work. During the day a deputation of representatives from the city duma called on Kaul'bars and asked him to take over control of the city in order to put an end to the disorders. One of the representatives repeatedly asserted that the chief culprit in the pogrom was City Governor Neidhardt and that only his removal would restore calm to the city. The police were also charged with complicity, and it was asked that they be disarmed.[55] Kaul'bars answered that he had no authority to take over the city and to do the things that were asked of him.

Late in the day Neidhardt finally asked Kaul'bars to take more energetic steps to stop the disorders.[56] In the evening an order was sent to all military units under the signature of the chief-of-staff, Lieutenant-General Bezradetsky:

1. Take the most decisive measures against those houses from which shots are fired and bombs are thrown, if necessary destroying them.

2. Shoot at the robbers, and after each incident report to the commander the number killed and injured.[57]

At daybreak on October 21 fighting was renewed in various parts of the city. Now, however, the rioters were met with armed resistance from the military. For the first time during these four days a real show of force by the government was exerted toward stopping the riots and pogroms. By five in the evening peace had returned to the city; the pogrom was over.[58]

To fix responsibility for the Odessa pogrom and to generalize about the causes of Russian pogroms generally is not an easy matter. Senator Kuzminsky concluded that the Odessa pogrom resulted from a thermidorean reaction by the Russian population to the revolutionary excesses they had experienced during the summer and fall of 1905—excesses which were blamed on the Jews.[59] On the other hand, Kuzminsky suggested that the "spontaneous patriotic demonstrations" may have been initiated by "outside sources" although he neither identified such sources nor attempted to prove his suspicions. Kuzminsky noted that both the police and the army participated in the pogrom and that Neidhardt had prior knowledge of the "patriotic demonstrations" which ended in attacks on Jews but took no action to prevent them.[60]

Some authors have blamed the government, including the tsar, for the pogroms.[61] There is no doubt that Nicholas II was hostile to the Jews; by word and deed he revealed this antagonism. On October 27 he wrote to his mother that "because nine-tenths of the troublemakers are Jews, the People's whole anger turned against them. That's how the pogroms happened."[62] In the same letter, however, the tsar expressed his amazement that pogroms took place at the same time in many Russian cities and towns and denied that the government had arranged them. Nevertheless, on June 9, 1906, Prince Sergei D. Urusov, assistant minister of the Interior in Witte's cabinet and later a Kadet member of the First Duma, in an address to that Duma charged that "some kind of uniform and widely-planned organization" was behind the pogroms.[63] He noted that

the pogroms developed in a similar way in all the various com-
munities and that they always ceased abruptly as soon as the authorities announced they would act to end them. Moreover, in
areas where the police and army took quick and decisive action, no
pogroms occurred. Urusov charged that those directly responsible
for the pogroms were the "patriotic" societies who hoped to use
them as a means of rallying support for the monarchy and of de-
fending their own interests. He concluded that the government itself was not behind the pogroms, but that individuals in the government, often without the knowledge of their own superiors, assisted
and even participated in the pogroms. Sometimes these minor
government officials were prompted and paid by reactionary
groups; sometimes they acted voluntarily in a defensive response to
revolutionary attacks, from a sense of frustration, or out of mis-
guided patriotism and loyalty to autocracy and Orthodoxy.

The government was sensitive to the widespread public suspicion that it had a hand in instigating the pogroms, but it did little
to clear its name. On November 24 the Council of Ministers made a
very modest concession to the Jews by adding 100 towns to the list
of places in south and southwest Russia (the Pale of Settlement)
where Jews were permitted to live.[64] On February 28, 1906, after
the worst pogroms were over, the Council of Ministers belatedly
presented a memorandum to the tsar containing its judgment of a
particular outrage in the town of Gomel', which had occurred on
January 13–14, with some casualties and considerable property
damage. A high functionary of the Ministry of Interior, G. G.
Savich, had investigated the affair for Durnovo, and under pressure
from Witte the full Council considered Savich's report. The ministers endorsed Savich's conclusions, which blamed local authorities
for failure to stop the pogrom and accused Count M. A. Podgori-
chani-Petrovich, a local police official, of helping to organize and
conduct the riot by supplying firearms and a printing press to a
local "Black-Hundred" organization and by arresting leaders of the
Jewish community without cause. They also approved the measures
proposed by Durnovo, which included suppression of both revolutionary and counterrevolutionary organizations in the area, the
strengthening of police detachments, and the firing of Podgorichani,
but the Council went on to say: "These disorders were not simply
expressions of racial or religious hostility between Christians and
Jews but were the result, in a significant degree, of the incorrect

action of local authorities and the failure on their part to supervise responsibly the preservation of order." The ministers concluded by pointing out that they did not want to discourage legal action to oppose the revolution but that acts of the kind committed by Podgorichani were completely inadmissible and all civil servants should be informed of this. They recommended that Podgorichani not only be dismissed but be prosecuted as well. On this very damning report of his ministers the tsar noted, "What business is this of mine?" ("Kakoe mne do etovo delo?"), and ordered the Ministry of Interior to pursue consideration of the whole matter. In his memoirs Witte charged that this was the kind of issue which precipitated his growing distrust of Durnovo and his conflict with the tsar over his own role as chairman of the Council of Ministers. The tsar, according to Witte, decided that the affair in Gomel' and the fate of Podgorichani were not Witte's business but that of the minister of the Interior.[65]

Shortly after this Prince Urusov, as assistant minister of Interior, uncovered what he considered to be clear evidence that a police functionary in St. Petersburg, one Komissarov, had been using a government press to print inflammatory and pogromatic materials, but although, according to Urusov, Witte had an attack of nervous asthma when he learned about it, the chairman of the Council of Ministers declined to make a big issue of the affair, and Urusov subsequently resigned in disgust.[66]

Whatever the kind and degree of official complicity in the pogroms of 1905–06 (a matter which can probably never be determined with exactitude although the conclusions reached in Urusov's speech summarized above seem closest to the truth), it is also clear that these terrible events were in part based on a long history and evolution of anti-Semitic feeling in Russia and were prompted to a considerable degree by a mixture of religious bigotry and real or imagined economic grievances. In 1905 an additional element was added—a revolutionary movement led in part by Jews and directed against the autocracy. Those who wanted most to preserve the autocracy and to destroy the fruits of the Manifesto found it relatively easy to exploit old prejudices and fears and thereby present a serious challenge to Witte in his attempt to restore order and to offer reform.

Witte was not responsible for the pogroms; though somewhat anti-Semitic himself, he opposed all such forms of narrow nationalism and bigotry. But the government which he directed was not without guilt, and as the leader of that government, Witte received the condemnation of society. Witte was trying to lead Russia down new political paths; the pogroms, which were reflections of the old order, did nothing to increase public confidence in the new government.

First Steps

THERE IS LITTLE DIRECT EVIDENCE concerning Witte's personal attitude toward the varied responses the October 17 Manifesto produced in Russia. Yet he must have been both pleased and dismayed. As we saw in the preceding chapter, Witte had opposed publication of the Manifesto, fearing it would only create fresh unrest and raise false hopes of immediate change and reform. In this he proved to be quite correct: new disturbances, both for and against the government, broke out, and many segments of society demanded instant fulfillment of the promises made. But, without question, the disorders turned out to be more widespread, serious, and ugly, and public hostility more entrenched than Witte had expected. There is no reason to accept as his considered judgment the remark attributed to Witte a week after publication of the Manifesto—"If Christ himself were placed at the head of the government in the present circumstances, no one would have confidence in him"—but Witte undoubtedly began to experience almost from the beginning the sense of futility and isolation which so depressed and unnerved him from December on.[67] Moreover, he must have soon sensed the impatient and critical attitude of the tsar, which the latter expressed so early in the letters to his mother quoted at the beginning of this chapter. In a note of November 7, replying to Witte's query of what to do about the flood of congratulatory telegrams and resolutions pouring into St. Petersburg, Nicholas wrote: "You should reply that I have read them with pleasure. I am happy the senseless railroad strike is over—this is a great moral victory for the Government. Now the chief thing is not to yield further, strongly to stand our ground and decisively to achieve order."[68] What the tsar wanted from the Manifesto and from Witte was abundantly clear.

On the other hand, despite the ferment throughout the country, the feelings of the tsar, and the continuing opposition of some liberal and all radical circles, Witte's aim of pacifying "society" through the Manifesto had to a limited extent succeeded. Some moderates, many enlightened landowners and bureaucrats, and even some workers either swung over to support of the government or adopted a "wait-and-see" attitude. The monolithic opposition which had so nearly toppled the dynasty in early October was definitely broken. As a consequence, Witte determined, if one can judge his thoughts by his actions, to pursue steadfastly the twin goals he had set for himself: the introduction of reform and the reestablishment of order. Both, however, proved more difficult than he anticipated. At the same time it is clear that the widespread interpretation in Soviet texts and in some Western accounts that Witte immediately launched a policy of repression and a counterattack on the revolution is misleading. As we will attempt to demonstrate, both strands of Witte's policy evolved in the first weeks of his premiership—and indeed throughout it.

Witte's dilemma was dramatized on his very first day in office. The Manifesto had promised freedom of speech, and this was widely interpreted to mean freedom of publication as well. In a startling innovation in tsarist governmental practice, on October 18 Witte held a press conference, to which were invited the editors of newspapers and journals in St. Petersburg.[69] Witte began by telling the editors that the security of the government depended upon a favorable public opinion. Since the editors and their publications were molders of public opinion, he was asking for their help. By working together, Witte said they could quiet the population and then the government could "play a role such as it does in cultured countries." He asked them to do this not for him, or for the government, but for the good of all of Russia.

The editors were not sympathetic. Several demanded immediate amnesty for all political prisoners as evidence of the government's good faith, and others asked that General Trepov, governor-general of St. Petersburg, be fired at once. Witte agreed that reforms were necessary, but first of all, order must be restored; shooting in the streets had to be stopped. One editor raised the question of censorship. Witte promised freedom of the press, but he said editors must be patient as on occasion they might be asked "to drop a line." An editor retorted that freedom of the press was impossible until soldiers were removed. Witte answered, "Remove the army! No, it would be better to remain without newspapers than without electricity.[70] If I took away the soldiers, then 100,000 women and children would say 'Witte is mad'!" Witte promised, however, that as soon as order was restored, the military would be withdrawn.

The entire session was marked by stormy debate, signaling the chasm that still separated the government from the public. The following day, October 19, the government issued an administrative directive to censors. It called attention to the freedom promised by the Manifesto and pledged that new laws would soon be written which were in keeping with that document. Until such laws appeared censors were to continue to operate under the old laws but within the spirit of the Manifesto. "Radical" statements which were intended to inflame the population and to create revolution were not to be permitted.[71] On November 24 the Council of Ministers issued a set of "temporary" regulations on the press which provided on the one hand for swift prosecution and stiff penalties (in some cases more severe than before) for those responsible for violating restrictions on the press in the criminal code and on the other for abolition of preliminary censorship for publications issued in cities (though not outside). Under these rules editors and publishers were still subject to later court action for what they printed.[72] As we shall see in the next chapter, these "temporary" regulations were replaced by tougher rules after the turn of the year, but the problem of freedom of the press well illustrated Witte's efforts to balance order and reform in his first weeks in office. Actually government pronouncements on the subject of censorship meant little in these early exuberant days of "freedom" anyway. In the spirit of "October," publishers and editors simply ignored the censors and printed pretty much what they wished. Moreover, new journals and newspapers sprang up, representing a wide spectrum of opinions, and what amounted to a truly free press flourished in Russia's cities for several months.[73]

One of Witte's first actions met what was almost a universal demand of all liberal and oppositional elements, though it is difficult to estimate what effect it had in placating "society." On October 21, in the spirit of the Manifesto's pledge concerning the inviolability of persons, the government issued a decree granting full amnesty to certain categories of political prisoners, including participants in strikes, and partial amnesty to other groups (some sentences were cut in half, while those sentenced to life imprisonment or death had their sentences commuted to fifteen years at hard labor).[74]

Another early measure was designed to help calm the rebellious peasantry. On November 3 the government issued a decree, "About Improving the Living Conditions and Lightening the Situation of the Peasant Population." This provided that the burdensome redemption dues the peasants had been paying since their emancipation in 1861 would be cut in half on January 1, 1906, and abolished entirely as of January 1, 1907. It also promised that the activity of the Peasant Land Bank would be broadened to facilitate the purchase of private landholdings on favorable terms. Finally, the decree hinted that the Duma, in which the peasants would be represented, would act in cooperation with the government to satisfy "the further urgent needs of the peasantry," who until then should "everywhere preserve peace and order."[75] Later, as we shall see in chapter six, Witte attempted to work out more fundamental solutions to the peasant problem.

Witte also took steps to end the general strike, which in any case had probably spent its force. Immediately after publication of the Manifesto the Moscow city strike committee, which was dominated by liberals and representatives of the unions of professions (lawyers, teachers, engineers), appealed to the workers to return to work. Since the most disruptive strike was that on the railroads, which had touched off the general strike and which was still paralyzing the country, Witte authorized the Ministry of Communications to send a telegram on October 21 to all railroad lines promising that "the government will take immediate and decisive measures to improve the conditions of workers and employees of the railroads" and that workers who returned to work within twenty-four hours or no later than October 24 would not be penalized for participating in the strike and would be paid for the days they were on strike. The same day Witte persuaded representatives of the striking railroad workers to send a telegram to all the railroad strike committees promising, "in agreement with Count Witte," improved pay, the lifting of martial law on the railroads, freedom of assembly for workers, reinstatement of workers dismissed because of the strike, and immunity for those participating in the strike. On October 26, however, the Ministry of Communications disavowed these promises, claiming they were simply private opinions and that the matter of improving the workers' conditions was being studied and specific remedies would have to await completion of that study.[76] Witte's strategy, though clearly devious, worked. The railroad strike ended, and on October 21 the St. Petersburg Soviet called off the general strike in the capital.

In addition to measures designed to meet urgent demands of the public and to calm the situation, Witte began almost at once to implement certain reforms of the governmental structure which he believed would make it more responsive and efficient. As we saw in chapter two, in early October he had argued vigorously for a strengthened and revamped Council of Ministers, and had insisted that only if it were altered along the lines he considered desirable would he consent to serve as its chairman and head of the government. On October 19 an imperial decree did reorganize the Council of Ministers, giving Witte substantially what he wanted. The chairman of the new Council had the right to recommend to the tsar for appointment all ministers and heads of major administrative departments except the ministers of War, the Navy, Foreign Affairs, and the Imperial Court and Lands. Moreover, the chairman was empowered to coordinate and supervise the activities of all the ministries: he could ask for information and explanations from each minister, who, in turn, was required to submit to the chairman all legislative proposals and the most important administrative orders before they were discussed by the full Council and presented to the tsar. The only exceptions were the ministers noted above who were not nominated by the chairman—they had to submit to the chairman only those measures which it was essential for the full Council to discuss. Finally, the Council was to meet regularly two or three times a week, with a record being kept of its deliberations.[77] In practice, Witte's design for the Council never really worked. Several ministers, such as Minister of War Rediger, attended Council meetings infrequently, reported directly to Nicholas, and took a number of independent actions without consulting Witte, as we shall see later. Witte's most notorious failure to establish unified and centralized direction of the government was the case of his own nominee, Acting Minister of the Interior Durnovo, who almost from the beginning acted independently and worked directly with the tsar and his advisers at court. Moreover, the tsar himself did not hesitate to ignore Witte and the Council and to initiate his own policies and measures, prompted often by General Trepov, the court commandant, and other imperial advisers who were responsible to no one but Nicholas.

At this time Witte was also striving to put into effect a reform of the State Council which he had first proposed in his memorandum of October 9 to the tsar and which had been promised in his report published together with the Manifesto. During the nineteenth century this imperial and conservative institution, whose members the tsar appointed, had served as an advisory body, usually without much influence or power. In the 1860's and again in the 1880's, as a means of opening the way toward some form of representative government in Russia, the idea had been broached of reforming the State Council by including in it members elected by the zemstvos and city dumas. Under the pressure of the liberation movement of 1904 the idea was revived in governmental circles, but the tsar turned it down, finally agreeing after "Bloody Sunday" to substitute for it the advisory Duma which he promised in his imperial rescript of February 18, 1905. When the details of the proposed Bulygin Duma were made public in August, no reform of the State Council was envisaged; it was to have equal rights with the consultative Duma and was apparently to serve as a buffer between the tsar and the elected representatives in the Duma. There was widespread criticism of this failure to transform the State Council by adding elected members to it, criticism which Witte soon supported.

On October 9 Kryzhanovskii, a leading official in the Ministry of Interior, submitted a memorandum to the chairman of the State Council, Count Dmitri Sol'sky, recommending a reform along the lines desired by the liberals—but for conservative reasons. Kryzhanovskii argued that the Duma would be liberal and would be dominated by the intelligentsia. Therefore a conservative counterweight to it was needed in the form of the State Council, the authority of which, however, would be much strengthened if it contained some elected members from the gentry, clergy, upper bourgeoisie, and Moscow and St. Petersburg universities. In this way the Council could unite and make into an effective force the most reasonable elements in the country.[78] Kryzhanovskii's proposal was discussed informally by a small group of officials, including Witte, who finally agreed that one-half of the members of the Council should be elected by large landowners, by the Academy of Sciences and the universities, by all-Russian congresses of representatives of trade and industry. Also elected would be ten representatives of the Orthodox clergy and one representative of other Christian faiths. Around October 18 a draft ukase was prepared for the tsar, but he finally decided on October 28, for reasons that are not clear from the available evidence, to have the whole matter studied further by a special commission headed by Count Sol'sky, which included all the ministers, as well as seven other statesmen and bureaucrats. This commission held ten meetings during November, December, and January, and its recommendations were adopted without significant changes in February, as we shall see in chapter nine.[79]

In the commission Witte began by urging that the revamped State Council have only an advisory role in relation to the government and the Duma, but in late November he suddenly changed his mind and supported the position that the Council should have authority equal to that of the Duma, should in other words be a genuine second house, on the grounds that in this way the Council could act as a buffer between the tsar and the Duma and would serve as a necessary conservative counterweight to the Duma. Despite the opposition of two of his own appointees (Kutler, acting minister of Agriculture, and Obolensky, procurator of the Holy Synod), this point of view carried the day.[80] Witte's failure to institute immediately a reform of the State Council and his altered view of its role illustrate both the difficulties he faced in pursuing his twin aims of order and reform and his growing conservatism.

At the same time there were other indications in the early days of Witte's premiership of the complex course he was attempting to follow. One of the most difficult problems Witte confronted on taking office was the widespread revolt against Russian rule in the non-Russian regions of the empire. It is clear from Witte's actions and words he had no intention of presiding over the breakup of the Russian Empire. He believed that the policy of Russification which Nicholas II had pursued was stupid and a basic reason for present difficulties in the provinces. Witte conceded that Russia might be better off if the nation consisted only of Russians, but to free all the non-Russian peoples would have been unthinkable to the tsar. Equally unthinkable, from Witte's point of view, was the attempt to transform all of a many-cultured people into "true Russians."[81]

The October Manifesto further encouraged demands for national independence or at least cultural autonomy which had arisen in the last decades of the nineteenth century in many parts of the empire and which had reached a peak in 1904–05. In Poland, the Ukraine, White Russia, and Bessarabia, nationalist parties struggled for political autonomy; in the Baltic provinces the source of unrest was a combination of labor and peasant dissatisfaction fed by resentment against Russification and by the Baltic people's hatred for the German landlords in the area. The Finns rebelled in an effort to win restoration of their autonomy, which had been systematically abridged between 1899–1904. The Caucasus was torn by religious and nationalist ferment and by social unrest, and Tatars and other Moslem groups organized the All-Russian Moslem League at Nizhnii Novgorod in August 1905, in a bid for political and religious recognition. By concession, conciliation, or conquest Witte had to deal with this array of nationalist problems.

The two regions which demanded the most urgent attention—urgent in the sense that rebellions there threatened Russian control of them and that they were very close to the center of tsarist power—were Poland and Finland. Moreover, these two cases well illustrate the two sides of Witte's policy of order and reform. In Poland the cause of the unrest was labor and agrarian dissatisfaction combined with nationalism. When Witte assumed control of the Russian government Poland was in a state of anarchy.[82] On October 26 the governor-general, G. A. Skalon, asked Trepov and Witte for permission to declare a state of emergency and to enforce martial law.[83] Martial law was declared on October 29, and troops were sent to crush all signs of opposition to the government.[84]

For this action Witte was bitterly attacked by both the liberals and the radicals in Russia. To them it was an open violation of the spirit of the Manifesto. Witte explained: "It was clear to me that in our enthusiasm for political emancipation, we Russians had lost all respect for our glorious history and its product, the great Russian Empire. The radicals confused emancipation from the misrule of bureaucrats and courtiers with emancipation from all the traditions of our historical existence."[85] Therefore, to save Poland, Witte used force.

With Finland, Witte adopted a different approach. Whereas in Poland Witte believed that a successful revolution would result in the separation of Poland from the Russian Empire, in Finland he was convinced that the Finns desired only restoration of their autonomy. The Finns had participated vigorously in the October general strike, and as a result of the inaction and panic of the governor-general, I. M. Obolenskii, authority in Helsinki passed almost completely into the hands of a group of moderate Finnish leaders. One of them, Professor Mekhelin, called on Witte in mid-October and convinced him that all except the most radical elements were prepared to accept the Manifesto and that order and the Russian position in Finland could be restored if the government reestablished the Finns' traditional rights which they had enjoyed earlier in the nineteenth century and if the tsar appointed a new governor-general and reorganized the Finnish Senate.[86] The tsar accepted Witte's advice that the best policy toward Finland was conciliation. On October 22 he issued a decree which restored Finnish autonomy, and he soon appointed N. N. Gerard as the new governor-general.[87] This brought an end to the unrest although Finland continued to be a haven for Russian radicals, and Witte later expressed concern over the problem of closing off Finland as a place of refuge and an arms depot for the revolutionaries.[88]

Unfortunately for Witte Russian society as a whole did not prove to be as reasonable as the Finnish moderates. There is little doubt that Witte had expected most elements in Russian public life to respond favorably and sensibly to the Manifesto and to his first measures of reform outlined above. Yet while almost everyone savored the new taste of freedom and some waxed lyrical over it, Witte soon concluded that the sense of responsibility and cooperation he had hoped for were sadly lacking, not only among the editors he had confronted on October 18 but among the public at large. In a memorandum prepared by Vuich (but undoubtedly reflecting Witte's views) which summarized the history and achievements of Witte's premiership it was plaintively pointed out that after promulgation of the Manifesto, instead of calm, dedication, and good sense, the moderate elements in society were passive and refused to undertake the hard work necessary to effect reform, limiting themselves to Platonic agreement and cooperation with the government, while right-wing circles incited unrest and dissatisfaction and the revolutionaries continued to attack the government and to spread rumors and panic.[89]

In an apparent effort to explain his dual policy of order and reform and to win the support of "society" Witte's government issued several public statements in the first week after he had assumed power. The first and most important of these pronouncements was issued on October 20 and appeared in the official government organ, *Pravitel'stvennyi vestnik* [Government Herald]. Be cause it appears to sum up so well Witte's attitude and his dilemma at this time, it is worth quoting a substantial part of it:

> To establish a new order in the country requires hard work, steadfastness, and consistency. Society should recognize that it is not feasible to change at once the whole order of state life in Russia, and that to replace the existing structure with a new one requires legal determinations, as well as a series of administrative actions. Until this can be done the former laws must remain in force. The government will make every effort to act in the spirit of the Manifesto of October 17. The government ought to be given time to carry out its program, and the prime requisite for its success in this effort is the reestablishment of order. Nevertheless certain elements in society are trying to shake the people's faith in the government and to spur unrest among the population. If the majority of society considers that its duty is to aid the government, then the situation will quickly improve; otherwise the government ought not to be blamed for the difficult events that may occur and for not fulfilling the tasks before it as quickly as conditions demand and as it itself fervently wishes.[90]

This appeal for patience, a return to order, and assistance in carrying out reform apparently fell on deaf ears. On October 21 the government issued a declaration warning of the dangers illustrated by the fact that many high school students were participating in street demonstrations, and on October 24 a government statement appeared calling for an end to disorders and affirming that the promises made in the Manifesto were inviolable and "unswerving."[91] All to little or no avail. Finally, in the second week of November Witte appealed for support to the Congress of Zemstvo and City Leaders meeting in Moscow. In part his telegram said:

> The decisions of the congress will be read by all of Russia and will undoubtedly have considerable influence on public opinion. I suspect that some decisions of the congress would be different if its members were fully acquainted with what is happening in the country. The most dangerous thing is propaganda in the army. The fruits of this propaganda were reflected to some extent in the events at Kronstadt, and now are fully evident at Sevastopol. . . . If the congress does not take into account these circumstances . . . it can play an extremely unfortunate role in the immediate future of Russia. I consider it

necessary to communicate this to you, having no doubts about your patriotism.[92]

But the majority of the congress rejected Witte's appeal and refused to give full support to the government.

Forming a Cabinet

ONE OF THE KEY WAYS in which Witte hoped to enlist the aid of society in his endeavor to restore order and begin reform was by selecting a cabinet that would command the confidence of most elements in Russian public life. In accord with the decree of October 19 reforming the Council of Ministers the cabinet was slated to play a far more crucial role in state policy (though it was *not* to be responsible to the Duma) than it had in previous ministries, and Witte undoubtedly hoped that the cabinet could provide the sort of leadership he had called upon the government to exert in his report to the tsar of October 9. To achieve this end it was clearly necessary to add liberals to the cabinet. These should be men of influence who were well known for their reformist views but who would not try to run the government according to their own liberal theories. Any government which deviated too radically from what the tsar judged to be wise would be dismissed. Therefore, Witte needed to attract men who had reputations as leaders of the liberal opposition yet who were willing to set aside their roles as opposition leaders to assist Witte in restoring order and in initiating reform.

Witte's task was not an easy one. One factor which increased his difficulties was that he was in charge of a Western-type cabinet which, however, was responsible to the tsar and which had no pro-government party upon which to rely for support. Every prime minister expects to fight for his political life each day against the attacks of one or more opposition parties, but he makes this fight with the backing of a party that shares in his defeat if he loses. This was not the case with Witte. There was a fierce and determined opposition ranging from liberal to revolutionary; there was no pro-government party. Witte could not depend for support on the "conservatives" at the court. Nicholas II was not genuinely in favor of the new government. He desired most of all a return to order. Those in and around the court joined another kind of opposition, the reactionary parties, which presented as great an obstacle to

Witte as did the revolutionaries. In truth, Witte assumed control of the government in a political vacuum. Somehow, he had to break his isolation and to draw support from some quarter of the public.

It was natural that Witte should turn first to the zemstvo group for assistance. Zemstvo leaders had directed the fight for liberal reform and constitutional government; they had proved to be dedicated and honest public servants in affairs at the local level; and their demands on the government had never been set in the shrill and harsh language which characterized many of the intelligentsia and socialists. During the struggle to force liberal reforms from the government they had seemed to act more in the manner of a "loyal opposition" than had other liberal and certainly all the revolutionary groups.

On October 18 Dmitrii Nikolaevich Shipov, well-known zemstvo figure and later a founder of the Union of October 17, received a wire from Witte, requesting him to come to St. Petersburg.[93] Shipov was one of the most respected figures of this time. People looked to him for wise counsel and leadership. Even his enemies acknowledged his moral irreproachability and political honesty. His reputation and his prominent role in the zemstvo movement made him a most desirable man to attract to Witte's cabinet. The only drawback was that since the First Zemstvo Conference, November 6–9, 1904, he had become the leader of a minority or conservative faction within the zemstvo circle. Shipov had opposed the resolution at the First Congress calling for a legislative Duma and had argued for only a consultative Duma. Therefore, the left zemstvoists who were ultimately to find their place in the Kadet party no longer responded to Shipov's leadership as they once had.[94]

Shipov arrived in St. Petersburg on October 19, to learn from Alexei Obolensky that Witte wanted him to join the cabinet. Later Witte put his request directly to Shipov, indicating that he wished Shipov to accept the post of state comptroller. Witte urged Shipov to enter the cabinet, pointing out that it would build public confidence in the government. Shipov agreed to accept the position only if he were convinced that there was a real chance for a change in the policies of the government. To assure that such a change would be forthcoming, Shipov stated that Witte must include other "public men" in the cabinet, especially members representing the "left" faction of the zemstvo movement. Witte agreed and asked how he could make contact with such men. Shipov suggested that he wire F. A. Golovin, chairman of the Congress of Zemstvo and City Leaders, requesting that a delegation be sent to meet with Witte. Shipov thought the Bureau of the Congress would probably choose I. I. Petrunkevich, S. A. Muromtsev, and Prince G. E. L'vov to represent the left-wing zemstvoists. Shipov further suggested that Muromtsev would be ideal for the post of minister of Justice, while L'vov and Petrunkevich seemed suited for ministers of Interior and Agriculture respectively.[95] Witte told Shipov he already had in mind two other zemstvoists, Prince E. N. Trubetskoi and A. I. Guchkov, to head the Ministries of Education and of Commerce and Industry respectively.[96]

On October 20 a delegation representing the Bureau of the Congress left Moscow for St. Petersburg to meet with Witte. The delegation had been hastily selected and consisted of F. A. Golovin, F. F. Kokoshkin, and Prince G. E. L'vov. Whether this group represented the best thinking of the zemstvo movement is difficult to say, but there is no doubt that they expected to use the opportunity to make demands on the government rather than to attempt some sort of compromise.[97] Kokoshkin, for one, was captivated by the slogans of the Kadet party, which had just organized and which had pledged itself to oppose the government. The delegation met with Witte on October 21. They first demanded that their discussion be made public. Witte agreed, and it was published on October 23 in *Russkie vedomosti* [Russian gazette]. The delegation then presented Witte with an ultimatum. They demanded an immediate constituent assembly to work out new basic laws, the assembly to be chosen according to the "four-tailed" formula (which meant universal, direct, equal, and secret elections), and full political amnesty for all political prisoners.[98] Witte, of course, could not go this far and the attitude of the delegation made it impossible for Witte to cooperate with them. They were apparently less interested in joining his government than in overthrowing it.[99]

After the zemstvo delegation left, Witte wired to Shipov to return to St. Petersburg. On October 22 Shipov once again met with Witte. Witte told him what had taken place the day before; he also told Shipov that the tsar approved his nomination as state comptroller and was prepared to receive him for the purpose of confirming the appointment. Shipov immediately reminded Witte of his conditions for entering the cabinet. Therefore, he was unable at that moment to accept the appointment. The following day Shipov went to see the tsar. He told Nicholas that he was flattered to be offered the post, but unless more "public men" were included in the cabinet, his own appointment might do the government more harm than good. The tsar agreed and told Shipov to tell Witte the same thing.[100]

Later on October 23 and again on October 24 Witte met with Shipov and other zemstvoists. Witte said that the posts of Finance and of Ways and Communication required people with special training. Therefore, he had already chosen I. P. Shipov as minister of Finance and K. S. Nemeshaev as minister of Ways and Communication. I. P. Shipov had been Witte's long-time associate in the Ministry of Finance; Nemeshaev's experience had been chiefly with the southwestern railways. On October 24 Prince E. N. Trubetskoi, one of the zemstvoists Witte hoped to add to his cabinet as minister of Education, arrived in St. Petersburg and declared that he would accept the post only if Witte endorsed in advance Trubetskoi's entire program. When Witte declined to provide such a blank check, Trubetskoi refused to enter the cabinet.[101] Later, after the negotiations to bring "public men" into the cabinet had collapsed, Trubetskoi explained in a letter to Witte that he had felt unable to join the government because, as a leading Kadet, he had made publicly a number of political promises which he did not think the cabinet could at that time fulfill.[102]

In the renewed discussions between Witte and the Shipov zemstvoists concerning the formation of a cabinet a major point of disagreement was over selecting the minister of Interior. Witte insisted that it was important to have a man in this position who was familiar with police work and who was competent to take responsibility for restoring peace and order to Russia. Witte argued that he knew of only two men qualified for the job, Petr Nikolaevich Durnovo and General D. F. Trepov. Neither was acceptable to the "public men." Shipov and his colleagues maintained that the minister of Interior must be a person who embraced the ideas of civil freedom contained in the Manifesto and who would see that they were fulfilled. They acknowledged Trepov was a proper selection by the tsar for court commandant as a forceful man was needed to protect the tsar's life, but the minister of Interior should be a liberal as defined by the zemstvoists. Both Guchkov and Shipov said they would not enter the cabinet if Durnovo were appointed minister of Interior.[103] Witte then suggested that Prince Sergei D. Urusov—zemstvoist, governor of Tver in 1904, and later a Kadet member of the First Duma—be named as minister of Interior, with Durnovo assigned as assistant minister as Urusov was not so familiar with police work. This arrangement satisfied Shipov and Guchkov, and they left St. Petersburg for Moscow on October 24 only to receive word to return on October 25.

On October 26 Guchkov, Trubetskoi, M. A. Stakhovich, and Shipov went to see Witte. There they found Urusov, who, Witte announced, had agreed to accept the post of assistant minister of Interior under Durnovo as first minister. Shipov and Guchkov were incensed at having been deceived by Witte. Both were adamant in their refusals to join the cabinet with Durnovo as minister of Interior. Urusov sought to sway them, but they would not listen.[104]

Why Witte insisted on Durnovo is as much a mystery today as it was in 1905. The few whom Witte had already selected for the cabinet opposed Durnovo;[105] the tsar disliked the appointment, refused to accept Durnovo as a minister, but finally agreed to name him as acting head of the ministry.[106] Trepov opposed Durnovo's appointment, a fact that strengthened Durnovo in Witte's eyes. Witte said he chose Durnovo because he was "known for his sane, liberal ideas."[107] This opinion of Durnovo was not shared by others, especially the liberals.

Somewhat different reasons were offered by Gurko, who said Witte preferred Urusov as minister of Interior, but Durnovo forced Witte to choose him instead. According to Gurko, Witte submitted Durnovo's name to the tsar as minister of Interior but in such a way that the tsar at first refused to accept him. In this way Witte hoped to get Durnovo to accept the post of assistant minister. Gurko, who saw Durnovo shortly after the tsar had turned down Witte's request to appoint him as first minister, said Durnovo was in a rage and shouted, "I'll show him [Witte]! I'll show him!" Shortly thereafter Witte gained the tsar's assent to Durnovo but only as one in charge of the ministry. Gurko wrote that Durnovo had in his possession certain letters whose publication would have hurt Witte's career and that Durnovo used these letters to blackmail Witte into appointing him.[108]

It is difficult to know how much credence to give to Gurko's narrative. Gurko was no friend of Witte and did not avoid opportunities to criticize him. On the other hand, it is strange that Witte would have gone to such lengths to add Durnovo to his cabinet. Durnovo's appointment cost Witte whatever chance for liberal support he may have had and left him with no other choice than to select his ministers from bureaucrats. Among the liberals only Urusov agreed to join the cabinet, and then as an assistant minister; this hardly compensated for all the bureaucrats who headed the other ministries. Witte was not blind to Durnovo's faults. Because of the latter's questionable moral reputation, Witte told Shipov it would be necessary to silence the newspapers.[109] One can speculate that the appointment of Durnovo was the sort of devious stratagem Witte liked to employ. If he could get both some liberals *and* Durnovo in the cabinet, he would satisfy not only those who were clamoring for reform but also the elements who were demanding a forceful policy and a prompt return to order. He could then initiate the reforms he believed necessary while having in Durnovo a convenient scapegoat on whom to blame the measures of repression that Witte realized would be required to quell the revolution. In short, he could have his cake and eat it too. But this must remain speculation since in Witte's memoirs and papers no really credible explanation of his appointment of Durnovo emerges.

For whatever reasons Witte had, his insistence on Durnovo was his first major mistake as chairman of the Council of Ministers. Not only did Durnovo's appointment help prevent Witte from obtaining the potential and much-needed support of the liberal community, but Durnovo's loyalty to Witte was less than satisfactory. He rarely attended cabinet meetings, and he seemed more intent on making his presence welcome with the court at Tsarskoe Selo than with Witte in St. Petersburg.[110] Witte wrote that Durnovo was both energetic and competent and would have been satisfactory had he been told by Nicholas that he must work through Witte, but Witte was forced to admit: "Durnovo's appointment was one of the greatest errors I made during my administration."[111]

Although there is little doubt that Witte's determination to appoint Durnovo was a major stumbling block in his effort to add "public men" to the cabinet, the usual explanation that this alone largely explains the failure of the negotiations between Witte and the zemstvoists is an oversimplification. Just as important were three other factors: One was a vague but strongly felt sense of mistrust of the government on the part of men who had been vigorously opposing the old order for the past several years. The issue of

Durnovo, of course, did little to dispel these doubts. Could the tsarist leopard really change his spots?[112] Related to this feeling was the firm and honest commitment of the liberal leaders to their principles and program, which, as in the case of Trubetskoi, they believed were not fully represented in Witte's platform. Some things they espoused Witte promised to do; others he would or could not do. Could they support and work for half a loaf? Finally, some of them, such as Shipov and Stakhovich, genuinely believed that unless the cabinet could include representatives of all shades of liberal sentiment, who would then carry sufficient weight to counterbalance the influence of bureaucratic ministers, they could work more effectively for the goals they espoused outside the government, continuing and strengthening their role as leaders of society and molders of public opinion by forming an active and viable political organization or party of moderate elements.[113]

Failing to get support from the zemstvoists, Witte in desperation turned to the Kadets for counsel. He found Miliukov even less responsive than were the right-wing zemstvoists. Miliukov gave two reasons why the Kadets could not join Witte's cabinet: first, the Kadets feared they would be asked to compromise their principles; they were willing to take control of the government but not to become part of a bureaucratic government. Second, Witte was only the representative of the tsar and could be replaced whenever the tsar chose; therefore, in the Kadets' estimation nothing of value could be given permanence by the Witte government. In a meeting with Witte in late October or early November, Miliukov asked Witte why he had thus far avoided using the word constitution. "Witte answered sadly, 'I am not able to because the tsar does not want this.'" Miliukov broke off their discussion saying, "Then it is useless for us to continue our conversation. I am not able to offer you any kind of serious advice."[114]

By refusing to assist Witte except on its own terms, which required in essence the capitulation of the government, the liberal camp demonstrated its own political immaturity. For years the government had been the enemy; now the enemy was mortally wounded. It was time not for a truce but for unconditional surrender. Some of the liberals—Shipov and his colleagues—were too proud to compromise their ideals a whit. They were men of principle; such men find it difficult to be expedient. Other liberals—Miliukov and the Kadets—preferred continuing the struggle against the government in the forthcoming Duma rather than joining the government. The Kadets were far more critical of the government than of the revolutionaries who wished to continue the revolution, thereby giving the impression that only the reactionaries wanted peace and order reestablished. Witte assumed power on the theory that a program of reform would lead to order. The Kadets did not wish order until a full constitutional regime had been established. Witte, on the other hand, could hardly accept as ministers those who were committed to furthering disorder. Witte wished to be eclectic; the liberals were doctrinaire. Witte hoped to compromise; the liberals wanted the government to capitulate.[115] While the liberals mistrusted the government and concluded correctly that Witte's concept of political reform was not the same as their own, by refusing to cooperate with him, they created a situation which made it most unlikely that any real reform would result. The liberals chose the easy path. They stood on the sidelines, jeering and criticizing, clothed in their principles and doctrines while Witte struggled to implement some programs in which they presumably had a stake. Witte may have begun his administration with little real chance of achieving his objectives, but what chance there had been was dashed by the cold aloofness with which the liberals greeted his requests for support.[116]

Failing to add liberals to his cabinet, Witte had no other recourse than to fill the posts with bureaucrats, however distasteful such a government might be to the public. At least, under the new organization of the Council of Ministers he might select those bureaucrats whom he trusted and could control. Most of those who headed the ministries prior to October 17 either submitted their resignations or were forced to resign by Witte. Witte's attitude toward former ministers he did not like was demonstrated by his relationship with Count V. N. Kokovtsov. Kokovtsov, who had been assistant minister of Finance under Witte from 1896 to 1902 and became minister of Finance in 1904, had opposed both Witte's plan to reorganize the Council of Ministers and his program of reform which resulted in the October 17 Manifesto.[117] Therefore, Witte insisted he be replaced by I. P. Shipov, a protégé of Witte when he was minister of Finance.[118] The tsar agreed and offered Kokovtsov as an alternative position the post of head of the Department of State Economy in the State Council, an advisory group that reviewed the policies of the Ministry of Finance. Witte was infuriated and threatened to resign if Kokovtsov were given this position.[119] The tsar relented but noted that he would never forgive such impudence on Witte's part.[120] Witte also forced the resignation of procurator of the Holy Synod, K. P. Pobedonostsev, whose identification with reactionary policies made his continuation in office incompatible with the new regime and who was replaced by Prince Alexei D. Obolensky, principal author of the Manifesto.

Five ministers remained in office: General Aleksander F. Rediger, minister of War; Admiral Aleksei A. Birilev, minister of the Navy; Baron Vladimir B. Fredericks, minister of the Imperial Court; Count V. N. Lamsdorff, minister of Foreign Affairs; and S. S. Manukhin, minister of Justice. The first three occupied posts, appointment to which was the prerogative of the tsar. Witte admired both Lamsdorff and Manukhin, and he, therefore, chose to retain them. Witte's own appointments to the Council as it began to work in October 1905, were the following: Petr. N. Durnovo, acting minister of Interior; Alexei D. Obolensky, over-procurator of the Holy Synod; Ivan P. Shipov, minister of Finance; Dmitrii A. Filosofov, state comptroller; Nikolai N. Kutler, acting minister of Agriculture; Klavdi S. Nemeshaev, minister of Ways and Communication; Vasilii I. Timiriazev, minister of Commerce and Industry (a new ministry); and Count Ivan I. Tolstoi, minister of Education.[121] Of his cabinet, Witte gained the total support of Shipov, Kutler, and Nemeshaev; Kutler, as was true of Shipov, had formerly worked under Witte in the Ministry of Finance. Another group consisting of Tolstoi, Timiriazev, Filosofov, and Lamsdorff were more or less independent but generally supported Witte. A third group consisting of Fredericks, Rediger, and Birilev rarely took active part in the deliberations of the Council and considered themselves apart from it. The last two—Durnovo and Mikhail G. Akimov, who succeeded S. S. Manukhin when he was forced to resign by Nicholas for being too "soft"—paid little attention to Witte and, working behind his back, reported directly to the tsar.[122]

By the time of his resignation in April 1906, Witte had been forced to replace three of his original ministers. Manukhin's resignation has been indicated. The forced resignation of Timiriazev, minister of Commerce and Industry, is discussed in the next section of this chapter. Kutler's resignation was a result of an agricultural program he devised which angered the conservatives near the court.[123] Witte was forced to ask Kutler to resign in February 1906. The choice of a new minister provoked a quarrel between Witte and Nicholas, with Witte threatening to resign. Nicholas wished to appoint Aleksandr V. Krivoshein, who Witte believed was nothing more than a spy for Trepov. Finally after a number of names were posed and rejected by one or the other, Nicholas agreed to the appointment of A. P. Nikol'skii not as minister but as acting minister of Agriculture.[124]

In summary, it is clear that Witte's cabinet did not approach his original conception of what the government should be. He had wanted a cabinet consisting of men who represented various shades of opinion but who would unite to restore order and to initiate a program of positive reform. Rebuffed by the liberal camp, Witte resigned himself to a cabinet of whose members only a few were even mildly committed to the spirit of the Manifesto. Others showed themselves later to be openly hostile to its provisions. Rather than ministers who worked only under his direction and gave him their unqualified support, some ignored him completely and negotiated directly with the tsar, pursuing on some occasions policies which were incompatible with Witte's program. This was not a very propitious beginning for a government committed to leading Russia down the path of political reform.

The Need and Concern for Order

WHILE WITTE was introducing his first measures of political and administrative reform, attempting to enlist public sympathy and support for his government, and forming his cabinet, he was also confronted by continuing disorder and unrest, in addition to the demonstrations and pogroms described earlier. At first he attempted to deal with these manifestations of the on-going revolution either with moderation or by letting them run their course in the hope that rebellious attitudes would subside and the bulk of the population would come to support or at least to acquiesce in his combined program of reform and order. Gradually during November, however, his attitude stiffened and he felt forced to take certain repressive steps to maintain the authority of the government and to quell disorder.

Although the railroad and general strikes had come to an end shortly after Witte took office, as the weeks passed new outbreaks of strikes and worker unrest developed in various parts of Russia, often accompanied by the rise of soviets, or councils of workers' deputies.[125] The fresh wave of strikes and the power of the soviets both crested in early December. This development and the government's reaction to it will be described in chapter five. But Witte's early attitude and policies toward the workers' movement are illustrated by several incidents that occurred in the first weeks of his premiership. In the face of a call by the St. Petersburg Soviet on November 1 for a new general strike (a major goal of which was achievement of an eight-hour day but which was unsuccessful), Witte decided to appeal directly to the Soviet to call off the strike, wiring them:

> Brother workers! Remain at work, avoid trouble, protect your wives and children. Do not listen to other advice. The tsar has ordered us to turn our total attention to the worker question. For this his imperial majesty formed a ministry of commerce and industry, which must establish a just relationship between workers and owners. Give us time—all that is possible for you will be done.
>
> Listen to the advice of men who are well disposed toward you and who wish you well.[126]

Witte said that he intended to appeal to the workers "in a spirit of comradeship" in the hope that this would move them, but his tone was more paternalistic than fraternal, and his telegram did not have the desired effect.[127] Rather than winning the support of the Soviet, it angered some of its members that Witte would refer to them as his "brothers." Woytinsky, who was present when the telegram was read, wrote that it introduced a note of hilarity into the situation.[128] The Soviet immediately rejected the note as being another example of the government's treachery and deceit. "Bloody Sunday" was recalled as an illustration of the tsar's concern for the workers. It was agreed that workers would be safe only when the control of government was in their own hands.[129] Witte's note was also read in the factories on November 4 with no apparent effect. One factory committee replied to his appeal: "We have read it and we have struck!" The principal reaction came from those in and near the court who were angered that Witte would so demean himself and the government.

On November 4 in a meeting of the Council of Ministers

called to discuss the new general strike, an advisor of Witte, V. Litvinov-Falinskii, argued that the situation was quite different from that during the October general strike, when the industrialists had supported the workers. Now the owners of enterprises, satisfied by the political concessions of the Manifesto and feeling directly threatened by the demand for an eight-hour day, opposed the strike and were acting vigorously against it by locking out the workers. Thus the government was in a much stronger position and should simply wait until the revolutionary fever of the workers subsided and the economic action of the industrialists began to have its effect. Durnovo opposed this counsel, urging the arrest of the Soviet and the leaders of the Union of Unions. Litvinov-Falinskii replied that repressive action would only inflame the masses and that in any case new revolutionary organs would spring up to replace those suppressed by the government. He again advised riding out the storm, and Witte and the Council apparently adopted his policy since no action was taken against the Soviet until the very end of November, as we shall see in chapter five. Moreover, the strike movement did subside temporarily.[130]

Ten days later, however, Durnovo—whether on his own or with the consent of Witte and the Council of Ministers is not clear —did take more drastic action against the strike movement. In this case the issue was whether government employees, which included not only civil servants but employees of the state-owned railroads and communication lines as well as some industrial enterprises, had the right to strike—a problem which had been plaguing the government for some time and which was not resolved in the Council of Ministers until early December, as we shall see in chapter five. In mid-November Durnovo forbade the organization of a union of postal-telegraph workers, threatening to dismiss workers who joined it. In defiance the First Congress of Postal-Telegraph Employees declared on November 15 a strike of protest and expressed its sympathy with the Russian labor movement as personified by the St. Petersburg Soviet. Although the leaders of the Congress were promptly arrested, the strike met with some success and helped touch off new railroad strikes during the latter part of the month.[131] While this was only a preliminary skirmish between the new government and the labor movement, it foreshadowed the bigger battles that lay ahead.

A more disingenuous effort to deal with worker unrest in St.

Petersburg, in which Witte acquiesced, was broached at about this same time. Someone—who it is not clear—decided it might be useful to encourage Father Gapon of "Bloody-Sunday" fame to renew his organizational and agitational activity among the workers in the capital. An appeal to the workers which called on them to avoid bloodshed, to hold the gains they had won, and to support the Manifesto and the Duma was drafted and sent to Gapon in Paris for his approval and signature. The police financed the printing of a large number of copies of this appeal but whether it was widely distributed is not clear.[132] Gapon then came to Finland and, through intermediaries, offered to sell his organization and contacts to Witte and Durnovo for 100,000 rubles. This offer was apparently rejected but a journalist contact of Gapon, Matiushenskii, approached Minister of Trade and Industry Timiriazev, saying he had been sent by Witte. Timiriazev gave Matiushenskii 30,000 rubles to help get Gapon's organization going again. Matiushenskii, however, gave only 7,000 to Gapon's cohorts and pocketed the rest, which resulted in the press breaking open the whole scandal. Witte's refutation of his complicity in the affair in later press polemics over it and in his memoirs is not very convincing. He claimed that he was not aware of the plan to revive Gapon's organization, and that he authorized the money for Matiushenskii on the understanding it was to be only 7,000 rubles and was to be used, under strict control, to reopen libraries and reading rooms for the workers which the police had closed after January 9. Witte also asserted that he had ordered Gapon to be sent abroad on pain of arrest if he stayed. In any event, the plan collapsed, Timiriazev became the scapegoat, and after the tsar had ordered an investigation of the whole matter, Timiriazev resigned.[133]

Besides continuing worker unrest Witte's government had to deal with a rapidly growing peasant rebellion in the countryside. Beginning with October and extending through December 1905, more than 300 districts of gubernias were embroiled in peasant uprisings. Not only did incidents increase in frequency, but they grew in the degree of violence as well. There was much more pillaging, burning, and robbing than before. Few landowners were killed, but many were beaten. From October through December more than 1,000 manor houses were burned and sacked.[134] In some provinces violence became so great that both landowners and government administrators fled, thereby leaving the estates open to pillage.[135]

The most serious agrarian riots occurred in the middle Volga and in the central black-earth region where communal ownership was prevalent and the depression of peasant farming most acute.

While the increase in peasant unrest after October 17 and the acceleration of Socialist-Revolutionary and other radical agitation in the villages imply strong political motivations behind peasant rebellions, in fact the growth of peasant violence was probably as closely linked to the season of the year as to any political circumstances. Peasants became restive *after* the termination of field work and *after* the crops had been harvested. Extensive rioting before the crops were gathered threatened their own self-interest. By the end of October the major agricultural tasks were completed until spring, and the peasants could turn their attention to rectifying grievances.[136] However, a marked decline in unrest in January and February 1906 was prompted no doubt by the full onslaught of winter and by the effectiveness of the punitive expeditions described below.

The peaking of the revolutionary movement in the countryside after the harvest is illustrated by the following estimate of the number of peasant outbreaks per month: September—71; October—219; November—796; December—575. Together these accounted for almost half the total number of agrarian disorders throughout 1905.[137] Many of the peasant actions began simply with the illegal cutting of timber or pasturing of animals and the theft of stored grain, but when local authorities or police interfered at the request of the landowner or his steward, violence and more aggressive acts often resulted. And in the most severely afflicted black-earth regions the peasant mutinies soon took on an anarchistic hue, with attacks on local officials, government institutions, and even bridges, telegraph stations, and railways.[138]

In response to this situation and apparently because of his growing dissatisfaction with what he considered the inaction of Witte, the tsar decided, only two weeks after issuance of the Manifesto, to take decisive measures to restore order in the worst areas of peasant unrest. Although the evidence is not entirely clear on this point, in the absence of documentation to the contrary it seems likely that these actions were taken without consulting Witte or the Council of Ministers,[139] though there is also no reason to believe that Witte and his colleagues necessarily disapproved of them. On October 30 Baron Fredericks at the court wrote to Witte transmitting the tsar's orders that a series of adjutant-generals (specially designated generals) be dispatched with sufficient forces to a number of provinces in south-central Russia in order "to investigate the reasons for the outbreak of disorders and to take immediate action in the name of His Imperial Majesty to suppress them."[140] In early November General Count Ignatiev was sent to Kherson, General Strukov to Tambov and Voronezh, General Sakharov to Saratov and Penza, Admiral Dubasov to Chernigov, Orel, and Kursk, and General Prince Engalychev to Stavropol. General Pantaleev replaced Dubasov in early December after the latter was named governor-general of Moscow, and General Maksimovich replaced Sakharov after the latter was assassinated November 22 in Saratov.[141] At the same time a state of "strengthened security" was declared in many of these provinces, and the adjutant-generals were given extensive powers: they were to have authority over the local army, police, and civil administrations except the courts; they could draft any government servant; they could subject to personal detention anyone considered dangerous to social order; they could close wine shops and trade and industrial enterprises; they could prohibit the issuing of newspapers and other publications; and they could issue obligatory decrees in the name of the tsar for the sake of preserving order.[142] Though hampered by inadequate forces, by the widespread nature of the rebellion, and by the continuing mutinous attitude of the desperate peasantry, whose economic grievances and hunger for land remained unredressed, these military expeditions did succeed, by force, in restoring a semblance of order and authority in the affected areas by early January.

A number of government reports of this period blamed the peasant jacqueries on the leadership and agitation of the All-Russian Peasants' Union, which had grown remarkably since its founding in the summer of 1905 and which at its Second Congress in early November displayed increasingly radical, if not quite revolutionary, tendencies. As a result, the government arrested on November 15 the leaders of the Union, which substantially crippled its activities as a national organization. A swing to a more forceful policy had clearly begun.

But the trouble was that if the government were to suppress the revolution by force, reliable troops in sufficient numbers were needed. Yet a large part of the army remained in Manchuria, and mutinies in the army and navy raised serious doubts about the steadfastness, as agents of repression, of the units in European Russia. Typical of numerous appeals for more troops in this period was that of Governor Zinov'iev of the province of St. Petersburg, who on November 23 called urgently for help in order to control disturbances in the Peterhof and Iamburg districts. Recognizing that "because of limitations on the availability of military detachments I can ask to use the army only in cases of extreme urgency," Zinov'iev ingeniously suggested that normal cavalry maneuvers and drills of the troops of the St. Petersburg garrison be combined into "one such lengthy exercise in areas I designate as needing pacification." His request was granted.[143] And on November 20 Witte reported to the tsar the opinion of the Moscow city governor that it would be impossible to provide adequate protection and security in the city until the return of the army from Manchuria.[144]

At the same time both Soviet and Western authors have tended to exaggerate troop shortages and the extent of trouble and disaffection in the Russian armed forces in 1905, the former for political reasons, the latter because mutinies and revolutionary disorders in the army and navy provide dramatic and well-documented material. In fact, as it turned out, the army proved to be both numerous and loyal enough to quell the revolution. In 1904, 55,525 troops were employed to assist the civil authorities in maintaining order, while in 1905 the figure swelled to 3,398,361. Obviously many units were used a number of times since the whole army in 1905 was only about a million and a half men.[145] Even allowing for the roughness of the estimate and for deliberate exaggeration on the part of army bureaucrats, it is abundantly clear that the tsarist government did not lack for troops to deal with the revolutionary movement in 1905. On the other hand, one must recognize that in the chaotic and unsettling atmosphere of the times, with the countryside aflame, and the national minorities busily ousting their Russian overlords, the authorities—not surprisingly—were suddenly overcome with grave doubts concerning that ancient and ultimate weapon of the tsarist autocracy—the army. Even the Decembrist revolt of 1825 had not affected the rank and file, and until the revolution of 1905 there had never been any occasion seriously to question the reliability of the army as an instrument to protect the government. Now widely scattered mutinies and disturbances, though no one of them was really threatening in itself, spread anxiety and uncertainty. Rumors about the extent of revolutionary agitation in the army and about the widespread discontent of the average soldier passed quickly from one panicky official to another. Thus, while the autocracy was never in any grave danger on this score, many of its own adherents feared that it was. And Witte himself expressed deep concern over the shortage and possible unreliability of troops, making a major effort to rectify the situation as part of his policy of restoring order.

To understand this aspect of Witte's premiership it is necessary to review briefly the situation in the armed forces in the fall of 1905 and some of the specific and widely publicized incidents which gave rise to governmental qualms about using the army against the revolution. Estimates of the number of mutinies or disorders by groups of soldiers or sailors (as against individual acts) in 1905 vary widely. At one extreme a leading Soviet specialist on this subject has calculated one hundred ninety-five outbreaks from October 1, 1905, to the end of the year (with seventy-six for the first nine months of 1905); at the other an official report of the Ministry of War counted thirty-three disorders for 1905, while John Maynard comes up with a figure of eighty-nine for November and December 1905.[146] Whatever the exact number, the majority of these incidents were minor, posed no serious threat to the government, and were suppressed with local forces. The few major ones, most of which required the dispatch of reliable troops from the outside to restore order, are discussed briefly below.

The causes of these mutinies varied, but the bulk of them stemmed from grievances over general conditions of service or particularly bad local circumstances. To be sure, in some cases political or even revolutionary demands were also included, sometimes spontaneously, sometimes at the instigation of radical or socialist agitators who were in the service or who were connected with revolutionary organizations in localities where the disaffected troops were stationed. And, as we saw earlier in this chapter, the October Manifesto did encourage a number of disgruntled servicemen to press their demands, both military and political. But much of the generalized discontent stemmed from the strong desire of reservists and conscripts called up during the Russo-Japanese war to be demobilized and returned home once a peace treaty was signed. This category of servicemen accounted for over half of the mutinies and violent disorders, according to Petrov, which is not surprising when one considers that 1,200,000 men were mobilized during the war.

These conscripts also served under abominable conditions.[147]

The soldier's lot was certainly not a happy one. Of eighty-four demands of mutineers analyzed by Petrov, eighty-six percent of them contained complaints against low pay, inadequate clothing allowances, excessive hours of duty, poor food and sanitary facilities, and minimal provisions for rest and leave. In over half the cases a demand for demobilization was included, and in fifteen instances this was the *only* claim presented. There were also objections to too rigid discipline, to the attitudes of officers, to saluting, and to the censorship of mail. In over fifty percent of the cases demands for political or civil rights were included, and in one-third of them protests against participating in police actions against the revolution were listed.[148] Yet in almost all the principal disorders in the armed services in the fall of 1905 (the Sevastopol mutiny is a possible exception) the chief causes were not revolutionary or political, but military or local. The Ministry of War belatedly acknowledged this fact when in December 1905 and January 1906, it ordered an improvement in pay, food, and clothing and offered better conditions of service for reenlistees.[149]

The first serious disturbance in the armed forces Witte faced occurred a week after he took office when, on October 26, a mutiny broke out at the Kronstadt naval base and fortress. The exact cause of the disorder is difficult to determine. The Social Democrats said that the incident began when a marine battalion refused to eat wormy pork. Some of the marines were arrested and, while they were being transported to a military prison, their colleagues stopped the vans, disarmed the guards, and freed the prisoners. This was the signal for a general revolt. The mutineers disarmed the military police and arrested their officers.[150] The official version showed the mutineers to be far less heroic. According to the chief of the Kronstadt police department, the rebellion began with a number of soldiers who started a brawl in a Kronstadt saloon. As the military police were hauling away the ringleaders, other soldiers stopped the arrest and freed the prisoners.[151]

Whichever version is correct, there is no doubt that from that point the island fortress became a scene of anarchy. Liquor stores were raided and soldiers, sailors, and Kronstadt citizens engaged in an orgy of drunkenness. The mutiny took on less the appearance of a revolt to settle grievances than a mob of soldiers and sailors on the rampage. On October 27 Trepov arrived with troops from St.

Petersburg and easily brought the revolt to a halt. Altogether, seventeen people were killed and eighty-two injured during the two-day riot.[152] Several hundred soldiers and sailors were arrested and brought before courts-martial. The rumor that they would all be shot helped stimulate a new general strike in the capital in the first days of November.[153]

In Sevastopol a revolt occurred from November 11 to 15,[154] which had it coincided with the general strike in October could have had a significant impact on the government. The discontent in the Black Sea fleet had been demonstrated by the *Potemkin* mutiny in June. In June, however, the rebels on the *Potemkin* had been unable to gain support of other military units, while in the Sevastopol mutiny rebellion occurred among both sailors of the fleet and soldiers in the Sevastopol garrison, with some support from radical elements in the town. There had been some agitation in Sevastopol after promulgation of the October Manifesto, but a serious revolt began on November 11. Leadership of the rebellion soon passed to Lieutenant N. P. Shmidt, a retired naval officer who assumed command of the rebellious crusier *Ochakov*, ran up a red flag, and proclaimed himself head of the Black Sea fleet.[155] Although part of the Brestsky infantry regiment joined the rebellion, the forces remaining loyal to the government outnumbered and out-gunned the mutineers.

Lieutenant-General Baron A. N. Meller-Zakomel'sky was sent to put down the rebellion and so distinguished himself that he was later chosen to head a punitive expedition to the Far East. On November 15 the cruiser *Ochakov* was forced to surrender; Shmidt was arrested and later shot;[156] and the five-day rebellion came to a close. At the peak of the mutiny Meller-Zakomel'sky estimated that the mutineers numbered between two and six thousand. About thirty people were killed, and seventy were injured in the uprising.[157]

Perhaps the most troublesome problem involved the Far Eastern army. This army, consisting primarily of peasants under arms, had been sent to the Far East during the Russo-Japanese war. Following the close of the war, the government was slow in demobilizing the Far Eastern army, and as a result there were serious disorders in Vladivostok at the end of October. Between the signing and the ratification of the peace treaty no plans for evacuation were made. Finally, a plan for demobilization appeared which was designed to return soldiers in the following order: (1) cavalry and Cossacks, (2) the Siberian corps, and (3) the balance of the army.[158] This plan was put into operation on October 13, but came to a halt on October 15, when the Trans-Baikal and Siberian railroads joined the general strike. When the strike ended, there were a few days of undisturbed travel; but in mid-November the railroad workers once again voted to strike. According to the commander of the Far Eastern army, General N. P. Linevich, from November 15 his army was completely cut off from Russia. He said they received no information and did not know what to do.[159]

The problem was disturbing because Witte was counting on Linevich's troops to help restore order in European Russia. Therefore, he wanted to evacuate them as rapidly as possible. Linevich was also conscious that the longer his troops remained in the Far East the more restive they became. He was plagued with desertions; even one of his generals threatened to resign unless he were promised leave for the Christmas holidays. The soldiers were unusually susceptible to revolutionary appeals because they were dissatisfied with the slow evacuation. But this also caused them to become greatly irritated at the strikers who impeded their return home.[160] Once they were returned to European Russia, moreover, they were to prove loyal to the tsar.

As Linevich saw his problem, there were two possible solutions. He could concentrate his efforts on putting down unrest in the Far East, as strikes there were part of the general revolutionary movement. However, his army was a Russian army; the soldiers disliked the East and wished to return home. Or he could take every step possible to see to it that his army returned to the West. Since there were no steamships, this meant returning them by rail, which required in turn cooperating with the railroad strike committee.[161] Linevich took the latter action at severe risks to his own career. General A. N. Kuropatkin opposed it and carried on secret negotiations with an officer on Linevich's staff encouraging him to seize control of the army from Linevich.[162] As a result of his decision, Linevich was relieved of his command in February 1906, and was brought before an investigating commission, which dropped the charges only after the intercession of the tsar.[163]

The group with which Linevich chose to cooperate was an organization that called itself the "Government of the Russian Far East." Its president was Ferdinand Ossendowski, who had been sent to Harbin during the war to expedite transportation of goods to supply the army. In the third week of November Ossendowski was chosen to head the strike committee of the Chinese Eastern railway and was given the title of President of the Committee of the Government of the Russian Far East.[164] Ossendowski's first order was to send word to the army that the committee had taken over the administration of the Far East and that passenger service to the West had been interrupted to free more trains to carry troops back to European Russia.

It is clear that Ossendowski and Linevich shared a similar goal but for different reasons. Both wanted the army returned to European Russia as rapidly as possible. Ossendowski desired this because if the strike continued to impede the troops' evacuation, Linevich might choose to use the army to end the rebellion in the Far East. Moreover, Ossendowski hoped that once the troops returned they might intervene to protect the populace from government repression. In a meeting of the strike committee on November 27 the representatives agreed to continue to run the railroad until all troops were evacuated "in order to attain our general political goals."[165]

General Linevich accepted the program of the strike committee and pledged his support. Ossendowski's principal challenge came not from Linevich, the army, or the city officials of Harbin but from the Union of Russian People, who opposed his usurpation of power, and from the Social Democrats, for whom he was insufficiently radical.[166] When Ossendowski tried to resign after being subjected to intimidation and attack from both right and left, Linevich asked him to continue his duties. Linevich's actions met with sharp disapproval in St. Petersburg, and in January 1906, he finally felt compelled to arrest Ossendowski and his cohorts. Witte commented with bitter sarcasm in a note to the tsar on January 23:

> In the furthest reaches where the imperial army operates, in foreign territory, under the eyes of our recent enemies, the chief communication line, the Chinese Eastern Railway, was taken over by some sort of self-constituted committee of strikers who for whole months ran the railroad on their own authority, while the commander of the Russian—not Japanese—army, with good-natured naiveté looked on as this shameful and outrageous affair took place. Yesterday Gen. Linevich communicated to me that he had arrested this committee, but he did not explain what he proposed to do with them.

Does he perhaps intend to give them a deluxe train and send them, for the edification of all the railroad employees, to your majesty's capital in honor? Wouldn't it be more appropriate to order the guilty judged on the spot by a military court?[167]

In other areas of Siberia and the Far East the sort of cooperation between the authorities and the strikers that developed in Harbin under the aegis of Linevich and Ossendowski failed signally to materialize. In fact, as the disgruntled returning soldiers moved slowly westwards along the Trans-Siberian railroad they frequently fell into common rebellious action with local workers and radicals. Acts of insubordination, small mutinies, strikes, and general unrest flared up, turning, in such important centers as Chita, Irkutsk, and Krasnoiarsk, into major disturbances which threatened temporarily the control of the local authorities. Finally, as we shall see in the next chapter, the government was forced to dispatch two punitive military expeditions along the railroad, one from Harbin, the other from Moscow, to restore order in Siberia.

Nevertheless, whatever the exaggerated fears at the time, the mutinies and disorders in the army and navy never posed a serious threat to the government as a whole. As even Soviet historians admit, the soldiers generally lacked "class" or revolutionary consciousness (most were peasants in uniform), they had weak ties with the radical workers, they were poorly organized and led (despite occasional extravagant Bolshevik claims to the contrary), their goals were primarily personal and *ad hoc*—demobilization, better conditions—and the outbreaks were too widely scattered, localized, and sporadic to permit any coordinated assault on the government.[168] That fatal link between the radical worker and the soldier-peasant which was to seal the fate of the autocracy in 1917 was yet to develop.

To draw up a balance sheet of Witte's first weeks in office is not easy. On one side of the ledger, it is clear that Witte's hope that the promises of the October Manifesto and his first measures of political and administrative reform would serve to calm society and to enlist its cooperation and assistance in effecting further reform and in restoring order went largely unfulfilled. On the other side, it is equally evident that the united front of opposition to the government that had existed prior to the Manifesto was broken, and that preliminary steps toward reform and the reestablishment of order were indeed taken. Moreover, in our view, Witte, though shaken by the difficulties that arose, remained committed to his twin goals of order and reform throughout this period.

But the obstacles he faced were formidable. First, the reaction to the Manifesto was more violent, ugly, and disruptive on the part of the extreme left and extreme right and more passive, critical, and demanding on the part of the center than he had expected. He had propounded what he considered a reasonable and moderate program to meet Russia's most urgent problems and had, with difficulty, secured the assent of the tsar to it, but the majority of Russian society did not respond to it reasonably or moderately. Second, he had genuinely hoped to secure the aid and collaboration of some of the best elements in public life in carrying out his plans, but this was denied him, partly because of his own deviousness and his ill-advised insistence on including Durnovo in the cabinet and partly because the liberals, nurtured in the spirit of opposition and high-mindedly devoted to their principles, could not bring themselves to act expediently, to compromise, and to bear a burden of active public responsibility. Whether it would have made much difference if Witte had succeeded in adding "public men" to his cabinet is a moot point. It would have made Nicholas and his reactionary advisors even more suspicious of Witte's government and policies, and it is doubtful that the liberals, after October, could have exerted much influence over the increasingly radical workers, peasants, and national minorities, who in the succeeding weeks posed the chief threat to the stability and order of society and to the success of Witte's program. "Public men" might have pushed the government to take somewhat more liberal measures, but it is unlikely that the reforms they favored would have satisfied the revolutionary masses and their leaders. And if they had gone too far, the tsar would unquestionably have dismissed them.

Third, Witte almost immediately found himself in an isolated and exposed position, partly because of circumstances beyond his control, partly because of his own attitude and outlook. It was not just that he was unable to develop any base of support among the liberals, for whatever use that might have been, but that he had no source of real backing anywhere. The tsar rapidly lost confidence in him; Witte wanted no part of the right-wing, proto-fascists symbolized by the Union of the Russian People; the army was basically apolitical; and the Octobrists were a small and relatively ineffectual group. He had to fall back on a small coterie of bureaucrats, men of his own stripe, who believed in orderly and efficient government; but they were scattered throughout a conservative and tradition-laden civil service and were without organization, a voice, or any real means of exerting influence. Witte failed signally to understand that to carry through economic modernization and the rationalization of government also required a political strategy and a broad political base as an instrument of power. His attitude is well illustrated by his reply on December 1 to an appeal for a broadening and acceleration of reforms from the Fourth Congress of Zemstvo and City Leaders, which met in Moscow, November 6–12. Witte declared that the aim of his government was to fulfill the program of the October Manifesto and that it could not go beyond that to satisfy the other demands of the congress. He promised that although the matter was a complicated one, the government was making every effort to arrange as quickly as possible for the election and convocation of the Duma, and that in the interim he did not exclude the possibility of issuing temporary laws to implement further reforms. Nevertheless the government had a clear responsibility to maintain order. It could not be beholden to or influenced by the views of any party or organization but had to fulfill its duty to the Manifesto and to the country.[169] In a similar, though slightly more arrogant, vein Witte told a deputation of Octobrists that he knew what was best for Russia and that the government did not need the trust of society.[170] This attitude clearly revealed Witte's political naiveté and shortsightedness.

Finally, Witte had to deal with broad and anarchic trends in Russian society, for which he was quite unprepared. He believed that these manifestations of disorder had to be brought to an end, both to permit the institution of the reforms he desired and because he knew that the foreign loan which he believed was so essential to save Russia from bankruptcy and to support his program of modernization would not be forthcoming while the country remained in turmoil.[171] To halt the disturbances Witte sometimes acted in a conciliatory manner, at other times with force. Whatever course he followed was too slow and cowardly to suit the tsar and much too repressive to satisfy the liberals. Gradually and somewhat reluctantly, he moved toward a policy of forcibly repressing the peasant riots, the renewed strikes, the mutinies in the army and navy, and the rebellions in Poland, the Baltic, and the Caucasus. His growing concern was reflected in his query to the tsar on November 20: "I know nothing about the commander of the army there [in Moscow]. Is is possible to count on his energy and foresightedness?"[172] The agrarian disorders were the most serious, and Witte thoroughly understood that they stemmed from deep-seated grievances, as we shall see in chapter six. But until fundamental reforms for the peasantry could be worked out, Witte believed he must act to restore order in the countryside. He also decided that the other disorders had to be quelled if he were to protect society and get on with his program.

Yet Witte did not develop any coordinated plan of action or apply a systematic policy of repression. He dealt with the outbreaks as they occurred, which left him harassed and weakened and which gave the impression that he was inconsistent and unsure of himself. At the same time he continued to work for reform, discussing a number of projects in the Council of Ministers and actively participating in a whole series of meetings in November designed to modify the electoral law and to reform the State Council. Nor was Nicholas himself as bloodthirsty in this period—at least in public pronouncements—as he is sometimes portrayed. To be sure, under heavy pressure from the gentry, he ordered punitive expeditions into the worst regions of peasant violence. But on November 24 he told a delegation from the Tula zemstvo that while "in order to realize fully the freedoms I have granted it is first of all necessary to restore order," he recognized the need in this effort for the assistance and cooperation of the true sons of Russia and that a prime necessity was to aid the peasants and to improve their lot. And on December 1 to a mixed delegation of right-wing groups Nicholas declared:

> ... I call upon you to tell all those who cherish our beloved fatherland that the manifesto I gave on October 17 is the full and convinced expression of my inflexible and immutable will and act, which cannot be changed.
>
> For the most rapid realization of the reforms I have granted it is necessary, with just, strict, and firm authority, to restore calm and order to the Russian Land which has been torn by strife.[173]

In our opinion, most secondary accounts of the first weeks of Witte's premiership are misleading or inaccurate. It is certainly not true that Witte and the tsar embarked on a course of bloody repression immediately after promulgation of the Manifesto, thereby revealing the deceit of the government in issuing it, as some of the Soviet texts would have one believe. But neither is the picture painted of 1905 in two recent Western accounts a faithful delineation of the situation. Both the American historian Harcave and the British historian Kochan describe the weeks after October 17 as a stalemate, a sort of uneasy equilibrium, between the revolution and the government.[174] The metaphor is of a battlefield with two armies maneuvering before being locked in combat, or of a boxing ring with two opponents sparring for position before launching an attack. But for neither side is this accurate.

The revolution was not an anthropomorphic force, with a goal, a will, a central direction, and a calculated consideration of whether to advance or to retreat. It was rather a mélange of uncoordinated, often disparate, groups who acted instinctively and anarchically for the most part. Varying aims were sought, different tactics used, and the outcomes were often dissimilar. The St. Petersburg Soviet did not provide any real national leadership, and one simply cannot speak about the revolution in the autumn of 1905 as a unified, purposeful movement. There were many revolutions, which caused Witte and the government great anguish but which they could hardly deal with as a common enemy. Yet neither is it correct to depict the government as a monolithic force biding its time and reviving its strength until it could smash the revolution. As we have seen, the government did not speak or act as one; among the tsar, Witte, the Council of Ministers, the army and police, and the local authorities there was little common cause or centralized direction. Partly because of its diverse nature, partly because of the variety of the opposition it had to confront, the government behaved inconsistently, pragmatically, here putting out rebellious fires, there trying to conciliate its opponents and reform the system. On both sides the picture is one of expediency, of confusion, of bitter but aimless struggle, and of uncertainty about where it would all lead.

In this situation Witte's position was not an enviable one. He still wanted order and reform, but he was trapped between what the tsar would allow and what the radical elements in society demanded. And as he tried to set about the task of renovating the old structure, arsonists of various hues were busy trying to raze the whole building. It is little wonder that, isolated and put upon, Witte found his first weeks in office a nightmare and his efforts largely unsuccessful.

IV

THE BALANCE SHIFTS:

ORDER TAKES PRIORITY

I order that any infringement of the legal order must evoke from local authorities the sternest opposition, within the limits set by law . . .

—*Circular of Minister of Interior*
P. N. Durnovo, *December 23, 1905*

I F Witte faced disorders, difficulties, and disappointment in his first four or five weeks in office, these were only a mild preliminary to the upheavals, increased repression, and growing despair which marked the next few weeks of his tenure as Russia's first prime minister. Not only did the calm, cooperation, and change that he had expected the October Manifesto to bring not materialize, but beginning in mid-November Witte had to deal with a resurgence of the strike movement, continued rural unrest, and growing public dissatisfaction and criticism. Badgered by right and even moderate circles to adopt a sterner line and openly challenged and scorned by radical groups anxious to extend the revolution, Witte moved slowly toward more repressive policies, encouraging measures designed to break the strikes, supporting the dispatch of armed punitive expeditions to the Baltic to restore order and along the Trans-Siberian railroad to reopen that line to the unhindered return of the Manchurian army, and adopting extraordinary security measures against violence and insurrection. At the same time, however, the prime minister pushed forward plans for creating Russia's first national representative assembly. In what seemed paradoxical, if not downright contradictory, efforts the sending of punitive expeditions and the use of special security measures were accompanied by the drafting and promulgating of an electoral law for the new Duma. It was a compromise measure but nevertheless greatly extended the franchise offered on August 6.

Thus, the few weeks from the middle of November to the first part of December reflected anew the difficult dilemma of reform and order that Witte confronted. It was a period of transition from the high hopes of post-October to the violence and repression of December; Witte had not yet decided to attempt fully to suppress the revolutionaries, but it was becoming increasingly clear that the promises of the Manifesto and his subsequent policies of moderation had not succeeded in restoring domestic tranquillity and setting Russia on the road to peaceful change. Gradually Witte began to realize that reform was difficult, if not impossible, in the midst of chaos, and that the continuation of discontent and rebellion endangered not only social order but the tsarist system as a whole, including his own government. In this way the groundwork was laid for the bitter struggle between the government and the revolution which the armed uprisings of December climaxed.

As we suggested, there was a good deal of confusion and disorganization toward the end of November among both the revolutionaries and the government. The only decisive step that had been taken was the sending of military expeditions to put down the peasant rebellions in the south-central provinces, but this did not affect the main centers of power and struggle. The strikers in the cities and along the railroads and the dissident national minorities sporadically renewed their opposition and voiced their dissatisfaction, but without any central leadership or common goal, unless it was the vague cry for convocation of an all-Russian constituent assembly. The revolutionaries did not quite know what to do next nor how best to continue their assault on the tsarist system. As we shall see shortly, they were as much pushed by events as they were consciously directing them. Similarly, the government was indecisive and perplexed. Although the tsar and Durnovo undoubtedly wished to take more vigorous action, Witte and his cabinet were still pursuing a generally "soft" line and tended to react to individual crises rather than to follow a consistent and carefully considered course of action. On both sides there were some who wished to avoid a showdown, a direct clash with its inevitable bloodshed and violence. Thus, although it was obvious to all that tension and uneasiness were mounting, both the government and the revolutionaries (with the possible exception of some radical Social Democrats) tended to drift, uncertain how to proceed or what might happen.

A symptom of this attitude on the part of the government was its rather fruitless effort to enlist the services of the church, both Orthodox and Roman Catholic, in the task of calming the country. A circular from the Holy Synod at about this time urged the faithful to support the throne and eschew disorder, and in early December, Pope Pius X, after representations from the Russian envoy to the Vatican, sent an encyclical (*Poloniae populum*) to the archbishops and bishops of the Roman Catholic church in Poland, which asked them to encourage their parishioners to obey the duly constituted authorities and to oppose the revolution.[1] At Foreign Minister Lamsdorff's urging the tsar sent a special note of appreciation to the pope on January 5. Lamsdorff also proposed that the encyclical be translated and widely circulated throughout Russia, but the Vatican demurred, agreeing only that it be made known in private communications that the encyclical should also apply to other Catholic dioceses of the empire, as well as to those in Russian Poland.[2]

Despite marginal efforts such as this, signs of a gathering storm multiplied. On November 17 in a report to the tsar on the state of internal security in the country General Trepov noted the ominous fact that the workers in St. Petersburg and elsewhere were beginning to collect weapons and to arm themselves. He added that the question of an armed uprising was a lively current topic of discussion in revolutionary circles.[3] A week later, in an effort to deal with this situation, the Council of Ministers ordered all governors to issue special regulations controlling and limiting the selling and storing of firearms. The same day, November 24, the Council forbade the import of weapons into Russia.[4] The danger of an armed confrontation between the government and the workers was clearly increasing.

The Strike Movement

IN THE LATTER PART of November the government was confronted with two serious strikes, which, although not nearly as widespread and disruptive as the October general strike, were annoying and unsettling. One was a strike of post and telegraph employees, the other—partly stimulated by the first—a renewed strike of railroad workers. These succeeded in harassing the government for two reasons: first, Witte and the cabinet opposed in principle strikes and the formation of unions among government employees (which most of the postal-telegraph and railroad workers were), and second, at a time of continuing unrest the strikes severely interrupted communications from the capital to provincial and local authorities and hindered the rapid return of the army from the Far East.

As we saw in the preceding chapter, Durnovo had attempted to prevent formation of a postal-telegraph union and had arrested the leaders of the First Congress of Postal-Telegraph Employees, actions which had led to the strike call. In a report to the tsar on November 20 Witte noted that the postal-telegraph strike was continuing, and shortly thereafter the government resorted to more forceful measures to break the strike. In instructions from Durnovo and from the minister of Communications local authorities were ordered to fire, with no opportunity of being rehired, postal-telegraph workers involved in the strike and to bring to trial the ringleaders; on December 2 Durnovo arrested the members of the new Central Bureau of the Organization of Postal-Telegraph Workers. On November 29 the tsar confirmed an ukase prepared by the Council of Ministers which gave governors-general and city governors the right, on their own authority, to declare regions under their control in a state of "strengthened" or of "extraordinary" security if this were necessary to deal with the railroad or postal-telegraph strikes locally. In addition, on December 14 the minister of Communications and the heads of railroad systems were empowered to declare martial law on the railroads and to form special committees to punish strikers.[5]

The Council of Ministers, which for some time had been concerned about the participation of civil servants and state employees in strikes and in antigovernment activity, followed up these actions by issuing on December 2 a set of temporary regulations concerning strikes. These provided that in state enterprises, including railroads and the postal-telegraph system, and in other enterprises "the closing or interrupted production of which threatened the security of the state or caused social harm," participants in strikes could be sentenced to eight to sixteen months in prison while those guilty of inciting strikes in such enterprises could receive prison terms of sixteen months to four years.[6] On December 16 Durnovo, in an instruction to all subordinates, added his strong recommendation that any teachers or medical personnel who engaged in antigovernment activity should be fired.[7] This tougher line taken by the government toward the strike movement was one factor precipitating the showdown between the government and the workers that culminated in armed uprisings in early December in Moscow and other cities. These will be discussed a bit later since first we must examine a particularly harsh aspect of government policy which was instituted several weeks before the December insurrections.

Punitive Expeditions

THE DECISION to extend the practice of sending military expeditions to "pacify" areas where rebellion was most serious, a tactic that had first been employed in early November in the south-central provinces of extreme peasant unrest, was another sign of the hardening of the government's position. As with the earlier instance, the evidence is conflicting concerning the attitude of Witte and the cabinet toward the new punitive expeditions which were dispatched to the Baltic and then along the Trans-Siberian railroad in December of 1905. There are some indications that these decisions were taken by the tsar, his court advisers, and the military authorities, with little reference to the Council of Ministers or its chairman. Other testimony suggests Witte initiated the plans, at least in regard to the Trans-Siberian railroad, and vigorously supported the suppressive activities of the expeditions in December —only later, in January and February 1906, when the worst danger was past, did he have second thoughts and attempt to restrain the military commanders of the expeditions and to prevent some of the cruelest excesses of the actions being taken.

Through much of 1905 Russia's Baltic provinces had been the scene of widespread unrest, verging on open revolt. The cause was a mixture of grievances. Among a growing and increasingly politically conscious native middle class and intelligentsia, opposition both to general tsarist oppression and to specific policies of Russification led to demands for civil freedom and national autonomy. Socialists of various kinds were active among the workers in the cities, and there was also very serious agrarian discontent. The situation was complicated by the fact that the hostility of all oppositional groups, though arising in large part from the same dissatisfactions that had sparked the liberation and revolutionary movements in Russia proper, was intensified by nationalistic resentment of the Baltic Germans, who in the early twentieth century were still the chief landowners of the region and dominated its economic and political life on behalf of the tsarist government.

The October Manifesto signally failed to calm the unrest in the Baltic, in part because, unlike Finland, there were no previous autonomous rights to be restored to its peoples. Strikes broke out again in November, and the peasant rebellion, if anything, worsened. As a result, in response to an appeal to Durnovo from the governor of Lithuania, martial law was declared for the province on November 22 and was reaffirmed for the province of Courland (Estonia), where it had originally been proclaimed in August. This did not improve matters much, and in late November the governors in the region appealed urgently for more help, reporting they had insufficient forces effectively to preserve order.[8]

Finally, on November 28 the tsar appointed Lieutenant-General V. U. Sollogub governor-general of the whole Baltic region, with extensive powers. In a meeting two days later with Grand Duke Nikolai Nikolaevich and other military authorities, General Sollogub worked out plans for sending several punitive expeditions to the area; the most important were one under Major-General A. A. Orlov in the north and another under Major-General V. V. Meinhard in the south. At the same time, either out of recognition that repression alone was insufficient or in an attempt to pursue a "carrot-and-stick" policy, General Sollogub was ordered to convoke a special conference "to develop legal projects on all local questions, especially the introduction of local self-government, improvement of the lot of the peasantry, and the reform of revenue-collecting institutions."[9] But force was first on the order of the day.

In the second week of December, Sollogub and the military detachments arrived in the Baltic and began their repressive work. They acted with efficiency and cruelty. At first Witte, whether or not he was privy to the original decision to send the punitive expeditions, approved their actions, telegraphing Sollogub on December 18 that the units would succeed only if they used "decisive and stern measures against the insurgents."[10] Later, as we shall see, he changed his mind. The tsar was delighted, writing his mother on December 12 that Orlov was "acting splendidly" and asserting that "terror must be met by terror."[11] Even taking into account that revolutionary violence in the preceding months and years had resulted in the murder of Nicholas' relatives, high officials of his regime, landowners, and ordinary citizens and that the tsar considered the revolutionaries disloyal, treasonous, and betrayers of the true interest of the people for whose welfare he was responsible, it is still difficult to credit, much less to comprehend, the bloodthirsty reaction of Nicholas, who by all accounts was personally a gentle man, to the terror he encouraged his subalterns to exercise in the Baltic. In an undated telegram to General Sollogub in December the symbolic father of all the Russian peoples urged his governor-general not to negotiate with the revolutionaries but "to act with full energy, dealing with the rebels and their followers by means of the most decisive repressive measures *on the spot* of the commission of their most odious crimes"; on the margin of a telegram of December 28 from General Sollogub, which reported that in suppressing the revolutionary movement in Estonia Captain Rikhter had shot and hung the chief agitators, the tsar noted: "Well done!" Moreover, despite the objections of the local authorities, Nicholas personally supported the formation and dispatch to the Baltic, because of the general shortage of troops, of a battalion of mutinous sailors from the prison at Kronstadt, who acted in the area with particular savagery.[12]

For a number of weeks a virtual reign of terror seized the Baltic. To assist the generals in their task, the Baltic landowners prepared a proscription list and went with the army from one village to another, watching while some peasants were flogged and others executed. Often the accused were brought before hastily organized field courts-martial, sometimes they were shot without the semblance of a trial. In a telegram to the tsar on January 9, 1906, General Orlov reported proudly that at a cost of one casualty he had burned seventy buildings, killed twenty-two rebels in armed clashes, shot seventy-eight others, and sentenced many more to be executed.[13]

As might be expected, actions such as this provoked outraged protests from various segments of Russian and Baltic society. As early as January 7, General Sollogub, who Witte claimed was an intelligent and just man, felt compelled to warn the commanders of all military detachments in the Baltic that the practice of burning the homes of suspected agitators must cease since innocent relatives and young people suffered and since the property destroyed often belonged to or was mortgaged to landowners or credit institutions. Moreover, Sollogub ordered, cases in which whole assemblies or groups were subjected to punishment instead of a few guilty individuals must not be repeated since this both violated legality and aroused the general hostility of the population.[14] In addition, Sollogub, convinced that excesses were taking place, appealed to Witte to intervene with the tsar for moderation and condemned the extreme cruelty displayed by General Orlov and Captain Rikhter. After Witte's dismissal in April, Sollogub was replaced by General Meller-Zakomel'sky, apparently because it was felt that Sollogub was not sufficiently decisive and stern.[15] As we shall see later in this chapter, Witte himself finally felt outraged enough to attempt to curb the extremes of repression in the Baltic provinces, with not entirely successful results. In any case, whatever illegalities and violence the revolutionaries in the Baltic perpetrated in 1905–06, it is almost impossible to justify, at least in the more humane terms of pretotalitarian modern history, the extreme measures taken against them or the delighted attitude of the tsar and the initially passive response of Count Witte.

Hardly more honorable was the behavior of similar punitive expeditions which were dispatched to restore order along the Trans-Siberian railroad. In his memoirs Witte, who toward the end of November and early in December became virtually obsessed with the necessity of rapidly bringing troops back from the Far East to European Russia to reinforce the inadequate forces available there to preserve order, asserted that the plan for reopening the Trans-Siberian railroad by force was originally his. Indirect but not conclusive substantiation of his claim is contained in a report Witte made to the tsar on December 21, in which the prime minister recalled his appeals from mid-October on for repatriation of the Manchurian army and his earlier proposal to send armed expeditions by train to reopen the rail line.[16] Yet one Soviet author attributes the idea to Grand Duke Nikolai Nikolaevich, and another Soviet source states that the evidence as to who originated the proposal is unclear and conflicting.[17]

Whoever first conceived the scheme, it worked effectively, if ruthlessly. In consultations among Witte and the military authorities it was decided in mid-December to send General P. K. Rennenkampf with an armored train and sufficient forces westward along the Trans-Siberian line from Harbin, and General A. N. Meller-Zakomel'sky, similarly equipped, eastward from Moscow. Rennenkampf was appointed December 13, but since telegraphic communications with the Far East were cut by the strike, orders had to be sent to him via London and Peking; and he did not start out until January 9, 1906. On New Year's Day General Meller-Zakomel'sky departed from Moscow. The two units were to move along the Trans-Siberian railroad, restoring it to government control and pacifying the nearby countryside as they traveled. Martial law was proclaimed on the railroad, and the two generals were ordered "*at all costs* to reestablish order on the line" and to reopen it to normal movement so that the return of the army from the Far East could proceed apace. In supplementary instructions to General Rennenkampf the tsar admonished him "not to be stopped by any obstacles in breaking the spirit of opposition and mutiny" on the line and "to eliminate any interference or agitation quickly and ruthlessly using all necessary measures."[18]

Both commanders carried out their orders faithfully, although Meller-Zakomel'sky accused Rennenkampf of insufficient decisiveness, a judgment with which the tsar agreed.[19] From the record it is hard to tell which man acted more ruthlessly. For example, on March 1 the expedition of Meller-Zakomel'sky met a returning troop train filled with rebellious soldiers. The general ordered his men to fire at it. The soldiers were forced off the train and beaten with whips and rifle butts. The considerably sobered mutineers were then reloaded onto the train and sent on their way. Similar tactics were used whenever mutinous soldiers were encountered. When revolutionary agitators were found aboard the trains, they were taken off and executed. Each time Meller-Zakomel'sky's army approached a railroad station, they rounded up the members of the strike committee and either beat them severely or shot them.[20] In this manner he gradually pacified the railroad and restored the stations to government control.

Rennenkampf, moving westward, headed for Chita, which had been largely under revolutionary control since December 21, when a deputation of members of the city duma and representatives of the workers had agreed to end the postal-telegraph strike if the local commander, Lieutenant-General I. V. Kholshchevnikov, would turn the postal-telegraph over to them.[21] He had agreed to do so, as he sympathized with the liberation movement and, in any case, his forces were too weak to do otherwise. On January 21 Rennenkampf arrived in Chita and quickly restored order.[22] Rennenkampf noted that the city had been thrown into a panic as his army approached and that it surrendered with very little bloodshed, an embarrassing capitulation which Soviet historians hasten to attribute to the Menshevik orientation of the Social-Democratic leadership in Chita. Rennenkampf indicated that he had arrested strikers, mutinous soldiers, and the editors and publishers of revolutionary newspapers. Officers of the mutineers were shot during the arrest.[23] Moreover, according to the records of only ten trials conducted by field courts-martial under Rennenkampf, seventy-seven men were sentenced to death, fifteen to hard labor, and eighteen to prison.[24] General Kholshchevnikov was tried and sentenced to sixteen months in prison for having cooperated with the revolutionaries.

By early February 1906, the Trans-Siberian railroad was once again in government hands and open to regular traffic. During December 1905 and the early part of 1906 similar military expeditions were sent to the Caucasus and to some parts of southern Russia, where they also employed harsh methods and succeeded eventually in restoring order. The various punitive expeditions achieved their purpose but at the cost of many lives and heedless of legal safeguards. In many instances civilians and soldiers who were suspected of aiding or abetting the revolution were beaten or executed without trial. In his memoirs Witte deplored the excessive use of violence in combatting the revolution and argued that as prime minister he could do little to prevent such outrages, as he had almost no control over the army or the Ministry of

Interior. Although, as we shall see later in this chapter, Witte did make some effort in late January and in February to curb the excesses of the military suppression of the revolution, these belated remonstrances do not erase the fact of his earlier encouragement of the use of "drastic measures" against the rebels.[25]

Electoral Law of December 11

YET WHILE THESE HARSH STEPS to quell the revolution in various parts of Russia were being planned and launched and at the very moment when the government began to act to break the urban strike movement, Witte was also deeply involved in working out one of the key planks of his reform platform—the broadening of the basis for electing representatives of the people to the Duma. The contrast is startling and instructive. Witte could think, at one and the same time, of encouraging means for the free expression of the will of Russia's citizens and of suppressing their antigovernment activity by force and in disregard of other freedoms promised in the October Manifesto. His attitude toward extending the suffrage became quixotic and unclear, perhaps as a result of his simultaneous concern with quelling revolutionary disturbances, but he did not abandon his aim of providing Russia with some sort of representative assembly. The dilemma of order and reform remained the key to his policy and activity.

The October Manifesto had promised a legislative Duma and its second provision had announced:

> Without halting the scheduled elections to the State Duma, to admit to participation in the Duma, as far as is possible in the short time remaining before its call, all classes of the population which at present are altogether deprived of the franchise, leaving the further development of the principle of universal suffrage to the new legislative order.

Witte and Obolensky had been purposely vague about the terms of a new election law at the time they drafted the Manifesto. Obolensky desired universal suffrage; Witte was not convinced. Therefore, they agreed on a general statement which merely indicated that changes in the law of August 6 were necessary and promised such changes would be made insofar as they were "possible."

Recognizing the importance of convening the Duma as quickly as possible, Witte in his very first days in office initiated steps to fulfill the promise of point two of the Manifesto. The day after promulgation of the Manifesto he called in S. E. Kryzhanovskii, a senior official in the Ministry of Interior who was in charge of organizing the elections, and asked him how the electoral law could be broadened, without disturbing the preparations already under way. According to Kryzhanovskii, Witte was confused and indecisive, toying with various ideas as the basis for the franchise —general for all, limited by property, determined by profession or class, etc. In response Kryzhanovskii pointed out that if the prime minister wanted to arrange the elections as soon as possible, then the system set up for the Bulygin Duma, preparations for which were already well advanced since the elections had been scheduled for December 10, would have to be retained, though the Bulygin provisions could be expanded to include new categories of voters and to reduce those deprived of the vote. If a new basis were selected, then the preparations would have to be begun all over again and convocation of the Duma would be delayed. As a result, Witte finally instructed Kryzhanovskii to draw up draft regulations which utilized the existing principles but broadened the circle of electors.[26]

During the next few weeks Witte consulted several times with Shipov and other "public men" concerning revision of the suffrage. They tried to persuade him to accept a general electoral law. Though he was moved by their arguments, Witte remained doubtful "since in the absence of well-organized political parties and because of the unpreparedness of the government and the illiteracy of the population, direct and general elections would undoubtedly place the Duma in the hands of those who would promise the voters the greatest material benefits, and first of all the division of the land and the seizure of factories." Finally, Witte, still confused, decided to have the Council of Ministers consider the several alternatives.[27]

To understand the discussions which then ensued it is necessary to review the main electoral provisions of the Bulygin Manifesto of August 6. While there was no pratical reason why these, though written with a consultative Duma in mind, could not, broadened and strengthened, serve to elect the legislative Duma promised in October, some potential voters would inevitably be excluded and a general electoral law was an important point in the democratic program of the liberals. The Bulygin system divided the population into classes for the preliminary stages of voting.[28] Property qualifications restricted the number who were permitted to vote, and elections were multi-staged or indirect rather than direct. All Duma deputies were to be chosen by provincial assemblies, but it required, in some cases, several elections before an elector was finally sent to the provincial assembly.

The first curia consisted of landowners. These were divided into two groups. Large landowners who held property valued at a minimum of 5,000 rubles voted directly for electors to gubernia (provincial) assemblies by casting their votes at uezd or district electoral assemblies of landowners. Clergy using church lands in the uezd and landowners whose holdings were valued at no less than 1,500 rubles nor more than 5,000 rubles elected their representatives to the uezd assemblies of landowners at preliminary electoral meetings, with one representative being chosen for every 5,000 rubles in property represented. The value of landed property varied for each gubernia and was calculated from a minimum number of desiatins the landowner must possess before he was judged to own land of the requisite value. This varied from 100 to 800 desiatins but averaged 200 to 300 desiatins in central Russia.

Voting separately from landed and peasant voters at the uezd level were uezd burghers who owned real estate worth at least 1,500 rubles in provincial cities, individuals who owned highly taxed commercial and industrial enterprises, and tenants paying high apartment taxes. For voting, uezd towns were divided into electoral districts (which corresponded to police districts), each of which voted for electors to the town electoral assembly.

A third category—and the largest in numbers of people—was the peasantry holding commune land. The Cossacks of Astrakhan, Orenburg, and the Don were also included within this curia. In a four-step system these voters first had to elect one representative from every ten householders to a volost assembly, at which two delegates were chosen to sit at uezd assemblies; these in turn chose electors to the gubernia assemblies, at which deputies to the

Duma were selected. Peasants, therefore, initially chose representatives from their own class, but their representatives ultimately joined with those of other classes at the provincial assembly to choose deputies to represent the province. However, as a special concession to the peasantry and to those nobles and bureaucrats who believed the simple muzhik was basically conservative and loyal to the throne, peasant electors at each gubernia assembly were given the right to choose separately and directly one Duma deputy. It was not a large concession; it gave to the representatives of the peasantry, who were at least seventy percent of the population, the right to elect on their own some fifteen percent of the Duma deputies.

Special representation was given to twenty large Russian cities which chose their own deputies to the Duma via city electoral assemblies. St. Petersburg was given six deputies; Moscow was awarded four; and the other eighteen cities were each permitted one deputy. Suffrage requirements were somewhat higher than for uezd towns. The cities, as the towns, were divided into electoral districts.

The purpose of the Bulygin system was to weight representation so that those considered most loyal to the government, primarily gentry and communal peasants, would be elected. Those elements considered to be "untrustworthy" were not franchised; these included small industrial and commercial elements, many professionals and intellectuals, the city proletariat, landless peasants, agricultural laborers, and some three million nomadic and non-Russian peoples of Central Asia and the Caucasus. Both the Bulygin system and its revision of December 11 excluded from the franchise entirely men under the age of twenty-five, all women, students, those in military service, certain high civil servants, and individuals who had criminal records or who were on trial.

The liberals saw in the October 17 Manifesto the opportunity to discard the Bulygin electoral system, which had not won broad support, and to substitute the liberal "four-tailed" formula, i.e., universal, direct, and equal suffrage according to secret ballot. On the other hand, Witte, though uncertain, seemed to favor "liberalizing" the Bulygin project to include those classes which had originally been excluded and thereby to provide for almost universal male suffrage, while maintaining indirect elections.[29] To some degree Witte's stance reflected the conflicting pressures to which he was subject on this issue. Whatever the tsar had promised in the October Manifesto, it soon became clear that Nicholas, while not intending to renege on his pledge, was anxious to keep the Duma as restricted as possible. In November, when Witte and Kryzhanovskii went to see the tsar concerning revision of the Bulygin electoral law, the tsar replied to Witte's assertion that His Imperial Majesty and the government would find the new institution of popular representation useful and helpful:

> Don't speak to me of this, Sergei Iulevich; I understand perfectly well that I am creating not a helper but an enemy. Nevertheless I console myself with the thought that I must strengthen the state in this way so that in the future Russia will be guaranteed an opportunity for peaceful development, without in any way infringing those principles on which it has rested for such a long time.[30]

Concerning proposals for electoral reform Nicholas wrote to his mother: "God alone knows how far people will go with their fantastic ideas," and at the conference which finally decided on the electoral law of December 11, Nicholas declared bluntly: "To take too big steps is impossible. Today a general election law, and then it is not far to a democratic republic."[31]

On the other hand from all sides arose a clamor that the only way to save the country from revolution and anarchy was the speediest convocation of the Duma. Octobrists and Kadets, as well as other liberals and moderates, preferred a general electoral law, but urged above all else a quick calling of the Duma, on whatever basis it was constituted. Even some in court circles and the tsar himself were anxious to hasten the Duma into being, believing it would help quell the revolution. Typical was the statement of Baron Korff at the December conference on the new law: "The calling of the Duma—that is the end of the revolution."[32] Because of the great public interest in progress toward developing a new electoral law the government took the unusual step of issuing in late November and early December several quite frank and detailed explanations of what was being done and where the matter stood, which were published in *Pravitel'stvennyi vestnik*.[33]

Part of the explanation for this widespread sense of urgency was the deteriorating situation in the country, and it is important to recall that the negotiations for the electoral law took place at the very time that Witte was facing the most serious problems of his six months in office. He had failed to win public acceptance of his program; revolution was still raging in the countryside and endangering the cities. On December 5 he exclaimed to the special conference working on the new election law that the domestic situation was a "nightmare" to him. The government was trying to suppress disorder while the Far Eastern army was isolated 12,000 versts away.[34] The result was that during the discussions relating to the election law Witte was upset and performed far below his capacity. He was irresolute, indecisive, and vague.

Illustrative of Witte's lack of a clear-cut policy on this issue was his presentation on November 19 of three distinct proposals to the Council of Ministers, which together with several representative "public men," including Shipov and Guchkov, plus some invited members of the State Council constituted a small special conference on the electoral law under Witte's chairmanship.[35] One project, which probably reflected the personal views of Witte, who had urged as far back as July that workers be given the vote, provided for a broadening of the franchise based on the Bulygin system but suggested that the workers should have a separate curia, electing their deputies directly to the Duma. A second draft proposed a similar broadening of the Bulygin franchise but did not give the workers a separate vote for Duma deputies, providing instead that electors chosen by the workers participate jointly with representatives of other classes in provincial and city electoral assemblies, which would then elect deputies to the Duma (the system finally adopted). A third proposal, presented by Shipov, called for a general, but indirect, two-staged electoral law.[36] Only brief consideration was given to the possibility that the elections be by separate estates (*soslovie*)—nobility, burghers, peasants—a proposal which had been discussed but rejected at the time the Bulygin project was drafted on the grounds that this would freeze people into estates which were in the process of change and that it would not give sufficient weight to the most cultured and reliable elements in society, the gentry and the bourgeoisie.

In the discussions of the special conference on November 19 and 20 Durnovo opposed any broadening of the electoral law (this was only a month after Witte had appointed him because of his supposed liberal views), while Witte rejected Shipov's plan because, he argued, only through preliminary voting by classes could the peasants be assured of adequate representation in the Duma.

Shocked by the stand taken by Witte, who the liberals had hoped would champion a general electoral law, Shipov and his supporters accused the prime minister of violating the October Manifesto. Witte retorted that the Manifesto had promised only that new classes would be admitted to the franchise and had not said anything about universal suffrage or a general electoral law, except that these might be worked out by the new Duma. Although some of his own ministers, notably Kutler, head of the Ministry of Agriculture, Minister of Communications Nemeshaev, and Minister of Trade Filosofov, supported Shipov's proposal, the majority of the conference finally rejected it, arguing that it ignored Russian conditions in which a literate and educated citizenry did not yet exist and that it therefore might lead to "a despotism of the masses" and the domination of the Duma by the extreme parties, who were better organized than the more moderate groups.

Since the special conference had revealed a sharp division of opinion, Witte proposed to the tsar on November 30 a new and broadened conference under the chairmanship of Nicholas himself to make a final decision. Presented to this Crown Council, which met on December 5, 7, and 9, with the participation of the Council of Ministers, members of the State Council, Grand Duke Mihkail Aleksandrovich, Trepov, and others from court circles, and four invited "public men" (Shipov, Guchkov, Count Bobrinskoi, and Baron Korff) were the Shipov proposal and the first project considered by the previous special conference, which broadened the Bulygin system on the grounds that this was the only way to avoid delaying the elections but gave a separate vote to the workers. The latter was justified in a memorandum which argued rather defensively that unless the workers were allotted a separate curia, the electors they chose would be lost among the mass of gentry, town, and peasant electors in the provincial electoral assemblies; thus deprived of the hope of direct representation and of having their most urgent needs satisfied through the Duma, the voting proletariat would become prey to propaganda and revolutionary agitation. While recognizing that separate elections for workers might lead to a bloc of socialist deputies in the Duma, the memorandum asserted that this was the lesser of two evils.

Before the first Crown Council meeting, an amazing private conversation occurred between Witte and Shipov.[37] At this meeting Witte recalled to Shipov the latter's surprise on November 19 when Witte had opposed his plan for universal suffrage, as it appeared Witte was thereby violating the spirit of the October Manifesto. Witte then told Shipov that if he had agreed with Shipov at that time, Witte's many opponents would have said that he wished to head off any debate on the election law and wanted to present for the tsar's signature a law based on universal suffrage. Witte said that he actually supported Shipov's point of view but had deliberately argued from the other side, confident that when the time came for a decision Shipov would present a strong case and that it would be better if such a proposal seemed to come from the initiative of the "public men." Witte said he wished Shipov to become aware of his position in advance of the Crown Council sessions and warned him not to refer to the Manifesto in constructing his case before the tsar. This is an almost incredible account and can be believed only because it is supported by Witte's actions during the three sessions of the Crown Council. If Witte's conversation with Shipov is accepted as evidence of his true beliefs, then Witte was guilty of securing the Council of Ministers' acceptance of an election formula in which he had little or no confidence himself.

At the first session of the Crown Council on December 5, Shipov was invited to present the arguments in favor of his proposal. He told the tsar that a great gulf existed between the government and the public and that this could best be closed by devising a proper election law for the First Duma. This election system, Shipov said, "must be founded on the principle of democracy."[38] Shipov suggested that Russia be divided into representative districts according to population. Each uezd with 300,000 residents would get one representative; each uezd with less than 100,000 residents would have to join with another uezd to form an election district. Each uezd over 300,000 population would be divided into two districts. The result would be 600–650 representative districts roughly equal in population sending that number of representatives to the Duma, representatives who were elected across classes. Shipov justified the majority position which the peasantry would hold under such a system by asserting, in the Slavophile tradition, that while the peasants would be radical on the question of land, they would be conservative on political issues.

Guchkov noted that, under Witte's plan in which representatives were chosen by classes, the workers would receive fourteen special deputies. According to Guchkov, this would be a built-in strike committee. He added that there was no reason to fear the public. Moreover, since a general electorate was inevitable, it would be better to grant it now than have it extracted by force later. Shipov said that his party, the Union of October 17, was formed to protect the government and to encourage reform. A good election law would elect his party to the Duma; a bad law—that proposed by the government—would find the Duma filled with radicals.[39]

Various members of the council opposed the liberals' plan. State Councillor Rikhter said that the peasants were not interested in anything but land. Therefore, accepting a general election law would be opening the door to the intelligentsia and the proletariat. This, he believed, would create a most undesirable situation in the Duma. On the other hand, Prince Alexei D. Obolensky, pro-curator of the Holy Synod, said he favored full equality for all Russians before the tsar, supported Shipov's plan, and argued that such a program was after all "quite Russian." The head of the Ministry of Agriculture, N. N. Kutler, spoke against the government's report because he said it would include only about one-tenth of the population. In St. Petersburg, for example, he said, only 100,000 would be permitted to vote.[40] Therefore, he favored Shipov's report.

Witte was slow to speak, and when he did, he vacillated back and forth between the two reports. He seemed excited and irritated and spoke standing, with extravagant gestures, while the tsar sat, fidgeting at the table, dejectedly looking at his prime minister.[41] Early in the meeting Witte asked how any kind of real elections could be held in the countryside which the conservatives had de-serted and left to the control of revolutionaries. Later, he stated that above all "we must not have a Duma which will transform itself into a constituent assembly." Then he seemed to contradict himself by saying that in view of the lack of sufficient force to restore order it was imperative that the Duma satisfy all the population and not just two or three of its elements. Therefore, the government must adopt "that principle which will satisfy all the people." Witte said that if the government report were adopted, the "third element" would have no voice but that this would not prevent it from stirring up the people. According to Witte, the government's report would be one with more faith in the tsar, but no one would have faith in it. Furthermore, Witte said it seemed impossible to adopt the gov-ernment's report and still retain a separate vote for workers. Yet, if one wished to exclude workers, one might as well adopt the law of August 6; but such a Duma would be respected by no one.[42]

Witte's actions were no less puzzling at the next session of the Crown Council. On December 7 he spoke out even more forcefully against his own report. Whereas on December 5 he had asked how elections could be held in the midst of revolution, he now insisted that it was necessary to convene a Duma very soon; but it was not possible to do so according to the law of August 6. Witte stated flatly that his report was "impossible." Like it or not, Witte said, the twentieth century was one in which workers would grow in importance. Therefore, his report was unfair; Shipov's report was most just. In a burst of enthusiasm he said "Russia is one of the most democratic countries." Then in almost the next breath Witte did an inexplicable thing. After speaking strongly for Shipov's report and undermining his own, he ended his remarks by saying: "When I think about it, I incline in favor of the second [Shipov's] report, but when I begin to act according to it, I fear this report."[43]

One cannot be sure what Witte hoped to accomplish by his actions or whether he had a clear plan in mind. The tsar finally chose the government's report because according to Nicholas, "it is better and less dangerous to take report number one. . . . The first report gives more guarantees."[44] If Witte had intended to secure acceptance of Shipov's report, as he told Shipov on December 3, he failed miserably. Kryzhanovskii later told Shipov that the tsar made the decision he did because of Witte's uncertainty and unsteadiness. Kryzhanovskii added in his memoirs that Witte gave the impression of being afraid to take the responsibility for a new electoral law on himself and trying to force it on the tsar; as a result his prestige and reputation among both bureaucrats and public leaders suffered a serious blow.[45] Clearly, such exhibitions helped cost Witte whatever confidence the tsar had once had in him.

On December 9 the Crown Council, having heard the news of the Moscow uprising, met once again to discuss the provisions for the new election law based on Witte's report. Witte expressed his dissatisfaction with the final product saying "[the] results will be bad," that it would not quiet the revolutionaries nor even the moderate groups.[46] Witte's memoirs completely falsify his position. Witte wrote that the tsar could not decide between the two reports. Therefore, one day before the last Crown Council session, Witte spoke to the tsarina and convinced her that Shipov's proposal was far too democratic and would endanger the throne. Whereupon, according to Witte, the tsar, under the influence of his wife, decided to adopt Witte's report.[47] This story cannot be supported in the least from the minutes of the three Crown Council sessions.

The election law published on December 11 retained the basic features of the Bulygin formula; it simply added new groups of people, notably industrial workers, the lower-middle class, intellectuals, and the smallest landowners.[48] The new law recognized four categories of voters: landowners, burghers, peasants and Cossacks, and workers. All persons owning land or real estate regardless of its value were admitted to the category of landowners, but preliminary elections were retained for small landowners. For city dwellers the terms were liberalized so that anyone who for one year had owned a commerical or industrial establishment, paid a professional tax, rented an apartment, or received support or pensions for state service could vote. The provisions for peasants and Cossacks remained essentially the same as those in the law of August 6.

New regulations to include workers as voters specified that workers employed for at least six months in factories, mills, mines, metal works, and railroads which employed over 50 workers were to choose electors. Enterprises employing between 50 and 1,000 workers were entitled to one elector; large enterprises employing more than 1,000 workers were awarded one elector for every full 1,000 workers. By this tactic the government hoped to balance the large and more militant labor force in the big factories against the presumably more politically reliable workers in small factories. Thus a factory with 50 workers and one with 1,999 each had one elector, and according to one calculation, 145,234 workers in factories of between 50 and 100 workers had the right to elect 2,072 electors, while 475,111 workers in 212 large factories were able to choose only 424 electors.[49]

The Crown Council rejected Witte's plan for permitting workers to elect Duma deputies directly. Instead in a three-step system workers first voted in their own shops; then their representatives met to choose electors to city and provincial assemblies. From these assemblies the deputies to the Duma were elected. Moreover, the law was weighted so that electors from the workers represented a very small percentage of the total number of electors in provincial and city assemblies, even in the main industrial regions of the empire, ranging from a high of 15.6 percent in Moscow gubernia to a low of 1.2 percent in the cities of Ekaterinoslav and Baku.[50]

Finally, it should be noted that while many workers received the vote under the December 11 law, many others were excluded from the franchise. Those without electoral rights included workers in factories employing less than fifty men, artisans, casual laborers, and workers in nonindustrial enterprises such as bakeries, produce factories, the building trades, and state and public institutions. It has been variously estimated that sixty-three percent, or some two million, of the working population was not franchised.[51]

There were, of course, other groups of males who did not receive the right to vote. Since many people did not live in an apartment or own property, they were disenfranchised; landless peasants, agricultural laborers, and nomadic peoples, as we saw earlier, were disenfranchised. Moreover, in Russian Asia the vote was heavily weighted against the non-Russian peoples; for example, in Turkestan 322,000 Russians and other non-natives chose seven deputies, while 5,378,000 natives chose six.

In general the law of December 11 was weighted to favor the gentry and bourgeoisie out of proportion to their numbers in the population. In the fifty gubernias of European Russia, of the total electors peasant electors made up forty-two percent, landowners thirty-two percent, city dwellers twenty-three percent, and workers three percent. Thus one elector represented 2,000 landowners, 7,000 city dwellers, 30,000 peasants, and 90,000 workers. Or, to put it another way, the vote of one landowner was equal to that of three and one-half city dwellers, of fifteen peasants, and of forty-five workers.[52]

Fearful of unfavorable public reaction to the law, the government issued with it a statement which explained that while the idea of the workers directly electing their representatives to the Duma had certain advantages, it had been dropped because it would set the workers apart from the rest of society and would establish a special category which would be difficult to change in the future when a new and even broader electoral law were decided on. Moreover, the government explained, it had not gone as far as introducing a general electoral law because point two of the Manifesto had promised that this matter would be up to the new Duma. Finally, admitting that the law was a compromise and had deficiencies, the government statement argued that it was the best that could be done without greatly prolonging convocation of the Duma and that the provisions of December 11 did correspond to the existing structure and contemporary state of Russian society, giving a voice to almost all of the male population but granting greater weight to those who had the greatest influence in public life.[53]

Yet in many respects the government had little reason to feel ashamed. The December 11 law was a notable advance over that of August 6, and the formula worked out was not unrealistic for a traditional society in the process of change and for a nation unaccustomed to elections and to representative government. In a country so enormous and with an electorate so largely illiterate a system of indirect and weighted elections made some sense. Although the results of the elections, discussed in chapter eight, confirmed Shipov's fears of an opposition Duma, it is hardly likely that his formula would have provided a Duma more favorable to the government. The unfortunate thing was that whatever credit and good will the new law might have engendered for the government was overshadowed and vitiated by the fear, excitement, and horror produced by the armed rebellions that broke out in Moscow and other cities just as the electoral law was being announced and that the government sternly suppressed by force. As Sir Bernard Pares noted, "The importance of these measures [the new electoral provisions] was overlooked in the noise of the Moscow rising and in the general bitterness against the subsequent repression."[54]

Extraordinary Security Measures

BEFORE TURNING to a discussion of the St. Petersburg Soviet and the Moscow uprising, the chief threats to the government in this period, it is necessary to review first a number of special measures to deal with the revolution that the government began to consider before the crises in the two capitals. Some of these were effected during the dangerous days of December, or later; some were never put into effect; but the fact that they were being discussed before the most serious cases of open defiance of the government and simultaneously with the government's efforts to grant more Russian citizens voting rights clearly reflects both the stiffening stance of the government toward the revolution and the quandary in which Witte found himself. His actions and views concerning these extraordinary measures strongly suggest he personally was beginning to feel a growing urgency to put the restoration of order first, on the grounds that genuine reform was only possible when the chaos that ruled the country was ended.

In his memoirs Witte attempted to justify his position in regard to repression in two ways. First, he argued that it was necessary to meet force with force, sternly and without compassion, but that once order was restored, legal norms should be strictly observed. Second, he explained that much of his effort in taking steps to restore order was motivated by an endeavor to establish clear legal limits for repressive action, to abolish the arbitrary application of force and to regularize its use by law and clear regulations instead of leaving it to administrative decision and the personal whim of local authorities.[55] To some extent the evidence supports this *apologia,* particularly as far as Witte's attitude and actions after the middle of January 1906 are concerned. On the other hand, as we shall see shortly, the record clearly indicates that there was a period when Witte was prepared to see any measures, no matter how ruthless, taken to quell revolutionary disturbances.

The related questions of the imposition of the death penalty and of the use of special or field military courts are a case in point. In his memoirs Witte maintained that during 1905, as the revolutionary movement developed, as the number of places subject to martial law grew, and as the designation of special governors-general and commanders of punitive expeditions with broad powers increased, application of the death penalty and the use of military courts to judge accused revolutionaries (which usually resulted in the death penalty) became arbitrary and uncontrolled.[56] As a result, according to Witte, he attempted to clarify the regulations pertaining to these matters. The record, however, shows Witte not to have been quite so altruistic.

Following the Manifesto of October 17 and the partial political amnesty granted on October 21, one of the chief and most loudly voiced demands of "society" was for abolition of the death penalty. Consequently, on November 12 Witte wrote his minister of Justice, Manukhin. Noting that the issue of the death penalty was a topic of current discussion, Witte suggested that if the Ministry of Justice had views on the matter, "then it would, of course, be desirable for the government itself to raise this question so that subsequent discussion of it would not appear to be merely a concession to public opinion." On November 20 Manukhin sent the prime minister a long memorandum which reviewed the issue historically and legally and concluded, though somewhat equivocally, that the majority of legal experts seemed to oppose imposition of the death penalty. Although attached to this was a draft ukase abolishing the death penalty for civilians, Manukhin's covering letter stated that while he personally and in principle disapproved of the death penalty, he believed that acting to abolish it at that moment would clearly be bowing to the pressure of public opinion and "would not fully correspond with the extraordinary measures against the revolutionary movement now being applied." On the margin of Manukhin's letter was the notation: "left without action."[57] Whether Witte dropped the matter because of Manukhin's opinion, or because the latter had already displeased the tsar and was shortly to be dismissed, is unknown.

In any case a related matter, the question of establishing special or field military courts, soon raised the issue again. Sometime early in December the chief military procurator, General I. V. Pavlov, presented to Witte a draft set of regulations designed primarily to protect the armed services from demoralization and to prevent revolutionary agitation among the ranks. On the grounds that trials of those accused of spreading antigovernment propaganda and of organizing revolutionary activity in the army and navy generally dragged out, even when they were conducted in regular military courts, and that the punishments meted out were too lenient, General Pavlov proposed that such individuals be remanded to special military courts, which would act within twenty-four hours and which would be expected to impose the death penalty. On December 15 Witte reported to the tsar that the Council of Ministers had reviewed the proposal and rejected it, primarily on the grounds that establishment of such special military courts was unnecessary.[58] In a somewhat equivocal fashion Witte explained in the memorandum that he did not oppose the draft regulations in principle but that "the introduction of special military courts would not actually change matters." Under existing law the army could act decisively when it met armed opposition, and in areas under martial law or "strengthened" or "extraordinary" security local authorities could, without consulting the minister of Interior or minister of Justice as was normally the case, transfer the accused to the jurisdiction of regular military courts, "which operated quite swiftly."[59]

Witte then went on to take up a theme which was to become a major concern of his in succeeding weeks, as we shall see in chapter five. He expressed his anxiety about the reliability of the army but suggested it was becoming demoralized primarily because the circumstances and procedures under which it was called in to assist civilian authorities in suppressing disorder and rebellion were poorly defined and confusing. As a result the army, in some cases, acted too energetically and stayed too long, thus provoking hostility among the local population and unrest in its own ranks. Witte noted that new rules governing the use of the army against the revolution had already been presented to the State Council with a request for speedy action, and he closed sternly by requesting the tsar "to order the Minister of War to issue categorical instructions for the army to use decisive action and full armed force against anyone who opposed it with weapons or who attempted to disrupt its activity." Thus, in the end, though the draft law on field courts-martial was turned down, Witte's concern about possible excesses in suppressing the revolution was outweighed by his conviction that the army must meet force with force. When necessary the army could shoot to kill, though it should be called upon sparingly.

In yet another form the question of imposing the death penalty and of the use of military courts for this purpose was raised again at about this same time. Apparently in an effort to deter terrorist acts Witte insisted that a law be drafted which would establish mandatory transfer to the jurisdiction of military courts for all cases involving either an attempt on the life or health of government authorities or the preparation or use of explosives and bombs. If the accused were found guilty, the court was obliged to impose the death sentence, which could be reduced to life at hard labor only under special circumstances calling for the granting of mercy.[60] Witte argued that such a law would clarify and limit application of the death penalty and the use of military courts and would reduce the existing administrative arbitrariness in these matters. A number of officials, however, including several members of his own cabinet, strongly opposed this measure, primarily on the grounds that it extended arbitrary and undesirable features of martial law and military justice into the regular legal code, and the measure was finally never enacted fully.[61]

When Witte first presented his draft of the proposed law to the Council of Ministers, Procurator Obolensky and Minister of Trade and Industry Timiriazev objected to it strongly. Apparently they carried the majority of the cabinet with them, although Timiriazev later claimed in a polemic with Witte that he had resigned from the Council of Ministers because of the pressure Witte put on him in an effort to force through approval of the prime minister's scheme.[62] After the replacement of Manukhin by a new and presumably tougher minister of Justice, M. G. Akimov, Witte again submitted his pet project to the Council of Ministers. But even Akimov did not support it entirely, and the full Council turned it down once more. Around December 20, the tsar, for reasons that are unclear, asked Witte, through Durnovo, to revive the plan. Thus yet a third time the draft law was presented to the Council of Ministers. Still the vote was divided, whereupon Witte asked the tsar to have the whole question reviewed by the State Council.[63] In mid-January Witte's proposal was extensively discussed in the State Council, with fifty-one members supporting it and twenty-two opposed. The matter was then passed to the tsar for decision. He refused to promulgate the whole law, affirming only that in certain cases and with the consent of civilian judicial authorities, cases involving terroristic bombings could be transferred to military courts. A subsequent decree provided sentences of four to fifteen years at hard labor for the use of bombs or explosives.[64]

While these various discussions of the use of military courts were taking place, the government also endeavored to speed up the trials of revolutionaries in the regular courts. In a circular of December 29 Minister of Justice Akimov scolded all court procurators that in some investigations "excessive leniency" was being shown toward people accused of belonging to antigovernment political societies, and he exhorted his subordinates to display unusual energy in prosecuting such people. In a similar circular of January 5, 1906, Akimov criticized the slowness of prosecutions of those responsible for agrarian disorders and urged investigations be limited and accelerated, methods be simplified, and the procurators concentrate on the chief culprits and ringleaders.[65]

Although Witte's government successfully blocked the establishment of field courts-martial, its overall record was not particularly praiseworthy. It refused to abolish the death penalty, and it tolerated its widespread use in military courts that functioned in areas under martial law or special security and in regions to which military expeditions were sent. We have reviewed numerous instances of this in discussing the punitive expeditions, but also instructive is an appeal from the lawyers of Warsaw to Witte on January 27 protesting seventeen summary executions there without any trial.[66] Such occurrences do no honor to the history of Witte's premiership.

Another extraordinary security measure discussed in December was a proposal from the army chief of staff that militia and guards units be formed in certain localities to oppose the revolutionary movement. The Council of Ministers reviewed this plan around December 20, but led by the ministers of Justice and Interior, they decided to reject it on the grounds that it would be impossible to count on the local population formed into militia units acting energetically against their fellow citizens, that such groups, if they were not strictly controlled, might even be dangerous, and that if militia members were paid more than the regular soldiers, this would cause trouble among the army. On December 24 Nicholas wrote to Witte: "I am not sympathetic to the idea of forming a militia. It is complex, probably expensive, and would require much time." The tsar added that he thought it was much more important to reinforce and improve the regular police.[67]

Concurrently the government sought to stiffen the backbone of local authorities and to stop civil servants from participating in the revolutionary movement. In early December the Council of Ministers considered a proposal from one of the generals leading the punitive expeditions against the agrarian disturbances in south-central Russia that special courts should be set up to try civil servants accused of indecisiveness or of engaging in antigovernment activity. Although the Council rejected this suggestion, it recommended a stern reminder to all governors of their responsibility for ensuring the loyalty of civil servants under their supervision.[68] On December 16 the tsar approved a decree of the Council of Ministers forbidding military personnel to participate in political parties or meetings, and on January 12 another decree declared that while civil servants might join political parties, they could not affiliate with those that strove to violate state order; high bureaucrats, including heads of major administrative units and of separate local institutions, were forbidden to play a leading role or become officers in any party.[69]

On December 23 Durnovo sent a secret telegram to all governors and heads of administration under the Ministry of Interior; it is particularly interesting because it suggests the existence of a considerable degree of weakness, laxness, and even veiled defiance of the capital among the local agents of the highly centralized tsarist government. At times it reads almost like one of the numerous calls for "vigilance" that the Soviet Communist party has periodically issued in recent years. Durnovo began by warning that the state was in grave danger because the peaceful part of the population was losing faith in the ability of the government to protect their lives and property in the face of the revolutionary movement. For this the minister of Interior blamed the local authorities "who in these difficult times did not always display a sufficiently firm understanding of their responsibilities" and who in dealing with the growing turmoil failed to act "with that decisiveness, energy, and steadfastness, or with that resourcefulness in skillful methods of administration which they ought to have, quite apart from any personal talent or creativity." As a result, their defense of state institutions, as in the recent railroad and postal-telegraph strikes, had been weak and slow; many governors had not even used the broad powers the tsar had given them, had refused to interfere, and had looked on passively. Then Durnovo complained concerning the postal-telegraph strike:

> To my demand for the arrest of the guilty parties were sent replies either that fulfillment of this order was difficult because of the inadequacy of the army or that local procurators, after investigating the matter, did not believe the participation of state employees in a strike was a criminal act. Finally, there were cases when, because of a failure to understand the dangerous significance of the disloyalty of civil servants, I was asked to spare the guilty since "they sought only the improvement of the economic welfare."

Durnovo continued that many police chiefs did not even assist the governors in dealing with the strikes, the special railroad police were even more ineffective, and the law regulating the freedom of public meetings was not enforced.[70]

The minister of the Interior concluded with a sharp demand for the display of decisiveness and strict discipline and obedience, adding:

> I order that any infringement of the legal order must evoke from local

authorities the sternest opposition, within the limits set by law, in the consciousness that stopping each separate violation of security is the most effective method of government, which will assure the population that its legal rights are being defended. . . .

The slightest connivance, passivity, or indecisiveness in fulfilling their responsibilities will lead to the dismissal of civil servants under the jurisdiction of the Ministry of Interior.

Durnovo warned the governors that they had a special duty to ensure the effectiveness and loyalty of all employees of the ministry and to prevent public institutions such as the zemstvos from usurping authority and acting in matters outside their rightful concern. He declared that the *principal* task of the governors was to restore order and that all their efforts should be bent to this end.[71]

In addition to this severe reprimand and exhortation, Durnovo deemed it necessary to address a further circular to the governors on January 10, calling their special attention to the need to prevent the large-scale agrarian disorders which the government expected would break out in the spring.[72] He urged that opposition in the countryside be crushed by the sternest measures, including, where necessary, the use of weapons and the destruction of separate dwellings or even of whole villages.

Clearly repression was the order of the day, and the government was prepared to take extreme measures to preserve the security of the state. The ensuing struggle cost thousands of casualties on both sides and incalculable property damage. By harsh and merciless measures such as those already discussed, and with the support of the army, Witte's government was eventually able to reestablish order though its reputation became considerably sullied in the process. But first it had to face the serious challenges presented by the emergence and growth of the St. Petersburg Soviet and by the December armed uprising in Moscow.

V

THE DECISIVE STRUGGLE

AND ITS AFTERMATH

*In a short time the Duma will open . . . and I will be obliged to give
an explanation for actions in which I did not participate, for the lack
of success of measures which I did not have the chance to fulfill, and
for projects I did not support.*

—Count Witte to Nicholas II,
February 12, 1906

F ROM EARLY DECEMBER 1905 to the middle of February 1906,
Witte had to deal with a series of challenges and crises that
brought him to the verge of nervous collapse and his government
to the brink of defeat—or dismissal. The revolutionaries and radical
workers embarked on a major and final test of strength with the
government in December. Although the government triumphed,
and order was restored, the resulting violence, repression, and
open violation of the October Manifesto's promises affected tens of
thousands of innocent people, called into serious question the
government's good faith, and helped discredit Witte and his cabinet, both with the public and at court. In the heat of the battle
Witte suffered a crisis of nerves which led him to agitated advocacy of forcible suppression of the revolutionary movement. This
only weakened his position with the tsar and further tarnished his
reputation in the eyes of "society." As a result, his leadership role
was much diminished and he became essentially head of a "care-
taker" government until the Duma could be convened. Despite this
Witte made some progress on his reform program, and he took

steps, after December, to check some of the worst excesses of the government's repressive policies.

The St. Petersburg Soviet

A MAJOR PROBLEM for Witte in his first two months in office was the existence of the St. Petersburg Soviet, or Council of Workers' Deputies. The soviets, which Lenin dramatized in 1917 with his demand that they be awarded all political power, were first born in the revolution of 1905 as the natural progeny of the strike movement. Although the soviets did not play a decisive revolutionary role until the summer and fall of 1917, as early as the fall of 1905, only a few months after their founding, they succeeded in posing a significant challenge to Witte's government. In particular, the St. Petersburg Soviet, located at the seat of power, by rallying considerable popular support around it, by organizing and staging strikes, by exercising a kind of anti-censorship over the press, by threatening the government's financial credit, by arming some of the workers, and by serving as a vague symbol of inspiration and leadership for the revolutionary movement throughout Russia, created one problem after another for Witte and his cabinet. Although its own deputies then and Soviet historians later exaggerated the strength and prestige of the St. Petersburg Soviet, it is clear that Witte's dismissal of it in his memoirs as not important is equally wide of the mark. The Soviet was an incipient revolutionary body which presented a distinct threat to the government; it impeded Witte's efforts to restore order and to initiate reform and it hampered his freedom of action.

The soviets arose in 1905 as groups representing the interests, predominantly economic at first, of factory workers in their struggle with the owners and with the government, and as organs providing organization, direction, and discipline for the chief weapon of the workers, the strike movement.[1] At times of general strike they also carried out certain economic and civil functions when workers refused to cooperate with official and legal organs. Beginning primarily as strike or grievance committees, the soviets, as the revolutionary movement swelled, often began to advance political goals and some even became embryonic battle organizations fighting for revolution. Yet, because they quite accurately represented the chief interests of their constituency and their power was more moral and inspirational than physical, their dominant function remained the organization and coordination of strikes and their principal aims continued to be improvement of the economic conditions of the workers. Most of the soviets were in theory, and usually in fact, non-party; that is, though leaders and members of revolutionary parties were generally well represented, directly or indirectly, the soviets were not intended to be, and seldom were, the instrument of one revolutionary organization.[2]

The first soviet grew out of a strike which began on May 12, 1905, in Ivanovo-Vosnesensk, a textile district near Moscow. A few others arose during the summer, and the October general strike led to the organization of many soviets. Not only did workers' soviets emerge in cities, but soviets representing other groups appeared as well. For example, in four volosts of Tver in November and December 1905, peasant soviets were formed. Soviets arose also in universities and secondary schools, and were organized in the army and navy, as in Sevastopol in November, and in Krasnoiarsk, Chita, and Moscow in December. Altogether, approximately eighty soviets were established in 1905.[3] In some cases these soviets gained considerable power. On December 9 the Soviet of Novorossiisk assumed control of the local government and proclaimed the "Novorossiisk Republic." The governor and police chief fled to save their lives, and the troops joined with the workers.[4] The Novorossiisk Republic and other such soviets were suppressed by the punitive expeditions of December 1905–January 1906; but for a brief period a few were successful in their challenges to the government. Others, such as the Moscow Soviet, made unsuccessful attempts to overthrow the government by armed rebellion.

By far the most important of the many soviets in 1905 was the St. Petersburg Soviet, not because it seized control of the government, for it did not; nor was it either the first or the most successful of the soviets. It was significant because it spoke for the many workers in the capital city and for a time defied the government. For fifty days it flourished under Witte's very nose to his embarrassment and discomfiture. In a bit of journalistic exaggeration *Novoe vremia* noted that there were actually two governments in St. Petersburg—Witte's and the Soviet's—and it was a question who would arrest whom.[5] At the same time it is important to recall that the St. Petersburg Soviet did not create the 1905 revolution nor even the October general strike; rather the Soviet was a product of these two phenomena.[6] Although it represented the workers, it never in fact became their leader any more than the rider of a runaway horse actually determines the direction or speed of his mount. The Soviet held the reins; it spoke for the workers; but when the workers decided to end the strikes, no threats or appeals could spur them to further efforts. In addition, workers occasionally took action which the Soviet opposed but which it ultimately had to endorse if it were to retain its leadership.

On October 13–14, during the general strike, a Workers' Committee (essentially a strike committee) was formed in St. Petersburg, on the basis of one representative chosen in the factories for each five hundred workers; this group elected Georgii Stepanovich Nosar' (also known as Khrustalev or Khrustalev-Nosar') as chairman. Nosar', a young and previously little-known radical lawyer who just a few weeks before had been serving time in the Peter and Paul fortress for antigovernment activity, was not a member of any of the revolutionary parties, although of the delegates to the Committee who belonged to a party, a majority were Mensheviks.[7] At a meeting on October 17 Nosar' gave the organization the title, the St. Petersburg Council (Soviet) of Workers' Deputies, and thus the symbol of the revolution was officially founded on the same day the October Manifesto was promulgated. At its maximum strength, in late November, the Soviet had 562 deputies from 181 enterprises and 16 unions, plus 10 representatives each from the Mensheviks, Bolsheviks, and Socialist Revolutionaries. Even then the Soviet probably represented only about half the St. Petersburg proletariat. It had an elected Executive Committee which considered policies and programs to be presented later to the entire Soviet and which played a considerable leadership role. Yet, as Nosar' himself noted, "the Executive Committee proposed, the Soviet discussed and disposed."[8]

The representatives of the radical parties in the Soviet gave it a good deal of direction and often provided ideas and inspiration, but they by no means dominated it. Trotsky, who as vice-chairman and through his energy and gift for oratory played a prominent role in the Soviet, was at that time not formally affiliated with any of the socialist parties. Fearful of the dangers of "spontaneity" and wary of nonparty organizations on principle, the Bolsheviks supported the Soviet rather reluctantly and primarily because they could not afford to stand apart from such an influential and active workers' organization. The Mensheviks warmly embraced the Soviet but were not always certain exactly what it was or what it should do. Yet all involved in this surprising body were soon caught up in a mystique of revolution which led them to exaggerate their own ability to assault the forces of order, to emphasize the dramatic and symbolic effect of their actions as against pragmatic results, and to be militant and heroic, though often unrealistic. Their chief weapon was the strike, but when the workers wearied of this and found the results not consonant with the heavy economic losses they suffered as a result of loss of pay and of lockouts, the power and influence of the Soviet rapidly waned.[9] Nosar' explained that workers obeyed the Soviet *imperio rationis sed non ratione imperii* [by order of reason, but not by reason of orders].[10] The Soviet had no way of compelling obedience. Therefore, it could depend upon the loyalty of the workers only if it led in the direction they wished to go.

Following publication of the October Manifesto, the newly created St. Petersburg Soviet suddenly found itself acclaimed as head of the opposition which had forced the government to capitulate. As we saw, the Soviet had not started the general strike; but once the Soviet assumed its direction, workers and much of the rest of the St. Petersburg populace looked to it for leadership. The Union of Unions asked permission to send deputies to sit in the Soviet. "Officials and the employees of banks, offices, railways, post, telegraph, and telephone sent representatives to the Council and submitted to its decisions."[11]

The Soviet took this responsibility quite seriously. On October 18 a crowd gathered in front of the women's college in which the Executive Committee of the Soviet was meeting and asked it to lead an assault on the jails to free all political prisoners. Three men from the Executive Committee led by Trotsky took the crowd on a long march down side streets. Finally, Trotsky stopped and asked the crowd to scatter as he was afraid the civilians would be slaughtered by troops should they attempt to open the jails.[12]

That evening the Soviet, with 250 delegates from 111 plants present, voted to continue the general strike until a democratic republic was established. This seemed to demonstrate the political orientation and potential power of the Soviet. On the other hand, many St. Petersburg workers believed the October Manifesto gave them most of what they wanted. They wished to return to work, and they did so in great numbers on October 18 and 19. The Soviet, faced with the possibility of losing its support, voted on October 19 to end the strike at noon on October 21.[13] This was a gesture of weakness as most workers had returned to their jobs before the deadline. Moreover, on the night of October 20 the Soviet cancelled at the last minute a large demonstration which Witte had authorized and which was planned for October 21 to honor casualties of street riots that had occurred October 18; Soviet leaders feared clashes with "Black-Hundred" gangs would develop and lead to more bloodshed.

The Soviet also gave its attention to other activities. One was formation of a workers' militia. With the army still occupying the city and with the ever-present danger of "Black-Hundred" riots, the Soviet decided to organize its own self-defense brigade. The workers armed themselves with knives, daggers, and pikes which they made while they were at their jobs, as well as with a few revolvers and rifles the Soviet was able to acquire. A worker could secure a rifle or a revolver from the Soviet on payment of a ruble deposit. After taking the gun, he had to appear for review once a week or face punishment.[14] Trepov estimated the number of workers who possessed arms at about six thousand. From this group about three hundred were selected as a "self-defense corps" or "militia." The militia patrolled the streets each night from 8:00 P.M. to 6:00 A.M. in groups of eight to ten. Trepov wrote that "supposedly" the militia had been formed to protect the workers and to preserve peace against the pogromists, but "actually" their goal was to prevent the police and army from arresting revolutionaries.

The Soviet also turned to censorship. First of all it ignored the tsarist censors and published what it wished in its own paper, *Izvestiia*, which was first issued on October 17. In addition, the printers who were allied with the Soviet refused to set type for pogrom appeals, reactionary articles, etc. The Soviet called this "legitimate" censorship. Soon printers refused to print anything that attacked the Soviet and later anything which had been first submitted to government censors.[15] Newspapers also found it advisable to print articles from time to time which came from the

Soviet. The Soviet also collected money for a strike fund, established pharmacies, and took charge of workers' relief funds.

Some of its leaders also believed the Soviet should act, when necessary, as an intermediary between the workers and the government. Thus, as noted earlier, they approached Witte for permission to hold a memorial demonstration on October 21, and a delegation of Soviet deputies went to Witte on October 19 and asked him to release three Soviet deputies who were being held in the Kazan jail. According to the Soviet's records, Witte complied immediately.[16] Witte has, however, denied that he had direct contact with the Soviet or that it even had great influence.[17] This is not true. Witte and some of his ministers often received deputies from the Soviet to settle various points of disagreement. On one occasion Witte had to appeal to the Soviet to persuade the telegraph workers to send a telegram to the Central Asiatic fortress of Kuska.[18] On the other hand, more radical members of the Soviet opposed these contacts with the government.

Workers' demands to reduce the workday to eight hours soon demonstrated the basic dilemma which beset the St. Petersburg Soviet. Some Soviet leaders, especially the representatives of radical parties, wished to turn the Soviet into a kind of revolutionary government. For this purpose, economic goals were less important than political ones. Strikes, they held, should be used first to bring political pressure on the government and only secondarily to solve economic grievances. The Soviet leaders conceived a strike and the threat of a strike as weapons to hold over the government to force one political concession after another. To be effective, however, the strike had to be used only at the proper moment and with full force; to use it frivolously and haphazardly would be only to dull the weapon. The workers, on the other hand, had supported the Soviet when it seemed to assist them in achieving their goals. These goals were partially political, but for many they were primarily economic. Therefore, since the strike as an instrument of pressure had succeeded during the general strike of October, many workers questioned why it should not be used again to force further economic concessions. The workers naturally expected the Soviet to endorse and to support their actions toward this end.

On October 27 workmen in several mills and plants in St. Petersburg walked off the job after working eight hours.[19] It was not a strike but simply an attempt to compel employers to adopt the eight-hour workday. (The average workday in St. Petersburg in 1905 was ten hours, plus one and three-quarters hours for lunch.) The response of the industrialists to this movement, which soon spread to other plants, was far different from their attitude during the general strike, when many employers, sympathizing with the opposition to the autocracy, had continued to pay workers wages during the strike. But after October 17, when the employers were largely satisfied with the political concessions wrested from the tsar, they banded together to resist new economic demands from the workers. To those trying to force an eight-hour workday, management paid pieceworkers for what they produced; hourly workers were paid four-fifths of their normal wage. Employers, with encouragement from the government, circulated "black lists," gave financial aid to associates hit by strikes, and conducted lockouts.[20]

The workers naturally turned for support to the Soviet, which on October 29 resolved to back introduction of the eight-hour workday and ordered workers in all plants and factories beginning October 31 to "struggle" for that goal[21]—a clear illustration of the leaders being led by the followers. But workers had picked a very poor time to press their demands. The end of the war had already brought about a decrease in the demand for certain articles of heavy industry produced in many of the large St. Petersburg plants. This, and the increase in labor unrest, caused many owners to close their factories. Workers who walked off the job after eight hours returned the next day to find the doors of the plants locked against them.

By November 12 the St. Petersburg Soviet was forced to face the consequences of the faltering campaign for an eight-hour workday. In a meeting that day the Soviet agreed that there had been some successes, but more and more plants were closing, putting an increasing number of people out of work. Unable to control the situation and disturbed by the prospect of mass unemployment for its constituents, the Soviet decided "to suspend quickly everywhere the attempt to bring about an eight-hour day by revolutionary means."[22] It was a humiliating defeat for the Soviet, and a defeat that resulted from a campaign it had not started. The aftermath of the defeat caused more work for the Soviet as distributing relief funds for unemployed workers became a major responsibility.

While the campaign for an eight-hour day was in progress, the

Soviet called a second general strike with political rather than economic goals. In late October rumors circulated in St. Petersburg that all the Kronstadt mutineers were to be tried by special courts-martial, and shot as an example to others. On November 1 a young sailor from Kronstadt addressed the Soviet and pleaded for all the assistance it could give. Thereupon the Soviet decreed a general political strike to begin at noon the following day in order to protest against the extreme measures to be applied to those "who sought to defend their rights and the people's freedom in Kronstadt." In addition, the strike was aimed against the introduction of martial law in Poland and was to show the solidarity of St. Petersburg workers with the "revolutionary workers in Poland." The slogans for the strike were: "Down with field courts-martial! Down with capital punishment! Down with martial law in Poland and in all of Russia!"[23]

The strike seemed at first to be very effective. Representatives of the Soviet went from plant to plant giving speeches, telling workers about the strike, and urging them to leave their machines. The government estimated that 112,493 men struck on November 2.[24] However, the strike did not command the support of other groups as the October strike had. Factory workers struck, but storekeepers, clerks, office workers, and professional men continued business as usual. For the strike to result in the political success desired, the Soviet needed wider support than it received. As it was, the strike simply came to be linked with the effort to secure an eight-hour workday for factory workers.

Nevertheless, as we saw in chapter three, the government was sufficiently concerned to lead Witte to address a personal appeal to the workers, though in vain. A day later, however, on November 4, with the strike not going well, the Executive Committee tentatively recommended ending it, but the full Soviet overruled it and voted overwhelmingly to continue the strike. On November 5 the government announced that the Kronstadt mutineers would not be tried by field courts-martial but by regular military courts, and indicated that martial law might soon be lifted in Poland (it was on November 17, only to be reimposed three weeks later). With this apparent victory over the government and with more and more workers refusing to strike and returning to their jobs in fear that they would lose them, the Soviet decided on November 5 to end the strike as of noon on November 7.[25] On balance the strike was a sharp setback for the Soviet, which had used the only real weapon at its disposal but found that it no longer cut as deeply as it had in October.

As a result, and recognizing it could not stand still without losing its support, the Soviet began to consider other possible courses of action in its struggle with the tsarist system. It made some feeble attempts to organize a national workers' congress.[26] It toyed with the idea of an armed assault on the government, but recognized this meant "marching with open eyes to a defeat, preferring a horrible end to endless horrors."[27] Finally, the Soviet concluded it should lay siege to the government by harassing it without giving direct cause for the government to crush it in return; so the Soviet launched an attack on the government through its credit. The Soviet asked all workers to withdraw their savings from banks and savings institutions, demanding payment in gold. In addition, workers were told to demand their wages in gold rather than in currency. The object was to force the government to withhold payments of deposits, thereby destroying its credit abroad.

Nosar' claimed that the plan was nearly successful. In St. Petersburg alone, he wrote, 100 million rubles were withdrawn in just a few days and the government bordered on bankruptcy.[28] Woytinsky, on the other hand, said the entire plan was a farce. The workers had little or no savings, and paymasters could either pay workers as usual or not at all. They had no gold.[29] Farce or not, the government's financial situation was so serious in December, as we shall see in chapter seven, that it could ill afford any additional threat to its solvency. This tactic by the Soviet forced the government into action.

On November 25 the Soviet chose a commission to draft a special manifesto designed to attract wider support for its "financial war" on the government. The following day the government retaliated by arresting Nosar'.[30] Nosar' believed it was a trap: the government wanted to provoke the Soviet into an action which would then justify crushing it. The Soviet could either protest Nosar's arrest by leading workers into the streets, which Nosar' believed would have resulted in another "Bloody Sunday," or the Soviet could wait and do nothing. It chose the latter course although many workers wished to strike, and some even suggested that they attempt to arrest Witte and Durnovo.[31] For a few days the government also took no further action, Witte claiming later that the government bided its time because Durnovo feared that if he attempted to arrest the Soviet deputies individually, many would escape.[32]

Finally, on December 2 the Soviet responded to Nosar's arrest. Along with the Social Democrats, Socialist Revolutionaries, the Peasants' Union, and the Polish Socialist party, the Soviet published a "Financial Manifesto" which called on the public to refuse to pay taxes or debts, to insist on gold in all transactions and payments of accounts, to demand silver or other metal for all sums less than five rubles, and to insist on payment in gold on all savings in banks and other savings institutions as long as the government continued "to make war on its own people."[33] The "Manifesto" was published in all the liberal and radical newspapers, and the government retaliated by closing all printing shops that published it and confiscating their papers.

On the evening of the following day, December 3, police surrounded the building of the Free Economic Society, where the Soviet was meeting, and arrested thirty-odd members of the Executive Committee and over two hundred members of the Council of Workers' Deputies.[34] In his memoirs, Witte wrote that he ordered the arrest of the Soviet. This accords with the stiffening of his attitude toward the revolution at this time and is more or less supported by the tsar, who on December 1 wrote that "he [Witte] is now prepared to order the arrest of all the principal leaders of the outbreak."[35] Gurko, on the other hand, recalled that when Durnovo announced to the Council of Ministers that he had just arrested the Soviet, Witte turned white and cried that all was lost.[36] On December 5 the government issued a public statement justifying the arrest on the grounds that the radicals had been acting against the best interests of the majority of the Russian people, had been attempting to wreck the government's effort to build a new order based on the October Manifesto, and had been abusing the new freedoms by imposing their will by force on others.[37]

Regardless of who was responsible, the mass arrest on December 3 brought to a close the fifty-day existence of what Nosar' termed "a most democratic 'working man's parliament.'"[38] Although a second Soviet was formed to take the place of the first, it never achieved the power and prestige of the former. A call for a third general strike fell on deaf ears, and the new Soviet spent part of its time issuing proclamations from Finland in order to avoid arrest. On January 2, 1906, its members, too, were taken into custody.[39]

The strength of the St. Petersburg Soviet, and of other soviets as well, lay in the revolutionary attitude of the masses of the people, in the "battle atmosphere" of the major cities, and in the uncertainty of the government.[40] The success of the October general strike confounded both the revolutionaries and the government. It caused the revolutionaries to overestimate their strength and to underestimate the power of the old regime. In turn, the government falsely evaluated the relative power balance; in addition, some in the government conscientiously tried to find new ways to solve domestic problems other than resorting to the traditional, but much-abused use of force.

Although several soviets were able to arm some of their members, they were no match, as the Moscow rising showed, for the tsar's police and armies. The strike was not a sufficient weapon. Although it could wound the enemy, it could never destroy him. Furthermore, it dulled with use. Whenever the strikers disrupted the economic life of the city or provoked lockouts, they invariably damaged their own economic position as well. Moreover, if the soviets hoped to get aid from other groups, they were disappointed. Their efforts by and large were restricted to towns and cities. Not that disorder was absent in the countryside, but peasant riots were directed primarily at landowners rather than at the government. Strikes which tied up commerce and caused the peasants' produce to spoil on the way to market alienated rather than captured peasant support.

Overall, the soviets negatively influenced the cause of constitutionalism in Russia. By their unbending opposition to the government, they made a rapprochement between the government and the people they represented difficult, if not impossible. From Witte's appeal to "Brother Workers" on November 3 to the arrest of the St. Petersburg Soviet on December 3 was only one month, but it reflected a major shift in Witte's attitude and approach. The inability of the government and the soviets to find any common ground hardened the determination on both sides. It was only a matter of time until one would have to yield to the other.

The Moscow Uprising

THE FINAL SIGNIFICANT TEST of strength between the government and the revolutionaries during the revolution of 1905 took place in early and mid-December, when armed revolts broke out in a number of cities and the government suppressed them by force. Whether this was a foolish and costly gesture on the part of the radicals remains a moot point. But it is evident that these clashes reflected the growing desperation of the workers and their leaders as the revolutionary movement ebbed, as well as the increasing determination of Witte and the government to quell disorder and revolt ruthlessly. To be sure, the significance of these December rebellions has been greatly exaggerated in Bolshevik mythology; in fact, the uprisings were usually fairly minor skirmishes in a military sense; they had little real chance of overthrowing the government; and they resulted in unnecessary bloodshed and the erosion of many of the gains won by the workers earlier in 1905.[41] On the other hand, they did have symbolic importance, testifying to the fact that large numbers of Russia's urban populace were not satisfied with the concessions wrested from the government and wanted to go further. Moreover, they represented the final dashing of Witte's hopes that he could pacify the country exclusively by a policy of reform and moderation. The gradual movement of the government toward a policy of repression, which was capped by the arrest of the St. Petersburg Soviet, was now confirmed.

From the publication of the October Manifesto to early December, Witte had moved cautiously, using force when necessary and available to head off riots and to crush rebellions, but attempting generally to adhere to the spirit of the Manifesto. Newspapers published freely; political parties organized and met openly; and even groups loudly proclaiming the overthrow of the government were able to function almost without restriction. Undoubtedly, much of this freedom was a result of the conscious weakness of the government rather than its tolerance. Nevertheless, it was also a matter of Witte's design. But now, confronted by clear defiance and open rebellion and under increasing pressure from moderates, as well as reactionaries, to restore peace and order, the government was forced to act. Whether it had sufficient strength in December for the task for which it had insufficient strength in October was still to be determined, but the willingness to attempt the task was clear.

The government's suppression of the St. Petersburg Soviet sparked the last burst of revolutionary agitation and rebellion in the cities. Rather than watch while absolutism tried to reassert itself, the revolutionaries believed it necessary to call for an armed confrontation with the government. Overestimating their own strength while underestimating that of the government, misjudging the spirit of revolution among the soldiers, and ignoring the desertions by those groups that had once supported them, they took up arms against the government. But, as with a Roman candle whose last ball of fire is often the brightest, so the revolutionaries staged their most brilliant display in December only to have their hopes end in a smoking silence.

By far the most spectacular clash occurred in Moscow, but it was not the only city affected. In other cities, such as Nizhnii-Novgorod, Tver, Yaroslavl, Kostroma, Vladimir, Aleksandrev, Ufa, Saratov, Tambov, Kharkov, Poltava, Kremenchug, Ekaterinoslav, Rostov-on-the-Don, Odessa, Podolsk, Kiev, Chernigov, Gomel', Pinsk, Kovno, Reval, and Tiflis, the story was almost the same.[42] Rebellions began with strikes—in most cases to protest the arrest of the St. Petersburg Soviet and to support the Moscow rising—developed with attacks on police, the closure of stores, and the stoppage of railroads, and escalated into open street battles with police and soldiers confronting the armed strikers. The revolutionary fires burned throughout December until they were smothered one-by-one by the tsarist forces.

To one degree or another each of the rebellious cities was influenced by the Moscow uprising, which began on December 7. Witte had long believed Moscow to be the most revolutionary of all the cities of Russia.[43] Convinced that the Moscow officials were not competent for their responsibilities, Witte sought to have them replaced by more forceful men. Specifically, he recommended Admiral F. V. Dubasov to the tsar as the man he wished to have named as governor-general in Moscow. Witte first made the request on November 9, but it was not approved until late November, after an urgent note on November 20 in which Witte stressed the growth of the revolutionary movement in Moscow and the necessity to send a strong man there.[44] Dubasov was soon dubbed "Commander of the Kremlin Fleet."

In Moscow the growing unrest which alarmed Witte was a result not only of the weakness of the local authorities but of the aggressive policies of the Social Democrats there. The October general strike in Moscow had been directed by a broadly based committee which was non-party and which included liberals as well as radicals. Revolutionaries and representatives of the industrial workers were in a minority. After the strike the attitude of the proletariat became increasingly radical, and leadership of the workers' movement passed fully to the Social Democrats, who relied primarily on party and interparty organizations. Drawing upon the experience of the St. Petersburg Soviet, however, the Social Democrats decided it would be useful to establish a similar Soviet as a class, antiliberal, antigovernment body. Thus, on November 22 the Moscow Soviet was formed. It differed from the St. Petersburg Soviet in that elections were indirect, it was controlled from the center rather than by the workers, and its policies were set by the Social Democrats, primarily the Bolsheviks. Consequently, it never became the kind of vital and representative organ the St. Petersburg Soviet did; it always remained somewhat the creature of the parties. Nevertheless the Moscow Soviet served as a useful facade and as a suitable spokesman for the alleged interests of the workers.[45]

When the Witte government arrested the members of the St. Petersburg Soviet, the Moscow Soviet protested in two proclamations issued on December 4. One anounced the Moscow Soviet's compliance with the "Financial Manifesto" of the St. Petersburg Soviet and called on all Muscovites to adhere to its terms. A second declaration asserted that in arresting the St. Petersburg Soviet and closing the newspapers which had published the "Financial Manifesto" the government was attempting to seize absolute power once again and that all Moscow soldiers and workers should be prepared to resist this renewal of repression.[46] For the Moscow Soviet this was a significant step on the road to armed insurrection, and it was taken only after considerable debate and with some misgivings.

The leaders of the Moscow Soviet were aware the workers in St. Petersburg were exhausted and demoralized, the representatives of the railroad workers were reluctant to support a general strike that might turn into an armed uprising, and the attitude of the soldiers of the Moscow garrison, despite recent unrest among them, was not clearly rebellious. Yet, pressured by the militant mood of the Moscow workers themselves and entranced by their own mystique of revolution, the heads of the Moscow Soviet decided on December 4 the government's action in St. Petersburg was a deliberate effort to destroy the revolutionary movement and this challenge had to be met with "a policy of resistance, if necessary including armed struggle, even though the most clear-sighted among them realized how woefully inadequate their preparations for the struggle were."[47]

This decision was referred to the rank-and-file workers for confirmation, and two days later—on December 6—the Moscow Soviet voted unanimously to begin a general political strike at noon on December 7.[48] The avowed purpose of the strike was to protest the arrest of the St. Petersburg Soviet, but it was clearly intended that the strike develop into an armed rebellion and the slogans adopted by the Soviet for whipping up public support reflected this expectation:

> Down with the criminal tsarist government!
> Hurrah for the general strike and armed rising!
> Hurrah for a general constituent assembly!
> Hurrah for a democratic republic![49]

In making this bold move the Moscow Soviet acted independently, not at the behest of the Soviet or the parties in St. Petersburg. In the words of Robert Slusser, "the Moscow Soviet consciously assumed responsibility for the continuation and development of the revolutionary movement as a whole."[50] A day later the reconstituted Soviet in St. Petersburg also issued a call for a general strike, but without effect.

The aggressive action of the Moscow Soviet alarmed the government because it doubted the reliability of the troops in Moscow. Shortly after his arrival in Moscow in the last week of November to take up the post of governor-general, Admiral Dubasov had appealed directly to Witte for more troops, telling the prime minister privately that neither the army command nor the soldiers in Moscow could be depended upon. Minister of War Rediger ordered reinforcements sent from Poland, but they were delayed in transit by the renewed railroad strike. On December 2–3 a serious mutiny occurred in the Rostov regiment stationed in Moscow. Although quelled without too much difficulty, it stimulated exaggerated hopes among the revolutionaries that the army was on the verge of joining them; and it further frightened the government. After the Moscow Soviet issued its strike call, Dubasov again appealed to Witte for help. The latter was told by the tsar to request reinforcements for Moscow from Grand Duke Nikolai Nikolaevich, commander of the St. Petersburg military district. But, according to Witte, the grand duke at first absolutely refused to send any troops, arguing that it was better to let Moscow fall than to weaken the St. Petersburg garrison and thereby endanger the capital and the royal family. He relented only after receiving a personal note from the tsar; the Semenovsky regiment was ordered to Moscow from St. Petersburg on December 12.[51]

In fact, the government had enough forces in Moscow to handle the uprising as the revolutionaries apparently never disposed of much over a thousand militia, inadequately armed. The difficulty was, however, that since most of the army and police were tied down guarding various military and governmental offices and installations, or were confined to their barracks because of doubts about their reliability, Dubasov had only a small mobile force with which to deal with insurrectionary activity in various parts of the city. As it turned out, few troops actually joined the rebelling workers, and by the time reinforcements arrived on December 15, Dubasov had the situation largely under control.[52] At the same time the government's anxiety over the military situation in Moscow was reflected in the quick and vigorous steps it took to encourage and exhort the army in the struggle with the Moscow uprising. On December 13 the Council of Ministers ordered the army not to hesitate to resort to firing on the revolutionaries when this was necessary for the prompt suppression of disorders. This was followed by an imperial ukase to all army commanders to employ whatever force was necessary to restore order. And in instructions to General Min, commander of the Semenovsky regiment, the tsar declared that while every effort should be made to avoid opening fire, when it was necessary to do so, the action taken should be "extremely energetic" and should not cease until all opposition had been eliminated. This would quickly restore order and prevent new disturbances from arising.[53]

The general strike, which led to the armed rising, began on schedule on December 7. In the beginning it met with considerable success. Trains came to a halt (except for one line running into Moscow from the northwest and St. Petersburg which the government was able to keep secure by force and which later served to bring in reinforcements); electric power ended; stores closed; workers left the plants, and mills, attended meetings, marched through the streets, and listened to street-corner orators urge the populace onward in an assault against the government. During the first few days there were frequent clashes between the strikers' militia and government forces, but these were skirmishes not battles and one group or the other always retired before they became such.[54] The workers, moreover, had no concerted plan or strategy, were disorganized and poorly led, and made no attempt to seize the key points and institutions of the city from the relatively dispersed and weak government forces.

Governor Dubasov declared a state of emergency, took steps to defend the center of the city and important enterprises, and had a number of revolutionaries arrested, including, unbeknownst to the government, several members of the Executive Committee of the Soviet. In these actions he had the support of much of the citizenry of Moscow. The situation was therefore quite different from that in October. For example, the bourgeoisie, who in the earlier general strike had generally supported the workers, now strongly opposed them. The city duma, dominated by liberals and industrialists, appealed to the population on December 15 "to end the struggle and bloodshed in the name of Christian love, charity, and devotion to the fatherland." It also elected two representatives to work with Dubasov in restoring order and assigned 5,000 rubles to help the army and police suppress the rebellion. The committee of the Moscow stock exchange voted an additional extensive sum to be placed at the disposal of Dubasov.[55] The typical citizen was apparently either hostile or apathetic toward the workers' revolution. The strike and the barricades erected by the revolutionaries interfered with normal daily life, and in the words of a contemporary English observer, "the attitude of the man in the street is curious: sometimes he is indignant with the strikers, sometimes indignant with the Government . . . [it] seems to be one of skeptical indifference in spite of all, in spite of trade ceasing, houses being fired at, and the hospitals being filled to overflowing of dead and wounded."[56] Thus, without widespread support and sympathy in the country as a whole, or even in Moscow itself, the revolutionaries soon found themselves isolated, carrying on a lonely and increasingly fruitless struggle.

On December 9 the government began to take the offensive, arresting several militia units and using artillery to attack an important command post of the revolutionaries. In response the rebels resorted to guerrillalike tactics; rather than challenge the better armed government forces in the streets, the revolutionaries took refuge in houses and buildings and became snipers, firing at those few soldiers and police who were patrolling the streets.[57] The government, in turn, employed artillery fire against buildings in which snipers were concealed, with the result that innocent inhabitants were killed and much property was destroyed. By the time the Semenovsky regiment arrived in Moscow on December 15, the main body of the revolutionaries had been forced into one area of Moscow, the Presnia district. On December 17–18 a full assault on Presnia took place, followed by brutal repression throughout the city. General Min carried out to the letter the tsar's personal orders to use the severest measures in suppressing the rebellion. Although privately Nicholas expressed concern that the uprising had been put down with excessive ruthlessness, he officially commended the regiment as follows: "From the bottom of my heart I warmly thank you for your service. Thanks to your valor, steadfastness, and loyalty the rebellion in Moscow was overcome."[58]

On December 18 the Moscow Soviet voted to end the uprising. It appealed to the workers to be ready to fight again in the future, but for the moment the political strike was called off.[59] The losses suffered by the revolutionaries during the struggle were high. Although only estimates are available, it seems likely that five hundred to a thousand were killed and several thousand wounded. Official government losses were seventy killed and wounded. Some two hundred leaders of the rebellion were arrested and finally tried in December 1906.[60]

Although there was no fight left in the Moscow proletariat, Dubasov attempted to hold on to the Semenovsky regiment. Witte explained to the tsar on December 23: "Since nowhere are there enough troops, every commander tries to keep what he is once given. . . . But I think it [the regiment] should be returned to St. Petersburg before New Year's." After first requesting Dubasov to release the regiment, Nicholas finally ordered its return to the capital by January 1.[61]

However, several troublesome questions remained. Although much of public opinion welcomed the government's firm action against the rebels, there was also sharp criticism of the severity of the repression from some Kadets and a few moderate papers. It was evident that many innocent people had suffered in the course of the fighting, and a few days after the defeat of the rebels the tsar placed 100,000 rubles at the disposal of Dubasov for the relief of the city. On December 21 Witte, apparently stung by criticism of the government and somewhat conscience-stricken over his own support for the ruthless suppression of the uprising, reported to the tsar that "the many human sacrifices and the extensive material damage in Moscow as a whole, as well as for individuals and for particular institutions, place a heavy moral responsibility on the government." Witte noted that since it required the specially energetic action of the army and quite extraordinary measures to overcome the rebellion, many would be quick to blame the government for lack of foresight and for failing to take necessary preventive steps. He continued:

> Responsibility for this affair will turn out to fall, perhaps correctly, not only on individual responsible local authorities but also on the central government, in the person of the chairman of the Council of Ministers, the heads of the Ministry of Interior, and former governors-general. In such circumstances the best thing would seem to be the immediate appointment of an impartial body, designated by a decree of Your Imperial Majesty as a supreme criminal court, to investigate the events in Moscow under procedures established by law for judging the guilt of higher members of the state administration.

Witte went on to suggest that the department of civil and spiritual affairs of the State Council be entrusted with this task, and concluded that only such an investigation could give the government the moral support it might need in the future, "when it again may find it necessary not to be deterred, by the possible heavy costs to the populace, from taking extraordinary measures."[62] Although Nicholas took no action on this suggestion, it is interesting to speculate why Witte proposed such an inquiry. Was he genuinely contrite and sincerely anxious to have the blame (as he saw it, not for the severity of the repression, but for letting the rebellion break out) apportioned impartially among members of the government, including himself? Did he hope through such an investigation to shift responsibility for the affair to Durnovo and the local authorities and thus to clear his own name with the tsar and before public opinion? Or, did he, as his conclusion implies, hope to "whitewash" the government and to establish a position which would justify its taking severe action against future outbreaks? Probably Witte was not sure himself; all of these considerations undoubtedly motivated him to some extent. In any case, this unusual proposal is another measure of the complexity of the man.

In the aftermath of the uprising two other nettlesome issues had to be settled. One was the fate of the arrested revolutionaries. There was considerable pressure for remanding them to military courts, which could be expected to impose the death sentence in most cases. Dubasov, although he had condoned the extreme measures used in suppressing the revolt and must certainly share the guilt for the excesses committed, strongly opposed trying the rebels in military courts. Witte fully supported him, and those arrested were eventually tried in the regular courts a year later.

Another question was whether and how Dubasov should be rewarded. As we saw earlier, Dubasov was reluctant to take the post of Moscow governor-general; before finally agreeing to do so, he extracted a promise from Witte that the latter would recommend the admiral's appointment to the State Council if Dubasov did a good job. (If Dubasov were assassinated, Witte was to petition the tsar to take care of his family.) In a rather pitiable letter to Witte on January 7, Dubasov complained that though he had succeeded in restoring order in Moscow, he had been neither promoted nor decorated; as a result, everyone was concluding that the government did not approve of his actions. He begged for some sort of reward and reminded Witte of the latter's promise to have him appointed to the State Council. Witte transmitted this letter to the tsar, who ordered Witte and Durnovo to prepare an imperial rescript expressing both gratitude for Dubasov's service and an expectation that he would be rewarded in the future. The rescript was never issued, however, and in April, when Witte resigned, Dubasov was relieved of his post as governor-general in Moscow (although he was then finally appointed to the State Council). In his memoirs Witte insisted that Nicholas failed to reward Dubasov because the tsar was annoyed at Dubasov's refusal to turn the rebels over to military courts. On the other hand, Soviet historians have suggested it was because Nicholas did not wish publicly to honor the man most closely connected with the bloody events in Moscow.[63] Although the former interpretation seems more likely, it is also possible that Nicholas failed to act simply because Dubasov was Witte's man and the tsar did not want any glory reflected on the prime minister, whom by now he thoroughly disliked and distrusted.

The Moscow uprising, as those in other cities—the high point of the revolution of 1905, as Soviet historiography puts it—failed essentially because the government possessed sufficient reliable armed forces to crush it and because the revolutionaries were isolated from other elements in Russian society. In 1917 neither of these conditions obtained. But in December 1905 few troops came over to the side of the rebels, there was no link to the peasants, who were largely disinterested in the efforts of the city revolutionaries and who were in any case busy either with their own anarchic activity or hiding from punitive detachments, the bourgeoisie and liberals were either aloof or hostile, and workers in other cities, as well as many in Moscow itself, failed fully to support the uprising. The result was that the revolt did not become a general armed insurrection of the masses but rather a series of growingly one-sided street fights between superior government forces and ill-equipped and disorganized detachments of workers' militia and revolutionaries.[64] For the government, suppression of the rebellion, however much its brutal aspects might be criticized, was a major victory. Although the revolution as a whole was by no means over, the government now clearly had the upper hand. The revolutionaries were disorganized, divided, and scattered, while the government's strength was growing, as the army began to return from the Far East and more and more elements in society called for an end to bloodshed and a return to order. The revolutionaries' direct challenge to the government by armed attack had forced the government to respond in kind, and its success in defeating the rebels emboldened it to continue to suppress unrest and to preserve order by force. A reactionary tide set in, and the policy of repression toward which the government had been moving since mid-November became solidly established.

Witte's Crisis

BUT WHAT DID ALL THIS MEAN for Count Witte, inspirer of the October Manifesto and champion of reform? Witte, as indicated earlier, became increasingly concerned during late November and early December with the threat the revolutionaries posed to the security of the state and with the problem of restoring order. His behavior during the final deliberations concerning the new electoral law was erratic and peculiar, to say the least. From the time of the outbreak of the Moscow uprising in the second week of December to the middle of January, Witte suffered, it is apparent from his actions, from his reports to the tsar, and from the testimony of contemporaries, a serious crisis of nerves, which markedly affected his attitude and his activity. This phase eventually passed, and he regained a more composed, rational outlook and approach to Russia's problems and was able to conduct the business of state normally and effectively, though his views seemed then to become somewhat embittered and more conservative.

It has been suggested that Witte's strange behavior in this period, marked as it was by an unrelenting, almost violent determination on his part to exterminate the revolution, resulted from his growing realization that he was losing favor with the tsar; and that it reflected a desperate attempt by Witte to ingratiate himself with Nicholas and the tsar's advisers by being "more royalist than the king," that is, by being even more hostile and repressive as regards the revolution than the most conservative court circles were. While this may indeed have been one factor motivating Witte, consciously or subconsciously, this is rather belied by the critical, forceful, far from submissive tone of his reports to the tsar in this period. Moreover, there are other, more direct and more persuasive explanations for his bout of panic and nervous instability in these few weeks. First, Witte was confronted by an overwhelming array of very serious problems—issues and dangers which would have taxed the resources and confidence of the doughtiest of statesmen. Even to list them is to begin to understand Witte's hapless position: widespread anarchy and disorder in much of rural Russia, with the expectation of worse to come in the spring; violent national rebellions in the Baltic, Poland, and the Caucasus; major challenges to the authority of the government and the security of the state in St. Petersburg, Moscow, and many other cities; exaggerated but nonetheless genuine concern about the reliability of the army; difficulties inspired by strikers and revolutionaries in bringing the troops from Manchuria back home; and a major financial crisis which threatened the country with bankruptcy.[65] In short, the government seemed endangered from every side, and Witte had good reason to be deeply alarmed. But even worse, and adding a note of despair to the urgency of the situation, was Witte's clear realization that order must first be restored before he could achieve his most important goals: execution of the reform program he had set forth in October, and completion of the large international loan which he believed was so essential to Russia's future well-being. It is little wonder, then, that Witte began to advocate suppression of the revolution and the meeting of force with force.

Yet Witte might have been able to cope more effectively and less emotionally with even such a formidable series of problems but for a second set of circumstances—the conditions and psychological atmosphere under which he had to try to deal with them. Surrounded by a cabinet of relatively mediocre and undistinguished men, Witte worked virtually alone, without the support, assistance, and counsel of close and able advisers and colleagues. As a result, he was overworked and by early December was emotionally and physically exhausted. Moreover, he was a terribly disappointed and frustrated man. He had sincerely thought that his moderate and rational program presented to the nation in October would succeed, that it would lead to a restoration of order and tranquillity and the intiation of needed reforms. To put it mildly, these expectations had not been fulfilled. Much of society had rebuffed him, disorders of the right and left had ensued, and now the revolution was flaring up again everywhere. If anything, the situation in early December seemed worse than it had been six weeks before. This was certainly a grievous shock to Witte. Finally, Witte found himself almost completely isolated. Scorned by the liberals, despised by the tsar, intrigued against by court circles, ignored by some of his own ministers, Witte discovered in late November that even his only erstwhile supporters, the Octobrists and industrialists, had turned against him, criticizing him for being too indecisive and vacillating.[66] It must have seemed as if every hand were raised against him.

Under these conditions, and in view of the problems he faced,

Witte's reaction of fear, anger, and despair and his emotional behavior in December and early January are hardly surprising. These
attitudes are not fully reflected in Witte's memoirs, although he
admitted there that he generally approved the policies of Durnovo
and that he believed open rebellion should be suppressed decisively, energetically, and without sentimentality.[67] Nevertheless, it
is easy to trace the course of Witte's crisis on the basis of contemporary evidence. As we have seen, the Moscow uprising evoked
a strong response from Witte. He took an active personal role in
urging that reinforcements be sent and in arranging for their dispatch. On December 13 the Council of Ministers ordered the army
to fire on revolutionaries "without any hesitation," and on December 15 Witte reported to the tsar that although the Council disapproved the establishment of field military courts, it favored
ordering the army to use whatever force was necessary to end disturbances. Witte's aggressive attitude at this time prompted the
first of several surprised comments on his behavior by contemporaries. After listening to Witte express his desire for energetic
action against the Moscow rebels, Major-General G. O. Raukh,
aide to the Grand Duke Nikolai Nikolaevich, wrote in his diary:
"What does this man [Witte] want? I don't understand him, and
for me he is almost a sphinx. Undoubtedly this is a man possessing
an infinite ambition and craving for power . . . they are convinced
he is sick with this, that this is an illness such as madness."[68]

Next, the punitive expeditions and uprisings in outlying places
absorbed Witte's attention. In a rather panicky tone Witte reported
to the tsar on December 17 that rebels had seized the Ekaterinskii
railway and that a military expedition like that under Rennenkampf should be sent there at once, but the difficulty was that not
enough reliable troops were available.[69] Two days later Witte urged
Sollogub, governor-general in the Baltic provinces, to use ruthless
measures to quell the rebellion there. On December 21 Witte presented a long report to Nicholas reviewing the general situation; its
tone was at once hurt and aggressive, and it reflected the strain,
anger, and frustration Witte obviously felt at this time.[70] The prime
minister began by pointing out that the task of restoring order was
extremely difficult not only because of the size of the country but
also because the bulk of the field army was still in the Far East,
because demobilization was proceeding too rapidly, because lower-

rank officers were weak and unreliable, and because there was no coordination of action between the civil and military authorities. He reminded the tsar that he had been urging the prompt return of the army from Manchuria ever since assuming office; yet when punitive expeditions were finally ordered to clear the Trans-Siberian railway, he had learned of this only from the newspapers. "If the military trains had been sent a month ago, we would perhaps now have several extra divisions on hand."[71] Then Witte reviewed his pleas to bolster the military command in Moscow, but "what was done in this regard is unknown to me." He then recalled that "reinforcements were sent to Moscow only after the governor-general and I had pleaded unsuccessfully for several days for their dispatch." Witte finally argued the necessity for civilian authorities to have a say in the disposition of the army, a subject of great concern to him at this time, as we shall see below. Clearly Witte was alarmed and annoyed.

Two days later Witte's mood had not changed, as his two reports of December 23 to Nicholas demonstrate. Witte told the tsar that to suppress revolts in Rostov-on-Don and in Novorossiisk he had ordered the atamans of the Don and Kuban Cossack armies, respectively, to take the necessary action. He also reported that he had ordered the governor-general of Turkestan to introduce martial law there. He reviewed the progress of the punitive expeditions in the Baltic and along the Trans-Siberian railroad, noting that "it is necessary with bloodthirsty mutineers to use the most merciless measures."[72]

Throughout this period and as a common thread running through all the reports reviewed, Witte was infuriated by the lack of army units available to deal with revolution and particularly by the fact that he, as head of the government, had no control over where troops would be allocated and sent. In each separate case he had to ask the Ministry of War and the high command to order forces to a trouble spot. He first raised the issue in his report of December 17, pointing out that the army should be assigned with due regard to the needs of internal security as well as to strategic considerations of defense and suggesting the tsar appoint a commission of the chief military authorities plus Durnovo and himself to examine the question. By December 21 Witte, repeating himself several times, was almost violent on the subject:

At this time the army ought to be assigned mainly to the struggle against the revolution and in support of state order. It is evident that under present conditions disposition of the army should be judged according to the internal needs of the country and by people on whom Your Imperial Majesty has placed responsibility for domestic policy. Not only are neither I nor the Minister of Interior informed about the number and allocation of the army, but our whole effort in calling on the army for help is limited to requests submitted to the Minister of War. . . . For example, it is clear to me that we have too few troops in the Baltic . . . but whether it is possible to send reinforcements or not, I do not know.[73]

Witte concluded his tirade by reminding the tsar of the slowness of the State Council in acting on an earlier proposal by Witte for regulating the procedures under which the army would come to the assistance of civil authorities and by recalling his suggestion of December 17 that a special commission on the issue of the disposition of the army be formed. Witte then said: "But perhaps a radical decision of this question would consist of putting at the head of the government a military man and of entrusting to him, with the participation of the ministers, the coordination of all government activity, including that of the military." This was a renewal of Witte's suggestion in October that an alternative to reform would be appointment of a military dictator, and it was a forerunner of his later efforts to resign, but it was probably not meant seriously—rather it reflected his anger and frustration.

In response to this emotional appeal, the tsar acted promptly, appointing the very next day the commission Witte wanted; the prime minister was to chair it, and its members were Durnovo, the Grand Duke Nikolai Nikolaevich, Minister of War Rediger, and Generals Palitsyn and Polivanov.[74] After meetings on January 28 and March 1, 1906, and considerable wrangling, Witte had his way, and it was agreed that troops would be distributed in European Russia with due regard for the need to avert or suppress revolutionary activity. Nicholas confirmed this decision in an ukase of March 12.[75]

Although these agitated reports to Nicholas in mid-December marked the high point of Witte's crisis and of his concern with using maximum force to quell disorders, he continued in early January to press for aggressive action against the revolution, on two occasions deliberately attempting to circumvent the reluctance of the tsar. On January 10 the Council of Ministers renewed an earlier discussion of how best to prevent the widespread peasant uprisings which everyone expected to occur in the spring.[76] Recognizing the impossibility of using the army widely as a preventive force guarding the countryside, the cabinet nevertheless foresaw the possibility that the army would need to be called in not only to suppress riots that had broken out but also to restore property that had been seized by the rebels and to compel the arrest and forcible migration from the trouble spot of the ringleaders of the disturbances.[77] On January 23 the tsar approved the proposal that the army be given the right to arrest rebels and transport them from the scene of disorders, but he asked that this be reviewed by the State Council, which was still trying to work out new rules to govern the action of the army when it was asked to assist civil authorities in suppressing rebellion. Witte objected to this procedure as causing further delay, and on January 27 got Nicholas to agree that Witte might transmit the wishes of the Council of Ministers directly to the ministers of War and Interior for action.

Similarly, Witte sent the tsar on January 11 a memoir of the Council of Ministers dated January 3 on "the need to take decisive measures against civil servants who violate their obligations," with a draft ukase attached.[78] Nicholas refused to sign the ukase, noting "I find that Section I of the decision of the Council of Ministers gives sufficient authority to gubernia authorities to permit them to remove from his post any civil servant who violates his oath." Witte was furious, replying on January 14:

> . . . I consider it my duty to say that Section I of our memoir does not contain *any* new provisions. Therefore, the matter remains in the *same* position, and the governors will be powerless, now as formerly, to combat the revolutionary tendencies of many civil servants. . . . I, for my part, am sure that not taking decisive measures against the mass of provincial civil servants who act beyond the bounds of duty and loyalty will leave the governors largely *paralyzed in the struggle with the revolution* [Witte's italics].

Two days later Witte sent Nicholas, without comment, a report showing the widespread participation of civil servants in the strikes and turmoil on the Trans-Siberian railroad, but the tsar was unmoved, noting on January 18: "I leave in force my earlier decision."

Witte's remarkable about-face in this period startled and puzzled those in and near the court. General N. N. Levashov observed that Witte's change in disposition "staggered" him. Witte, author of a liberal constitution, was now expressing ideas which were not only ultraconservative but even fanatical. Levashov said that Witte now favored the "most decisive measures of coercion, firing squad executions without court trial, the most energetic activities of the army and so on. . . ."[79] On January 12 Nicholas wrote that Witte had changed radically since the Moscow uprising and exclaimed, "I have never seen such a chameleon of a man."[80] According to Nicholas, now Witte wanted "to hang and shoot everybody." As a result of these actions, Nicholas said that no one believed in Witte anymore and that he was "absolutely discredited with everybody except perhaps the Jews abroad." Even in late January Witte told Polovtsev that Russia had proved to be true to the monarchical principle and that it was now possible to place faith in the army. Polovtsev concluded, "This opinion, evidently, is his new general policy."[81]

Witte's sudden change of heart and emotional behavior had no effect on the tsar's basic attitude and outlook toward the revolution and only served to lower further his esteem of Witte. The tsar remained determined both to preserve the autocracy and to abide by his promise in October of a Duma, apparently seeing no contradiction between these equally staunch views. On December 23 Nicholas received a delegation from the Union of Russian People led by its head, Dr. Alexander I. Dubrovin. After accepting badges of the Union for himself and his son, the tsar thanked the Union for its support and said: "I myself will carry the burden of authority laid on me in the Moscow Kremlin [at his coronation], and I am sure that the Russian people will help me. In exercising that authority I am responsible before God." Later in the audience Nicholas stated that with the continued support of the Union and of the Russian people he believed he could defeat Russia's enemies. Then, poetically he exclaimed: "Soon, soon the sun of truth will shine on the Russian Land, and it will then dispel all doubts. I thank you for your sincere feelings. I believe in the Russian people. Unite the Russian people! I am counting on you."[82] Yet on January

18, 1906, the tsar declared to a delegation of peasants from Kursk province:

> I will not forget the peasants, your needs are dear to Me, and I will continually take care of them, as My beloved Father did. A State Duma is being called, and together with Me it will discuss how this can best be done. All of you can count on Me, I will help you, but always remember that the right of property is sacred and cannot be violated.[83]

At about the same time Nicholas told Kokovtsov that if the government stopped wavering, the future would be bright. The tsar indicated that he was determined to stand by the promises he had made in October and would give the people "legislative rights within established limits," but he had no intention of having the Duma strip him of his authority.[84]

Moreover, Nicholas did not forget his continuing concern for order under the new freedoms. On February 10 he wrote to Witte suggesting an imperial manifesto setting the date for the convocation of the Duma which would also explain to his people that the rights he had granted in October were to be exercised only on the basis of special laws that had been issued or were being worked out. In addition, the manifesto should contain a precise and clear reminder that everyone was obliged to obey all existing laws,

> . . . especially those which on behalf of the whole people and the state protect the property rights of individuals, families, institutions, societies, rights which extend not only to immovable and movable possessions but to everything that is in the control of or at the disposition of another person and the deprivation of which would cause harm, for example, hindrances to the use of property, obstacles to pursuing work, infringements on the exercise of legal freedoms.

The tsar went on to urge that the proposed manifesto make plain that violations of such rights would be severely punished and that the guilty would have to answer with their own property or personal labor for damages caused.[85] The tsar's firm but rather paradoxical position was summed up in his words to a delegation from the Autocratic-Monarchical party, which visited him on February 16: "Tell all of your electors that the reforms set forth in My manifesto of October 17 will be realized without change, and the rights which I have given equally to all the population are inalienable. My autocracy remains just as it was of old.[86]

Witte's Isolation and Loss of Influence

IN ADDITION to Nicholas' personal disgust with Witte and the tsar's growing lack of confidence in him as head of the government, widespread criticism of Witte from various moderate and conservative circles further weakened the Count's position at this time. The Octobrists, who a few weeks before had been chastising Witte for indecisiveness and lack of energy, now began to fear that he might undermine the promises of the October Manifesto. In their first party congress, meeting in Moscow, February 8–12, 1906, they criticized the prime minister both for slowness in initiating reforms and for the indiscriminate application of force in controlling the revolution. The Octobrists also demanded immediate promulgation of temporary laws protecting civil liberties and a firm promise that the Duma would be convened no later than April 25–a promise which Witte gave (see p. 175).[87]

From more conservative and from reactionary groups came sharp attacks on Witte and demands that Nicholas remove him and restore the government to his own hands.[88] A congress of gubernia and uezd marshals of nobility which met in Moscow on January 7–11, 1906, expressed concern that Witte might attempt to issue a law on land reform before the Duma opened, and demanded affirmation of the inalienability of private property.[89] A particularly scurrilous criticism of Witte and his government was contained in a petition of large landowners to the tsar which was printed in Kiev but widely circulated in St. Petersburg and elsewhere. Infuriated by this attack, Witte wrote Nicholas on February 2, transmitting a copy of the petition:

Of course I could find out the authors and instigators of this but I consider it a pointless waste of time, especially since to me, as to all those active in public life, it is known that the initiative for this affair comes from what we in the State Council call "the black hundreds of the Council." And so whether the idea of such a petition comes from Count Ignatiev, or Stishinskii, or Shturmer, or Goremykin, or Admiral Abaza, or some other member of such a cabal, it is all the same. I think, however, these honored leaders are not really seeking power for themselves because they don't want to run any risks but prefer to act by spreading secretively all sorts of lies through the reactionary press.[90]

Whatever the effect of this sort of intrigue, a dispute between Witte and Nicholas over appointments to the cabinet and over its role and responsibility flared up in January and further weakened the already strained relations between the tsar and his prime minister. First, early in the month Nicholas appointed Durnovo full minister of the Interior without consulting Witte. The tsar had been unenthusiastic about Durnovo when Witte had proposed him back in October, and Nicholas had agreed only to appoint Durnovo as acting minister at that time. But Durnovo had assiduously worked his way into the good graces of Trepov and court circles, and the tsar had been pleased with Durnovo's firm actions against the revolution. So now Durnovo was rewarded, much to Witte's annoyance.

Next, Witte proposed to the tsar on January 29 that in view of the formation of parties and of the lively election campaign then in progress, the government, under Witte's personal supervision, should collect and analyze all the political brochures, papers, and party platforms appearing in order to obtain "a clear chronicle of contemporary events and a full picture of the electioneering." Witte concluded that this would be extremely useful in assisting the government to prepare its program for the Duma and in facing that body when it convened. Nicholas was unenthusiastic, simply noting on Witte's proposal that this task should be entrusted to the Main Administration for Press Affairs, which was under the Ministry of Interior. Witte apparently protested orally, for on February 2 the tsar added a further note, saying that Witte could do it if he insisted, but "in my opinion the role of the chairman of the Council of Ministers ought to be limited to coordinating the activities of the ministers, while all executive work should remain the responsibility of the specific ministries."[91] Clearly Nicholas had a quite different view of the role and function of the Council of Ministers from that held by Witte.

Finally, Nicholas and Witte clashed head-on early in February over the appointment of new ministers to replace Timiriazev at the Ministry of Commerce and Industry and Kutler, whom the tsar forced to resign as acting minister of Agriculture in late January.[92] The tsar wished to appoint A. V. Krivoshein as minister of Agriculture, but Witte considered him nothing more than a spy for Trepov. After a number of candidates had been posed and rejected between Nicholas and Witte, the prime minister told the Council of Ministers that his position had become intolerable and that he planned to resign. The Council persuaded him to make a last appeal to Nicholas, with their full support, and on February 12 in a long and heated letter to the tsar, Witte said:

> All the censure, blame, and criticism for the activity of the Government is directed first of all against me. This follows naturally from the law about the Council of Ministers, although this law in fact is not fully carried out and I learn about very serious and grievous measures, especially of local authorities, from the press. All this puts me in a very difficult position which I endure, in spite of weariness and poor health, because of the critical condition of the state, my oath of allegiance to Your Imperial Majesty, and my love of country.
>
> But now I am deprived of the possibility of conducting the activity of the Government in a responsible way. In a short time the Duma will open . . . and I will be obliged to give an explanation for actions in which I did not participate, for the lack of success of measures which I did not have the chance to fulfill, and for projects which I did not support.
>
> As things have turned out, it is quite impossible to run the Government when it is not only not united by conviction but is not even firm in the relations among its own members. I do not find in either Krivoshein or Rukhlov those elementary attitudes which would give me the possibility of working with them. . . . The Council of Ministers decided . . . that their designation would completely complicate the further conduct of its business, while it would place me in a still more difficult position. . . . [The Council] asks that you give the government a chance, without upsetting its composition, to carry out the extremely difficult responsibility placed on it until the convocation of the State Duma.[93]

At this the tsar yielded and gave Witte the ministers the latter finally proposed: A. P. Nikol'skii as acting minister of Agriculture and M. M. Fedorov as minister of Commerce and Industry. Yet, as Witte's letter so clearly and pathetically explains, his position was an isolated and unfortunate one: he was not even master in his own house, the Council of Ministers.

Despite this, and in sharp contrast to his ruthless attitude a few weeks earlier, Witte now made several major attempts to bring under control the policy of repression and to curb excesses that were occurring because of it. For example, he proposed to the tsar that law students be drafted for temporary service as assistants to prosecutors and judges in order to relieve the burden on the overtaxed civil courts and to insure that accused insurgents were provided with normal, legal safeguards and fairly rapid trials and that they were not left to the jurisdiction of military courts.[94] In late January, moreover, Witte returned to a theme which had evoked his concern and attention off and on ever since he had taken office. The problem was how to define and regulate the circumstances and procedures under which the army acted to assist civil authorities in putting down disorder. Witte had no compunction about using the army to suppress rebellion, but he came increasingly to believe that such intervention should be employed only when absolutely necessary, that it should be firm and expeditious, but that once order had been restored, the army should withdraw and the rule of law and civilian authority should replace the rule of force. At the same time he recognized that things often did not work out this way, as it was difficult to restrain the military authorites.[95]

Sometime toward the end of January or in early February Witte submitted to Nicholas a long draft report which was apparently intended to be issued as an official government statement. It defended the use of the army against disorders in cases of extreme necessity and when no other measures to restore order were left, and it argued that the army should be given a free hand as long as the rebels continued to resist and to use force. The statement went on, however, to note that in a few cases military action had gone beyond what the circumstances warranted and army units had punished insurgents who had already stopped their aggressive activity. The report warned that such zeal, while natural in an aggravated situation, was totally unjustifiable. The army should fulfill the specific task set for it in agreement with the civil authorities and should then promptly withdraw, turning the guilty over to the civil courts and permitting prompt reestablishment of the normal legal order. On February 7 Nicholas wrote on this report: "I find this communication unnecessary and it discredits the army, *which I will never permit* [Nicholas' italics].[96] In addition to this rebuff to Witte, the same day the State Council finally issued the new regulations governing the calling in of the army to suppress civil disorder on which it had been working for over two months. These must have been a disappointment to Witte since the Council's rules dealt at length with the army's use of weapons, recommending that shooting into the air be banned as dangerous to innocent bystanders, that firing blanks be prohibited as ineffective, and that when necessary the army should fire live cartridges against the rebels since once this were known, it would have the maximum deterrent effect. The regulations did provide, however, that the army should be used only as a last resort and not for preventive or police purposes, that it should employ weapons only when all other methods of restoring order had been exhausted, that the civil authorities should specify exactly what task the army was to fulfill, and that once this was accomplished, the army should depart and return control to the civil authorities—all points for which Witte had campaigned.[97]

At the same time Witte did have some success in establishing regulations designed to restrain the army, although individual commanders did their best to evade them. Toward the end of January the Council of Ministers, with the approval of Nicholas, instructed the minister of War to send all army units orders that rebels who were not punished during the course of their armed resistance or during the actual commission of crimes and who were transferred to the custody of civil authorities could not be taken from the jurisdiction of the latter and should be judged according to law. In regard to this instruction the tsar noted: "Of course, I never had any thoughts that it could be otherwise."[98] Yet only a few weeks later Witte heard that troops under General Bekman in the Baltic had taken five peasants accused of destroying an estate from jail, without the knowledge of the judicial authorities, and had hung two of them and shot the rest. Nicholas approved Witte's demand for an immediate investigation, but the military authorities had their story ready. According to the reply from General Bekman, the peasants in question were being taken from jail to the scene of their crime, so that testimony for their trial could be elicited, when they tried to run away and had to be shot while attempting to escape, in accord with Article 153 of military regulations—and to show how poorly informed the civilian government was, the fact was that none of them had been hung but all were shot![99] In early February Witte also sharply criticized Baron Kaul'bars, commander of the Odessa military district, for shooting people without trial in violation of the government's instructions but how much good his reprimand did is questionable.

Besides trying to bridle the forces of repression, Witte continued in this period, as before, to work toward bringing his reform program into being and advancing the negotiations for a foreign loan. Despite rumors that suggested just the opposite, Witte remained determined to carry out the October Manifesto, telling a group of public leaders in January: "The tsar decided the question about the structure of the state for himself and for the people irrevocably. From now on there is no autocracy in Russia, nor can there be in the future."[100] On January 10 Witte guided a long review in the Council of Ministers of agrarian problems and set in motion development of a program of agrarian reform that laid the basis for the later Stolypin land reforms. In a report to Nicholas dated January 24 Witte explained that the Council of Ministers was working out a full program of governmental proposals to be presented to the Duma, after approval by the tsar, since this would help direct the Duma toward definite, businesslike, and constructive activity and would permit the government to present a united front before it. Witte declared that the peasant question in both its legal and economic aspects would have first priority in the Council's program, and he outlined his views on the necessity for abolishing the commune and on other measures of agrarian reform.[101] Moreover, during the first six weeks of 1906 Witte continued to press ahead with preparations for the Duma elections, eventually in mid-February setting firm dates for the final step in the electoral process and for convocation of the Duma. The prime minister also played an active role in conferences at this time which worked out the final provisions for reorganizing the State Council and which began to draw up the Fundamental Laws, or the new constitution of Russia, developments which are discussed in chapter nine.

In this period, as we have seen, Witte personally and the government as a whole were subject to heavy criticism from all sides. Feeling cut off from literate society and public opinion, Witte, with the assistance of Durnovo and the support of the other ministers, decided to found a newspaper to expound the government's position and to serve as a mouthpiece for his own views. Before then the government had had only the official gazette, *Pravitel'-stvennyi vestnik*, and it offered little opportunity for getting the views of the government before society or for influencing public opinion. In hopes of explaining government policies, of winning popular understanding and support for them, and of combatting antigovernment propaganda and agitation, Witte established in February, with funds from the Ministry of Interior, *Russkoe gosu-*

darstvo [The Russian state]. It continued to be published through most of 1906 until Stolypin replaced it with *Rossiia,* but it does not appear to have been very influential.[102]

Witte's efforts to check the excesses of the army, to further his reform program, and to establish contact with public opinion took place under most unfavorable circumstances, as his relations with the tsar worsened and his ability to influence policy declined. Nicholas retained a formal and correct attitude toward Witte, but the tsar came increasingly to rely on the advice of Trepov, Durnovo, and the new minister of Justice, Akimov. On January 12 Nicholas wrote that both Akimov and Durnovo were doing splendid work but "the rest of the ministers are people without importance." In a letter on January 26 Nicholas noted that Trepov had become "indispensable" to him, explaining: "I give him Witte's bulky memoranda to read, then he reports on them quickly and concisely," a fact which the tsar said was a secret between the two of them.[103]

Witte was aware that his position at court was weak and that his influence was waning. Early in January a discouraged Witte confided to Kokovtsov his belief that the tsar had no intention of permitting further reform and of introducing a real constitution. Realizing that he was now little more than a figurehead yet subject to public abuse and reactionary intrigues, the prime minister offered to resign. Whether the offer was meant seriously, or was intended as a means of pressure in an effort to bolster his position, is unclear. In his memoirs Witte maintained that he did not resign before April despite the knowledge he was in disfavor and things were being done behind his back because he felt obligated to complete the foreign loan and the return of the army from the Far East, because he felt a sense of duty to his country and did not want to leave it in the hands of Trepov and his cohorts, and because of personal and monarchical loyalty to the tsar and to the throne. Yet in January he was certainly tired, frustrated, and disillusioned, and he might well have left office if the tsar had permitted it. Witte first asked Trepov, then Grand Duke Nikolai Nikolaevich, to intercede on his behalf with the tsar, but without result. Finally, the prime minister asked Nicholas directly for permission to resign, but the tsar refused on the grounds that there were still important state tasks to be done, notably conclusion of the international loan.[104] As we saw, Witte also threatened to resign during his quarrel with Nicholas over the appointment of new ministers but relented when the tsar gave in.

Nevertheless, it was clear that Witte no longer set the pace or direction of domestic policy. Distrusted by the public and discredited with the court, he was kept on until the opening of the Duma, but his chances for realizing significant reforms had almost ended. As French Ambassador Bompard reported to Paris on February 6: "Count Witte is no more than a simple spectator in his own government; without authority, without the power of decision, he leads no one anywhere. He is the plaything of events and the post of prime minister remains to be occupied."[105]

The Strengthened Position of the Government

It is ironic but perhaps not accidental that Witte's fall from favor and the futility of his own role developed at the very time when the overall position of the tsarist government was substantially improving. In October, when the security of the system and of the state had been seriously endangered, Witte had served a useful purpose, suggesting a way out of the threatening situation and symbolizing a program of moderate reform which appealed to some elements in Russian society. But now, with the December armed uprising suppressed, with an uneasy order restored, at least temporarily, in the countryside and in the Baltic by force, and with the army coming back in good array from Manchuria, the tsarist administration began to regain control of the situation and the need for reform seemed far less pressing. Moreover, the government drew strength from the changed mood of much of the country. During the first weeks of the new year, the strike movement declined sharply and a defeatist attitude spread among the workers. In the winter the peasant rebellion became quiescent, and there were no further signficant mutinies in the armed forces. Most of the general public was sick of the turmoil and violence of the revolution and longed for a return to civil peace and order. The typical citizen wanted to get back to a regular, normal way of life and to see business and commercial activity restored.[106] Several contemporary observers noted that if the elections to the Duma had been held in January, that body would have had a far more conservative hue than it eventually had.[107]

Moreover, liberal and moderate opinion generally supported the government, albeit with reservations. At their February congress the Octobrists approved the quelling of open armed rebellion, deploring, however, the fact that innocent victims had also suffered in the process and opposing the continuation of repression against peaceful elements in the population. The Octobrists, as well as several independent groups of industrialists, urged a prompt calling of the Duma as the surest means of averting reaction and of preventing future uprisings and disorders. They maintained, besides, that delay or failure to convene the Duma would only play into the hands of the revolutionaries and bring back the chaos and violence of the preceding fall. The Kadets, though more sharply critical of the government, also opposed armed revolution, while urging rapid fulfillment of the reforms promised in October.[108]

A further indication of the general swing to the right throughout the country was the changing attitude of the zemstvos. In response to a query from the minister of the Interior on February 14, governors in twenty-four provinces reported that the mood of their gubernia zemstvo assemblies had taken a definite turn toward a more moderate, security-conscious point of view, while only seven governors recorded no such shift of opinion. Moreover, in the elections to the State Council conducted during the following two months in gubernia zemstvo assemblies, the seed-bed of Russian liberalism, candidates from the Kadets, Octobrists, and Progressists won only fifteen seats (forty-four percent) as against nineteen seats (fifty-six percent) obtained by rightest groups.[109]

Despite this, Durnovo did not trust the zemstvo organizations, and on January 10 he asked the Council of Ministers for authority to close down the work of zemstvo statistical bureaus on the grounds that their distribution among the population of census and other questionnaires stirred up revolutionary feelings and that many members of such bureaus were engaged in antigovernmental activity. Although the Council rejected this proposal, Durnovo sent a circular dated January 13 to all governors and mayors calling for full reports from them on the activities of gubernia and uezd zemstvos and of city dumas. The local authorities were to describe the general attitude and policies of these bodies, noting especially any deviations from the areas of activity prescribed for them by law and any antigovernment agitation or views. Finally, Durnovo wanted submitted on a regular basis the times and agendas for all zemstvo and city duma meetings.[110]

This increased surveillance of public organizations was accompanied by growing restrictions Durnovo imposed on the press and on the holding of meetings and by fairly widespread arrests conducted during the winter. These new actions violated the October Manifesto's promises of personal inviolability and of freedom of the press and of meetings and were sharply criticized, especially by the Kadets. But bolstered by the more conservative mood of the country as a whole, the government went ahead with these efforts to control opposition and to prevent further development of the revolutionary movement. While the methods used were less drastic and violent than those employed in December, and the effect was less inhibiting than the situation that had existed before October 17, this policy of limited repression was nonetheless a significant step backward.

There are no precise figures on the number of people arrested in this period, but it is clear that the total ran well into the tens of thousands. Beginning with the arrest of the St. Petersburg Soviet and the crushing of the December armed uprisings, the government clearly returned to practices of arrest and personal detention which it had found so useful in its more absolutist days. Throughout the succeeding few months there was a wave of arrests of suspected revolutionaries.[111] One estimate states that in St. Petersburg alone in the month from December 25, 1905, to January 25, 1906, 1,716 people were arrested. The English journalist Baring, who was in Moscow, wrote on January 7 that people were being arrested there every day, many seemingly without cause. Another author concluded that during the half year of Witte's premiership, from mid-October 1905 to mid-April 1906, the number of persons either imprisoned or exiled to Siberia amounted to seventy thousand.[112]

As we saw in chapter three, the freedom of speech and press promised by the Manifesto of October 17 brought many new papers and journals into existence. Some were satirical, others were socialist, still others were openly revolutionary; nearly all were antigovernment. The temporary press regulations issued November 24 lifted preliminary censorship for periodicals published in cities but also tightened procedures for regulating and prosecuting papers accused of violating their legal responsibilities not to print inflammatory material. These regulations failed completely to satisfy the editors and publishers and liberal public opinion. Yet for a number of weeks genuine freedom of publication existed. The first repressive step was taken on December 2, when the government closed all papers and publishing houses which issued the "Financial Manifesto" of the St. Petersburg Soviet. Within several days many of the newspapers reappeared under new names only to be closed again as the government launched a campaign of censorship.[113]

Witte defended the government's policy by insisting considerable freedom was granted to the press, and only newspapers which published "inflammatory revolutionary propaganda" were closed. Witte argued that any society would prohibit publication of appeals to overthrow the legal government.[114] In actual fact, many papers were shut down for quite different reasons, including satire of government officials and pro-Jewish sentiment. Beginning in December 1905, a majority of those papers closed were silenced and their editors and publishers jailed simply because their views were too openly hostile to the regime.[115] Despite these measures the government felt it had inadequate control of the situation, and a memoir of the Council of Ministers dated January 27, 1906, declared the "temporary" rules adopted November 24 had proved to be unsatisfactory and new, more stringent regulations concerning the press should be adopted. This was finally done on March 18 and April 26.[116] From then on the government possessed fairly broad powers of regulation over the press.

The October Manifesto promised not only freedom of the press but freedom of assembly as well. In fact, the latter right had been a troublesome subject of discussion in government circles for a number of weeks before the October Manifesto was conceived. Following the tsar's decree of August 6, 1905, which had promised a consultative (the so-called Bulygin) Duma, a special commission under Count Sol'sky had been formed to work out the details of the new project. Early in its deliberations it became clear that if elections were to be held, even to a consultative Duma, there would have to be an opportunity for candidates to be presented and policies to be discussed, and this would require the holding of campaign and electoral meetings. The majority of the commission urged that the elections be entirely free and representative and recommended that the Ministry of the Interior work out regulations providing for unhindered electoral meetings. Durnovo, a member of the commission, who was then head of the department of police in the Ministry of the Interior, objected strongly, insisting that free meetings could be held only in cities, but not in other places where there were insufficient police to permit proper control of meetings.[117]

A limited compromise was eventually worked out and embodied in a Senate decree issued on October 12, 1905, which established temporary regulations governing meetings. These provided that public meetings could be held only if permission were obtained from the local authorities not less than three days in advance. Meetings were to take place indoors, special permission of the governor or mayor being needed to hold them in the open air, and soldiers could not attend. Even after permission had been granted, local officials had the right to close meetings. To convene a congress the personal permission of the minister of Interior was needed.[118]

In practice these rules apparently were often ignored in the succeeding few months when, stimulated by the promise of free assembly in the October Manifesto, all sorts of groups, including political parties and soviets, held meetings freely and openly, some of them dedicated to violent attacks on the government. With the arrest of the St. Petersburg Soviet, however, and the dominance in the government of a policy of repression, the situation changed and efforts were made to enforce the October 12 regulations. The difficulty was that Witte and the government as a whole were firmly committed to encouraging the electoral campaign to the Duma and to making the elections as free as possible, as we shall see in chapter eight. Thus, the government could hardly oppose all public meetings or detain everyone who suggested an alternative to its own program. Nevertheless, on January 10 the Council of Ministers approved a recommendation that any meeting which endangered the security of the state should be closed, and on January 17 the minister of Education, in a circular to the heads of all regional departments of education, warned that educational lectures and literary readings were considered public meetings under the October 12 rules and that they therefore could be arranged only with prior police approval.[119]

On January 20 Durnovo sent a circular to all governors suggesting guidelines for the supervision of meetings. He urged that the governors exercise great care in permitting meetings, generally allowing only those of moderate views to hold them. They should also limit the number being held so that all meetings could be properly supervised and there would always be sufficient police to disperse a meeting, if this became necessary. Governors were also not to permit mass meetings in the guise of private ones and were not to allow meetings, "the aim of which was to propagandize revolutionary workers or the simple people." Durnovo then returned to his pre-October position, recommending that no meeting outside of cities or in the open air in cities be permitted. Only the moderate parties were to be permitted to hold meetings in public buildings, and if students or military personnel attended, they were to be removed, or the meeting closed.[120] In short, political meetings could be held, but they were to be closely watched and supervised. Moreover, on February 13 the State Council approved a proposal of the Council of Ministers that criminal penalties be applied to people who spread lies concerning the government or its officials or who made speeches inciting enmity between different classes or groups of the population and between owners and workers.[121] It is clear that under these various regulations some meetings were blocked and others broken up, but it is difficult to gauge how widespread this sort of harassment by the government was.[122]

Finally, on March 4 the government issued two decrees which had been worked out by the Council of Ministers and approved by the State Council. One established freedom of meetings and assembly but with the government retaining supervisory control of public meetings largely along the lines of the October 12 rules; the other created the legal right to form unions, parties, and societies although their constitutions and programs had to be registered with the government. The minister of Interior retained the authority to close meetings or unions if he considered that their activity endangered social peace or the security of the state.[123] These decrees were issued as temporary regulations pending definitive action by the Duma, but in fact they remained in force until World War I.

Despite the efforts of the government to control meetings, to restrict the press, and to round up suspected revolutionaries, a great deal of lively political activity took place in the first months of 1906, and a quite vigorous electoral campaign ensued. Both conservative and moderate circles exerted public pressure on the government to facilitate the elections and to accelerate the calling of the Duma, which many saw as the only guarantee against the renewal of violent revolution in the spring.[124] On January 27 Witte appealed urgently to all governors to speed up preparation and publication of the electoral lists. On February 7 and 8 the Council of Ministers decided to convoke the Duma on April 27, and on February 10 Durnovo ordered that preliminary stages in the electoral process begin February 20 and the final steps March 10.[125] Thus the machinery was set in motion to bring into being the long-awaited Duma.

The winter of 1905–06 provided the severest test for Witte's government and for everything for which the October reform program stood. Because either a liberal or a Marxist viewpoint has dominated the historiography of this period, it has come to be regarded as an era of reaction and of failure. And, to be sure, extreme and even bloodthirsty measures were taken, though at times without Witte's knowledge or against his wishes, and progress to effect Witte's program of reform was slow, even faltering, in the face of conservative, bureaucratic, and royal opposition. Neverthless, Witte's achievements in this period—at least from his own point of view—should not be overlooked. The revolutionary movement in the cities was suppressed, the agrarian uprising was brought under temporary control, and some degree of order and security was reestablished in the country as a whole. Preparations for the election went forward and a relatively free electoral campaign began. Various proposals to deal with the peasant question were considered, and the outlines of an agrarian reform program began to be developed, as we shall see in the next chapter. First steps toward reorganizing the state structure of Russia were taken, and negotiations for the foreign loan proceeded, although much too slowly to suit Witte.[126] Finally, Witte tried, albeit sporadically and not always consistently, to mitigate some of the worst excesses of the armed suppression of the revolution and to prevent enactment of some of the more Draconian measures proposed. In short, it is quite incorrect to depict Witte in this period as bent only on crushing the revolutionary opposition by force and violence in order to save the tsardom—and his own position. Driven by fear and his own crisis of nerves, he at times acted ruthlessly, but he did not entirely lose sight of the larger goals which he had set for himself in mid-October. Order had to come first, but reform was not abandoned.

At the same time Witte's own position became increasingly hopeless. Unable to find a locus of support among society in the relatively calmer times of the post-October euphoria, he increasingly alienated both liberals and conservatives not only by his policies but by his personal attitudes and behavior. The tsar and his advisers at court came only to tolerate him, the Octobrists and industrialists criticized him for inconsistency and inefficiency, and the liberals believed their worst fears about him were confirmed. The way he restored order antagonized some, the way he went about reform others. Witte lost power and influence and was soon almost completely isolated. The personal cost of what he achieved was indeed high. And to some extent the victories were not even his. The government defeated the revolution largely because at the crucial moment the army proved to be reliable and loyal. Its force was far superior to that of roving peasant marauders, disorganized, poorly armed workers, or bitter but powerless non-Russian minorities. On the other hand the reluctant progress toward a Duma, a reformed state structure, and a new agrarian order were less the result of Witte's leadership and vision, of any conviction to follow the path he had laid out, than of fear that if these minimal steps were not taken, the dangerous situation that had threatened the monarchy in early October might well recur.

Although Witte's government did not end officially until April 1906, in spirit it died in December 1905. Nicholas II, who would have preferred to use force in October but had lacked the strength, now saw the opportunity to reassert his power. Witte was still important to the tsar for the facade he provided the regime and for his influence abroad, but the new year saw Witte in decline at the court. Although he supported the policy of repression, he could not escape the stigma of appeasement associated with the October 17 Manifesto. Aware of his plight, Witte asked to resign; but his request was refused. Circumvented by his ministers, ignored by the tsar, and attacked by the public, Witte was forced to carry on until April.

Worst of all, the events of these few months seriously jeopardized the chances for genuine reform in Russian society. It was not only that the symbol of a new course, Witte himself, became isolated and discredited, but the use of force undercut whatever basis for peaceful change had existed after October 17. Because of the violence and repression there was no longer any modicum of trust, cooperation, or even communication between the government and the best elements in society. Instead of the link between tsar and people which some had thought the October Manifesto symbolized, the disasters of December and afterward intensified suspicion, hostility, and lack of understanding. The existence of "two Russias," the dichotomy of "we"—the people—and "they"—the government—was reinforced, and the possibilities of a common effort to work out a revised and modernized, but not radicalized, Russia faded to inconsequence. The government's success in quelling the revolution and restoring order failed to heal, and even widened, this fatal breach in Russian society and made the frustrations of the subsequent Duma period and the futility and collapse of 1917 all but inevitable. Sworn enemies could hardly be partners in a common cause, even as worthy a one as the gradual transformation of an outworn system. Whatever status the government had gained through the October Manifesto was soon negated by its repression and its infringement of the freedoms promised. With a limited and backward-looking tsar and with the ablest individuals in society alienated, the prospects for reform were hardly bright.

And yet how harshly can one judge Witte's actions and those of the government in these months? Could they stand idly by and see the revolutionaries seize the cities and destroy law and order in the countryside? Were the old system and way of life to be entirely sacrificed? And for what? It surely seemed at the time as if the whole country were threatened not just with revolution but with anarchy and chaos, the result of which might have meant far greater bloodshed and sacrifices than the forcible restoration of order. Was not order a prerequisite to reform?

VI

WITTE AND THE PEASANT QUESTION

A positive decision on the peasants' right of ownership and on permitting them to single out their allotment holdings from the land commonly held can have . . . a wholesome influence on the legal consciousness of the peasants, thereby introducing among the peasantry healthier views on the right of ownership.

I agree.

—REPORT OF WITTE TO NICHOLAS
January 10, 1906, Marginal Notation of Nicholas

WHEN WITTE BECAME CHAIRMAN of the Council of Ministers, one of the most serious and complex problems facing his government was agrarian unrest. It was not that the problem was new; in various forms and degrees it had troubled the government ever since the 1880's. Different commissions and special committees had investigated and discussed the need for agrarian reform for years, and as early as 1898 Witte himself had been seriously concerned over this issue. But in 1905 widespread and often violent rebellion in the countryside gave the problem an immediacy that had not existed before. The threat of a possible new *Pugachevshchina* was as important in wringing the October Manifesto from the tsar as any other factor.

Earlier consideration of the agrarian question had focused as much on the economic plight of the peasants and landlords as on the necessity for social and legal reform designed to strengthen the stability of rural society and the state. Now, however, the danger to social order and to the security of the whole tsarist system was patent. Thus Witte confronted the task both of restoring order in the countryside and of initiating sweeping changes in the structure of Russian agriculture which would make it not only more economically viable but also more politically reliable. Here, as elsewhere, he faced the dilemma of order and reform.

His task was complicated, moreover, by the previous record of conflict, uncertainty, and vacillation over agrarian policy both among "society" and within the highest circles of government, including Nicholas himself. Seldom was there agreement as to the causes of peasant unrest, and lacking this there was no consensus on a solution. Before October 1905, a few minor ameliorative measures had been adopted but no consistent or concerted general policy of reform existed. To a considerable extent the government had simply drifted, postponing a final decision as long as possible. The various alternatives, such as giving the peasants more land from state and private holdings or abolishing the commune, generally carried important social and political implications which would affect the entire tsarist system. The result was that the government waited until fall 1905, when the light of burning manor houses signaled the urgency of action. It became Witte's responsibility, therefore, to extinguish the fires of peasant rebellion and to develop a program of reform which would make the countryside less combustible. To a large extent he succeeded, though the fruits of his efforts were to be reaped by Stolypin.

The Nature of the Peasant Rebellion

WHILE THERE HAD BEEN a number of peasant uprisings in the preceding decade, and notably in 1902 and 1903, the revolutionary movement in the countryside which developed in the summer and autumn of 1905 was more intense, on a wider scale, more destructive, and more dangerous to public order than anything Russia had experienced in over one hundred years. Moreover, the October Manifesto seemed to have little effect on the rural population; if anything, the peasant rebellion intensified after its publication. This led in November, as we saw in chapter four, to the sending of punitive expeditions into the worst areas of peasant revolt. But this obviously was a stopgap measure. Basic reforms were clearly necessary.

In general the grievances and actions of the peasants seemed primarily economic in nature.[1] To be sure, the Peasants' Union, whose program included increasingly radical political demands, exerted some leadership and influence, and in a few areas the Socialist Revolutionaries made considerable headway. Yet by and large the peasants resisted efforts to politicize their struggle, and the revolutionaries had little success in channeling the peasant movement to their own advantage.[2] Instructive in this regard is the experience of the revolutionary Woytinsky, who with a fellow Social Democrat toured a number of peasant villages near Novgorod in an attempt to turn peasant dissatisfaction to political ends. In one village they were well received, but in all the others their political agitation and their attacks on the autocracy angered the peasants. After one village meeting the peasants threatened to hang them. When the antigovernmental Woytinsky decided to flee the countryside and to return to St. Petersburg, peasants at the Borovenka railroad station captured him and would have killed him had he not been saved at the last moment—ironically enough —by government troops.[3]

Peasant unrest was largely unrelated to and independent of the revolution in urban centers. Not only were peasants upset by the attacks on the tsar, but they were also annoyed by the strikes which disturbed the flow of commerce from the country to the city. A peasant described his attitude to Woytinsky as follows:

> A muzhik drives all the night to take his produce to the station —no train. The muzhik asks the gendarme, "When will the train come?" and the gendarme knows the answer. "Ask the strikers. They have stopped all the trains. Wait till tomorrow!" The muzhik waits the whole day and tomorrow it's the same story. . . . Much harm came from the strike.[4]

Nevertheless, even if the mutinous peasants had little in common with the striking proletariat or the revolutionary intelligentsia, their vigorous activities—illegal pasturing and timber cutting, the theft of grain and agricultural implements, the seizure of land, and on occasion the burning of manor houses, and the physical abuse of local authorities or landowners who interfered—betokened the existence of deep-seated problems in rural life and of a growing unwillingness on the part of the long-suffering villager to put up any longer with intolerable conditions.[5]

Any long-range program to quiet the countryside and to

remedy the grievances which sparked the rebellions obviously depended upon a proper analysis of the cause of peasant unrest. But when the government tried to identify those factors stimulating agricultural riots, it received conflicting explanations. A report to Witte from the police department cited seven reasons for peasant disorder, each of them to one degree or another economic in nature, including the insufficiency of land allotments, inadequacy or lack of pasture for cattle, prevalence of strip farming, the remoteness—in many cases—of land from peasant homes, and the absence of cheap credit.[6]

On the other hand, the minister of Interior presented a far different analysis in a report to Nicholas II based on answers from the governors of each of the provinces to an inquiry from Durnovo concerning the origins of peasant dissatisfaction.[7] All the governors belived that revolutionary agitation was the principal cause of peasant revolts and that, while other factors were also present, most agrarian unrest could be traced directly to agitators. This led to the second general conclusion of the governors—that the government had not reacted with sufficient energy and courage in the beginning, when peasant rebellions first occurred. Eight of the governors —those of Perm, Tambov, Kazan, Voronezh, Bessarabia, Poltava, Simbirsk, and Kursk—believed that the peasant who had little land was at the root of disorder as such peasants were more susceptible to revolutionary, socialistic propaganda. These governors pointed to the shortage of land, the lack of work for some members of peasant families, the inadequacy of the Peasants' Bank, and the need for timber. But ten governors disagreed totally with the eight. They did not see the land-poor peasant as the source of agrarian unrest, noting that many of the peasants who rebelled had substantial holdings and that poorer peasants were merely the chief targets of the propagandists.

The governors were divided over what course of action the government should pursue to remedy the problem. All agreed that the army and police should be strengthened, and some believed that the movement and activities of known revolutionaries should be curbed. A minority suggested that steps be taken to assist peasants in buying land and to extend peasant ownership of land. Taken as a whole the report stressed revolutionary agitation as of primary importance and economic grievances as a secondary factor.

Landowners tended to stress revolutionary agitation, peasant laziness and drunkenness, and class hostility as causes for the rebellion. Other reasons advanced at the time, and subsequently, were a poor harvest in some localities in 1905, high rents, restrictive leases, low wages, an excessive tax burden, and a peasant belief that the land by right belonged to those who worked it and that the October Manifesto had provided as much.[8]

From the foregoing it is clear that there was no general agreement concerning the basis of rural unrest. Without this, it was most difficult to gain assent to reform. Those who saw the rebellion as the work of agitators demanded a policy of force and punishment. Those who saw economic grievances at the root of the disturbances were anxious to initiate reforms. Since no one course could win the support of everyone concerned, Witte soon began to develop an agrarian program which embraced both the restoration of order and the launching of basic reforms.

Witte on Agrarian Reform Before October 1905

SINCE THE REFORM SIDE of Witte's agrarian policy when he was chairman of the Council of Ministers continued ideas he had advanced earlier, a brief description of Witte's concern for peasant problems before October 1905 is needed. As minister of Finance, Witte assumed responsibility for the entire Russian economy. A serious weakness in any one segment could endanger the whole. By the turn of the century it had become apparent that in spite of, or as a result of, Witte's policy of forced industrialization there was increasing impoverishment in the countryside, and this in turn was acting as a brake on the further economic growth and industrialization of the country.

As early as 1894 and again in 1896 Witte had suggested Russian agriculture follow "the road of capitalist development" and had opposed the communal structure of peasant life.[9] Finally, in October 1898, Witte addressed a letter to Nicholas in which he described clearly and completely for the first time the changes he felt were necessary to improve the position of the peasantry.[10] Witte began his note by reminding the tsar that Alexander II had abolished serfdom to revive prestige abroad and to strengthen Russia internally. Yet Alexander II had been uable to finish the task of agrarian reform, and it was now up to Nicholas to complete what his grandfather had begun.

"Why is our taxpaying capacity so low?" Witte asked. It was, according to him, a result of the depressed state of the Russian peasantry. Both France and Austria-Hungary collected far more tax revenue per capita than did the Russian government. The difference between Russia and these countries lay in their respective social organizations. Witte argued that only freedom sparked the best in man and drove him to operate at his fullest capacity whereas "slavery robs the individual of the impulse to improve himself." The Russian peasant was freed from the landowner, but he was still a slave to his own countrymen and to village authorities. Although the peasant was given land, his right to it was not clearly defined by law. Wherever the commune exists, Witte asserted, "the landowning peasant does not even know which plot of ground is his." Inheritance rights were regulated by custom rather than by law and, therefore, often by abritrary discretion. The family rights of peasants remained almost completely outside the scope of law.

Both taxes and justice were administered by local authorities in an arbitrary manner, practices which the central government was unable to check. The principle of mutual responsibility for communal dues furthered the peasant's sense of individual irresponsibility. Rural education was also in a deplorable condition. Witte said Russia "remained not only behind Europe but behind Asiatic and trans-Atlantic countries as well." He acknowledged that to educate people could be dangerous, but it had to be done if Russia were to move forward. "A dark people cannot be perfected. He who does not go foward will, for that very reason, go backward compared with those people who do go forward."

Above all, Witte exclaimed, it was necessary to raise the spirit of the peasants. "The peasant while personally free still finds slavery in arbitrariness, lawlessness, and ignorance." According to Witte, the peasant had become passive and spiritless, thus making him open to vices. The spirit of progress was paralyzed within him. He must be revived, and to do this, it was necessary to grant him the same civil rights other subjects of the tsar enjoyed. No longer should the peasant be treated as a half-person. Witte noted that widespread discussion had centered on which of the various individual classes in Russia was most loyal to the autocracy. Witte believed preservation of the country lay not in further pampering of the nobility but in treating all classes alike. "God preserve Russia from a throne not based on the entire nation but on separate classes," Witte warned.

The most significant and crucial problem facing Russia was not the land crisis, unorganized migrations, or the growth of the budget, but was rather confusion and disorder in the daily life of the peasants. Witte emphasized, "The peasant question, in my sincere opinion, appears presently to be the most vital question in Russian life. It must be solved immediately." At the close of his letter, he suggested that the tsar call a conference of top officials to consider the problem.

The significance of this letter is that as early as October 1898 Witte had concluded that the basic cause of the agrarian problem was the commune, and he urged the tsar to take steps to abolish it. Witte wanted capitalist landholders. He wanted peasants free to leave the commune and to join the urban labor market if they chose. He believed that only by creating conditions in which the peasant could exercise his own initiative could Russian agriculture flourish. Witte knew that a modern, industrialized state depended upon an advanced agriculture as well as upon an educated and highly skilled labor force. The state of the Russian peasant class at the turn of the century did not fit what Witte believed was required if Russia were to assume the role of a great power.

Witte's letter elicited no visible response from the tsar, who was apparently undecided about the desirability of breaking up the commune. In his budget report for 1899 Witte returned to the attack, concluding his discussion of the agrarian problem: "The final arrangement of the social conditions and property rights among the peasantry is the task for our generation."[11] But to no avail for the moment. Only several years later, when Witte was made chairman of a Special Commission on the Needs of Agricultural Industry, was he able to reopen his case against the commune.

The Commission, established on January 22, 1902, continued until the tsar dissolved it abruptly on March 30, 1905.[12] The Commission was interdepartmental and was composed of a number of high officials, including the ministers of Interior and of Agriculture, as well as selected experts. Shortly after the Commission began its work, Witte decided to enlist the support of "local men" by establishing committees at both the uezd and gubernia levels which met to discuss and to make recommendations on the problems of the rural economy. Only a few peasants served on these committees, which largely reflected zemstvo and small nobility opinion.

Altogether some 600 local committees numbering more than 11,000 people met to review the peasant question and to suggest solutions. As the reports from local committees began to arrive in St. Petersburg, it became clear that the majority of them opposed the commune and wished to have it abolished, or at least favored free exit from it. Most of the committees urged that the peasant be transformed into an individual landholder and be given civil equality with other citizens.

Despite this grass-roots support for Witte's position, the Commission failed to persuade the government to adopt a strong stand against the commune. Witte's ability to influence policy all but disappeared after his dismissal as minister of Finance in August 1902. Witte's political enemy, Minster of Interior Plehve, though in favor of private property rights for the peasants, wavered, as did the tsar. The conflict and confusion within the government were sharply revealed in part of the imperial ukase of February 3, 1903, which declared that new peasant legislation "shall be based on the inviolability of the communal organization of peasant landowner-ship, and at the same time shall endeavor to establish means whereby individual peasants may more easily leave the com-mune."[13] For the present the direction indicated by Witte's Special Commission, with its vast social implications for old Russia, was more than the tsar and his advisers could digest. It would take the revolutionary fires of 1905 to convince them that at last the commune would have to be abolished.

Although the Special Commission did not achieve all that its friends had desired, it was not a total failure. For one thing it amassed an immense quantity of statistics and information about the state of the rural economy. Second, it contributed to the development of lines of communication among local and bureaucratic levels committed to solving peasant problems, lines of communication which were to prove invaluable later. Third, certain laws directed toward the peasant did come into being during the life of the Commission. On March 12, 1903, a Witte-sponsored law ended in most provinces the practice of joint responsibility of the village commune for state taxes. Another law—this one of August 11, 1904 —abolished corporal punishment of peasants by local authorities.

[185

Finally, during the winter of 1904–05 the Special Commission worked out preliminary conclusions stating that dissolution of the commune should be encouraged, that measures to facilitate individual private landholding by peasants should be taken, and that peasants should be granted full legal equality.[14] Thus the first fully developed and well-documented formulation of what later became the Stolypin land reforms arose from the work of Witte's Special Commission. But in the spring of 1905, before the full onslaught of the peasant rebellion, the tsarist government was not yet ready to accept such a radical transformation of the countryside, for both principled and practical reasons. The tsar and his advisers still believed in the innate conservatism of the peasantry, as the great weight given to peasant votes in the electoral system for the Bulygin Duma, worked out in the summer of 1905, demonstrated. Besides, it was evident that Witte's proposals would require a long time to be put into effect, while immediate measures were needed to stem the growing revolutionary movement in the countryside. Consequently, the ideas of the Special Commission were shelved for the moment, and it was dissolved.[15]

To replace the Special Commission a new Conference on Measures to Strengthen Peasant Landholding was appointed in the spring of 1905, under the chairmanship of I. L. Goremykin, Witte's successor as prime minister in April 1906 and a strong supporter of the commune. This Conference, which was not dissolved until January 1906, contained a conservative majority, including the prominent Slavophiles, Khomiakov and Samarin. It also had, however, a minority group headed by A. I. Gurko, chief of the peasant section of the Ministry of Interior, and N. N. Kutler, Witte's first minister of Agriculture, who opposed the commune.[16] As a result, the proposals of Goremykin's Conference were mixed: while strongly supporting the inviolability of the nobles' land and minimizing land hunger as a cause for peasant unrest, it recommended an increase in peasant landholding through the renting of state lands, the encouragement of peasant land purchases through the Peasants' Bank, and the extending of the program of migration to Siberia and other "empty" lands. The conference defended the general principle of communal landholding and the special social and legal status of the peasantry, but at the same time it urged measures to facilitate the consolidation of strips of land into separate plots within the commune and the departure of some peasants from the commune. It also refused to endorse any further steps to protect the commune from natural processes of dissolution. Finally, Goremykin's Conference proposed a new body to unify and centralize agrarian policy—the Chief Administration of Land Organization and Agriculture—which was established on May 6, 1905, and which later became the administrative and legal model for implementing both Witte's agrarian program and Stolypin's reforms. Thus, the Conference made some contribution to the evolution of a new agrarian policy, even though it failed to continue Witte's direct assualt on the commune.

Proposals for Radical Reform—Autumn 1905

THE UPSURGE of the peasant revolution in the summer and fall of 1905 clearly conditioned the next phase in the government's handling of the agrarian question. When Witte came to power in October, many conservatives, thrown into panic by the anarchy in the countryside, were prepared to consider radical land-reform proposals in the hope that they could by such action save a portion of their holdings. Admiral Dubasov, commander of a punitive expedition to suppress agrarian riots, suggested letting the peasants keep the lands they had seized, and General Trepov told Witte in late October: "I myself am a landowner . . . and I would be very glad to give up half of my land if I were only certain that by this action I could retain for myself the other half."[17] And in early December a group of nobles from Simbirsk wrote Nicholas that they were prepared to make "the sacrifice" of selling part of their lands.[18]

It was in this atmosphere that on November 2 P. P. Migulin, a professor of economics at Kharkov University and a small landowner, addressed a letter to Witte warning of the dangers of a general peasant armed uprising and asserting the October Manifesto had done little to calm the peasants since they interpreted it as a call to rescue the tsar from the clutches of the "lords," who, with Jews and radical students, were preventing the Little Father from giving land to the peasants.[19] Therefore, Migulin proposed, the only solution was to issue at once, before the opening of the Duma, an imperial manifesto promising the peasants additional land but noting that rioters would not be eligible to receive this new land. Migulin declared: "There can be no discussion of the transfer of *all* landlord lands to the peasants, but *partial* alienation of private lands is quite feasible and should not provoke any serious opposition."

At about the same time Migulin, through his acquaintance with General Trepov, submitted a more detailed proposal to Nicholas, who gave a copy to Witte.[20] In this Migulin blamed the current crisis on the inadequacy of land allotments under the 1861 emancipation and on the subsequent neglect of agriculture by the government. After reviewing a number of palliative measures, such as increased migration, the stimulation of higher agricultural productivity, and the development of rural industry, Migulin asserted that the only lasting solution to the widespread land hunger (which he described well) was to sell to the peasants some ten to twenty million desiatins of state and crown lands and some twenty to twenty-five million desiatins of private lands, much of it land that was already being rented to peasants. He argued that the "majority of landowners will willingly agree to the alienation of their lands in favor of the peasants, even at very moderate prices, in order to preserve the remaining part and again to establish good relations with their neighbors, the peasants," but, drawing on what we would call the right of eminent domain, Migulin clearly implied that unwilling landholders should be forced to sell "in view of the state's right of full sovereignty and of the domination of its interests over private interests." He proposed 100 rubles per desiatin as a just average price and maintained that the whole matter could be financed through the Nobles', Peasants', and private banks by the grant of 2 billion rubles in advances to them. He declared that the able peasants would take maximum advantage of this opportunity, and warned that "the most dangerous person is the hungry peasant who has nothing to lose."

In writing of his proposal later, Migulin insisted that he had not intended to strip the large landowners of their lands, nor to confiscate church and monastery lands.[21] He said, in fact, that the large estates were the most productive and therefore to have expropriated them would have been to bring Russia to economic ruin. According to Migulin, he intended to make available to peasants large reserves of government land in Asiatic Russia, certain princely domains, and land formerly reserved for Cossacks. Migulin believed the land included in these categories would have been sufficient to meet most of the needs of the peasants, and little private land would have been required. He also pointed out that he had suggested steps be taken to improve peasant productivity by introducing them to modern techniques of agriculture. This implied, according to Migulin, the necessity of abolishing the commune.

Migulin's scheme was studied by the Council of Ministers and rejected because it was too radical and because they believed such a measure, affecting as it did the very social structure of the state, should await the opening of the Duma.[22] While turning down Migulin's proposal, the Council of Ministers did adopt two measures which affected peasant life. Confirmed by an imperial ukase on November 3, these, as we saw in chapter three, cut redemption payments in half for 1906 and abolished them for 1907, and also broadened the regulations of the Peasants' Bank, making it easier for peasants to borrow money to purchase land.[23] The Council of Ministers also created a special commission, under the chairmanship of N. N. Kutler, head of the Ministry of Agriculture, to prepare agrarian legislation which ultimately would be presented to the Duma.

Shortly after Migulin's proposal was rejected, another project embracing forced expropriation of land came before the Council of Ministers. The question of who initiated this proposal remains unanswered. According to Witte, who claimed he opposed the idea as soon as he learned of it, the plan originated with Kutler. Witte told Kokovtsov the project developed "only in the brain of our dear mutual friend Kutler." Yet Kokovtsov reported a conversation with Kutler after the Council of Ministers had turned down the plan, during which Kutler exclaimed:

> I received orders from Witte and had to comply, especially since we now have a unified government. Now that the project has failed, everybody repudiates all responsibility and says that it was entirely Kutler's idea. It is not the first time that a scapegoat has been needed. I was left no choice but too tender my resignation to Count Witte in order to show that I really was to blame for everything.[24]

According to Witte's account of the incident, sometime after Migulin's proposal was rejected Kutler stopped the prime minister after a Council of Ministers' meeting and told Witte that the more he thought about Migulin's report the more he had become convinced that some sort of expropriation of land was necessary. Kutler asked Witte's opinion, and Witte answered that in his view this would be possible only in exceptional circumstances.[25] Several days later, Witte wrote, he found a packet from Kutler on his desk, a packet which contained the report of Kutler's commission regarding the improvement of peasant life. Since the tsar had asked Witte to expedite all proposals aimed at alleviating peasant conditions, Witte ordered copies of Kutler's report sent to the members of the Council of Ministers and to certain members of the State Council even before he had read the report himself.

Later that evening Witte examined Kutler's report. He noticed immediately that it recommended forced expropriation, with compensation, of a portion of privately owned land in favor of land-poor peasants. Since the Council of Ministers had only recently reacted negatively to Migulin's report along the same lines and since Witte believed that those in important positions in and near the court were now set against any program involving expropriation, Witte decided that Kutler's project was at best inopportune. He ordered that those copies of the report already distributed be returned and asked Kutler to meet with him on the following day. The next morning, according to Witte, he told Kutler that it was not the proper time to introduce a project calling for forced alienation of land as he feared that it would be used as the basis for intrigue against him and his government. Kutler suggested that his project might be discussed at a private conference of the Council of Ministers.

Shortly thereafter a private meeting of the Council was indeed called, and Kutler presented his ideas. Kutler's project, which was drawn up with the assistance of Professor A. A. Kaufman, a Kadet specialist on agrarian affairs, stressed that the basic cause of the agrarian crisis and peasant discontent was population growth and land hunger.[26] Kutler acknowledged that it would be useful and beneficial to raise the efficiency and productivity of peasant agriculture by improving techniques of cultivation and by consolidating strips of land into plots (though he did not propose abolishing the commune), but he pointed out that this would require raising the cultural level and changing the basic attitudes of the peasantry and would therefore take a long time, while the need for more land was immediate and pressing. Kutler argued that in European Russia the number of land-hungry peasants had grown from twenty million in 1860 to over thirty-eight million in 1905. He estimated that even to achieve the minimum level of landholding per peasant household established as a desired norm in 1861 would require adding seventy-five million desiatins of land to the present eighty-six million desiatins held by the peasants— and yet the maximum his project proposed for transfer to the peasants was forty-eight million desiatins!

In this desperate situation, Kutler maintained, the only solution was to set up in each uezd a minimum level of land per household, taking account of the land available for transfer, and then to use first state, crown, monastery, and public lands and then, if necessary, private lands to give each household, both private and communal, below that level sufficient new land to bring it up to the established minimum. These transfers would be supervised by an all-Russian Chief Land Committee, composed equally of Duma and of government representatives, under which would work gubernia and uezd land committees, made up of representatives from the government, the peasants, and the landowners and/or the zemstvos. If a transfer of land through the Peasants' Bank could not be worked out voluntarily within six months, the committees could then forcibly expropriate private land in the following amounts: up to one-fifth of small estates, up to one-third of medium-size estates, and up to one-half of large estates. Owners would be compensated on the basis of a capitalization at five percent of the average rent over the previous five years.[27]

Kutler emphasized that his proposal was designed to assist only those in the direst need and was not intended to be a general redistribution of land. He pointed out that the private lands involved were to be primarily those being rented and that there was no thought of breaking up large estates worked by their owners since these were the most productive units in Russian agriculture. At the same time Kutler warned that the gradual transfer of land to the peasants through voluntary sales to the Peasants' Bank was too slow and inadequate a remedy, and concluded that his plan

. . . is necessary in the interests of the landowning class itself since only in this way is it possible, under contemporary conditions, to preserve the inviolability of a significant part of the estates of that class and to permit owners to receive a fair price; too firm insistence on the principle of the inviolability of private property and the freedom to dispose of it can lead, at the present, to the landowners being deprived of everything under conditions ruinous to themselves and to the country.

Despite Kutler's arguments and his warning of what might befall the landowners, the Council of Ministers rejected his proposal. Furthermore, they ordered Kutler to alter his project and to add certain conservatives who were known to oppose compulsory expropriation as members of his commission. Witte said he concurred with the Council in its decision. However, he wrote he did not oppose Kutler's program in principle as it was identical to that underlying the "great reforms" of the 1860's, but Russia's financial situation and military position would not permit such a project at that moment. Witte claimed that he would have supported Kutler's plan if he could have been certain that it would not have weakened Russia.[28]

It is difficult to ascertain Witte's real views on the question of alienating private land. He certainly had no concern to protect the nobility and landed gentry, whom he had long despised as an unproductive and backward element in the Russian economy. Yet he clearly and strongly believed in the sanctity of private property, and before the fall of 1905 he had always opposed the idea of forced expropriation of land. On the other hand, as the agrarian revolution became more menacing, Witte, with his pragmatic sense of the situation, must have realized that his own panacea for the peasants' problems, the dissolution of the commune, might require too much time to take effect, even if the tsar could be persuaded to support it, and that more immediate and radical measures were now needed. It is possible that even before coming to power Witte began to toy with the idea of compulsory alienation of some private land in favor of the peasants; in his first report to Nicholas on the revolutionary crisis, on October 9, Witte obliquely touched on the issue when he suggested that to help the peasantry the government might redeem for them some lands they were renting.[29] Witte certainly understood that expropriation would be very unsettling to the social order and the tsarist system and that it would provoke widespread opposition among the upper classes and at court. Yet when he learned of Migulin's project and that it had been circulated to the tsar, Witte may have decided it would be worth pursuing the idea of expropriation as an emergency measure. He perhaps encouraged Kutler's design as a trial balloon, wanting to see what the reaction would be and saying that he supported it in principle, though not in practice if it would weaken Russia—and threaten his own position. If strong opposition to the Kutler proposal arose, Witte was prepared to sacrifice Kutler in order to save his government and to preserve the possibility of initiating other measures to solve the peasant question.

And opposition did arise almost at once. Around November 20 a memorandum entitled "On the Inadmissibility of a General Distribution of Land to the Peasants" was drafted, apparently by Gurko, and was widely circulated and discussed during the next few months. The memorandum directly attacked the principle and bases of the Kutler proposal, maintaining that compulsory alienation would not only violate all the norms of legality and the rights of private property owners but would also lower the level of agricultural production and produce chaos in the countryside, thereby ruining the rural economy and undermining the strength of the whole country.[30] Moreover, the memorandum argued, the plan would not even work since the peasants' need for land was infinite and the distribution of some fifty million desiatins among one hundred million peasants would provide only half a desiatin additional land to each peasant, which would simply whet their appetites. Finally, it was asserted that the basic idea was wrong, since a general transfer of land to those most in need would benefit the weak and poor peasant when the government should be encouraging the advanced and able peasant (Gurko strongly favored abolishing the commune and assisting the better-off peasants).

During December and early January the Octobrists and various groups of landowners, including a congress of marshals of nobility meeting in Moscow, denounced the idea of forcible expropriation and urged that no major land reform be adopted before convocation of the Duma. The Kutler project was also the chief target of attack in a petition of landowners criticizing Witte and his government. This petition, drawn up in Kiev and circulated in St. Petersburg and elsewhere, prompted a rebuttal from Witte to the tsar, as we saw in chapter five. Moreover, by January, once the punitive expeditions to the south-central provinces had begun to restore order there and the December risings in Moscow and other cities had been put down, the danger of full-scale revolution seemed less immediate. As a result, those who had been willing to bribe the peasants with land in October now believed the government was sufficiently strong it need not yield to such radical proposals. Nicholas himself, undoubtedly prompted by his advisers and by influential members of the gentry, took a strong public stand against the expropriation of land. On January 18, 1906, the tsar told a delegation of peasants from Kursk that "all property rights are inviolable; therefore, what belongs to a landlord belongs to him, and what belongs to a peasant belongs to him. Land which belongs to a landlord is his under that same inalienable right as your land belongs to you." And on February 2 and February 9 Nicholas assured delegations of gentry from Tambov, Tula, and Vladimir that whatever measures to improve peasant life and to meet the need of the peasants for land were taken, they would not in any way infringe "the inviolability of private property."[31]

In this changed atmosphere it was clear that any program of land reform based on expropriation was bound to be rejected. Moreover, Kutler, as a symbol of this approach, had become a burden to Witte's government. When Nicholas asked to see a copy of Kutler's project, Witte explained to the tsar that it was not a definite proposal but only a rough outline which had been discussed privately with the ministers, which they had opposed, and which Kutler had agreed to revise. Nevertheless, in a letter to Witte on January 29, Nicholas said he wished Kutler replaced. The prime minister asked Kutler to resign and he did, promptly.[32]

Renewed Concern Over the Peasant Problem

ALTHOUGH IT WAS APPARENT that forcible alienation of private land was not a politically feasible solution to the agrarian question, and even though the peasant rebellion was temporarily quiescent, Witte recognized that the crisis was far from resolved and that some measures of relief for the peasants would have to be adopted as soon as possible. Consequently, in a report to Nicholas on December 23, 1905, only a few days after the Moscow uprising had been suppressed, Witte raised with the tsar, as an urgent question, the matter of agrarian policy.[33] The prime minister pointed out that even though the Council of Ministers had discussed the peasant problem three times and a majority of the ministers had favored not taking decisive measures until the Duma met, the danger of renewed peasant mutinies in the spring was so great that Witte believed the tsar in the near future should call and preside at a special conference to work out a draft program on the agrarian question. In accord with his panicky state of mind at the time Witte stressed the need for strong security measures, including the use of the army to preserve order in the countryside and perhaps formation of a special agrarian militia. The next day Nicholas replied that he disapproved the idea of creating a militia but that he wished the Council of Ministers to prepare draft proposals on agrarian security and reform to be discussed by a special conference which he would personally chair.[34]

In accord with the tsar's instructions the Council of Ministers returned on January 6, 1906, to a consideration of the peasant problem. In a report to Nicholas of that discussion, dated January 10, Witte stated that for the most part revolutionary disturbances had been brought under control—beside which the tsar noted, "Thank God!"[35] Only agrarian disorder continued to be a problem and, although for the moment unrest had quieted, new and more violent peasant uprisings were expected in the spring. As he had adumbrated in his letter to Nicholas of December 23 and in line with his attitude toward most issues, Witte then outlined a twofold approach to the peasant question: the restoration of order and the initiation of reform. Witte asserted that it was necessary to distinguish those measures which gave the external appearance of solving the problem from those that drove to the heart of the matter. The government was taking steps to end disorder by the use of force, but this merely put the lid on what was seething beneath. Measures of a "positive character" were also necessary to bring the boiling to an end.

In his report Witte turned first to temporary, defensive steps designed primarily to preserve order. We will treat these suggestions and subsequent measures along these lines as a unit, a single aspect of Witte's agrarian program, before taking up the reform side of his policy toward the peasantry, which he sketched in the report of January 10. To prevent further peasant revolts Witte recommended three measures. One was to strengthen village police forces by increasing their numbers and funds. A second was to disperse the army throughout Russia to supplement and to support the police and to help maintain civil order. Third, Witte argued that it was a poor practice to leave the dispensation of justice to military courts. A way had to be found to speed up the investigation and trial of suspected rebels in regular civil courts, which had insufficient personnel to handle the sudden upsurge of revolutionary cases. Therefore, Witte proposed that law students near the end of their studies be drafted into temporary duty to help relieve the crushing load on the regular courts and to help assure that most cases would be heard in civil, not military, courts.

To implement Witte's first point additional funds were given to the minister of Interior to bolster village police; the use of law students to assist judicial personnel, his third recommendation, was approved by the State Council on March 8 and by the tsar on March 18. The essence of his second proposal, the disposition of the army in accord with the needs of internal security, was substantially achieved, as we saw in chapter five, through conferences with the top military authorities during the winter and was confirmed by the tsar on March 12. There was, however, another, and more complicated, side to this last measure. At the same time that the Council of Ministers reviewed the larger aspects of the agrarian problem and recommended the desirability of using the army to maintain order in the countryside, it also considered a report dated December 21 from General Kryzhanovskii, commander of the Second Cavalry Division, which pointed out that employment of regular troops to suppress agrarian disorders and to stand guard in the countryside was having dangerous repercussions.[36] Because the army contained many recruits who had recently been peasants and because these men were being ordered to act repressively against their fellow citizens, the morale of the soldiers was being undercut and the troops were losing both their self-esteem and the respect of the population as a whole. General Kryzhanovskii strongly recommended that the army not be quartered among the peasants as a preventive force and that it be used against disorder only in extreme cases.

With the backing of Minister of Interior Durnovo the Council of Ministers acknowledged the validity of Kryzhanovskii's observations and concluded that the army should not generally be employed for police work or as a preventive guard. Consequently, Witte, in transmitting these conclusions to the ministers of War and Interior with the approval of the tsar, ordered that the chief responsibility for preventing agrarian disorders should lie with local authorities and the police at their disposal, while the army should only be used when absolutely necessary, should be assigned a definite task of suppression or punishment, and, once that had been fulfilled, should return to its barracks.[37] On the other hand, the Council of Ministers also recommended that the army be given the right to arrest suspected rebels at the scene of disorders and forcibly to remove them to the nearest city prison or even to another district before they were arraigned. Finally, the cabinet urged that the minister of Interior be asked specially "to inform the rural population before spring of the intention of the government to oppose in the most decisive way any attempt to violate private property and of its determination to suppress all disorders." Both these latter recommendations were also approved by Nicholas and sent to the ministers of War and Interior for action.[38]

In early February the idea of a warning statement to the peasantry was enlarged when the tsar received a memorandum recommending that the government issue a manifesto declaring the inviolability of private property and enjoining peasants who seized land from obtaining assistance from the Peasants' Bank. Nicholas, who was much concerned at this time about protecting the land rights of the nobility, seized upon this suggestion and, in turn, proposed a manifesto in his own name to reassert not only the sanctity of private property and the inadmissibility of any forcible or illegal seizures of land but also the absolute necessity of citizens' obeying all laws and of respecting all the rights of other persons.[39] The tsar submitted to Witte a draft manifesto which denied rumors of a general redistribution of land to the peasants, denounced the illegal seizure of land, rejected the idea of forcible expropriation, declared that peasants could obtain land by migration or by purchases through the Peasants' Bank, and warned that violators of legality would be deprived of the services of the Peasants' Bank.[40]

On February 17 and 24 the Council of Ministers discussed the tsar's proposal and his draft manifesto. Although they endorsed the general idea of issuing a manifesto, the ministers disapproved Nicholas' draft for three reasons: First, they felt any government statement would have to be phrased very carefully to avoid appearing to prejudge agrarian policy before the opening of the Duma; therefore they recommended that the manifesto "avoid any expression of principles concerning the direction of the government's agrarian policy which is not required by the specific purpose of the manifesto," and that it not include any blanket prohibition of compulsory alienation of land since in special circumstances, such as the need to eliminate the intermixture of peasant and landlord lands or to grant peasants land for essential watering and pasturing purposes, forced expropriation might occasionally have to be resorted to.[41] In the same breath, however, the cabinet rejected any thought of accepting violations of the right of private property or the compulsory alienation of gentry lands as bases for the overall agrarian program of the government. Second, the Council doubted that the tsar's proposed manifesto would, in fact, achieve its aim of calming the peasants, though the ministers acknowledged that some step should be taken to counter the rumors of a general redistribution of land agitators were spreading. Finally, the cabinet pointed out that the manifesto, because of its threatening tone, ran counter to a longstanding tradition that imperial manifestoes should be beneficent, positive, and kindly. The cabinet presented its own draft of a suitable imperial manifesto, but Nicholas rejected this on March 2. Although at about this time Durnovo, Gurko, and others also tried their hands at writing a satisfactory draft for the tsar, on March 5 Nicholas informed Witte, through Trepov, that he had now decided not to issue any manifesto on the subject of peasant disorders.[42]

Although as a result no authoritative government statement against peasant unrest was issued before the opening of the Duma, Witte's government did adopt two minor measures designed to control or punish agrarian disorder. On March 14 the Council of Ministers, noting that the antistrike law of December 2 (see chap. 4) did not cover agricultural laborers, recommended that rural workers be subject to varying prison terms for instigating a strike, for forcing other workers to participate, for seizing property, and for participating in groups or societies which advocated agricultural strikes. A law to this effect was approved by the tsar and promulgated on April 15.[43] As a final measure, Witte's cabinet approved, after considerable hesitation occasioned by a realization that such punishment would produce even more landless and hungry peasants, a law which reaffirmed an imperial ukase of April 15, 1905, that any landowner who had suffered damages as a result of peasant riots could receive appropriate compensation from the landed and movable property of peasants responsible for the disorder.[44]

In general, as this brief summary has suggested, Witte succeeded in achieving one of the two major goals of his agrarian policy, the restoration of order and the planning of measures to prevent further disorder in the countryside. When the peasant revolution flared up again later in 1906, Witte's successors, and especially Stolypin, profited from the arrangements Witte had made to have the army available to preserve internal security. Yet Witte considered this side of his agrarian program, as he had emphasized in his report to the tsar on January 10, far less important than the basic reforms he had in mind. For security measures could affect only what Witte had termed the "outward appearances" of order, and he was even more concerned about the core of the problem itself. In the last section of his report of January 10 Witte spoke out once again for the principles of agrarian reform he had been championing for almost eight years. He argued that the broadened activity of the Peasants' Bank and the cancellation of redemption dues had thoroughly undermined the commune and had given the peasants a healthier respect for private property. The next step should be to give the peasant his plot and free him from the commune.

Before developing this conclusion fully Witte reviewed the arguments pro and con regarding the major alternative reform program, the compulsory alienation of land as proposed by Migulin and Kutler.[45] Witte pointed out that the opponents of forcible expropriation objected strongly to the violation of the right of property it involved and alleged such a violation would undermine a chief basis of social life in Russia. Moreover, transfer of some land would not satisfy the peasants, whose land hunger was insatiable. Finally, Kutler's critics charged, agricultural production would decline disastrously since the large estates were the most productive and the majority of peasants worked their land poorly. On the other hand, proponents of the Kutler solution argued that land hunger was at the heart of the matter and violence could be ameliorated only by giving the peasants more land. Therefore, it might be preferable for the landlord to give up part of his land, as had been done in 1861, in order to save the rest of it. Alongside this observation the tsar noted: "Private property ought to remain inviolable."

Witte then reported to the tsar that because of the conflicting views and interests concerning this issue, as well as over the whole range of agrarian and peasant problems, the Council of Ministers had been unable to agree on a concerted agrarian program for the government and had concluded, in any case, that fundamental reform should await the opening of the Duma. Nevertheless, the cabinet had agreed that the agrarian question was of crucial importance and that the government should have carefully worked out proposals to present to the Duma as its first order of business. Consequently, while awaiting the decision of an imperial conference on agrarian policy (which Witte had recommended in December but which was never convened), the ministers intended to establish a special committee to review previous recommendations, including those of the Special Commission on the Needs of Agricultural Industry. In addition, the minister of Interior was specifically charged with preparing draft legislation on the peasants' social and legal order and on the improvement of land organization and utilization.

At the very end of his report Witte could not resist adding what was clearly his own personal and strongly held opinion, though he presented it as the consensus of the cabinet. He said that a follow-up to the November 3 decrees need not await the opening of the Duma and therefore measures to establish the right of peasants to their own allotments and to facilitate their withdrawal from the commune should be initiated right away. Witte concluded:

> A positive decision on the peasants' right of ownership and on permitting them to single out their allotment holdings from the land commonly held can have, in the opinion of the Council, a wholesome influence on the legal consciousness of the peasants, thereby introducing among the peasantry healthier views on the right of ownership.

To which the tsar noted: "I agree." The basis for the Stolypin reforms was laid.

Yet Witte was not destined to see his dream of dissolving the commune formally approved and implemented during his tenure in office. Instead the bureaucratic processes he had outlined in his report now began to operate, and the resulting conflicts and delays, plus the imminence of the opening of the Duma and the opposition of conservative circles, denied Witte the fruits of his efforts. Nevertheless, the trend of the discussion on agrarian policy that now took place within the government was clearly toward abolishing the commune. Witte's review of the arguments for and against forcible expropriation was the last presentation of that alternative; in a few weeks, as we saw earlier, the tsar fired Kutler and made abundantly clear in public statements and in his letter of February 10 to Witte that private property would be inalienable and that the peasants could expect to obtain additional land only through migration and by purchases, with government help, through the Peasants' Bank.[46]

In pursuit of the reform proposals of his report of January 10 Witte wrote Kutler on January 13, urging him, in view of Nicholas' approval of the report's conclusion, to form immediately an interdepartmental commission to draft detailed projects on the recognition of the peasant's right to consolidate and own his allotment land and on facilitating the peasant's exit from the commune. But Kutler's star was already on the wane, and he wrote Witte a few days later that when he had consulted Durnovo on forming such a commission, the minster of Interior informed him that the commission had already been created, with Gurko as its head.[47] Witte apparently did nothing to interfere in this bureaucratic struggle, and Gurko's commission, entitled "On the Preparatory Study of Questions, in accord with the Imperial Manifesto of November 3, of the Legal Issues Pertaining to the Right of Peasants to Allotment Lands," proceeded with its work. At about the same time another commission with an almost equally resounding title, "On the Study of Immediate Measures to Improve the Conditions of Peasant Landholding," was established under the chairmanship of A. P. Nikol'skii, Kutler's successor as head of the Ministry of Agriculture. Gurko also served on this commission.[48]

Before these commissions could complete their findings, however, Witte found another opportunity to advocate his position before Nicholas. In the third week of January the Council of Ministers, stimulated by a memorandum from the minister of Finance, decided that it should work out a full legislative program which the government would present to the Duma in order to maintain the unity of the government before the Duma and in hopes of directing the Duma toward "definite, strict, and business-like" activity. In reporting this decision to the tsar on January 24, Witte elaborated that the Council had agreed that the peasant question should have first priority in its program; and, in fact, Witte in his report became so excited and voluble on this one topic that he never got around to describing whatever other legislative proposals the cabinet may have decided to sponsor.[49] Witte asserted that the peasant question had to be attacked in both its economic and its legal aspects. As Witte shrewdly pointed out, however, the two were closely intertwined. As long as the peasant remained bound to the commune, he would remain both relatively unproductive and an inferior citizen existing in a separate class apart from the normal legal and social life of the country. Therefore, Witte concluded, this fundamental source of difficulty, i.e., the commune, must be attacked. Since the November 3 decrees had opened the way to the ending of communal responsibility for redemption dues, it should now be easier for the peasant to leave the commune, and the Council of Ministers had recently instructed that the necessary legal measures to encourage this (the Gurko commission) be worked out.

Then, Witte went on, once the peasantry had become a class of small property-owners, it would make no sense to maintain a separate class structure for them. In an incisive, almost sociological way, Witte continued by pointing out that a change in the legal position of the peasants would have extensive and deep-seated ramifications for local government, for the zemstvos, for tax and fiscal policies, for the judicial system, for Russia's administrative structure—in short, for almost every aspect of the whole tsarist system (though Witte did not tout peasant proprietors as a conservative political force). Witte concluded, not immodestly, that the Special Commission on the Needs of Agricultural Industry had studied most of these questions, and that its materials and findings could provide the basis for the Ministry of Interior to work out an entirely new legal order for the peasantry founded on the abolition of the commune. In essence, the prospect Witte sketched embraced a sweeping and profound transformation of much of Russian life, and it is a testimonial to his breadth of vision and understanding of social change that he foresaw how much an alteration in the status of the peasantry truly involved.

At about the same time that Witte was once more propounding his case against the commune to the tsar, an influential memorandum on peasant problems, which reflected the views of the Nikol'skii commission, was submitted to Nicholas, who approved it and asked the Council of Ministers to discuss it.[50] This report was apparently drawn up by A. V. Krivoshein, head of the migration department, who was serving on the Nikol'skii commission and who in early February published a similar proposal in *Novoe vremia*.[51] Although Krivoshein's memorandum admitted that it presented no clear-cut solution to the peasant problem, it suggested a four-fold program.

First, Krivoshein recommended that the government take a strong stand against peasant disorder by issuing a manifesto reaffirming the inviolability of private property and warning that peasants who participated in raids on estates would be deprived of assistance from the Peasants' Bank in acquiring private land, a suggestion picked up by the tsar, as we have just seen, but which never came to fruition.

Second, Krivoshein argued, although eighty percent of the Russian population was peasant, government officials were not sufficiently close to the peasantry to understand its problems. Therefore, special commissions at the gubernia and uezd levels consisting of both local leaders and government officials from various ministries should be established to study the particular conditions and needs of each locality and to assist in the implementation of measures best suited to improve peasant life in that area. Such measures might include, according to Krivoshein, better demarcation and cultivation of peasant land, increased migration to free lands, promotion of the purchase of landlord lands by peasants at fair prices, and encouragement of the right of peasants to own and consolidate their own plots apart from the commune.

Third, Krivoshein suggested that the Peasants' and the Nobles' Banks be merged into a consolidated governmental bank under the Ministry of Agriculture.

Fourth, Krivoshein proposed that the Chief Administration of Land Organization and Agriculture be charged with stimulating and providing credit to local peasant and artisan industry, with accelerating the rate of migration, with improving the utilization of government lands, and with regulating the renting of land.

Apart from these recommendations, but obviously closely tied to the second, Krivoshein echoed Witte's favorite theme, urging in passing that even before the opening of the Duma temporary regulations should be issued to assist peasants to consolidate their allotment lands into privately owned plots. Krivoshein declared:

By making it easier for each member of the commune to separate from it with his portion of the allotment lands an understanding of the inviolability of private property can be developed in the consciousness of the peasantry in comparatively short order. It is enough to make the peasant an owner for him to recognize the full monstrosity of the expropriation of property, to create in him determined opposition to the forcible alienation of someone else's property.

The memorandum as a whole is important not only because it contained in this last observation the basic rationale of the later Stolypin land reform but also because it included all the essential points of the agrarian reform program finally adopted by Witte and the cabinet in March. Though few of its ideas were new, it provided the blueprint for future tsarist agrarian policy.

On February 10 and 17 the Council of Ministers discussed both Krivoshein's memorandum and the recommendations of the Congress of Marshals of Nobility which met in Moscow from January 7–11.[52] Among other things the nobles' leaders had urged that the transfer of peasants from the commune to private, individual plots be facilitated.[53] In reviewing Krivoshein's report the ministers approved in principle the idea of issuing a manifesto reaffirming the inviolability of private property but noted that its contents would have to be carefully worked out. The members of the cabinet were also sympathetic to Krivoshein's second proposal, the creation of local Land Organization commissions, and asked for a more detailed project on this. But they could not agree on the establishment of a centralized land bank, some ministers arguing that since such an institution would be a powerful force in agrarian affairs, it should not be under one ministry but should be interdepartmental in structure and control. Pending further study, the Council left the Peasants' Bank as it was, under the Ministry of Finance.

On February 24, the Council of Ministers took up the findings of the Nikol'skii commission, which had met January 31, February 7, and February 10. Its report was almost identical in content with Krivoshein's memorandum, though a bit more specific.[54] The commission proposed that a national Land Organization committee be formed and that it be broadly interdepartmental and include elected zemstvo members. Land Organization commissions at the gubernia level were to be chaired by the governor and would include the gubernia marshal of nobility, representatives from various ministries, and six zemstvo members, of whom three were to be peasants. The uezd commissions would be composed similarly. The functions of the local commissions would be primarily advisory and supportive along the lines suggested in the second and fourth points of Krivoshein's memorandum. In addition, however, the commissions were charged with mediating between peasants and landlords, where necessary, and with supervising local operations of the Peasants' Bank. As a separate and final point, the Nikol'skii commission recommended that the various ministries prepare suitable draft legislation for the Duma designed, among other things, to assist the peasants to consolidate their strips of allotment land and to establish their right of private ownership over the resulting separate plot, and to permit the Peasants' Bank to accept allotment land as security for loans.

The Council of Ministers generally endorsed these recommendations but sounded a note of caution.[55] Some ministers expressed concern that governmental promulgation of the program recommended might appear to be prejudging Duma action on the agrarian question. Others warned that the local commissions, under the composition proposed, might fall under the control of the zemstvo or of political parties which would attempt to implement through the commissions a radical reform program. The Council decided that the participation of elected zemstvo representatives in the national Land Organization committee was too difficult and complicated, but that zemstvo presidents should sit on the local commissions. The cabinet also recommended that the commissions stress practical activity rather than research and study of local conditions, but that they should begin with limited aims and a small budget, proceeding slowly and cautiously. In the view of the ministers, the commissions should not control but only advise the Peasants' Bank locally. Finally, the Council suggested that the views of Krivoshein and the Nikol'skii commission on encouraging the transfer of communal land to private ownership and the departure of the peasant from the commune be transmitted to the ministries and departments which were already studying this question, and that this issue be settled when draft legislation on it was submitted to the cabinet.

On March 4 Nicholas approved the chief recommendations of the Nikol'skii commission, and an ukase was issued which embodied them. As suggested by the Council of Ministers, the Land Organization commissions were not to control the Peasants' Bank, and nothing was said about peasant proprietorship or withdrawal from the commune. The Land Organization commissions set up in the decree retained most of the functions proposed by Krivoshein and by the Nikol'skii commission, but the ukase put greatest emphasis on the role of the commissions in assisting and facilitating peasant land purchases through the Peasants' Bank. This was done, the preamble to the ukase declared, in the hope that "through the joint efforts in these commissions of landowners and peasants the urgent needs of the agricultural population will gradually be met, under the indispensable condition of not infringing the right of private property as a basic foundation of state order and public welfare."[56] Thus it was a very modest program intended to allay the fears of the landowners yet to make a start on improving peasant life. It did not attack the commune directly, and the Land Organization commissions were clearly "service agencies without statutory power. The local commissions could carry out only those programs which they could persuade the peasants to accept."[57] The decree of March 4 could hardly have satisfied the desperate peasantry; nevertheless, it was a beginning, however cautious and limited, and it established both the structure and mechanism for the Stolypin land reform begun in the fall of 1906. Tsarist agrarian policy was now definitely set on a new course.

But from Witte's point of view the reform of March 4 clearly did not go far enough. As a result, he attempted to press forward with his long-standing ambition of dissolving the commune and turning the peasant into a free private landowner. In this he was helped by the report of the Gurko commission, which had met five times in January and early February to review the recommendation of the Council of Ministers that steps be taken to assist the withdrawal of peasants from the commue. Gurko, though no friend of Witte and a strong opponent of forced expropriation of land, had long favored the breakup of the commune. In the fall of 1905, during the final meetings of the Goremykin commission, he staunchly defended the prospective efficiency and political conservatism of abler and more prosperous peasants, once they were made private proprietors, against the doubts of the majority that they would remain loyal to the tsar and state.[58] Nevertheless, the recommendations of his commission were fairly moderate: under certain conditions peasants were to be granted the right to own and consolidate their share of allotment land, and their eventual withdrawal from the commune was to be facilitated.[59]

Witte wished both to incorporate these proposals into the legislative program the government was preparing for the Duma and to issue them as temporary regulations, pending definitive action by the Duma. However, for reasons that are not clear from the available evidence, but presumably because conservative forces in the government and at court were not yet convinced of the desirability of abolishing the commune and therefore forced a review of the issue, the recommendations of the Gurko commission were submitted to the State Council for discussion and approval before any further action was taken on them. In that body by the narrow margin of twenty-three votes to seventeen the proposals were turned down on March 18 on the grounds that such a radical reform should await the opening of the Duma and that it was impossible to decide so finally the peasant problem without hearing the opinions of the peasants themselves, who would be represented in the Duma.[60] Thus by six votes Witte was deprived of the credit for a radical change in tsarist policy and for one of the most fundamental reforms undertaken in modern history, affecting as it did a hundred million people in their social, economic, legal, and political life. The agrarian legislation of 1906–11, which would have transformed the Russian countryside had its implementation not been interrupted by the war, became inevitably associated with the name of Stolypin, and Witte's major contribution to this result was largely forgotten.

Despite this last-minute failure to obtain what he most wanted, Witte's achievements in agrarian policy were considerable. It is clear that while directing the government Witte held two objectives uppermost in the attempt to solve Russia's rural problem. One was to bring a halt to the anarchy which plagued the countryside, and here he was largely successful. He managed to restore a semblance of order in the villages, though primarily by the use of force, and he made reasonably effective arrangements to deal with future outbreaks of peasant violence.

On the other hand, in the pursuit of his second objective—the most fundamental one in Witte's eyes—he did not entirely succeed. Since 1898 all his memoranda, reports, and letters to the tsar on peasant reform had been directed toward the goal of dissolving the commune and setting up the peasant as a small proprietor with full social and legal equality. Private ownership would spark peasant initiative, lead to improved agricultural techniques and increased production, and end rural depression. Thus peasants would be able to buy and rent more land, productivity would rise, and the whole economy would benefit. Witte said little about what would happen to poor or lazy peasants, but presumably he thought they would enter the industrial proletariat or become agricultural laborers. Witte brilliantly envisaged the far-reaching effects of such a reform and fully comprehended the fundamental changes in the social, legal, and administrative system of tsarist Russia that it would entail. Though he did not specify the political effects of such a program, Witte undoubtedly shared the view of Gurko and others that becoming masters of their own property would instill a sense of responsibility and a respect for the property of others and for state order in the peasants.

Witte remained convinced that his prescription was the best solution for Russia's agrarian crisis, even though he may have toyed briefly with the idea of a redistribution of land through compulsory alienation at a time when the fire of peasant rebellion blazed most brightly. Since cancelling redemption dues and enlarging the operations of the Peasants' Bank weakened the commune and encouraged the abler peasants, Witte warmly supported the decrees of November 3 which enacted those measures. Through these and other inducements peasant landholdings—and probably prosperity —did increase during Witte's premiership. While peasants had purchased altogether an estimated 13,812,000 desiatins of land in the forty-two years from 1863–1904, in the one year alone from November 1905 to November 1906, peasants and the Peasants' Bank purchased almost as much, 12,360,000 desiatins.[61] Yet even this was not enough, and a definitive solution remained to be found.

Thus, Witte in his reports to Nicholas on January 10 and January 24 renewed his pleas, with both conviction and a good deal of persuasiveness, for a program based on dissolving the commune. Though the tsar agreed Witte was right, there was still enough residual support for the commune to delay a final decision. Nevertheless, to his credit if not his fame, Witte did establish the bases for a new approach to Russia's agrarian ills.

VII

THE LOAN THAT "SAVED" RUSSIA

The successful completion of the loan forms the best page in the history of your ministerial activity. It is for the Government a great moral triumph and a pledge of Russia's undisturbed and peaceful development in the future.

—Tsar Nicholas II to Witte
April 15, 1906

WITTE'S AGRARIAN PROPOSALS, though not fully adopted at that moment, laid the foundation for tsarist policy toward the peasants for the next decade. In chapter nine we shall see that Witte also played a significant role in shaping the legal-political structure that was to govern Russia to 1917. Yet in many respects the single act of Witte which had the greatest impact at the time and the most significant and far-reaching results for the future of Russia was his negotiation of the international loan of April 1906. This loan, which Witte, immodestly but probably accurately, described as the largest in modern history to that time, is of crucial importance not only in understanding Witte himself and the events of his six-month stewardship of the Russian government but also because of its effects on later Russian and European history.[1] Without the desperate necessity to conclude the loan Witte might have acted differently in December and January, when he determined to suppress the revolution; on the other hand, if the tsar had not felt that Witte was the person most capable of completing the loan, Nicholas might have dismissed Witte much earlier than he did. Finally, the loan strengthened the government's position before

[209

the Duma and oriented Russian foreign policy firmly toward France, its chief creditor, and toward the Entente Cordiale, with fateful consequences in 1914.

Concerning Witte's character and outlook the story of the loan reveals much: his *amour-propre*, jealousy, and spite; his vision and concern for the future of Russia; his adroitness and skill in negotiation and in matters of high finance; his passion and zeal for fiscal stability and economic progress in Russia; and his pettiness and knack for damaging himself by arrogance and intolerance. These contradictions, of course, appear repeatedly throughout his entire career. But to a remarkable degree the challenge of the loan epitomized Witte's personal and political dilemma in 1905–06. In this matter he wished desperately to succeed but once he had, he was ignominiously discharged. He wanted very much to provide a sound fiscal basis for Russia's gradual reform and for her future growth but in doing so he weakened the Duma which should have been the chief vehicle for such reform and growth. He was anxious to secure Russia's international position but ended by cementing Russia into an alliance that helped ensure her participation in a disastrous world war.

Once Witte had determined, in the fall of 1905, that he *had* to secure a large loan, both for his own glory and to save Russia from bankruptcy, he was forced to contravene a number of his own views and to act in ways which eventually harmed his own interests—and probably those of Russia as well. In December, as in October, he would probably have preferred to deal with the revolution moderately, drawing its sting by reform, but he felt driven to take speedy and stern measures to restore order because, among other reasons, international bankers were unlikely to risk money in a country torn by continuing violence and instability. Witte had to surrender his dream of a grand continental alliance of Russia, Germany, and France as he found the diplomatic price of the loan meant closer ties with France and, through her, with England, as well as growing estrangement from Germany. Harassed by these contradictions yet convinced that the loan was essential to preserve Russia, Witte drove ahead with negotiations for it, sacrificing whenever necessary his design for the future peace of Europe and his reform program. In this sense, then, the loan becomes the key to Witte's whole effort in 1905–06. He believed that he had "saved" Russia through the loan, but to obtain it Witte gave up much that might have been far more useful to her true salvation.

That Russia needed money in 1905 no one could doubt. Because of the almost unanimous belief in government circles in 1904 that the war with Japan would be brief and victorious, no long-range plans for financing it were made; the government relied instead on attempts to cut back domestic expenditures to balance the budget and to avoid new taxation. It also resorted to two short-term loans from Germany and France. In early 1905, with the outcome of the war still in doubt and with growing signs of open rebellion at home, it became clear that deficits due to war and revolution were going to be immense. As a result, Russia turned to France, its chief creditor since 1888, for a large long-term loan.[2] At the end of February, French bankers in St. Petersburg had reached all but final agreement with Russian Minister of Finance Kokovtsov on a 600 million franc loan, when news of the Russian defeat at Mudken arrived. On the very eve of signing the loan contract the French representatives in St. Petersburg were instructed to break off the negotiations and to return home. There were two reasons for this sudden French about-face: Although on most occasions French banking houses largely dictated what French investors would buy, in this instance continued Russian defeats and the prolongation of the war had so upset French public opinion that the bankers finally decided it was too inopportune a time to attempt to float a new large Russian loan. Second, Premier Rouvier of France was increasingly concerned over Russia's disastrous involvement in the Far East and the consequent disability of France's chief ally in Europe. Although the French foreign office insisted that direct French intervention to persuade Russia to make peace would provoke Russian resentment and bitterness, Rouvier decided that Russia could be pressured to the peace table by withholding from her the funds needed to continue the war, an indirect strategy that indeed soon worked.[3]

Needless to say, the Russians were incensed at this high-handed treatment by their ally, but there was little they could do. Throughout the spring and summer, despite Russia's obvious need and several indirect attempts to reopen negotiations for a loan, Rouvier maintained that while France was anxious to assist Russia, a large loan would be possible only after hostilities were concluded. Meanwhile Russia's financial position continued to deteriorate. The war cost over two billion rubles, which created huge budgetary deficits for 1905 and 1906, depleted Russia's gold reserves, and led to the currency in circulation being more than doubled.[4] In addition, during 1905 the revolutionary movement further strained Russia's finances. Not only did the government have to increase expenditures in an effort to keep order, but there was a poor harvest, with a resultant drop in export and tax proceeds, while strikes and the constant interruption of the railway service curtailed production and disrupted trade so that revenues declined sharply, particularly in the last quarter of 1905. Moreover, it was difficult to collect taxes, and even the movement of funds among banks was severely hindered.[5] Revolutionary propaganda incited runs on the savings banks and demands for payments in gold, which resulted in an estimated drop in deposits of one hundred fifty million rubles. Another two hundred million rubles was lost through the outflow of gold and securities abroad as a result of the panicky flight to Western Europe of nobles, landowners, and others frightened by the revolutionary disturbances in the fall of 1905.[6]

By the end of 1905 the gold standard, so dear to Witte's heart, was seriously threatened; and Russian credit abroad was so low that no new loans were immediately possible. Yet the budget deficit for 1905 was 158 million rubles, the estimated deficit for 1906 was a huge 481 million rubles, and another 144 million rubles was needed to cover a short-term loan from Germany, which was to fall due in early 1906. Thus, a total of 783 million rubles was urgently needed.[7] As the State Finance Committee reported to Nicholas on December 29, it was "an extraordinarily difficult period for the finances of our country." The report then summed up the disastrous situation:

> The enormous expenditures for the liquidation of the war, the demands of depositors on the savings banks, the flow of capital abroad, the curtailment of foreign credit for our banks and industrial enterprises have caused a great need for credit, without which it will be very difficult to maintain the credit of the State.[8]

In the face of imminent bankruptcy the tsar's financial advisers even recommended in early January 1906 broadening the right of emission of the State Bank and reducing the gold backing on notes and currency, but Nicholas and Witte disapproved these steps away from a fully-backed gold monetary system.[9] Instead Witte redoubled his efforts to secure the substantial foreign loan which, even before taking office, he had been convinced Russia needed to liquidate the cost of the war, to preserve the gold standard, and to fight the revolution.[10] As early as the summer of 1905 he had conceived a plan for a large loan which would be international in character in that German, American, Dutch, and British, as well as French, institutions would participate.

Witte's Conception of the Loan and First Negotiations

IN JULY 1905, while on his way to the peace conference at Portsmouth, Witte stopped in Paris and met with both President Loubet and Premier Rouvier.[11] Discussion centered on a possible loan, but the French leaders reasserted that nothing could be done until peace had been concluded with Japan. While he was in the United States, Witte sought and gained the support of John Pierpont Morgan for a future international loan. Morgan hoped his participation would lead to large Russian orders for industrial equipment.[12] Returning to Paris in early September after the peace conference, Witte found Loubet and Rouvier concerned by the growing crisis with Germany over Morocco. The Franco-German dispute over rights in Morocco had been intensified by the kaiser's surprise visit to Tangier in March 1905. The Anglo-French Entente had been concluded the year before, and the German leaders felt that while Russia was heavily and disastrously engaged in the Far East it would be an opportune moment to test that alliance and to attempt to split France and England. France, backed by England, stood firm and the danger of an armed clash loomed large. In April, at the instigation of the Germans, the sultan of Morocco proposed an international conference to settle the problem. Eventually the French, with considerable reluctance, agreed to the proposed conference, but the Germans then began to stall on technicalities and in September, when Witte was in Paris, they were still holding up convocation of the conference. As a result, Rouvier told Witte that any international loan to Russia was out of the question until the Moroccan dispute had been settled. However, Rouvier said France would then be willing to assist in a large-scale loan based solely on

French and British participation.[13] Witte countered this offer by suggesting that he intervene with the Germans to attempt to persuade them to adopt a more conciliatory attitude. Rouvier promised that should Witte succeed in getting Germany to the conference table and should the dispute be settled on terms favorable to France, Russia could rely upon the support of the French government for the loan it required.[14]

After leaving Paris, Witte went to Germany, where he arrived at Rominten, a favorite hunting lodge of the kaiser, on September 13.[15] He and William II discussed Witte's cherished plan for a continental alliance of Germany, Russia, and France in order to offset the growing domination of England and the United States in the world.[16] The kaiser then revealed to Witte that the meeting between the tsar and himself at Björkö in July 1905 had not been a purely personal exchange as the press had been led to believe (and as Witte's information from St. Petersburg had reported). Rather they had signed a defensive alliance between Germany and Russia as the first step in the establishment of a European coalition. Witte did not see the text of the agreement and was at first delighted. Later, after learning its detailed terms, he opposed the Björkö Treaty.

In the discussions at Rominten after the revelation of the Björkö Treaty, Witte urged the kaiser to round out the European alliance plan by arranging for a peaceful solution of the Moroccan crisis as a means of encouraging a rapprochement between France and Germany. He told William that French public opinion would accept Germany's terms only if they were not dictated but were the decision of an international conference.[17] This line of reasoning persuaded the kaiser, and he at once issued instructions for German participation in the conference. Thus, Witte had fulfilled his promise to the French by obtaining a more conciliatory German position.[18] After Witte's visit to William, the Germans continued to raise objections, but the negotiations now proceeded more conclusively; and in October both France and Germany consented to a conference to meet in Algeciras in January.

En route to Rominten Witte had stopped briefly in Berlin to see the German foreign minister, Count von Bülow, to whom Witte gave the impression that he had "succeeded at the last moment in preventing conclusion of a Russian loan in France and England."[19] Clearly Witte was attempting to throw the Germans off the track and to influence them to open the German money market to him. He was anxious both to base the loan broadly enough so that Russia would not have to pledge too much to any one country and to keep open the possibility of a tripartite continental alliance.

The complex international ramifications of the loan and the somewhat contradictory actions of Witte make sense only if we consider Witte's own words: ". . . this circumstance [the desperate need for a loan] significantly determined my policy and form of action."[20] Witte knew that obtaining a loan depended on relaxation of the international tension and that consequently he must bring France and Germany together. Therefore, he played a dual game, attempting to pressure or entice both parties into agreement over Morocco and eventually into a rapprochement. He tried to use Russian friendship with each side as the instrument of conciliation. The success of such a move would not only assure conclusion of his loan but would have other satisfactory consequences: it might pave the way for substantial Russian entry into the German money market and it might in the long run set the stage for his "chief political idea" of a continental alliance against England. For her part France wished to use the loan as a lever to pry greater support from Russia against Germany and to bring England and Russia, her two allies, together. The kaiser, fresh from his success at Björkö, now looked forward to entering into discussions which might splinter the Franco-Russian alliance forever.

Witte undoubtedly believed at the time that his post-Portsmouth efforts in Paris, Berlin, and Rominten were highly effective in furthering his plans for an international loan.[21] But upon his return to St. Petersburg the contents of the Björkö Treaty were revealed to him by Minister of Foreign Affairs Count Lamsdorff.[22] Although the treaty provided that every effort would be made to draw France into the agreement, its terms envisaged mutual assistance in case a foreign power should attack either Germany or Russia. Nicholas conceived of the treaty as directed against England, but its provisions were irreconcilable with Russia's alliance with France. Witte realized this at once, and he believed that in concluding the treaty the tsar had gone too far, too quickly.

In a last effort to bring together the continental powers Witte had the Russian ambassador in Paris sound out Rouvier on possible French interest in cooperating in a Russia-German-French concert, but the French flatly rejected the idea.[23] Witte knew that French participation was crucial to his scheme for a continental bloc. He also recognized the existing alliance with France was vital to Russia's national interests and maintenance of that alliance was essential to conclusion of his cherished loan. The French government would not open the Paris money markets if the alliance were endangered, and the Germans alone could not supply the total amount needed. Consequently, Witte joined Lamsdorff in persuading Nicholas that the Björkö agreement had to be abrogated. The kaiser, who already hated Lamsdorff, never forgave Witte for this, and the annulment of the Björkö Treaty was later a factor influencing the German government to oppose Witte's loan. From the time of the abrogation of the treaty Witte's chances of succeeding, diplomatically and financially, with both Germany and France were slim, and he swung more and more definitely to the side of France, supporting her unconditionally at Algeciras and negotiating the greater part of the loan with France. Björkö and Rominten proved to be the zenith of Russo-German relations before the World War.[24]

As the first step in direct negotiations for the international loan, representatives of French, British, German, and American banks arrived in St. Petersburg in October on Witte's initiative and Kokovtsov's invitation.[25] It is difficult to understand Witte's motives in agreeing to these talks. Although virtual agreement was soon reached on the financial details of a loan, the general situation outside and inside Russia was hardly propitious for its conclusion. To be sure, Rouvier, unaware of the existence of the Björkö Treaty and grateful for Witte's assistance at Rominten in getting the kaiser to remove the last obstacles to an international conference on Morocco, encouraged the negotiations.[26] Nevertheless, Witte must have wondered whether final French approval would be forthcoming until after the Moroccan crisis was settled to French satisfaction, the condition stipulated by Rouvier in September in Paris. Moreover, Witte must have realized that it was still too early to tell whether his plan, which he had not confided to his colleagues, for including Germany in the loan as a step toward drawing her into a tripartite continental alliance was yet dead as a result of Russian abrogation of the Björkö Treaty. Thus, at this time the diplomatic conditions for the loan were not fully clarified.

Domestically the moment was also inopportune. The bankers, arriving at the peak of the October general strike in Russia and just before Witte assumed office, could not have come at a more un-settling time. With no electric power the city was in darkness. The visitors were forced to move about under armed guard; and even the negotiations for the loan, which were conducted in Kokovtsov's house, were carried on under police protection. Moreover, it was generally known that Kokovtsov was on his way out as minister of Finance. Although some of the bankers became worried and upset in these circumstances, others were willing to stay, and it is prob-able a loan agreement could have been reached. In fact, the chief French representative, Eduard Noetzlin, offered the support of the French banks in case the others withdrew. Yet there were several reasons which apparently led Witte to break off the negotiations, telling Noetzlin in a secret conversation that to continue them in the midst of such turmoil was incompatible with the dignity of the Russian government.[27] In the first place, Witte, just coming to power and only shortly returned from abroad, may have believed he could conclude the loan later on better terms and under more favorable domestic and international conditions. In any case, he gave Noetzlin the impression that Russia could wait several months for the loan; and he hinted that France should not take Russia's friendship for granted, while iterating that he would do nothing in regard to relations among Russia, Germany, and France without informing the French or behind their back.[28] Second, Witte was probably reluctant to conclude the loan at the very moment of his assuming office. It would have been both a sign of the weakness of the government and the subject of heavy criticism from both lib-erals and revolutionaries who would have interpreted it, as they did later, as an instrument for suppressing the revolution and as a token of Russia's subjugation to foreign capitalists. Third, it is possible that personal spite played a part in Witte's decision to suspend the talks. He simply did not want Kokovtsov to get credit for the loan as the latter's final and crowning achievement in the post of min-ister of Finance. Yet many of these considerations could have been foreseen before the negotiations began, and it remains something of a mystery as to why Witte endorsed the calling of the bankers to St. Petersburg. In any case, Kokovtsov in his memoirs accused Witte of torpedoing the negotiations for personal and selfish rea-sons and gave little credence to whatever larger financial and dip-lomatic purposes Witte may have had in mind.[29]

A "Stopgap" Loan: Kokovtsov's Mission to Paris

By the end of November Russia's financial position had become critical. At a meeting of a special Committee on Finances on December 3, Shipov, the minister of Finance, expressed his desire to halt payments in gold and to inflate the currency. Recognizing the dangers inherent in such a course of action, the Committee balked and urged that further study be given to the problem. At this point Witte suggested that Kokovtsov be appointed to review the policies and activities of the Ministry of Finance and the State Bank for the purpose of proposing new actions that might stave off collapse.[30] Kokovtsov agreed if P. K. Schwanebach might assist him in the task. On December 9 the Committee on Finances convened to hear Kokovtsov's report. He noted that as a result of the postal and railroad strike, communications were so badly disrupted that it was difficult to form an exact judgment as to how serious the problem really was. Therefore, he recommended that rather than adopting an extreme program such as that suggested by Shipov, it would be better to look for a temporary expedient and to try to win breathing space. Specifically, he suggested that Russia negotiate a small foreign loan which could be used temporarily to restore gold deposits until other actions could be undertaken.[31]

When Witte suggested that Kokovtsov should go to France to negotiate the loan, Kokovtsov refused, arguing that it would be more appropriate for Shipov to go. On December 13 and 14 Witte met privately with Kokovtsov and pleaded for his help, saying, according to Kokovtsov:

> . . . I wish you knew in what a blind alley I find myself. There are moments when I am ready to commit suicide, and at such moments I recall all my past and perceive how deeply I have wronged you; even today I said to the Emperor how painful and hard these memories are for me. . . . But now I beg of you, for my sake, do not refuse to comply with the Emperor's wishes.[32]

Witte then explained that the tsar wished to see Kokovtsov the next day. On December 15 Kokovtsov heard Nicholas II request that he go to Paris to secure a loan. Nicholas told Kokovtsov that he could promise the French, in return for French credits, Russian support at the Algeciras Conference that was due to begin in slightly over two weeks.[33] Kokovtsov answered that he could not refuse a request from the tsar, although he had serious misgivings about the probable success of the venture.

While he urged Kokovtsov to go, Witte knew that a loan of the type and scale he desired was not within reach at that time.[34] Conditions which would have made such a loan possible were, if anything, less promising in December than they had been in October. The Moscow rising was widely reported in the French press, and speculation grew that the Russian government might well collapse. The immediacy of the Algeciras Conference made French banks reluctant to release money in the event the Conference failed and war resulted. Therefore, when Kokovtsov arrived in Paris on the night of December 18, he was greeted with the news that the French banks were not interested in a loan at that time. That Kokovtsov was able to return to St. Petersburg with some success must be credited to the efforts of the French government rather than to the willingness of French investors. Both President Loubet and Premier Rouvier were alert to the fact that their major ally on Germany's flank could not be permitted to founder. Therefore, when Kokovtsov experienced failure with Crédit Lyonnais, he turned to the French government and gained a sympathetic ear.[35] Both Loubet and Rouvier told him that no major loan was possible until Russia had solved her internal problems and the Algeciras Conference had been brought to a successful close. However, France did not wish to see her ally weakened by financial chaos. Therefore, if France could count upon Russia's unqualified support at the Algeciras Conference, Loubet and Rouvier said they would intervene to see that Russia was given an advance of 100 million rubles on a future loan to be negotiated after the Conference ended.[36] Such a figure could be carried by the banks without resorting to the market, and it might be sufficient to tide Russia over until a large loan could be arranged. The French banks, under pressure from the government, therefore agreed to advance 100 million rubles against eleven months' treasury bills at 5½ percent. Kokovtsov, having received Witte's confirmation that he could promise France Russia's support at Algeciras, hastened to sign the contract in the belief that this was the best loan possible under the circumstances.[37]

On his return trip to St. Petersburg Kokovtsov stopped in Berlin and secured an extension on the German short-term bonds that were rapidly approaching their due-date. Germany, anxious to avoid offending Russia during the Algeciras Conference, granted the extension in spite of, or perhaps because of, the loan Russia had just received from France.[38] When Kokovtsov met the kaiser, William asked why the two monarchies could not get together instead of Russia turning to republican France. Besides his remark to Kokovtsov, the kaiser at the same time made another informal effort to realize his Björkö-Rominten policy of isolating France by drawing Russia to Germany. He sent Witte a picture postcard of the meeting of the emperors at Björkö and urged that the plans discussed at Rominten be effectuated. Evidently he still hoped that, despite the abrogation of Björkö and Russian support of the French position on Morocco, he could break up the Franco-Russian alliance by promises and visions of continental union.

With the extension on the German bonds and the advance of 100 million rubles from France to bolster her sagging gold deposits, Russia had the breathing space she needed to repair her financial fences. Moreover, with the pacification of Siberia and the quelling of the Moscow uprising, the revolutionary movement began to subside. Revenue started to approach a normal level, the clamor for payments in gold died away, savings bank deposits increased, and the treasury was even able to burn 100 million rubles of paper as a gesture of confidence. Fluctuations on the Paris Bourse were stabilized, and the credit of Russia improved.[39] Although the urgency of the situation had been relieved and the gold standard preserved, the need for a large loan was still great since the government wanted to reinforce its weakened financial position in general and also hoped to be financially solvent before the Duma. The Paris bankers were now satisfied with Russia's internal condition, but the Moroccan question still blocked conclusion of the loan.

The Loan and International Politics

IN THE EARLY FALL when Witte talked to Rouvier in Paris, the latter made conclusion of the loan in the French market dependent on successful settlement of the Moroccan question. From the point of view of the French government this was a purely political bargain in which it received Russia's support over Morrocco and the intervention of Nicholas and Witte with the kaiser in exchange for its pressure on the banks.[40] From the standpoint of the French banking houses, however, the loan was contingent on a Moroccan agreement because the international crisis adversely affected European financial markets and made subscription of a large foreign loan difficult. On the other hand, the Russian government was anxious to conclude the loan before the opening of the Duma; and they had no other market but the French in which to raise the bulk of the money. The Algeciras Conference opened in January 1906 and the Duma was to convene in late April—which did not give Witte much time. The combined effect of these factors produced a situation quite different from that suggested by Sir Edward Grey on January 15, 1906 (n. s.): "Russia demanded a loan on improper terms as the price of her support."[41] As a matter of fact just the reverse was true. The French had the whip hand and could dictate almost any terms to the hapless Russians, for the French knew that Russia needed money both desperately and quickly. Thus they were assured of unconditional Russian support at Algeciras, and they were able to extort a very high commission on the loan.[42] On the other hand, the French had eventually to make good on their promise of a loan in order to avoid losing their ally to the east and driving Russia into the waiting arms of Germany.

In December when Kokovtsov was in Paris, the French demanded that the Russian delegate at Algeciras, Count Cassini, be instructed to vote with them without reservation on all issues; he was not even to wire home for instructions. To this the Russian government agreed, and despite German-inspired rumors to the contrary, it kept its part of the bargain faithfully—Russian backing for the French never wavered. At the end of February the Rouvier government fell and a new ministry headed by Sarrien assumed power. Raymond Poincaré and Georges Clemenceau were minister of Finance and minister of the Interior, respectively. Witte at once instructed Rafalovich, the Russian financial agent in Paris, and Noetzlin, the representative of the French syndicate through whom most of the financial negotiations for the loan were conducted, to call on the new government and to inform its leaders of the pledges exchanged between the Russian government and Rouvier. The new cabinet proved to be favorable to the loan and acknowledged the bargain that its predecessor had made, but it too insisted that the loan could not be negotiated until the Algeciras Conference had been brought to a successful conclusion.

Although the Russians at Algeciras voted in all cases with the French, anxiety to clear the way for the projected loan soon placed them in the position of unofficial moderator between the French and Germans. Witte urged his agents in Paris to advise the French to take a conciliatory position, and he reported to the French that he had pushed the Germans to the limit of their concessions and that now the French must yield.[43] On January 30 Rafalovich transmitted to Rouvier a list of the services performed by Russia in fulfilling her part of the bargain: Witte's work at Rominten in getting the Germans to come to the conference, two letters from Nicholas to William urging a conciliatory attitude on the part of Germany, and the instructions for Count Cassini to go "hand in hand" with the French.[44] The implication was clear: We have done our part; how about you? But Witte himself realized that his pressure on the French was to little avail. Since they were assured of unqualified British and Russian support, they could afford to be intractable on most points.[45]

Russian attempts to force the Germans to yield were more frequent and more forceful than those directed against the French. Pressure was brought to bear from every possible angle. Lamsdorff worked through normal diplomatic channels by sending long notes to Berlin to be presented to the German government by the Russian ambassador, Count Osten-Sacken. He protested against the possible breakup of the conference that German obstructionist tactics threatened, while frankly admitting that the loan depended on the conference and that the quelling of the revolution depended on the loan. He warned that the revolution was a danger not only to Russia but to all monarchical countries. The German replies usually argued that it was not the Algeciras Conference but rather revolutionary unrest and the protests of Jewish bankers that were blocking the loan.[46] Lamsdorff was constantly reminded of his duty to influence Berlin by the French ambassador in St. Petersburg, Maurice Bompard, who was acting under instructions from his government. Bompard records in his memoirs: "I did this [saw Lamsdorff] . . . daily; I did not let Lamsdorff have a moment's respite."[47] Bompard also made representations to Witte and the tsar.

Kokovtsov and Witte were in touch at this time with their German banker, Ernst Mendelssohn-Bartholdy of Mendelssohn & Company. They advanced their arguments on Algeciras to him, but he maintained that Germany could not yield further; and he threatened the Russians with the possible failure of the conference and its grave consequences for the international situation and the loan.[48] Informal contacts were used at the highest level. Witte wrote to Count Eulenburg, the kaiser's personal confidant, but to no avail.[49] At last even the tsar felt constrained to intervene personally with the Germans and he addressed several letters to "Willy." Their influence on German policy may be judged by considering the kaiser's comment that an earlier letter from "Nicky" had "a slightly comic tone with both fatherly and threatening exhortations on the subject of Morocco."[50] Then William records that he wrote a reassuring reply.

Witte felt strongly that part of the reason for Germany's delaying tactics at the conference lay in a deliberate attempt to obstruct the foreign loan and thus to prevent Russia's recovery from the war. Witte also believed that "the Germans endeavored to drag out the negotiations so as to increase our difficulties and take revenge on me for the annulment of the Björkö Treaty."[51] It is difficult to assess German motives, but they certainly had everything to gain by blocking the loan, thus weakening France's ally in the east and perhaps forcing Russia closer to Germany. Even more difficult is the task of evaluating the actual effect of Russian pressure in bringing about a successful conclusion of the Algeciras Conference. Witte, of course, tried to convince the French that it was solely through Russia's efforts that Germany finally gave in. However, the role of the United States as a mediator between the two parties and the desertion of Austria and Italy from Germany's side were clearly important factors as well.

The outcome of the Algeciras Conference also affected the question of participation in the loan by German banking houses. As early as 1904, at the time of Russia's commercial treaty with Germany, Witte had secured Germany's permission to float part of a new loan there.[52] In mid-February 1906, Mendelssohn-Bartholdy wrote Kokovtsov that financial confidence in Russia had been somewhat restored; and he suggested the opening of serious talks about a loan in the near future. About two weeks later he arrived in St. Petersburg and conferred with Witte concerning the terms of German participation in the international loan.[53] Evidently a general agreement was reached; but on March 19, in an angry letter to Witte, Mendelssohn-Bartholdy charged that press reports indicated that the Russians were about to conclude a loan in France (which was quite true), and that this was a direct breach of their St. Petersburg agreement, in which Witte had promised to make his first efforts for the loan in Germany since the French market was closed until after Algeciras. He added indignantly: "To treat Germany, in the negotiations and in the press, as a second-rate power and a negligible quantity, it seems to me, is to increase tremendously the impediments to agreement and could easily make fruitless any attempt at an international operation in Germany."[54]

Witte, evidently in the belief that the chances of German participation were slim and in his anxiety to guarantee the fullest possible French participation, had failed to keep Mendelssohn-Bartholdy informed. Attempting to repair the damage, he now hastened to warn Noetzlin, the French negotiator, who was about to go to London to open talks there with English and American bankers, that it would be a mistake from the political and economic viewpoint to begin such negotiations before discussions with the Germans. Witte, still hoping to keep the Germans in, arranged for Fischel, a representative of Mendelssohn, to meet Noetzlin in London. In a further effort to placate the Germans, Kokovtsov wired Mendelssohn-Bartholdy on March 21 that he would stop at Berlin on his way to Paris and that he "assigned special significance to meeting with you before meeting with the others in Paris."[55] At the same time the Russian ambassador in Berlin reported to St. Petersburg that William II opposed German participation in the loan and urged that Nicholas intervene personally with his cousin, but the tsar refused to do so.[56]

On March 21, Mendelssohn-Bartholdy wired Witte, indicating that the Germans were on their way out: "I do not conceal from you that the extraordinary difficulties have not disappeared. . . . The imminent issue of nearly 600 millions of German securities complicates the situation." In his reply on March 22 Witte made a last desperate attempt to assure German participation by threatening them with the consequences of withdrawal:

> A loan made with the aid of France, England, and other countries but without Germany will mean for the whole world a rapprochement of Russia with a political grouping which does not correspond to the interests of Russia or Germany. This removes Russia and Germany still more from realization of the wise principles proclaimed at Björkö. All this is very distressing.[57]

Witte was convinced that the German internal loan was merely a pretext for the government's refusal to grant permission to Mendelssohn-Bartholdy, and both Kokovtsov and he believed that the action was German retribution for the support which Russia had given France at Algeciras. In this instance, however, the profit motive proved to be more powerful than the pressure of the German government for diplomatic vengeance, for in a letter to Witte on April 5 Mendelssohn-Bartholdy extended his congratulations on the loan (which had been signed April 3) and reported that his firm would support it secretly by private investments in Paris, London, Amsterdam, and St. Petersburg.[58]

Just as Germany's official withdrawal from the loan widened the chasm separating Russia and Germany, so conversely British participation was an important step in the political rapprochement between England and Russia which was to lead to the Anglo-Russian accord of the following year. Although British banks acted independently, the fact that they joined in the loan was regarded as a political token by both parties and also by Germany. Witte felt that it was a grave policy error for Germany to have permitted England and Russia to move closer together through the loan and through their common cooperation with France at Algeciras.

Throughout 1905 there had been faint feelers, encouraged by France, between London and St. Petersburg. In October Sir Edward Grey, representing a new government in Britain, pointed out in a speech the advantages of Russian friendship and suggested this as a goal toward which the new cabinet should work.[59] British bankers had accompanied their French counterparts to St. Petersburg for negotiations in the fall of 1905, and in December Grey expressed high hopes for an understanding to Count Benckendorf, the Russian ambassador in London.[60] From the Russian side, Witte's guidepost of policy—the need for financial assistance—compellingly pointed to England. Cecil Spring-Rice, chargé of the British embassy in St. Petersburg, reported that Witte believed "that Germany could give a finger's length of help and England an arm's length."[61] Despite his dislike for the English and the traditional antagonism between the two countries, Witte realized that England was a valuable political connection with strong financial means, and consequently he began to work toward possible English participation in the international loan.

Transforming his interest in English wealth into action, Witte in late December proposed to E. J. Dillon, noted British correspondent and expert on Russia, English participation in the loan in return for a political agreement between Russia and Britain, and a short time later he even suggested to the British ambassador that King Edward come to St. Petersburg to discuss the matter with the tsar.[62] According to the French ambassador in St. Petersburg, Witte also sent an emissary to London on December 20 to encourage British interest in the loan in exchange for Russian willingness "to begin discussion of the points of friction which separate the two countries."[63] When the loan contract was signed, the British banking house of Baring Brothers took a small share in the subscription. Significantly, this was the first important English participation in a Russian loan since 1875. There is some evidence that the Foreign Office had semi-officially urged English participation.[64] In any case, the loan had definite political overtones, and it helped pave the way for serious negotiations toward an Anglo-Russian understanding, which were begun in St. Petersburg in May 1906.

Witte felt that the more international the composition of the lenders, the greater would be the success of the loan. Thus, he welcomed the interest that J. P. Morgan had expressed in the loan the preceding summer. In March 1906, Morgan journeyed to Paris and London to join in the negotiations. However, at the last minute he backed out and refused to float any part of the sum. Witte was angered by Morgan's withdrawal, which he ascribed to pernicious German influence and pressure.[65] Although Kokovtsov complained that the failure of Morgan to participate was a severe setback during the final negotiations, Noetzlin minimized its effect, suggesting that he had expected it all along.[66]

The withdrawal of open German support and the refusal of Morgan to participate reduced the amount of the proposed loan from the figure that Witte had aimed for, about two and three-quarter billion francs, to about two billion francs, but some of the reduction was offset by the Russian banks subscribing more than they had originally planned. Also Poincaré intervened with the French banks in support of Kokovtsov's argument that they should now take more. This was done, raising the amount to two and one-quarter billion francs. Italian bankers withdrew because they feared that the resultant efflux of gold would destroy Italy's internal money market, but Italian participation had not been expected to be large anyway. Holland and Austria took trifling amounts to broaden the international character of the loan. Austria's participation was uncertain until the last minute, and it required French guarantees of her share to keep Austria in.

Final Negotiations for the Loan

THE CHIEF FOREIGN NEGOTIATOR for Witte in all the discussions, whether with the French government, the French bankers, or other foreign bankers, was Eduard Noetzlin of the Banque de Paris et des Pays Bas, who headed the Paris syndicate interested in the loan. Noetzlin was a faithful and untiring worker throughout the negotiations, and he certainly deserved a great deal of credit for the ultimate success of the loan. A typical example of Noetzlin's activity was his method of operation after the fall of the Rouvier cabinet. On February 27, in a letter to Witte, Noetzlin reported that he was busy influencing the financial leaders to whom the new minister of Finance, Poincaré, would have to turn for advice and support. He had seen the director of the Banque de France, the head of the syndicate of stock brokers, and the chief director of a large savings bank. He had also continued to call on President Loubet regularly.[67] Naturally Noetzlin's motives were not completely altruistic; in fact, one French critic of the loan charged that Noetzlin's commission as an intermediary and as one of the bankers was twelve million francs.[68]

Early in the year Rafalovich, the Russian financial agent in Paris, and Noetzlin had attempted to interest the Rothschilds in the loan. They had no luck in sounding out the Paris branch of the firm, so Rafalovich went to London. The Rothschilds there said that they would like to participate but that they could not do so unless the Russian government enacted laws to improve the hard lot of the Jews in Russia. Witte felt that this was interference in Russia's internal affairs and "beneath our dignity."[69] After this, all the negotiations were with the so-called Christian syndicate of banks.

At this stage in the negotiations it was decided that Noetzlin should come to Russia to discuss the basic terms of the loan with Witte and with Shipov, the minister of Finance. Witte arranged for Noetzlin to come incognito and to stay at Tsarskoe Selo under the name of his valet, Bernard. This secrecy was to obviate any bad effect which news of his trip might have on the Algeciras Conference or on the Russian market. The ruse was completely successful since not one paper reported his presence in Russia. Noetzlin arrived on February 2 and spent five days discussing the loan with Witte, Kokovtsov, and Shipov.[70] Witte was very optimistic at the time; he conceived of broad international backing for a 3 billion franc loan at no more than six percent. Noetzlin immediately dampened his enthusiasm: the total was too high and some of the countries were wavering. Noetzlin maintained that the very high costs of flotation would mean that they could offer the issue at only about eighty-five percent of par value; thus with a five percent interest the Russian government would realize about eighty percent. The Russian negotiators refused to accept this, and the terms were left in abeyance.

At these meetings Noetzlin first raised a question about the legality of the loan: In view of the Manifesto of October 17 could the government conclude it without the consent of the Duma? Witte replied that Professor F. F. Martens, a noted jurist and authority on international law, had studied the problem and reported that the government could.[71] Witte argued that the loan must be concluded before the Duma convened since consideration by the Duma would only delay it, and would lead to debate about a future war and other unrelated political matters, which would destroy the confidence of the foreign public in the loan. This picture of the agitation and protest which the loan would evoke if it were brought before the Duma and of the consequent effect on the market convinced Noetzlin, and he agreed that the loan should be concluded after the Algeciras Conference and before the Duma.

Members of the French government, however, were not so easily persuaded, and Poincaré, as a jurist, was particularly troubled by the question of whether the Russian government had the legal right to conclude the loan without regard to the Duma, which would be constituted as part of the Russian state system when the time came to repay the loan.[72] On learning of these doubts Witte hastened to have the brief of Professor Martens translated into French and transmitted to Poincaré. The crux of Martens' argument was that although the Manifesto of October 17 had given the Duma some power over finances and credit, these would not be operative until the Duma met and thus legal control over credit was still vested in the present government. Moreover, Article 6 of the new Fundamental Laws clearly stated that the Duma could not repudiate state debts.[73] Poincaré, also aware that Russia's financial collapse would ruin millions of French holders of Russian bonds, was finally convinced. Nevertheless, the French government had its own experts study the question. Despite strong liberal pressure against the legality of the loan, a French government memorandum agreed substantially with that of Martens and the validity of the loan was accepted.[74]

French fears concerning the legality of the loan stemmed not only from a desire to protect their investment but also from protests against the loan on the part of liberal and socialist circles in both Russia and France. In early 1905, as an outgrowth of public outrage over "Bloody Sunday," a loose organization was formed in France under the name Société des amis du peuple russe et des peuples annexés to support the liberation movement in Russia, to encourage the aspirations of national minorities in the Russian Empire, and to oppose the French alliance with and aid to the Russian autocracy. Composed largely of intellectuals, including such luminaries as Anatole France, with a sprinkling of Russian émigrés and the tacit support of French socialists, the Société des amis organized public meetings and disseminated literature in an attempt to provide accurate information on the "true" state of affairs in Russia.[75] It also campaigned actively against French loans to Russia. After a period of quiescence in the summer of 1905, it resumed its activities in the fall and winter of 1905–06, with the upsurge of the revolutionary movement and rumors of a new loan to Russia. Its efforts were considerably abetted by publication in many European newspapers in late March of an impassioned appeal from Maxim Gorky entitled "Do Not Give Money to the Russian Government." (Because of Russian bribes to the French press only the socialist *L'Humanité* printed Gorky's letter in Paris.) Members of the Société des amis and French socialists thereupon intensified their activity against the imminent loan, and the latter even made it an issue in their campaign for the forthcoming French parliamentary elections, though attacks on the loan apparently had little effect on French voters—or on French investors, who eagerly subscribed to the new loan when it was announced.[76]

French opponents of the loan received unexpected and welcome assistance when several prominent members of the Kadet party who happened to be in Paris at the time, led by V. A. Maklakov, were drawn into the agitation against the loan by émigré friends living in Paris. Through well-connected French acquaintances the Russian Kadets obtained interviews with Fallières, the newly elected president of the republic, with Clemenceau, and with Poincaré, but these had little effect since the French government had already decided to go ahead with the loan. Nevertheless, Maklakov addressed a memorandum to Poincaré in which he stated that the autocracy would use the loan to resist the Duma. Out of this clash between the tsardom and liberal forces would grow further revolutionary upheaval that would destroy the economy of Russia, causing the loss of not only the present loan but previous French investments as well.[77] In their campaign among French government circles the Kadets particularly stressed the unfortunate effect of the loan on liberal public opinion in Russia and on future Franco-Russian relations, once the new constitutional order was established in Russia.

Although those hostile to the loan in France did not hesitate to use the cooperation of Maklakov and his colleagues to imply that the Kadet party officially opposed the loan (which subsequently led to a widespread "myth" of Kadet resistance to the loan), in fact the Kadets involved were acting strictly on their own. When they asked the party in Russia for permission to lend their names as Kadet members to a widespread poster campaign against the loan, they received no reply; and they withdrew from that effort. As it turned out, this was the last major activity of the opponents of the loan in France and it also ended in failure—with the permission of Clemenceau (ironically a member of the Société des amis) the French police pasted over the antiloan placards as soon as they were put up.[78] Despite the barren outcome of the activities of Maklakov and his friends, Witte was sufficiently upset by their campaign against the loan to send several warning telegrams about them to Kokovtsov, then in Paris to complete the loan. The latter replied that the efforts of the Kadets there had no chance of success because the Chamber of Deputies was closed, everyone was involved in election agitation, and the government was tied too closely to the pending financial operation.[79]

In Russia itself the rumored loan evoked the full criticism and opposition of the revolutionary and socialist parties, which as early as the "Financial Manifesto" of December 2 had made clear that they considered any such transaction illegal and that they would repudiate the ensuing obligations at the first opportunity (which did not come until 1918). For the Kadets, however, the loan was a delicate and divisive issue. As early as the second party congress in January 1906, the Kadets, at the suggestion of Miliukov, had declared that they would not repudiate legally incurred debts and obligations of the Russian government and state. As good constitutionalists and legalists, they were always forced to acknowledge that the Witte government did in fact have the right to conclude a loan. Moreover, the Kadets, as opponents of anarchy and violent revolution, realized that the financial collapse of Russia could well lead to chaos and the ending of any chance for peaceful reform. Finally, the Kadets, who aspired to power, fully understood that a stable fiscal situation and sufficient funds were necessary to whatever measures of change they hoped to effectuate through the Duma.[80] Yet to protect their oppositional stance and because of their genuine hostility to the autocracy they could hardly condone the loan and had to criticize it. The line they finally took, set as usual by Miliukov, was designed to persuade France and England not to grant the loan to the Witte cabinet. The Kadets hoped, vainly, that the Entente powers would listen to their views, as the majority party in the forthcoming Duma.

In the Kadet party organ, *Rech'*, Miliukov published a series of articles criticizing the loan.[81] Miliukov's arguments were not polemical, angry ones but rather were reasoned and legalistic. He suggested to the French that it would be to their self-interest in the long run to maintain and expand the ties between the French and Russian liberal publics instead of alienating them as signing the loan would do. Miliukov refuted the argument of the government that it would invite bankruptcy if it waited for the Duma to convene by pointing out that the loan was to be concluded only weeks before the Duma was scheduled to open. Obviously the government deliberately intended to circumvent the Duma. The government further argued that its obligations were so great that there would be no spare sums remaining once its debts had been met.[82] Miliukov retorted that this was not the point; it was the principle of the thing. If the government asserted the right to act in credit matters once without the consent of the Duma, then it would try to do it again.

The leftist parties attacked the Kadets for their weak opposition to the loan, but Miliukov rejected their proposal of a financial boycott (non-recognition of any loans and refusal to pay interest) because "the [Kadet] Party has always considered that a government cannot deny fulfillment of the financial obligations assumed by a preceding legal government. . . . Therefore, to threaten financial bankruptcy in the event of the conclusion of the loan . . . the Party can and will not do."[83] In line with this position the Central Committee of the Kadets, while recognizing that the loan was "extremely harmful" to the interests of Russia, refused unanimously to take any official action in the name of the party to prevent the loan. Moreover, embarrassed by the actions of Maklakov and his friends, the Kadet Central Committee disavowed them, declaring it had taken no formal stand on the loan and that since it had not authorized anyone to speak for the Kadets, the group in Paris must be acting as private individuals.[84]

As we saw, Maklakov's activity had little impact, partly because of the complete silence about it in the venal Paris press, which the Russian government was then paying and which had presented a special problem throughout negotiation of the loan. At that time it was generally known that Paris newspapers, from the top-rank organs to the meanest pamphlets, were always ready to do the bidding of the government which paid them the most. In practically all financial transactions of the day some arrangement concerning the press had to be made since its unfavorable reports could create enough lack of confidence among the financial public to make bonds of a country it attacked fall disastrously on the exchange.

During the course of the Russo-Japanese war the Russian government disbursed almost two million francs to the French press in an attempt to eliminate news of military defeats and of revolutionary unrest. Since the Japanese were paying the press too, the results of the Russian expenditure were most unsatisfactory, but as Nelidov replied to Kokovtsov's complaint on this score: "Think what the reports would be if there were no bribes."[85] From May to September 1905, when Kokovtsov ordered the subsidies halved, the Russian government paid two hundred thousand francs a month to some fifty newspapers, journals, and news agencies and to thirty-eight publishers, editors, and correspondents.[86] In December of 1905 the Paris press resorted to outright blackmail, threatening to begin a campaign against Russia unless their bribes were increased. The allowances for the press were duly raised again to two hundred thousand francs per month in order to sweeten the atmosphere for the big loan.

To insure the success of the 1906 loan the Russian government made elaborate further plans to prevent the press from ruining its credit. Rafalovich was able to engage an experienced middleman, Monsieur Lenoir, to handle the dirty business of subsidies to the press, while Kokovtsov succeeded in forcing the French government and banks to assume the burden of the press bribes. A new tactic was tried in regard to the actual payments: Instead of a pay-as-you-go plan the press was told that if the loan were a success, they would receive a handsome commission. This gave the press a vested interest in the success of the loan, and the tactic worked perfectly. For fear of losing their reward, the papers closed their eyes and wrote nothing about the loan negotiations or about the protests of Russian liberals against the loan. Kokovtsov recorded that after agreement with the press had been reached, no more reporters pestered him and there was not even a hint that the Russian financiers were in Paris. According to the archives of the French Ministry of Finance, a week after the loan was concluded four papers were paid 100,000 francs each and others lesser amounts to a total of a million and a half francs.[87] But, having received its mess of pottage, the press soon began violent attacks against Russia.[88] The *Cri de Paris*, irked at not receiving a larger share of the rake-off, summed up the affair in this way:

> Note that the operation succeeded so brilliantly only thanks to the papers—the silence of one, the enthusiasm of another—thanks to the co-operation in the crime by them all. Republican, conservative, socialist papers, all shades, all circulations, all formats had a hand in the affair and worked in touching agreement and harmony for God, Tsar, and fatherland.[89]

With the press silenced and the legality of the loan settled satisfactorily to his own and French, if not the liberals', satisfaction, Witte became increasingly impatient to open final negotiations for the loan. But the Algeciras Conference dragged on, and the French government insisted the loan could not be concluded until the conference was over.[90] Witte's anxiety and frustration are quite comprehensible when one recalls the very close timing into which the loan had to fit—between the conclusion of the Algeciras

Conference and the convocation of the Duma in late April. Noetzlin was now back in Paris working with Rafalovich, and Witte's concern and pique were reflected in a telegram of March 7 to the latter, in which Witte forwarded a report from Lamsdorff that the Algeciras Conference would certainly conclude satisfactorily and without international complications. "Hence . . . the linking of the loan to the Moroccan affair is only a pretext for not effecting the operation." Witte began to doubt the good faith of Russia's ally, and the bargain he had made with the French suddenly seemed very one-sided to him. He was afraid that the French would reap the advantage of a successful end to the conference "thanks to our energetic activity, and then will find various pretexts to avoid making the loan."[91]

As the days passed, the French continued to stand upon the technical requirement of a formal agreement at Algeciras before they would permit Noetzlin to begin final negotiations with the French bankers. Noetzlin himself supported this attitude of the government, and on March 14 he wrote Witte that it was useless to chafe at the government's precondition since "in order to complete international operations of this type the political barometer must stand at 'clear.' "[92] But Witte was not at all convinced. On March 16 Rafalovich transmitted to Nelidov the text of one of Witte's letters in which Witte charged that France was "playing some kind of game." Witte noted that at Algeciras Russia had been living up to her part of the bargain, and that it was about time France fulfilled her part. Witte wrote that the situation in Russia was serious. Eighteen months of war and internal unrest had severely weakened her finances. He noted that 680 million rubles were needed immediately to balance accounts. As for the issue of whether a loan would be legal or not, Witte wrote, "Only a republican minister can doubt the sovereign right of a monarch to conclude a loan."[93] When Rafalovich transmitted Witte's wire to Nelidov, he told Nelidov to make it clear to Poincaré that by further stalling the French "would not be acting as a friend but would be playing into the hands of their worst enemies." But Poincaré still demurred.

Finally, on March 18 Count Cassini wired Lamsdorff from Algeciras that full agreement had been reached on all major points; all that remained was the drafting of the final protocol.[94] On the same day Poincaré notified Nelidov that he had ordered Noetzlin to begin final preparations for the loan. Witte must have been delighted, especially since the results of the elections to the Duma that were beginning to come in indicated that it would have a strong antigovernment majority, probably headed by the Kadets, who disapproved of the loan. From Witte's point of view it was a close call: If the negotiations had been delayed much longer, the government would have had to stand penniless before a hostile Duma.

In the final stages of the negotiations the chief issue was the cost of the loan, and the negotiations almost broke down on this point. The argument hinged on the offering price of the loan and the amount of the bankers' commission—or in other words on how much the Russian government would actually realize. Noetzlin maintained that the offering price would have to be 80 percent of par value, plus 6¼ percent interest, since people had to see a profit if there were to be broad support and the loan were to succeed. In the current condition of the market the public was speculatively minded, and therefore the offering price had to be low. Furthermore, flotation costs were high and he had to grease the "wheels" of the loan (the stockbrokers, the press, and other intermediaries).[95] On the other hand, Witte maintained just as firmly that a hostile public opinion in Russia would not permit more than 6 percent interest or as low a realization price as 80. He reaffirmed the proposal made on the very first day of negotiations with Noetzlin in Russia for an offering price of 83½, plus 5 percent interest. This meant that the bankers' commission would have to be cut and naturally their opposition was strong. Finally in a wire to Witte on March 29 Noetzlin suggested that he might be able to get 83½ if the Russian government would bear the expense of the stamp-duty (a French government tax of about 1 percent). After some bargaining the Russians finally accepted this compromise. Kokovtsov records that it was achieved only through the active cooperation of Monsieur de Verneuil, the representative of the stockbrokers' syndicate, who was a violent opponent of high bankers' commissions since they raised costs and limited the activity of the French market in advancing credits. Kokovtsov also pays tribute to the firm and powerful backing the Russians received on this point from Poincaré, the minister of Finance. "Poincaré's moral support of Russia at the moment was decisive."[96]

When the final negotiations began, Witte decided to send a

delegation to Paris to participate in them. Witte wished to have the director of the State Bank, S. I. Timashev, head the delegation rather than Kokovtsov because of the latter's "failure" in December. Nicholas II, however, insisted that Kokovtsov be the one to conclude the loan. According to Witte, he personally acquainted Kokovtsov with all the details of the loan before his departure so that all Kokovtsov really had to do was to appear and to sign the documents. In addition, Witte wrote that he sent A. I. Vyshnegradsky to assist Kokovtsov "in order that no blunder would be made."[97] Kokovtsov, of course, indignantly refuted these allegations, pointing out that Vyshnegradsky was already in Paris as a representative of the Russian banks and that he (Kokovtsov) had in fact to negotiate a number of final details of the loan, including the increased participation of French and Russian banks necessitated by the withdrawal of the Germans and of J. P. Morgan.[98]

On April 3, 1906, Kokovtsov signed the loan at the Russian embassy in Paris. The simultaneous announcement in the various capitals on April 9 and the issuing of the loan on April 12 were carefully timed to fall between Easter (April 2) and the French elections on April 23. The loan, which totaled 2¼ billion francs (843,750,000 rubles) at five percent interest, was subscribed to by French, British, Austrian, Dutch, and Russian banks, making it appear to be the international loan Witte had desired. Of these countries by far the greatest share was carried by France—1,200 million francs, plus guaranteeing Austria's share of 165 million. The British took 330 million francs, the Dutch 55 million, and the Russian banks 500 million francs.[99] A proviso added by the French government prohibited any new Russian loan in the French market for two years. This irked Witte, but Kokovtsov assured him it was only a political maneuver and was designed as a sop to the violent opposition against the loan. Moreover, Noetzlin confided to Witte he had given Kokovtsov a memorandum from Poincaré pertaining to this two-year prohibition, "which can have definite value in the future." Nevertheless, the two-year moratorium on new loans was enforced, despite Russia's need for more funds. This led to austerity budgets in 1907 and 1908, until a new loan was concluded in early 1909.[100]

Although the great loan of 1906 was half a billion francs smaller than Witte had hoped for in February and its terms were heavy because of the low issue price, it remained without doubt one of the single greatest accomplishments of his government. Its importance was not lost on Nicholas II. In a letter to Witte on April 15, 1906, he wrote: "The successful completion of the loan forms the best page in the history of your ministerial activity. It is for the Government a great moral triumph and a pledge of Russia's undisturbed and peaceful development in the future."[101] Yet these words of praise and recognition were written as the tsar promptly accepted Witte's resignation, which had been submitted the previous day—only two days after the issuing of the loan. For some time Witte had known he was out of favor at court, and indeed he had offered to resign several times during the winter but "the invariable reply was that this was impossible before the conclusion of the loan."[102] Thus it is quite clear that the tsar refrained from dismissing Witte, in whom he had lost what little confidence he had had in October, earlier in 1906 primarily because Nicholas felt he needed Witte to complete the loan successfully. Witte perhaps overstated his value when he asserted, "The tsar clearly realized that I was the only one able to conclude the loan, first of all because of my prestige in all the foreign monetary circles, and secondly, because of my experience," but there is no doubt that Witte inspired greater confidence abroad—at least among French banking and government officials—than did any other public figure in Russia and that the tsar fully appreciated this fact.[103] Once the loan was concluded, however, Witte was more a liability than an asset since the hostile opposition in the Duma, highly critical of the loan, could have used the loan to attack Witte and the cabinet responsible for it. For Nicholas it was better to have a new government untainted by any connection with the loan to face the Duma.

Witte found himself in an awkward position in the winter of 1906. Knowing that his influence was waning and isolated by bitter attacks on him from both liberal and conservative circles, he undoubtedly felt that the best and most dignified course of action would be for him to resign. Yet his offers to do so were half-hearted, for the loan was dear to his heart and central to his attempt to "save" Russia, and he was loath to give up until he had completed that masterwork. Moreover, immodest as he was, he sincerely believed that the success of the loan depended primarily on his personal supervision of its negotiation. So he hung on, a rather pathetic, lonely, and increasingly querulous figure who, it was common knowledge, would be forced to resign as soon as he fulfilled his appointed task of obtaining a loan and somehow keeping the country running until the Duma met.[104] As Witte himself recognized, his days in power were numbered by those remaining before the loan was concluded, yet he stayed on because he was convinced that the loan was crucial to the preservation of Russia and of the autocracy, to which he was devoted. He put it best in his letter of resignation of April 14, in which he stated that he would have resigned earlier but for an "obligation to make every effort to ward off Russia's final collapse and to prevent conditions under which the Duma, taking advantage of the Government's financial straits, might force it to make concessions . . . inimical to the interests of the State as a whole, with which interests Your Imperial Majesty is inseparably identified."[105]

Realization of how important the loan was to Witte is also vital in order to understand his "chameleonlike" behavior in December 1905 and January 1906. As we saw in chapter five, various members of the government, including the tsar himself, were amazed at what seemed to them to be a complete reversal in Witte's attitude toward the revolutionaries and to any who were responsible for unrest. There were several factors that help to explain Witte's changed view of the revolution but not least among these was his conviction that a large loan was desperately needed, and that chances of obtaining it from financial circles abroad were slim until order had been restored in Russia.

Once it was concluded, the loan significantly influenced the course of Russian domestic history. Its immediate economic results were to stabilize Russian finances, to enable Russia to remain on the gold standard, and generally to assist the country in recovering from the ravages of war and revolution. But its long-run political impact was even more important. When Witte first conceived of the loan in the summer of 1905, he had no idea of the role it was destined to play in regard to the Duma, but as events unfolded that fall, he soon decided it was important to conclude the loan before the Duma met and he bent every effort to achieve that end. Witte's own words clearly illuminate the relation between the Duma and the loan in the history of Russia.

> My intention was to conclude the loan before the opening of the Imperial Duma. As I felt sure that the First Duma would be unbalanced and to a certain extent revengeful, I was afraid that its interference might thwart the loan negotiations and render the bankers

less tractable. As a result, the government, without funds, would lose the *freedom of action* which is so essential during a period of upheaval [our italics].[106]

This paragraph holds the key to the problem: it was not so much a question of strict legality concerning who had control over financial matters as it was a desire by the government not to be dependent on the Duma. Therefore Witte's success in negotiating the loan contributed ultimately to undermining his own efforts to introduce civil freedom and political reform into Russia, because the autocracy, given considerable financial independence, was able to operate with less regard for the wishes of the representatives of the people in the Duma than might otherwise have been the case. A bankrupt government would inevitably have been far more beholden to the Duma.

Equally important to Russian history was the effect the international loan had on Russian foreign policy. With the lapse of the German-Russian treaty in 1890, the signing of the Franco-Russian alliance in 1894, and the growth of French credits and investments in Russia, Russia had developed increasingly close ties with France. Yet in 1905 there were many in Russia, including Witte and probably the tsar, who would have preferred an alliance with Germany as well and who considered England Russia's chief enemy. This was certainly the spirit behind the ill-considered Björkö Treaty. But, driven by his conviction of the importance of the loan to Russia, Witte took steps and offered guarantees which led Russia ultimately from the Björkö romance with Germany to a hardened position as a member of the Triple Entente against the Triple Alliance. Thus, the effect of the loan was to estrange Russia from Germany, to shatter Witte's dreams of a grand continental alliance, to bind Russia ever more tightly to France, and to help pave the way for the Anglo-Russian Entente. During 1905–06 Russia definitely became a subservient partner in the alliance with France. The French used the promise of a loan to help force Russia to make peace in the Far East, to prevent any Russian rapprochement with Germany, to extract unquestioning Russian support at Algeciras, and to bring Russia and England closer together.[107] Yet in a real sense France was also dependent on Russia; she could not allow her ally to collapse because of the disaster this would mean for French investors and because it might lead to a renewal of Russo-German ties. Although Witte had hoped to use his mediation in the Moroccan crisis and the international character of the loan as a means of drawing Germany and France together, the loan turned out not to be genuinely "international" but rather a surety on the part of France and Britain that Russia would line up against Germany. Consequently, when one considers the effect of the loan in freeing the autocracy from dependence on the Duma and its decisive role in cementing the combination of Allied Powers against Germany on the eve of the World War, it is perhaps not inappropriate to ask: Did the loan really save Russia?[108]

VIII

ELECTIONS TO THE FIRST DUMA

To satisfy by legal means the needs of all classes of society.
—A major promise of the Kadet
electoral program of 1905–06

The only hope remaining for escaping from this deep darkness
lies with our father-tsar and with our electors who go into the Duma
to champion peasant interests. *—From a peasant petition*
January 1906

T HE FIRST NATIONAL ELECTIONS in the history of modern Russia
were held in most regions of the country from the end of
February to the middle of April 1906. Although no exact figures
exist, probably twenty to twenty-five million citizens voted indirectly to elect deputies to the State Duma, the first all-Russian
legislative assembly, and a much smaller number chose, by classes,
deputies to the State Council, all of whose members had previously
been appointive. Some thought they were voting for the tsar; many
believed they were voting for more land; and others were convinced they were voting for freedom and for a new order for Russia.
The overwhelming majority voted against the existing system and
against the government, much to the latter's surprise and discomfiture. Yet to the credit of Witte and the government the elections
were conducted with considerable efficiency and with a minimum
of either disorder or government interference.

In letter the elections fulfilled the tsar's promise of October 17,
1905, to give most of the population representation in directing the
affairs of the country. In practice, as we shall see in the next chapter, this pledge had been considerably undercut, even before the

elections were completed, by unilateral government limitation of the rights of the Duma and by establishment of a second legislative body, the reorganized State Council. Nevertheless, many in all walks of Russian life, from simple peasants to prosperous bankers, from socialists to monarchists, pinned their differing hopes and aspirations on the elections and on the Duma the elections would bring into being. Some saw the promise of a return to order and stability; others envisioned reform and progress. Only a handful of radicals opposed the elections entirely, although many in all classes were disinterested or apathetic. Parties sprang up, and a lively electoral campaign ensued. When the vote was in, it was clear that the people of Russia desired a change. The government, however, did not.

For Witte the elections were a key element in his program of order and reform, and he struggled consistently to see that this plank of the October Manifesto was fulfilled. He believed that creation of a representative assembly would help restore order by satisfying a major demand of the oppositional intelligentsia, and of many moderates and conservatives as well. Moreover, he hoped that the electoral process might aid in reviving the people's faith in the tsar and the government. Finally, he thought that the elected Duma might serve as both a channel and a buffer between people and government, preventing radicalism and hostility while beginning the process of transforming the old order into a more efficient, rational, and modern one. He probably hoped against hope that he might be permitted to stay on as prime minister in order to attempt to work with the Duma in initiating "constructive and business-like activity," but the Duma, accurately reflecting the sentiment of the country, was more radical than Witte would have wished, and the tsar, setting his face against the Duma, sent Witte into retirement.

The Electoral System

THE ELECTIONS to the Duma were conducted on the basis of the imperial ukase of August 6, 1905, as elaborated by a special governmental commission in succeeding weeks and as extended by the electoral law of December 11. Suffrage was not universal, and the electoral system was unequal and indirect, with voting according to various curiae or classes of the population. Eligibility was generally determined on a property or tax basis. Yet the majority of male citizens had the right to express their preference by secret ballot, and probably no more than ten percent were deprived of the franchise by law or by administrative action. The weighting of the electoral system favored the gentry and the bourgeoisie on the ground that these were the most active and influential citizens, but the very numbers of the peasant mass of the population ensured that their force, which many incorrectly assumed would be conservative, would be felt. As we saw in chapter four, the electoral system was an enlargement of that established earlier for the consultative Bulygin Duma. The law provided that the Duma have 524 deputies, but elections in much of Siberia, Russian Central Asia, and the Russian Far East, which were conducted under special regulations favoring the Russian colonizers over the native population, were delayed, with some actually never being held because the First Duma was prorogued before the voting could be organized. Consequently, the First Duma never had over 500 deputies, fluctuating for most of its short life around 480. The Duma deputies were elected in three ways (see chart, p. 244): (1) by city electoral assemblies in the twenty-six largest cities of the empire, each choosing one deputy (except St. Petersburg selected six, Moscow four, and Warsaw two); (2) by peasant electors sitting in gubernia (provincial) electoral assemblies, who voted separately to choose one deputy from each province; (3) by gubernia electoral assemblies composed of electors from the landowners, peasants, town dwellers, and workers, which voted as a body to select the bulk of the Duma deputies, the number per gubernia being roughly proportionate to its population.

The essence of the electoral system was indirect voting according to four basic curiae: landowners, peasants, town dwellers, and workers.[1] Large landowners participated directly in uezd electoral assemblies of landowners which chose electors to the gubernia electoral assemblies. Small landowners met first in preliminary meetings to vote for delegates to the uezd electoral assemblies of landowners; these delegates then joined with the large landowners in selecting electors to the gubernia electoral assemblies. Peasants who owned private land, in addition to holding communal land, could vote as small landowners in the preliminary meetings of landowners and could also vote in the separate peasant elections. This was the only instance of double voting the law permitted,

[243

THE ELECTORAL SYSTEM FOR THE FIRST RUSSIAN DUMA

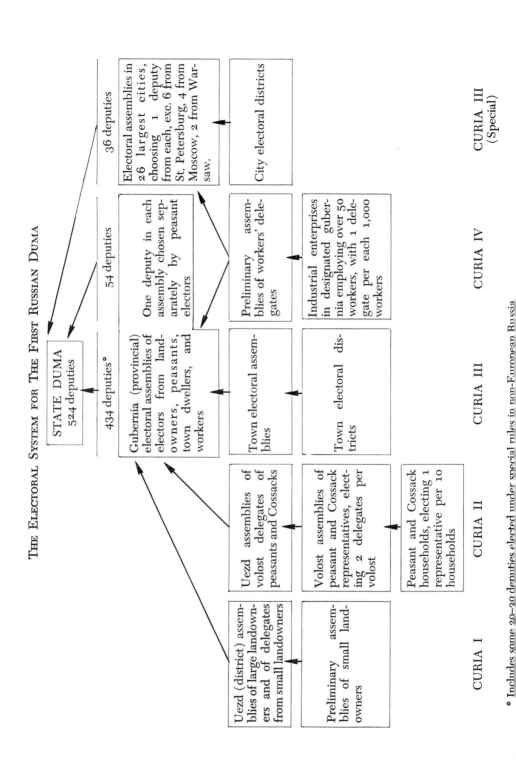

* Includes some 20–30 deputies elected under special rules in non-European Russia.

though in a number of cities some workers apparently voted both at the factories in their own curia and as renters of apartments in the curia of town or city dwellers. Partly because of the apathy of large landowners in many provinces, partly because of the sheer weight of numbers of the small landowners (many of whom were also apathetic), the latter often dominated the uezd assemblies of landowners, which therefore sent many "progressive" electors to the gubernia assemblies.

The second curia, that of peasants and Cossacks, was set up in four stages. First, every ten households elected one representative to volost assemblies; second, the volost assemblies picked two delegates each to uezd peasant assemblies; third, the uezd assemblies chose electors to the gubernia electoral assemblies; fourth, these peasant electors voted separately for one Duma deputy per gubernia and then joined with the other electors in selecting the remaining Duma deputies from the gubernia.

The curia of town and city dwellers voted in two ways. In the largest cities voters chose in electoral districts electors to a city electoral assembly, which elected Duma deputies directly [see chart, Curia III (Special)]. In smaller cities and towns voters chose in electoral districts delegates to town electoral assemblies; these in turn chose electors to the gubernia electoral assemblies, where they joined with other electors to select Duma deputies.

Workers in designated provinces and cities voted in a three-step process. First, they chose in the factories delegates to preliminary assemblies; these in turn sent workers' electors to either gubernia or city electoral assemblies, where they joined with other electors in selecting Duma deputies.

Organization and Supervision of the Elections

EVEN THIS SIMPLIFIED OUTLINE suggests the complexity of the electoral system, and it is remarkable that the government was able to organize and conduct the elections quite effectively in the short space of four months, in a period of turmoil and disturbance throughout much of the country. To be sure, unlike many developing societies in the twentieth century which have had to organize elections "from scratch," Russia benefited from an immediately preceding four decades of experience in elections to local zemstvo institutions and city dumas (the electoral regulations of August 6, 1905 were deliberately based on that existing system) and from a much longer tradition of elections and participation in village and communal assemblies. Moreover, preparations for the elections began in August 1905, and were already well advanced by December, when the new electoral law simply enlarged the existing Bulygin system, adding new voters to established curiae and a new curia for workers. Nevertheless, the successful conduct of the elections in the winter and spring of 1906 is a tribute to the efficiency, energy, and zeal of Witte's government, the bureaucracy, and the zemstvo institutions, all of which worked together in arranging and supervising the elections.

Overall control of the electoral process was vested in the Ministry of Interior, where a special but small section, headed by a seasoned bureaucrat, S. E. Kryzhanovskii, was established in September 1905, to oversee the elections. In each gubernia, uezd, and city, electoral commissions were set up, under the general supervision of the governor or mayor. These commissions were headed by the chairman or a member of the local okrug court and were composed of the local marshal of the nobility, the president of the local zemstvo, a representative of the city duma head, and two representatives of local branches of the central administration. The electoral commissions were empowered to approve electoral lists of voters and to hear complaints concerning the registration of voters or the elections themselves. Decisions on complaints could be appealed to the gubernia electoral commission and from there to the Senate in St. Petersburg.[2]

Registration of voters and compilation of electoral lists was the responsibility of city duma boards and of local zemstvos (or the local police administration, where no zemstvo existed). Lists of voters had to be published six weeks in advance of the elections, with protests over the inclusion or exclusion of voters submitted within two weeks (reduced to three weeks and one week, respectively, by the supplementary law of December 11). The actual voting was under the joint supervision of the electoral commissions and the local marshal of nobility or city duma head (or their representatives). The electoral assemblies at the various levels were chaired by the local marshal of nobility or city duma head (or persons they designated).³ Protests over the vote had to be submitted within three days but were not to void the results.

The institutions and procedures established for conducting the elections are significant, reflecting the spirit in which the government approached the elections. While obviously the central administration retained overall control and placed some of its representatives on the local commissions, the chief responsibility for arranging and supervising the elections was consciously given to local institutions of self-government (zemstvos and city dumas), the local judiciary, and local marshals of nobility (to be sure, most of the last were undoubtedly considered conservative watchdogs of the elections for the government). This, it was believed, would encourage the desire and the initiative of local citizens to participate in the electoral process and at the same time serve as a symbol and a safeguard of the impartiality and freedom with which the government hoped the elections would be conducted. In this way the trust which politically active people had developed in the elections and institutions of local self-government could be transferred to the national electoral process.

From the very beginning of the development of the electoral system, in July 1905, almost everyone in the central government, from Nicholas on down, including Durnovo, insisted that if national elections were indeed to be held, they should be as fair, free, and as open as possible. After publication of the ukase of August 6, a conference under Count Sol'sky was formed to work out details of the proposed elections to the consultative Bulygin Duma. In meetings on August 19, 20, and 22 one of the key issues the conference discussed was the necessity to ensure the propriety and freedom of the elections. To achieve this the conference recognized that the government would have to establish certain basic civil rights, the inviolability of persons, especially electors and Duma members, and freedom of assembly, speech, and the press being considered the most important. Some members pointed out that the existence of martial law or of states of "strengthened or extraordinary security" in numerous parts of the empire was a serious barrier to free elections. They recommended without success that such measures be suspended during the elections.⁴ Nevertheless, the opinions and activity of Sol'sky's conference regarding the significance of civil freedoms as a prerequisite to elections undoubtedly influenced the granting of such freedoms in the October Manifesto and bore specific fruit in new regulations providing limited freedom of assembly, which were issued on October 12, even before publication of the Manifesto.[5]

On September 9 and 15, 1905, the minister of Justice sent circulars to all okrug judges, reviewing their key role in the establishment of local electoral commissions and in supervising the electoral process. He urged them to bend every effort to accelerate the holding of the elections (those for the Bulygin Duma were originally scheduled for mid-December 1905) and to ensure that the elections were carried out correctly and without hindrance.[6] These instructions were elaborated in circulars from the Ministry of Interior to all governors and mayors on September 18 and 27, December 17, and January 11, 1906, which set forth schedules and detailed regulations for the elections. In these circulars it was stressed that the elections should be free, and that there should be no interference with them, generally, and especially none by government officials.[7] On February 26, 1906, in response to a request from Durnovo, the head of the department of police under the Ministry of Interior summarized the steps that had been taken to preserve the security and freedom of the elections. He reviewed circulars to governors and mayors of January 20 and February 16, which called for strict observance of the previously established regulations of October 12 and December 11 on the holding of meetings and which demanded the exercise of special efforts to protect the freedom and security of election meetings and especially to prevent the disruption of meetings and the pressuring of voters or electors by revolutionaries. The chief of police also reported the sending of a circular on February 25, requesting special measures be taken to preserve the security of the electoral assemblies where delegates, electors, and Duma deputies were chosen, and of circulars of February 10 and 18 to the departments of the local economy under the Ministry of Interior, calling for the guaranteeing of order in elections at the village and other local levels and for the protection of electoral lists of voters from theft or destruction (which had occurred in a few instances).[8] Finally, to supplement the existing regulation which provided that police and government officials not involved in the conduct of the elections could not attend electoral meetings and assemblies but could only check outside to see that no unauthorized voters or electors attended, the minister of Interior dispatched a circular on

February 4, ordering that no members of the provincial government, of the department of factory inspection, or of the management and administration of the factory could enter workers' polling places in the factories except on the specific invitation of the worker-voters and then only to clear up doubts and misunderstandings about the electoral law or process.[9]

The government did take one negative or punitive step in regard to the elections, but it regarded this as a measure to preserve the order and security of the elections not as any interference with free choice. Some Social Democrats and some Socialist Revolutionaries, as well as several minor radical and socialist parties, advocated a boycott of the elections on the ground that the promised Duma was a constitutional "deception" of the people, whose real interests lay in creating a constituent assembly and founding a revolutionary government. Under pressure from bourgeois and moderate parties and because of several instances in St. Petersburg and elsewhere of socialist agitators disrupting campaign meetings with fiery appeals not to vote and to go over from political to armed struggle against the government, the Council of Ministers issued a decree on March 8, providing four to eight months in prison for those guilty of inciting opposition to the elections or instigating mass abstention from them. The decree, entitled "Temporary Regulations Concerning Limitations of the Freedom and Legality of the Forthcoming Elections to the State Council and State Duma, and Concerning the Unhindered Activity of Those Institutions," was more familiarly known as "the law against the boycott."[10] It is not clear that this law led to many arrests, and, regardless, the boycott was not very successful.

The clear effort on the part of the bureaucracy to ensure the security and freedom of the elections reflected the strong concern of the leaders of the central government, both before and after publication of the October Manifesto, that the elections be fair, just, and open.[11] In September 1905, when detailed preparations for the elections first began, Bulygin, who was then minister of Interior and who had brought to fruition the ukase of August 6, told Kryzhanovskii, his subordinate in charge of organizing the elections, that he did not want to participate directly in supervision of the elections but wished only to be sure that they were held without any interference from gubernia or uezd authorities. "And," as Kryzhanovskii, who was a conservative, adds in his memoirs, rather regretfully, and therefore probably truthfully, "in fact neither central nor local officials made any attempt to exert the influence of the government to achieve electoral results favorable to it."[12]

Bulygin's successor, Durnovo, despite his generally repressive policies, acted, as we have seen, to implement the official concern of the government that the elections be free and encouraged the civil servants under him to protect the security and regularity of the elections. Durnovo did attempt, as we shall see shortly, to limit the holding of election meetings and rallies, but this was more out of anxiety that such meetings permitted revolutionary agitation, incited antigovernment attitudes, and could lead to disorders than it was from any desire to interfere directly in the elections or to turn them to the government's advantage. Durnovo's quite neutral stance toward the elections probably resulted from his belief, or at least hope, that as an institution the Duma would be relatively unimportant and impotent and from his conviction that political parties, platforms, and campaigning were really irrelevant and probably should not be allowed since, once elected to the Duma, every deputy would in any case vote according to his conscience.[13] Nevertheless, on one occasion, sometime in late January or in February 1906, Durnovo did suggest to Witte that the government should take a more active role in influencing the elections. Witte did not deny the desirability of such a step but pointed out that it was already too late and "that in any case it was probably impossible to have much effect and therefore it was not worth compromising the government with pointless measures of pressure."[14]

As this incident implies, Witte's attitude toward the elections was rather puzzling. As early as his memorandum to the tsar on October 9, he had insisted on the importance of making the elections free and of prohibiting any government interference with them so that "society" would have faith in them and the new Duma. And he maintained this position throughout his premiership. Yet it seems likely that his views on electoral freedom stemmed not from conviction nor from any lofty democratic principles but from pragmatism and disinterest. As we saw in chapter three in connection with his efforts to form a cabinet and to win public support, Witte, schooled in bureaucratic rivalry and court intrigue, knew little about, and rather disdained, politics at a public level and on a mass scale. He cared little for parties or organizations and made no effort to build either for himself. He envisioned not a democratic and politicized future Russian state but one of rationality and order managed by an efficient and able bureaucracy which would graciously accept the assistance of representatives of the people. The Duma was not an objective for Witte but simply a means to his end, a way of keeping people quiet by giving them a symbol of participation in the affairs of state and a method of enlisting the cooperation, or at least the lack of opposition, of "society" in what Witte wanted to do for Russia and what he believed was right for the country. Thus, as French Ambassador Bompard, often a shrewd observer, pointed out, Witte was not really interested in the elections nor even in the Duma, except as they might be useful instruments of support for the government in its task of modernization. Consequently, Witte largely ignored the elections, failing to do anything to get good people elected to the Duma, to indicate what the significance of the electoral process was, or what its outcome should be.[15] At the same time Witte did nothing to interfere with the elections, but this was chiefly because, as he told Durnovo, he thought little effective could be done, while such an effort would arouse the hostility of the public. So by and large Russian citizens were allowed to vote freely. For this Witte won no favor with the tsar and court circles, yet received no credit from the opposition. The result was an antigovernment Duma, which because of his dismissal he, perhaps gratefully, did not have to face. By encouraging free elections he had hoped to win the trust of "society" in the Duma and in his program of reform, but the ancient gap between government and people and the measures he felt he had to take to restore order defeated his purpose.

Parties and Programs in the Elections

THE VAST MAJORITY of Russian citizens were totally unprepared for national elections. Their previous electoral experience had been at the village or local level, where votes had been cast for individual personalities or for authority figures, and perhaps occasionally for or against some particularly burning local issue—but certainly not for parties or for any abstract general programs. Moreover, in the absence of a free press and because of widespread illiteracy, there was almost no possibility for the average citizen to be well informed on national political and social questions. Thus, most voters had only the haziest idea what the Duma meant, what an electoral campaign was, what the struggle between contending groups and candidates was all about. In view of this, the relative success of the elections is all the more remarkable.

To be sure, embryonic political parties had developed in the few years immediately preceding the elections, but these were either illegal, conspiratorial revolutionary organizations such as the Social Democrats and Socialist Revolutionaries, nationalist groups such as the Jewish Bund and the Dashnaks of the Caucasus, or broad, amorphous conglomerations of like-minded people as the Union of Unions, the Peasants' Union, and the Union of Russian People. The concept of an organized political party espousing a definite program and dedicated to winning votes was unknown to most Russians. Moreover, as we have seen, the government itself gave no lead to the voters, neither forming a party of its own nor openly supporting any of those that existed or came into being during the campaign. Therefore, it is hardly surprising that what party alignments there were in the elections were fluid and shifting, and that almost a third of the Duma deputies were either non-party or representatives of nationalist groups, while many others were affiliated only loosely with parties or with such broad fractions as the Toiling (*Trudovaia*) Group.

Nevertheless, parties of various kinds and of differing degrees of coherence and organization did play an important role in the elections, and the strongest and best-organized party, the Kadets, won a clear-cut victory. To survey the parties in the elections we will proceed in Chinese fashion, from right to left of the political spectrum (see chart, p. 253). Although a number of splinter parties and groups of the far right contested elections in various individual provinces and districts, including a few Russian nationalist monarchist groups in the non-Russian borderlands, such as the Bessarabian Party of the Center, the only national party of the extreme right was the Union of Russian People, founded in November 1905, whose pogromatic activities were discussed in chapter three. The Union, though opposed to the Duma, decided to enter the electoral contest in the hope of exerting influence in the Duma to restrict its authority and to turn it into at most a consultative assembly composed only of Russians. The Union presented candidates and campaigned in a number of provinces, though far from all, but was remarkably ineffective. Although some local officials and clerics

PARTIES IN THE ELECTIONS TO THE FIRST RUSSIAN DUMA

FAR LEFT		LEFT		CENTER			RIGHT		FAR RIGHT	
Socialist Revolutionaries	Social Democrats (Mensheviks and Bolsheviks)	Radical Democratic party; Party of Free Thinkers	Kadets (Party of the People's Freedom)	Party of Democratic Reform	Union of Oct. 17 (Octobrists)	Party of Legal Order	Progressive-Economic party (St. Petersburg)	Trade-Industrial party (Moscow)	Russian Assembly	Union of Russian People
and nationalist socialist parties									and nationalist conservative parties	

supported it and worked for it, neither the central government nor the Orthodox church officially endorsed or aided it. The Union published several newspapers, organized some meetings, distributed brochures, and held patriotic demonstrations to popularize among all classes its defense of autocracy, Orthodoxy, and Russianness, but its program was vague and had little appeal.[16] One older rightist group, slightly more moderate than the Union of Russian People, the Russian Assembly (*Russkoe Sobranie*), which was founded in St. Petersburg in 1900 as an upper-class, university-oriented body, attempted to form a right bloc for the elections but had little success.[17]

Of varying political hues but often quite conservative on social and general political questions was a series of non-Russian nationalist parties which supported cultural autonomy and equal rights for non-Russian peoples and espoused the particular interests of their own ethnic group. The most important and successful of these was the Polish National Democrats, whose candidates won an overwhelming victory in tsarist Poland and later were the core of the Polish Circle bloc within the First and later Dumas. Smaller and less cohesive were various Muslim groups which succeeded in electing some candidates from different regions of the empire. Most members and local committees of such radical nationalist parties as the Jewish Bund, the Polish Socialist party, and the Byelorussian Socialistic Gramad boycotted the elections. Many moderate Jews, though not forming a separate party, enthusiastically supported local Jewish candidates and backed the efforts of the nonparty League for the Attainment of Full Rights for the Jewish People of Russia, which in St. Petersburg and in areas of substantial Jewish population cooperated with the Kadets.[18]

Next along the political scale was a group of conservative and moderate parties, which Soviet historians have lumped together as the "bourgeois" parties. It is true that most of their leadership, membership, and funds came from merchants, bankers, and industrialists and that their programs generally reflected the interests of these classes, but they also included some moderate landowners, intelligentsia, and civil servants, and their platforms at times embraced broader political aims. The basis for these parties was laid in July 1905, at a congress of representatives of trade and industry that elected a bureau to prepare a political organization and program.[19] This bureau negotiated with the zemstvo-city oppositionists over a common program and electoral bloc for the elections to the Bulygin Duma, but agreement could not be reached on a platform of social and economic reform and the negotiations collapsed. As a result, the industrialists decided to form an independent party and tentative steps to this end, which Witte encouraged but did not participate in, were taken in early October. After the October Manifesto the necessity of broader political activity and organization became clear in view of the increased number of citizens who would vote, but the industrialists were unable to form a party with mass appeal or even to unite in one that represented their own interests, primarily because of minor differences over political and social aims and because of a long-standing rivalry between the industrialists of St. Petersburg and those of Moscow.

As a result, several "bourgeois" parties were formed in late October and early November, the most important being the Progressive-Economic party based in St. Petersburg and the Trade-Industrial party in Moscow. In general both parties supported the October Manifesto, the Duma, and civil rights, while opposing disorder, the eight-hour day, government interference in relations between factory owners and workers, and low tariffs. While both parties favored limitations on the right to strike, the preservation of the unity of Russia, and encouragement of peasant land purchases and of the dissolution of the commune, they had minor differences over the national, workers', and agrarian questions. (See table, p. 265, for a comparison of party attitudes on the chief issues.) Neither party was very successful in establishing branches outside of their respective capitals, and their main effort, and what little success they had, was concentrated in St. Petersburg and Moscow, where they swelled their membership rolls by pressuring salaried employees of their own factories to join. In an effort to mount broader appeal, the Progressive-Economic party published a paper; but it never caught on and was closed in April after ninety-one issues. Recognizing that not only their aims and platforms but even their names reflected too closely their special and vested interests and were hardly conducive to winning over the mass of voters, both parties entered a united electoral committee under the aegis of the Octobrists, and in several places they formed electoral agreements or blocs with Octobrist candidates. Generally unsuccessful, the parties dissolved or merged with the Octobrists during 1906.

The only other significant party of the right center was the Party of Legal Order, which drew heavily on merchants and industrialists but also included a large number of bureaucrats and retired military and civil servants. It was distinguished from the more narrowly "bourgeois" parties by its stronger emphasis on the restoration of order and on Russian nationalism, on the one hand, and by a somewhat more progressive social and economic platform, including reforms for peasants and workers, on the other. It, however, was also unable to develop wide appeal, and it joined the united electoral committee under the Octobrists. It lasted until the end of 1907. The Party of Legal Order, together with the Octobrists, was probably the closest thing to a government party that existed at the national level, but there is no evidence that Witte or the government ever gave it any direct support.

The largest and most important party of the center was the Union of October 17, or the Octobrists.[20] This grew out of the desire of some industrialists for a more politically active and broadly based organization than the "bourgeois" parties and out of a split in the zemstvo-city opposition movement which divided the more conservative zemstvo constitutionalists from the more progressive and intelligentsia-oriented "liberationists." The latter group, which held a majority at the November Congress of Zemstvo and City Leaders, formed the core of the Kadet party, while the former, under D. N. Shipov, joined with a group of predominantly Moscow industrialists under A. I. Guchkov to found the Octobrists. The central committee of the party, which consisted of eleven bankers and industrialists, six landowners, and five intellectuals, probably accurately reflected the basic make-up of the party as a whole. It also attracted some middle and lower bourgeoisie and traders, some civil servants at various levels, some Old Believers, and some Russified Germans; but it was never a mass party and it included few peasants or workers.[21]

Though its greatest strength was in Moscow and the central-industrial region in general, the Octobrist party established some seventy-eight branches in thirty-four gubernias and two regions, and it contested the election in a wide number of districts. It also published some thirty papers in the provinces. It is significant that the peak period for the formation of Octobrist branches was in December and January, the height of the reaction against revolutionary excesses; and there are some indications that a number of sections and members of the Octobrists suffered a loss of interest, enthusiasm, and activity in the crucial weeks of February and March, when the voting was taking place. Party membership may have been as high as twenty thousand, but some of these recruits were undoubtedly subordinates and office workers of industrialists and bureaucrats in the party.

As its name suggests, the Union of October 17 stood for the basic premises of the October Manifesto but did not advocate going beyond them. It supported civil freedoms, the Duma as proposed, and general though not necessarily direct elections. While the Octobrists favored constitutional monarchy and a modernized and more efficient though still centralized state, they also savored tradition and saw no objection to the tsar retaining the title "autocrat." They espoused industrial expansion and the increase of Russian military power and of Russia's prestige in the world. While generally supporting the government, the attitude of the Octobrists toward the Witte cabinet fluctuated. In November, as peasant rebellions continued and the strike movement flared up again, the Octobrists criticized Witte for weakness and indecisiveness. Though opposing armed uprising and recognizing the necessity of putting it down, the Octobrists in January and February accused Witte of backsliding on the October Manifesto, of using excessive force in repressing the December risings, and of continuing it too long afterward. Above all they urged the speediest convocation of the Duma as the surest means of avoiding both reaction and revolution.

Since the Octobrists aspired to unite a number of groups, interests, and classes in a great moderate coalition, their program was deliberately vague and general. As a consequence, several issues proved to be particularly troublesome for them. On the workers' question the Octobrists were anxious to avoid adopting a social and economic platform of special pleading like that of the "bourgeois" parties since they hoped to enlist the support of some workers. At the same time they could not advocate too radical measures because of their own constituency and because they sought the cooperation of parties slightly to the right of them. At the first full congress of the party in February 1906, the right wing favored taking a qualified stand against strikes, but the left wing opposed this, and finally no platform on this question was adopted. Similar difficulties confronted the party in regard to the agrarian question. The majority of Octobrists endorsed equal rights for peasants, increased peasant purchases of land, and the breakup of the commune. But over the dilemma of compulsory alienation of private lands the party could not agree: if it were to favor this, the result would be a loss of gentry support and perhaps even the splitting of the party; yet if the Octobrists did not advocate alienation, they would have little opportunity to capture peasant votes. As a result, the party program ignored this question also. Analogous was the problem of how to handle the national question. Though favoring the unity of Russia, the Octobrists feared that too strong a stand would alienate the national minority electorate. Yet if they favored autonomy, they risked losing some of their own constituents, as well as allied parties to the right. Once more the solution was to omit this issue from the party program.

By flexible rules which provided that anyone might join the party simply by endorsing the October Manifesto and which enabled individuals and groups to work within the Union of October 17 while retaining membership in other parties, the Octobrists tried to win broad support and to form a wide political front. In terms of mass backing they had little success but, as we saw earlier, the Octobrists did work out a unified electoral committee with the Party of Legal Order, the Progressive-Economic party, the Trade-Industrial party, and some fifteen other splinter parties and organizations. In city districts this often led to coordinated campaigns and, occasionally, to jointly supported candidates, who seldom won, however. In a few rural uezds and gubernias the Octobrists formed election blocs with far rightist groups, but again to little avail.

Except for a few isolated instances the Octobrists did not cooperate with and usually struggled against the Kadets. The parties were opposed to each other on programmatic and psychological grounds. The Kadet platform was too radical for the Octobrists on such key issues as strengthening the role of the Duma, introducing the eight-hour day, and forcibly expropriating private lands for the benefit of the peasants. Moreover, the Kadet attitude was one of hostility and distrust toward the government and the whole tsarist system, while the Octobrists fundamentally believed in the monarchy and in working within the system and with its officials. Although the two parties agreed on such basic questions as civil freedoms and economic development of the country, the gap between them was perhaps even wider than it appeared on the political spectrum.

Slightly left of center but a bit to the right of the Kadets stood the small Party of Democratic Reform, which was grouped around the magazine *Vestnik Evropy* and which contained a number of able intellectuals and civil servants, such as Professor M. M. Kovalevskii and Prince S. D. Urusov. But the left center was overwhelmingly dominated by the Constitutional-Democratic (Kadet) party.[22] This party grew out of the liberal Union of Liberation and the opposition movement in general of the preceding few years and drew heavily on the progressive majority of the zemstvo-city duma congresses. First steps toward organizing the Kadets were taken in July 1905, and its founding congress was held in mid-October, at the height of the general strike. The core of the party was the liberal intelligentsia and professional classes of Russia, rural as well as urban; but more than any other party in the campaign it attracted members and support from a wide variety of groups and classes in Russia. It included enlightened gentry, progressive bourgeoisie of various levels, forward-looking civil servants, national minority leaders, and some peasants and workers, especially skilled workers. Its appeal was deliberately designed to be above class and national factionalism, and in this it largely succeeded.

Yet this created two deep-rooted and perplexing problems for the party, one of tactics, the other of program, which it never completely solved, either in 1905–06 or in its subsequent history to its demise in 1917. If the Kadets were indeed to be an all-class party uniting the nation in a movement of democratic reform, constitutionalism, and economic growth, what should be its attitude toward the government and more conservative parties on the right and toward the socialist and revolutionary parties on the left? Throughout much of its life the party was torn between the so-called opening to the left and an alliance with parties and groups to its right, a dilemma which has sparked much debate in both party and historical literature. In 1905–06 the party deliberately opted for leftist tactics, which helped carry it to a clear victory in the elections. This, however, made it almost impossible for the party to work with the government, with consequences for the subsequent decade of Russian history that will undoubtedly be disputed for years. In any case, it is clear that if the Kadets desperately wanted to win the elections to the First Duma, as they surely did, then they chose the right course for the 1905–06 campaign.

The programmatic problem was simply that to ensure broad support the Kadets had virtually to promise all things to all people; this inevitably led to vagueness or compromises in their program and prompted disputes between left and right factions as well as opposition charges of demagoguery and unscrupulousness. Yet above all else, the Kadets came to stand for opposition to the old order, for change, and for improvement in the lot of the people; and this was clearly what the voters of Russia wanted in the winter and spring of 1906. Their opponents were able to make little capital out of the inconsistencies and indistinctness of the Kadet program. Most voters apparently decided that the Kadet party was espousing what they most wanted, whatever that happened to be.

From the beginning observers of every hue acknowledged that the Kadets were the most numerous, energetic, and effective party in the campaign. They conducted extensive oral and written propaganda and published twenty-five newspapers. The Kadets also established their branches in almost every district and gubernia, including regions on Russia's borderlands and even in Central Asia and the Far East. The party worked hard to recruit members from all classes of society, waiving membership dues where necessary. Unfortunately, no precise figures, or even reliable estimates, exist on the total membership of the party; but it probably surpassed one hundred thousand.

Rodichev, one of the leading Kadets, neatly epitomized the party's attitude toward its program, declaring: "A program is not a dogma, and there can only be agreement with it in principle."[23] Nevertheless, the party's general aim was clear and appealing—"to satisfy by legal means the needs of all classes of society"—and the Kadet platform set forth a number of points designed to win over a wide electorate. After flirting earlier with advocacy of a republic for Russia, the Kadets decided at their second congress in January 1906, that Russia should become "a constitutional and parliamentary monarchy." This permitted them both to tell the peasants that the party supported the tsar and to encourage the democratic hopes of others. Moreover, following considerable wavering, the Kadets finally remained silent in their program on the question of convoking an all-Russian constituent assembly, which was a major demand of the left but which all parties to the right of the Kadets strongly opposed. This, in turn, allowed the Kadets to hint to more radical citizens that the party would not be adverse to turning the Duma into a constituent assembly and yet to assure the more moderate-minded that the Kadets supported the Duma as simply a representative legislative assembly. The Kadets strongly espoused a general electoral law according to the "four-tailed" formula (universal, equal, direct, and secret suffrage) and promised that this would be one of their first and most important legislative concerns in the Duma.

At the same time the Kadet position on the Duma itself shifted toward the right from October to April. Some Kadets had urged the boycotting of the Bulygin Duma, but after October 1905 all agreed that the party should participate in the Duma promised in the October Manifesto and that the role and power of the Duma needed to be greatly enlarged and protected. Yet while in October the party had suggested that "organic" (i.e., legislative) work in the Duma would be impossible until its members had succeeded in passing a general election law and either reelecting the Duma or reconstructing it, by April, with their plurality in the Duma assured, the majority of Kadets were supporting the desirability of undertaking constructive work in the existing Duma, even though its representativeness and powers were unsatisfactory. Moreover, in April 1906, Miliukov, the Kadet leader, urged that for the moment no attempt be made to change the legislative structure and system established in the tsar's decree of February 20 and in the Fundamental Laws (both to be discussed in chap. 9); this was indeed a far cry from the Kadet position six months earlier.

On the national question the Kadets adopted a compromise position but still one considerably more radical than that of their rightist opponents. While opposing a federation for Russia, they urged that each nationality be given the right to use its own language; and they advocated autonomy for Poland. For the workers the Kadets proposed various welfare benefits and favored introduction of the eight-hour day "where this is possible in accord with technical conditions," a clever hedge designed not to alienate their bourgeois supporters.

The agrarian question caused more debate and rancor in the party than any other issue. In general the Kadets advocated forcible expropriation of private lands, but the exact terms and conditions under which this would be applied and carried out provoked lively discussion among left, center, and right factions in the party. The platform finally adopted at the third party congress in April provided for a slightly qualified version of the general principle of compulsory alienation with compensation, but this did not prevent Kadet agitators from suggesting to the peasants a widespread distribution of land, perhaps as a gift.

The attitude of the Kadets toward the government was hostile and suspicious. They criticized the Witte program as inadequate and limited, and urged a genuinely democratic constitution for Russia. They were quick to discover signs that the government was reneging on its October promises and paraded these as evidence that the government did not really trust the people and was not truly interested in reform. The Kadets deplored the excessive measures used to quell the December risings and the continuation of repressive policies afterward. At the same time the party's stance toward the revolutionary movement was a delicate one, for it was committed to using only legal, nonviolent means and it opposed armed rebellion. Thus, the party encouraged protests and other peaceful manifestations of the revolutionary movement, including even political strikes, but these had to stop short of armed or violent opposition. The Kadets opposed boycotting the Duma, a tactic some leftists favored, and urged legal, parliamentary struggle against the government. Nevertheless, by taking over some parts of the radicals' program and by depicting themselves as champions and defenders of the people's needs and rights against the government, the Kadets hoped to win numerous leftist votes. As part of this tactic and recognizing that the words "constitutional" and "democratic" in the party's name were foreign and meant little to the average voter, the Kadets changed their name during the campaign to the Party of the People's Freedom, with reportedly good results.

Just to the left of the Kadets were two small nonsocialist parties, the Radical-Democratic party and the Party of Free Thinkers, but these had little impact on the elections. The first was dissolved in early 1906, and the second in 1907.[24] Socialist parties, chiefly the Socialist Revolutionaries and the Social Democrats, small in numbers but extreme in program, dominated the left. Yet although the Kadet party considered them its main rival, their influence in the elections was limited, primarily because substantial elements in both socialist parties boycotted the elections and also because the electoral system disenfranchised groups (landless peasants, agricultural laborers, workers in small factories) from which they might have drawn the most support.

Since a good deal has been written about the program and tactics of the socialists in 1905–06, only a brief review will be given here.[25] The Socialist Revolutionaries, at that time still a rather inchoate peasant socialist and terrorist organization, generally favored boycotting the elections and succeeded in getting the Peasants' Union, over which the Socialist Revolutionaries were exercising growing influence, to endorse the boycott at its second congress in early November 1905. But the Socialist-Revolutionary party and the Peasants' Union were both rather loose and undisciplined groups, and many branches and individual members of both did not observe the boycott and participated in the elections. In any case, the influence of the Socialist Revolutionaries as a party, whatever the spread of their ideas, was not extensive in rural Russia in this period; and it is doubtful that their decision to boycott the elections had much effect on the peasants except in a few scattered districts.

The Social Democrats were better organized, but, torn by factional strife, they adopted several different tactics toward the elections. A number of units and individuals of the Menshevik wing of the party, though denying the legality of the Duma, participated fully in the elections as the best means, particularly after suppression of the December risings, of continuing active struggle against the government and for an eventual revolution. In their view, the Social Democrats should not sit idly by but should work with and lead the masses in the campaign, not to validate the Duma, but to gird the workers for the next round of armed insurrection against the government. Moreover, once in the Duma, socialist deputies could use it as a forum for revolutionary agitation and propaganda. Other Mensheviks favored participating only in the preliminary stages of the voting; they would then not elect deputies to the Duma but would attempt to turn the electoral assemblies of workers and of other groups into revolutionary organs of self-government. Finally a few Mensheviks encouraged those disenfranchised to elect representatives on their own who would form a people's Duma or a workers' congress. In fact, a number of Menshevik branches participated fully in the elections and succeeded in send-ing a handful of Menshevik deputies to the Duma, particularly from the Caucasus.

The Bolsheviks led by Lenin strongly urged a full boycott of the elections, a tactic which Lenin later called "a slight and easily corrected mistake." The Bolsheviks argued that the Duma was a treacherous fraud, an attempt to deceive the people with "constitu-tional illusions" and to divert them from their true goal—the over-throw of the system by armed struggle. At the same time, the Bolsheviks maintained that the electoral system and the govern-ment's policies of repression prevented any free and genuine ex-pression of the people's will or any truly representative Duma. If, they argued, the party entered the election lists, it would simply be playing into the hands of the police, who would close meetings and newspapers and arrest socialist candidates. (The Mensheviks retorted that to avoid a scandal over the freedom of the elections the government would not take such measures.) Nevertheless, the Bolsheviks urged their agitators to frequent electoral meetings of other parties in order to use them as an arena for spreading revo-lutionary propaganda and for organizing the masses. The Bolshevik attitude toward the Kadets was summed up in a resolution of the Fifth Social Democratic Congress, which recommended in part that

the Social Democrats should use their [the Kadets'] activity in the interests of the political education of the people, counterposing to their lying-democratic phraseology the consistent democratism of the proletariat, unmasking the constitutional illusions they spread, and steadfastly struggling against their hegemony over the democratic petty bourgeoisie.[26]

Those socialists who contested the election ran on an extreme platform. Though favoring civil freedoms, they opposed the Duma as illegal and unrepresentative and called for formation of a popular constituent assembly either through a general electoral law or by armed struggle against the government. The Socialist Revolutionaries urged socialization of the land but not of factories, while the Social Democrats espoused socialization of industry and nationalization of the land (or "municipalization," in the Menshe-viks' phrase). All urged equal rights for peasants and extended

A Comparison of the Attitudes of the Parties on the Chief Issues in the Elections

	SOCIALISTS	KADETS	OCTOBRISTS	"BOURGEOIS" PARTIES	FAR RIGHT
1. Monarchy:	No, a republic	Yes, but parliamentary and constitutional	Yes, but constitutional and headed by autocrat	Yes, but constitutional	Yes, unlimited
2. Constituent Assembly:	Yes, by vote or armed struggle	(silence)	No	No	No
3. General Electoral Law:	Yes, universal, equal, direct, secret	Yes, universal, equal, direct, secret	Yes, but indirect	Yes, but unequal	No, voting by *soslovie*
4. The Duma:	No, boycott (some for using it as a revolutionary forum)	Yes, but broaden its role	Yes, as is	Yes, as is	Yes, but limit it to a consultative body
5. Civil Freedoms:	Yes	Yes	Yes	Yes	Yes, within legal limits
6. Land:	Socialization or nationalization	Forced alienation with compensation	(silence)	Peasant land purchases and dissolution of commune; private property inviolable	Peasant land purchases only; private property inviolable
7. Workers:	8-hour day, etc. SD's for socialization	8-hour day, right to strike, benefits	(silence)	Restrict right to strike, no government interference	Strict controls
8. National Minorities:	Greater autonomy	Use own language, autonomy for Poland	(silence)	Unitary Russia	Unitary Russia, with Russian people dominant
9. Attitude toward Witte Cabinet:	Violent opposition	Strongly opposed, but also against armed rebellion	Generally support, sometimes critical	Support	Critical as weak and reformist

privileges and benefits for workers and for national minorities. The socialists also espoused creation of a people's militia and separation of church and state. But the Kadets had stolen some of their ammunition, and their impact on the elections was relatively slight.

The Electoral Campaign

ALTHOUGH MOST PARTIES had been formed in the fall, the campaign for the elections did not really get underway until after December, when the new electoral law was announced and armed uprisings in a number of cities were put down. The reaction against the revolutionary movement and the more conservative mood of the country in January stimulated a spate of activity and recruitment on the part of the Octobrists, who then experienced a fall-off of interest and a decline in their fortunes in February and March. Several contemporary observers noted that if the elections had been held in January, the Duma would have been considerably more conservative than it was. Suppression of the December risings was also a turning point for the Kadets, but for two different reasons. Shortly after its formation in October, the party had to endure a period of quiescence, the so-called dead season, first while everyone reveled in their newly won freedoms and waited for Witte to work miracles, and then, through the upsurge of the revolutionary movement in November and the December rebellions, which forced it into non-activity and relative silence since though the Kadets opposed armed insurrection, they were loath to criticize the revolutionaries openly for fear of alienating potential allies on the left. But once the radicals had made their desperate gambit and lost, leadership of the opposition movement passed readily into the hands of the Kadets. After December, amidst a population weary of revolution but still hostile to the government, they could pursue their electoral goals with confidence and at an increasing tempo. Moreover, as the weeks passed and the repressive stance of the government continued while the memory of revolutionary excesses faded from the public mind, the Kadets were able to capitalize not only on the weakness and disorganization of the radicals but on growing resentment against the government's policies. They could present themselves both as the chief exponent of the welfare of the people and the interests of the country and as a sincere ally of the left in its struggle against the government, a tactic which had considerable success.

For all parties the primary instruments of electioneering were public meetings and the distribution of newspapers and leaflets.[27] In both techniques the Kadets were the most energetic and active, followed by the Octobrists; but almost every party had at least one newspaper in St. Petersburg or in Moscow, held several meetings, and distributed some brochures. The Kadets, commanding the services of "the flower of the Russian intelligentsia," had the best orators and writers, and their agitation and propaganda were clearly the most effective. According to their opponents and some government officials, Kadet tactics were sometimes unscrupulous, ranging from the infiltration of other parties for disruptive and recruitment purposes to the inducement of peasant voters by offering them feasts and parties. The Kadets were widely accused of making extravagant and sometimes even contradictory promises, particularly regarding the eight-hour day for workers and land for the peasants, and of deliberately cloaking their true colors, as when they posed as supporters of the tsar before the peasants. Nevertheless, although the Kadets established a special central commission to coordinate their campaign among the workers and although they made particular efforts in a number of provinces to reach the peasants, the evidence indicates that Kadet success with these groups was limited and spotty. In some factories and villages they were shut out entirely by extreme influences from either the right or left, and in a number of districts the workers and peasants either did not understand the Kadets' program or wanted to go considerably beyond it. Despite this, some peasant and worker Duma deputies were Kadets or Kadet-oriented. Among the national minorities the Kadet campaign was quite successful, and they elected a number of their candidates from the non-Russian regions of the empire.

At times the tactics of the Kadets' opponents were also quite vigorous. In a few districts the Octobrists bought up whole issues of Kadet newspapers, and during the polling rightist agitators tore down Kadet banners and placards and seized Kadet pamphlets and election lists. In Mogilev and Chernigov extreme rightists threatened Jews with pogroms if the latter supported moderate or leftist candidates. Socialist hecklers disrupted Kadet meetings, as we shall shortly see, and rightist orators did not shrink from bitter personal attacks on Kadet candidates. Yet the other parties (except the socialists) had even less success than the Kadets among peasants and workers, and in general they were unable to cope with Kadet promises and activity. The platform and propaganda of the socialists were too radical for most voters, while the appeals of the Octobrists and the rightists were too conservative, heavy handed, and patronizing. For example, a leaflet of the Trade-Industrial party addressed to the peasants declared: "Now the Russian peasantry should not make a noise for nothing, drawing upon themselves the just punishment of the law for beatings, pillage, and burnings, but ought, praying to God, agree about whom to elect to the Duma."[28] Appeals to patriotism, to defend law and order, and to heed the tsar's word fell on deaf ears, since the mood of the masses was clearly against the government and for change. As one contemporary observer summed it up:

> It was very indicative of the general situation that during the elections the right [wing parties] was not heard. They were cast aside, washed away by the flood. In the provinces the defenders of unlimited autocracy soon rallied, organized demonstrations, pogroms, printed illiterate pamphlets and hand-outs, sent telegrams to the Tsar and the government. But all this was clumsy and weak, and it did not correspond at all to the strengths of that historic authority which the extreme right dreamed of preserving in all its autocratic fullness.[29]

In any case, Kadet speakers, ideas, and literature dominated the campaign.

The Kadets were also the best organized party. They had more branches than anyone else and better direction and leadership. They worked hard to register voters, to organize meetings at which they advanced their own program and attacked the platforms of others, and to present their candidates to the voters at meetings or personally. The best Kadet orators were made available to party branches that needed help, and the Kadets attracted the support and aid of students and young people, who were used for "doorbell ringing" and distributing literature outside meetings and polling places. The Kadets also enlisted the services of the town and rural intelligentsia, particularly members of zemstvo administrations and of their staffs, the so-called third element. During the voting the Kadets distributed lists with the names of Kadet candidates already printed in (which was not illegal but provoked much criticism). Finally, the Kadets cleverly concentrated much of their electioneering not on the voters at the lowest levels but on the delegates and electors to the higher electoral assemblies. They tried particularly to win over peasant electors, who were generally non-party, or to make election agreements with them, often with considerable success.

Unfortunately, there is practically no evidence on the financing of the campaign. Since the major parties printed and distributed brochures and leaflets in millions of copies and supported a number of branches, it is evident that they had substantial sums available, probably in the millions of rubles. This apparently came primarily from wealthy benefactors and supporters since party dues were low and were often waived.

The question of the freedom of the electoral campaign and of the elections themselves has been a rather murky one in historical literature. Some Soviet historians have hinted at or alleged widespread government interference in the electioneering and voting, while some Western writers have simply assumed that, given the situation at the time, there must have been some government pressure. In fact, as we have already seen, the official policy and action of the central government was not to interfere and to do everything possible to protect free choice. At the same time it must be recognized that the atmosphere of a revolutionary situation controlled but not yet mastered and the general policy of repression pursued by the government inevitably produced some constraints on the parties and on the voters. Moreover, there were clearly some instances of government interference or pressure at the local level. Yet these were relatively few in number for a country with a patriarchal and authoritarian tradition, the majority of whose citizens had only forty-five years earlier been emancipated from what amounted to slavery and which was essaying the first national elections in its history. In short, we have concluded that the elections were remarkably free and provided the most accurate reflection of the people's will possible at the time.

In analyzing the fairness of the elections two basic features of the contemporary Russian scene must be borne in mind. First, the bulk of peasant (and probably worker) voters were illiterate and therefore more easily subject to pressure and intimidation. Many peasants certainly had only the haziest notion what the elections were all about. One peasant, asked for whom he was going to vote, replied: "Yes, as God wills, the same Tsar, now and as in the past." Another, returning to his village quite drunk after attending an electoral assembly, was asked what had happened. "They gave us vodka, asked us if we all agreed, and then we came home," he replied with literal truthfulness but without any idea of who had been elected. Second, it must be remembered that all or parts of almost half the provinces of Russia were at this time under martial law or in states of "strengthened" or "extraordinary security," and some had been in this condition for six months or more. While there is almost no evidence that the governors used the broad powers these provisions gave them to interfere directly, it is evident that at least electioneering, if not voting, was necessarily circumscribed in the regions in this situation, as the Sol'sky commission had foreseen some months earlier.

The only direct ways in which the government intervened in the electoral campaign were by arresting "undesirables" and by prohibiting or closing meetings, yet even these steps were infrequent and had minimal effects. Although, as we saw in chapter five, Durnovo had several tens of thousands of citizens arrested in the winter of 1906, such arrests affected less than one percent of all electors (at the last stage of the elections) and Duma deputies. In fact, the reports from the gubernias list more instances of delegates, electors, and deputies being chosen who were or had been in detention or exile than of such people being barred from the elections. (People in prison, under prosecution, or with criminal records were, of course, disenfranchised by the electoral law, but in a few cases local authorities permitted particularly popular people in these categories to be candidates in the elections.) Moreover, very few instances were uncovered in which candidates or voters had been removed from the lists on technicalities or because of administrative pressure, and there were suprisingly few complaints to the electoral commissions on this (or for that matter, any other) score. The most famous example of a person barred on a technicality from running or voting, Paul Miliukov, the leader of the Kadets, was permitted, as were others in the same situation, to attend and address meetings and to participate fully in party work.

The holding of meetings confronted the government with a dilemma, as we have already seen in chapter five and earlier in this chapter. The Sol'sky commission had recognized in August 1905 the importance of free meetings to the elections, and the October Manifesto had promised the right of assembly. Yet some in the government, and particularly Durnovo, feared that meetings would become vehicles for revolutionary agitation and propaganda or staging points for revolutionary action. Moreover, in the provinces the local authorities had a good deal of discretion concerning the holding of meetings, and it is evident that in some areas few electoral meetings were permitted and others were closed. Yet the government's own reports on the elections clearly show that on balance many more meetings were held than were prohibited or terminated.

In St. Petersburg the question of meetings was particularly delicate, not only because it was the capital and a prime center for agitation but also because some of the best orators were concentrated there. In early February after several large meetings called by the Kadets had been interrupted by socialist hecklers and had turned into lively debates between the Kadet speakers and the hecklers, who called from the floor for boycotting the Duma and for armed struggle against the government, the mayor of St. Petersburg, supported by the police and Durnovo, forbade further Kadet meetings.[30] The Kadets protested arguing that

> such meetings, which give a chance to the representatives of the extreme parties openly to express their views, are very useful because the radicals' extreme ideas are countered by the calm and intelligent opposition of the Kadet speakers and such disputes weaken the force and influence of the revolutionary elements, who suffer an ideological defeat in the meetings; therefore it would seem the government itself, in its own interests, ought to encourage such meetings.

This shrewd argument did not convince the authorities, however, who concluded:

> In fact, the "defeats in debate" are in most cases suffered by the Kadet orators . . . partly because of the bigger impression on the crowd the straight-forward and inflammatory tone of the revolutionaries' speeches makes. . . . The rebuttals of the Kadets are usually weak and do not seriously influence either their own adherents or the whole audience who greets the fiery speeches of the extreme orators with applause.[31]

The Kadets, backed by a resolution of the St. Petersburg city duma, then carried their complaint to Witte. The latter took the matter up with the Council of Ministers and reported to the Kadets that while the mayor was within his rights to close any meeting that he felt was dangerous to public order and security, the Council of Ministers, "recognizing the necessity of minimal interference with any kind of meeting which does not have illegal aims, had called the attention of the mayor to the desirability of permitting meetings of the Kadet party" if they were requested by trustworthy people who would take the responsibility for carefully supervising them.[32] From later press and police reports it is clear that the Kadets continued to hold meetings and to be harassed as much by the socialists as by the police. In any case, this *contretemps* over meetings in St. Petersburg apparently affected the Kadets little since they won all the Duma seats from the capital. Moreover, Witte continued to support their right to meet, advising the Kadet central committee in early April that he had ordered the governor of Nizhnii Novgorod, who had forbidden a Kadet meeting, to reverse that decision and to allow the planned Kadet rally.

Even at the local level instances of direct government interference in the elections were rare. In a few gubernias local authorities encouraged subordinates to join the Octobrists or rightist parties, to attend their meetings, and to distribute their literature; and in Orlov the gubernia administration openly patronized and assisted a local conservative party formed under its tutelage, while preventing the printing and distribution of Kadet literature. But in many more gubernias the complaint was that the government did nothing, and that local civil servants refused to assist the moderates and rightists because they believed this was incompatible with their position or because they feared criticism from the Kadets. The only place where any notable number of cases of direct governmental interference or pressure was reported was at the village and volost level. This most often took the form of the peasants electing the village elder or some other official as their representative or delegate. In one instance a local official insisted upon his own candidacy, and would not let the assembly disperse until he had been elected. In a few villages local police or *zemskie nachal'-niki* illegally attended the polling and told the peasants how to vote.[33] Yet there are almost as many examples of peasants rebelling against local leaders and authorities, as well as against priests. In several villages and volosts peasants tore up the prepared voter lists and substituted their own, refused to select candidates suggested by the authorities, broke up the meetings unless police and officials withdrew, or declined to participate in the balloting together with priests. In one remarkable instance, in a volost in Kursk, the peasants, "suspecting the *starshina* of pressuring the balloting, ate all the ballot balls, pretending they were nuts, and then left the meeting without finishing the voting."[34] Occasionally peasants refused to vote, demanding the right to elect their deputies directly to the Duma, and in quite a few instances peasants refused to vote by secret ballot, insisting instead upon open voting by voice in accordance with their long-standing custom in village assemblies.

After the elections were over, Durnovo made a clumsy attempt to influence the peasant deputies selected. On the proposal of a rightist deputy, Colonel Egorin, the Ministry of Interior provided a special residence in St. Petersburg where it encouraged peasant deputies coming from the provinces to stay and where they were to be "educated" by Egorin and others. The latter attempted some heavy-handed indoctrination, but when news of the affair reached the press, the whole scheme collapsed.[35]

Results of the Elections

Despite the substantial politicization of Russia the revolution had produced, the vigor of the electoral campaign, and the considerable interest the promise of the Duma aroused, voter participation in the elections was quite low, probably falling somewhere between thirty and forty percent of those eligible to vote.[36] Since there were wide fluctuations in the voting patterns in various provinces and a number of exceptions, the following generalizations can be only tentative and suggestive. It does seem, however, that the poorest turnout of voters was, as one might expect, in the countryside. Village and volost assemblies usually met with less than half of those eligible to vote present, and often with many fewer. At least as poor, if not a worse, record was compiled by those voting in the preliminary assemblies of small landowners, which frequently convened with as few as five to ten percent of their authorized strength in attendance. In a number of instances complaints were lodged that this was because the voters eligible at this level and curia had not been notified of the meeting and of their right to vote. This was probably not deliberate disenfranchisement and is understandable when one recalls that many in this group had been added to the electoral rolls only by the law of December 11 and had been registered by zemstvo administrations on the basis of existing records, not through personal contact. Moreover, only a few weeks intervened between the completion of additional registration and the holding of preliminary assemblies of landowners in late February and early March. Finally, many peasant holders of private land probably did not realize they were eligible to vote as small-holders. In general, the poor rural turnout can probably be explained by the traditional passivity of Russia's agricultural population, rather than by political factors. A contributing problem may have been the season, which in some areas of Russia made travel difficult. Except in a few cases where absenteeism was so great as to make it impossible to hold elections, village, volost, and small-landowner assemblies voted for delegates to the next stage of the electoral system, although in several instances the few peasants present ended up by electing themselves as the winning candidates. As a result, attendance at the uezd or penultimate level of the elections was usually very high, averaging ninety percent or more.

More difficult to explain is the small number of large landowners attending many uezd assemblies of small and large landholders. For example, in one uezd of Vologda province only nine of twenty-six large landowners attended the electoral assembly. Parties of the right, and even some government officials, strongly criticized this failure of the Russian gentry, but it seems likely that absentee ownership and a general spirit of *Oblomovism* were the causes, as much as any dereliction of political duty. In many uezd assemblies of landowners and even in gubernia electoral assemblies, peasant owners or electors took an uncompromisingly hostile attitude toward the large landowners, at times much to the latter's surprise.

A technical problem which the government had not foreseen was that peasants in volost and uezd assemblies, coming from different villages, usually did not know each other. Since no provision had been made for preelectoral, get-acquainted meetings (and in a few cases where people tried to arrange them, the authorities prohibited them), peasant representatives and delegates often had no idea for whom to vote, particularly since at that level most people were non-party. Consequently, in a number of assemblies only a few of the authorized electors were chosen, or after one or two better-known individuals had been elected, the rest of the seats were filled by lot.

Voter participation in cities and towns was very irregular and spotty. For reasons that are unclear, some provincial towns turned out as little as ten to twenty-five percent of those eligible, while in others sixty to seventy percent voted. The average was apparently around fifty percent. The range in the larger cities was not quite as great, but there were still wide variations in participation. As with the curia of small landowners, the addition of many town and city dwellers to the electorate by the law of December 11 and their late registration in January and early February may be a partial explanation, yet one would suppose that with the better communication and the better organization of parties in the urban environment most voters would have learned of their new suffrage rights.

In the last curia, that of the workers, it is almost impossible to generalize either about the general level of participation of voters or about the effectiveness of the boycott espoused by some Socialist Revolutionaries and Social Democrats. For example, in Briansk in one large factory of almost ten thousand workers the boycott, under Socialist-Revolutionary instigation, was so effective that no elections were held, yet in other factories in the same city almost full participation of worker voters was reported. Soviet historians generally claim that forty-nine percent of the factories in St. Petersburg boycotted, twenty-three percent in Moscow, and up to seventy percent in some other cities; yet in almost the same breath they admit the boycott was not widely effective and failed to disrupt the workers' elections to the Duma.[37] Whatever the situation in individual factories, it is clear that almost all assemblies of workers' delegates were held and sent their electors to the gubernia electoral assemblies. In St. Petersburg and Moscow, twenty of the one hundred and eighty electors in the city assembly were workers, but in Moscow no workers' deputies were elected to the Duma.

In the various electoral assemblies beyond the first stage of voting some lively political struggles took place. Unfortunately insufficient data exist to analyze fully the composition of peasant delegates and electors at the uezd and gubernia level, but the scattered information available suggests they were a mixed and probably fairly representative lot. As one might expect, there was a preponderance of prosperous peasants (*kulaks*), rural traders and artisans, village and volost officials, and rural intelligentsia (scribes, teachers, agronomists, etc.) but few priests. Nevertheless, there was also a considerable number of poor peasants and those with little land, who generally had radical views. Underrepresented was the average or middle peasant. Most of the peasant delegates and electors were non-party, a few were Kadet- or socialist-oriented. With a few exceptions the peasants, both in the gubernia assemblies and in the uezd assemblies of landowners, where those who held private land participated, proved to be uncompromisingly hostile to the gentry in particular and to the rightist parties in general. They refused to support landlord candidates, advancing the slogan "not to elect the lord, but to choose from our own midst." Primarily this was because they believed only peasants, or those who endorsed the peasant demand for land, could adequately represent their interests in the Duma. Nevertheless, it was reported from several gubernias that some peasants were eager to go to the Duma because they had heard that deputies would be paid ten rubles a day.

Some uezd assemblies of landowners were dominated by small holders because of the weighting of the representation or because few large landowners showed up. As a result, almost a third of the landowners' electors (based on forty-five gubernias) were small owners, who were sometimes well-to-do peasants but who often had quite radical views. In other uezd landowner assemblies a three-way fight among gentry, clerical holders of church lands, and small owners developed. In a few cases this resulted in a stalemate, and the assembly was able to choose only one or two of the electors allotted to it. In most instances the large landholders prevailed, and about fifty-five percent of the landowners' electors were nobles. On occasion party struggles also took place at this level, with the Kadets generally supporting the small holders and peasants, and the Octobrists and right parties the large landowners. Of those landowner electors whose political affiliation was known a slight majority were Octobrists and rightists, but apparently most were non-party.[38]

As noted earlier, the Kadets made a vigorous effort to win over peasant electors to the gubernia assemblies, and it is clear that in general extensive electioneering and the bitterest political fights occurred at this level. The composition of the some 6,700 gubernia electors as a group was approximately as follows:

Peasants:	42%	Far left:	5.7%
Landowners:	32%	Kadets:	19.7%
City dwellers:	23%	Octobrists and rightists:	13.1%
Workers:	3%	Non-party or unknown:	61.5%
Total	100%	Total	100.0%

But even more important was the allocation of these electors among the fifty-one gubernias of European Russia. In only four gubernias did the landowner and city electors combined have a majority, while in over one-half, or twenty-seven gubernias, the peasants were in a majority—in thirteen by the allocation of electors under the electoral law, and in fourteen by combining their electors with small landholder or Cossack electors. Thus, in addition to the fifty-one deputies the law permitted them to elect separately, the peasants could optimally have elected another one hundred and eighty-four deputies, thus giving them a near majority in the Duma. But the peasant electors were neither united nor sophisticated enough to vote as a bloc, and the key to the elections then became whether the Kadets, as the largest party among the other electors, could win sufficient peasant support to carry them to victory. In fact, the Kadet triumph was not as easy as it has sometimes been depicted.

In three gubernias in which the peasants commanded a majority, only peasants or radicals were elected to the Duma. In one, Podolsk, this was accomplished only after a bitter struggle among the peasants themselves, with three-quarters of the assembly submitting themselves as candidates for the Duma. In Tambov, the election, controlled entirely by the peasants, was so obviously unfair and unpolitical that the parties protested and the election was subsequently voided, with the deputies being forced to withdraw from the Duma several weeks after it had started. In five other peasant-dominated gubernias, non-peasants were able to capture a quarter of the Duma seats, and in seventeen others almost half the deputies were not peasants. At the same time the peasants received a few extra seats in the gubernias where their electors did not have a majority. In the remaining twenty-six gubernias (including the area of the Don Cossacks) the following were elected to the Duma: forty-six landowners, forty peasants (twenty-six by law), nineteen intelligentsia, fifteen merchants and industrialists, eleven workers, seven employees and civil servants, five Orthodox and Catholic clergy, and four Cossacks. In all, the peasants won about one hundred and eighty seats; about fifty of these deputies were Ka-

[277

dets, with twenty or so belonging to the Octobrists or to rightist parties. The balance entered the leftist Toiling Group or were non-party.

The contest for peasant votes and support in the gubernia assemblies was hard-fought. In three provinces the Kadets and Octobrists even tried to join forces against the peasant majority, but these agreements either collapsed or were unsucessful. In Orlov under pressure from the marshal of nobility, M. A. Stakhovich, who was an Octobrist, the peasants rejected the Kadets and elected seven of their own members—and Stakhovich. In Riazan the Octobrists hinted that peasants might eventually receive land free because of an overpayment of redemption dues in the past; in this way they split the peasant vote and managed to get four Octobrists elected. But in most other provinces where inroads were made against the peasants, it was the Kadets who won. For example, in Poltava, where peasant and Cossack electors held a majority, six Kadet and six peasant and Cossack deputies were chosen. And in gubernias where the peasants did not have a majority, the Kadets, often with peasant support, usually captured a substantial share of the seats.

In this the Kadets were greatly assisted by their triumph in the town elections, where they won 38.5 percent of the electors as against 19.5 percent for the Octobrists and rightists. In addition, the Kadets swept the large city vote, winning 63 percent of the electors (as against 27 percent for the Octobrists and rightists) and almost 80 percent of the seats. The Kadets also benefited in a number of places in European Russia from the support of, or blocs with, national minority groups and candidates. Finally, in non-Russian areas the Kadets did well: In Poland they won four seats (the remaining twenty-nine going to the Polish National Democrats); in Kazakhstan and Eastern Siberia, six of ten seats; and in other scattered Asian districts, one-third of the deputies. It is important to note, however, that many Kadet victories in all curiae were by narrow margins.

The final outcome of the elections to the First Duma is shown in the table on p. 279.[39] Of 524 authorized deputies, 436 were elected before the opening session on April 27; because of late elections in the Caucasus and elsewhere, this figure grew to 448 by the end of May and to 499 by July 9, 1906, when the Duma was dissolved, with an average membership of about 480.

PARTIES IN THE FIRST RUSSIAN DUMA

May 1*		
Left	47 (10.5%)	
Progressists	36 (8.0%)	} 58.5%
Kadets	182 (40.0%)	
Democratic Reform	4 (1.0%)	
Octobrists	26 (6.0%)	} 9.5%
Trade-Industrial	2 (0.5%)	
Rights	8 (2.0%)	
National parties	60 (13.5%)	
Non-party	83 (18.5%)	
	448 deputies	

May 15**		
Toiling Group	107 (24.0%)	
Moderate progressives	2 (0.5%)	} 58.5%
Kadets	153 (34.0%)	
Democratic Reform	4 (1.0%)	
Octobrists	13 (3.0%)	
Trade-Industrial	1 (0.5%)	
Autonomists	63 (14.0%)	
Non-party	105 (23.0%)	
	448 deputies	

June 26***		
Toilers (Trudoviki)	94 (19.5%)	
Social Democrats	17 (3.5%)	} 61.0%
Kadets	184 (38.0%)	
Democratic Reform	6 (1.5%)	
Octobrists	32 (6.5%)	} 9.5%
Rights	7 (1.5%)	
Autonomists	44 (9.0%)	
Non-party	100 (20.5%)	
	484 deputies	

* S. M. Sidel'nikov, *Obrazovanie i deiatel'nost' pervoi Gosudarstvennoi dumy* [The formation and activity of the First State Duma] (Moscow 1962), 192.

** Based on a compilation in a Kadet collection of articles on the Duma, cited in ibid.

*** Based on ibid., 194 and 196, and on Alfred Levin, *The Second Duma*. (New Haven: 1940; 2nd ed., Hamden, Connecticut: 1966), 67.

As the Duma opened, a loose left amalgam, the Toiling Group, was formed under the leadership of several radical deputies who were close to the Socialist Revolutionaries. The majority of this faction later became the Trudoviki (Toilers), which included both peasants and workers. The Social Democrats, strengthened by Menshevik deputies from the Caucasus, eventually formed a separate faction of seventeen deputies (six were Bolsheviks). The Kadets lost some members both to the Toiling Group and into the non-party ranks, but these were largely compensated for by newly elected Kadet deputies from non-Russian areas and by some recruits from the left and the non-party groups. Thus, they about maintained their absolute numbers, though losing a little ground relatively.

The social composition of the Duma is shown in the table below:[40]

SOCIAL COMPOSITION OF THE FIRST DUMA*

	Nobles	*Peasants and Cossacks*	*Merchants*	*Others*	*Total*	
Large and middle holders of land and property:	105	1	14	8	128	143
Industrialists:	8	2	3	2	15	
Traders:	—	27	6	—	33	
Intelligentsia and professional classes:	51	39	11	7	106	151
Employees (primarily state service):	13	27	2	3	45	
Clergy:	3	6	1	7	17	
Agriculturalists:	—	125	—	2	127	152
Workers:	—	18	3	4	25	
	180	245	40	33	498	

* Modified from table in Sidel'nikov, 190. One of the 499 deputies elected resigned. See also the roughly proportionate breakdown of 160 deputies from 28 gubernias in TsGIAL, Fund 1276, op. 2, d. 8.

If one divides the traders and clergy equally among the other functional groups, as was probably the case, then it is clear that holders and managers of property (bourgeoisie, if one prefers), "brain" workers (intelligentsia and employees), and toilers (peasants and workers) each composed almost exactly one-third of the deputies. Though this was certainly not proportionate to their numbers in the population, it was not a bad equivalent of their political activity and weight in the country under relatively free conditions.

The Duma deputies were very young, only fifteen percent being over fifty, and forty-three percent under forty, which accorded with the age structure of the country but not of its governance and economic and social management. Duma deputies were clearly better educated than the average man, with some forty-two percent having a higher education, about the same number a primary education, and the rest with a secondary education (plus a few illiterates). Some eighty to eighty-five percent of the deputies were Orthodox, the rest scattered among Catholic, Jewish, Muslim, and Lutheran affiliations.[41]

The elections to the State Council were a much more restricted affair (see chap. 9) and, as might be expected, returned far more conservative representatives. The majority were large landowners; there were also some civil servants and industrialists (eight of whom were members of the central council of the Congress of Representatives of Trade and Industry). Of the ninety-eight members elected, twenty-eight were Octobrists and eleven were Kadets; there were a few scattered rightists, and the remainder were nonparty.[42]

As the discussion of the electoral campaign earlier in this chapter adumbrated, there is little mystery surrounding the ability of the Kadets to win a plurality in the Duma elections, though the margin of victory surprised the party's own leaders, such as Miliukov and Maklakov, and many government officials, including Witte, who had hoped against hope, pinning their faith on the peasantry, for a more conservative Duma. Contemporary observers, as well as subsequent writers, explained Kadet success primarily on three grounds: their energy, organization, and leadership; the weakness and inertness of their opponents (in part, the other side of the coin); and the antigovernment mood of the country as a whole. Rightists advanced a few other reasons, such as the breadth and weighting of the electoral system of December 11 and the general naiveté of the population, but almost everyone, from monarchist to socialist, agreed that the Kadets were the best organized and most popular party, that they promised what most people wanted, and that what opposition they encountered was feeble.

On March 29, when the extent of the Kadet plurality was already becoming clear, Durnovo addressed a circular to all governors asking for an analysis of the reasons for the success of the "extreme parties" (i.e., the Kadets) in the elections. With due allowance for bureaucratic self-interest and political conservatism on the part of the governors, the following tabulation of the replies from twenty-four gubernias is of considerable interest:[43]

A factor in Kadet success?	Yes	No
1. The electoral system	10	3
2. Organization, unity, and leadership	5	—
3. Energy and activity (meetings and agitation)	12	—
4. The press	8	—
5. Program and promises	13	—
6. Unscrupulous methods	10	—
7. Electoral illegalities	—	16
8. Disunity and inertness of opponents	19	—
9. Effects of government repression	17	6

Other factors noted by some governors were the general political immaturity and ignorance of the electorate, zemstvo support for the Kadets, Kadet success in exploiting local grievances, and Kadet efforts to win over electors, especially peasants; but none of these was mentioned more than a few times.

We have already commented, in an earlier section, on the vigor and excellent organization of the Kadet campaign, which produced widespread propagation of Kadet ideas orally and by the printed word in meetings and in literature of various kinds. Without denying the significance of this factor, it is also apparent that the Kadets capitalized on the temper of the times. This mood had two facets, a positive and a negative side. To most voters the Kadets represented a "new deal," "a new frontier," a hopeful future for Russia—and they symbolized opposition to the government, to the old order, and to the existing system. Whatever exaggerated promises the Kadets may have made in the heat of the campaign, the basic planks of their platform obviously came closer to the desires and aims of the majority of citizens than the programs of any other group: a legal, orderly representative government; civil and personal freedom; land; increased benefits and rights for workers and minority peoples. As their opponents charged, the Kadet program had something in it for everybody, but it was indeed what people wanted. Tired of violent struggle incited by the radicals, on the one hand, and of weak promises and inadequate performance by the government, on the other, the voters clearly expressed their wish that their needs and rights should be fulfilled and protected by peaceful, legal means.

Moreover, the Kadet appeal was direct and inviting, not ambiguous and condescending. The Kadets argued that the people's aspirations were legitimate and natural and that the citizens themselves should have a say in how they were to be met and in generally deciding their future destiny. As the governor of Simbirsk pointed out to Durnovo, the attitude common among the gentry and the government that "the people know us, they will follow us, they trust us" was completely unjustified now, whether it had ever been true. "The peasants believe," he went on, "that from the Tsar and from the Duma they will receive land and that their needs will be satisfied, but they consciously elect not landlords but educated people from their own ranks. . . ." The patriarchal attitude of the government and the upper classes no longer corresponded to the way people felt, and the Kadets deliberately and successfully held out before the voters the prospect of moderate reforms which would correspond to *their* needs and which they would have a share in shaping. To be sure, the Duma became an exaggerated symbol, evocative of false hopes and dreams, for almost everyone, the conservative seeing it as the surest safeguard against revolution, and the more radical as the path to democratic or revolutionary salvation. Yet the faith displayed toward the Duma by many citizens, and especially by peasants, who little understood it, is both touching and revealing. Many peasant voters believed that the Duma would correct and fulfill whatever grievances and claims they had; therefore hundreds of petitions were either sent along with peasant electors and deputies or addressed directly to the Duma. Many are moving testaments to the frightful conditions of peasant life, as the two quoted here suggest:

Ah, what a miserable position and what an unhappy life is that of the much-deprived man! The only hope remaining for escaping from this deep darkness lies with our father-tsar and with our electors who go into the Duma to champion peasant interests.

Members of the State Duma, you are our desire, our will, our good fortune, our life, our Sunday. Our hope is the State Duma, and we ask of it only amnesty, land, and freedom. Remember that! Without a lowering of taxes, without all the land, don't come back! We haven't the strength to endure any longer. Death is better than a black future.[44]

The Kadets bespoke not only the strongest aspirations of the people but also their deep and bitter hostility against the government. In fact, one contemporary observer believed that the anti-government sentiment in the country as a whole was far stronger than even the composition of the Duma reflected.[45] Time and again the reports of the governors, who had every reason to minimize this, attributed the Kadet victory primarily to antigovernment feeling. Moreover, as we saw earlier, the Kadets enormously profited from the timing of the elections, long enough after the December risings so that the memory of revolutionary violence had dimmed, yet in a period when the continued repression of the government loomed larger and larger in people's consciousness and daily lives. As Miliukov himself put it:

> Everyone realizes that the cannons and machineguns of Dubasov are more dangerous for the average citizen than the rifles of the revolutionary militia. Chaos, which should have inspired horror in the citizen against revolutionary terror, inspired in him to a far greater degree fear of the terror of the government; . . . Frightened of the revolutionaries, the citizen nevertheless did not trust the government.[46]

And therefore supported the Kadets, Miliukov might have added. Besides the citizen who was more bitter against the government than afraid of the revolutionaries, the Kadets drew strength from moderate radicals and disappointed or exhausted revolutionaries, who did not necessarily agree with the Kadet program or their adherence to peaceful parliamentary methods but who either disapproved of open rebellion or believed that it was useless in the current circumstances of defeat and despair. Since the socialists were relatively inactive, torn by dissension over the boycott issue, and since in any case their programs were too extreme for some who were to the left of the Kadets, the disillusioned revolutionary and disgruntled radical had nowhere to turn but to the Kadets, who, in Lenin's words, "seemed the most left party." Appealing, then, to the dissatisfied and needy, to the critic or victim of government repression, and to the disappointed rebel—and above all, to burning hatred and resentment of an unjust government and system pent up over centuries—it is little wonder that the Kadets became, in Lenin's phrase, "the fashionable party" and won an impressive plurality at the polls.

As noted earlier, however, the apathy and weakness of their

opponents also paved the way for Kadet success. Given the mood of the country, the socialists might have provided stiff opposition (and as we saw, the Kadets regarded them as the chief threat), but they were few in numbers and partly from self-denial, partly from disorganization, partly from the weighting of the electoral system, they were of relatively little consequence in the elections. The center and right, which theoretically should have been the chief counterforce to the Kadets, were obviously quite out of touch with both contemporary opinion and with the desires of the populace. They were also poorly organized and insufficiently active. And, as we have seen, they received no help from the government. Their own "post-mortems" touched on all these factors. In an editorial in *Slovo*, the Octobrist organ, on March 24, and in a meeting of the Octobrist central committee on April 25–28, it was acknowledged that the principal causes of the Octobrists' disastrous defeat had been ineptness and passivity, too loose an organization and coalition, an insufficiently democratic program and image, too close an identification with the special interests of landlords and factory owners, a failure to generate mass appeal, and a belief among the people that they were supporters of the government in a time of extensive antigovernment feeling. This self-analysis was essentially correct. To remedy the situation the Octobrist central committee recommended emphasizing the democratic aspects of their platform, taking a stand on the national question, distinguishing themselves more clearly from vague supporters to the right and left, and improving the press and agitational activities of the party.[47] The Octobrists, however, fared little better in the elections to the Second Duma.

The far rightists, who had done even worse than the Octobrists, blamed their defeat on the revolutionaries and Jews and on the failure of the government to assist them—which is further, if negative, evidence of our conclusion that the government did not interfere in the elections. Not discouraged, however, they "refused to accept the verdict of the elections as final" and campaigned actively in the elections to the Second (and also the Third and Fourth) Dumas.[48]

The tsar himself had no difficulty explaining the outcome of the elections, ascribing it in his letter accepting Witte's resignation to "the breadth of the electoral law of December 11, to the inertness of the conservative masses of the population, and to the complete withdrawal of the authorities from the electoral campaign, which does not occur in other states."[49] Nicholas did not lack for counsel on what should be done, monarchist and landlord circles advising him that "since the elections contradict the interests of Russia and the true opinion of the majority of citizens," he should prorogue the Duma and change the electoral law, in order not "to submerge the select elements of the Russian population in a wave of the lower social classes" and in order "to preserve for the landowners and bourgeoisie that character of representation of the most cultured and well-to-do classes which they received under the zemstvo reform of 1864."[50] In two months he took the first part of this advice and in a little over a year the second.

The successful conduct of the elections to the First Duma and their outcome were significant for Russia in several ways. In the first place, the elections demonstrated that the Russian people were ready for and capable of some sort of national self-government, some kind of a representative system. Contrary to the gloomy predictions of many conservatives and to the repressed fears of some liberals in the preceding few years and months, the elections, even though held in the aftermath of a great revolutionary upheaval and amid continuing turmoil, were not disorderly or violent, were conducted with considerable efficiency and generally without illegalities or interference from either the government or the revolutionaries, and did not result in unleashing the forces of the "dark people" or plunging the country into anarchy and chaos. The bulk of the Duma deputies were quite able and intelligent individuals dedicated to improving the lot of their constituents and to advancing the welfare of the country.

Second, the elections, if they fairly reflected the views and will of the people, as we believe they did, showed that above all else the average Russian citizen was desirous of change. He wanted some of his basic needs fulfilled, he insisted on a more just and humane system, and he was clearly opposed to the old government and old order. Yet he was, in the great majority, prepared to seek these goals by peaceful, legal means, by reform not revolution. The faith that some conservatives had placed, during the working out of the August 6 and December 11 electoral system, on the peasantry as an essentially conservative force proved to be totally unjustified; and it was evident that until the peasantry had more land

and a better and more decent way of life, the *muzhiks* would remain discontented and largely hostile to the government. Whether the agrarian program developed by Witte and taken over by Stolypin would in the long run have satisfied peasant needs and aspirations is a moot point, lying outside the scope of our inquiry, but at least the Witte proposals were a start on the problem. It is equally clear that fundamental reforms affecting other elements in the population, particularly the workers and the national minorities, were also desperately demanded and urgently needed.

Third, the elections, and the government's response to them, glaringly revealed the huge gulf between government and people, between rulers and "society," between the "two Russias." The plurality won by the Kadets, who had not expected to be in such a commanding position in the Duma, posed a dilemma for them. In a sense, they were now responsible both to the progressive sentiment which had elected them and for the stability and orderly development of the country. The electorate looked to them and the Duma for reform, for a fulfillment of their campaign promises, yet the Kadets realized that if they attempted to go too far too fast, they risked government intervention to crush the delicate beginnings of democracy and constitutionalism so recently and tenuously launched and invited a return to the stalemate and chaos of pre-October days. At their third party congress, a congress of "victors," convened on the eve of the opening of the Duma in an atmosphere of celebration and optimism, the Kadets adopted a compromise but responsible program and attitude for their participation in the Duma. While not abandoning their goal of eventually broadening the electoral law and the semiconstitutional system established in the Fundamental Laws, they proposed for the moment to work within the existing framework and to undertake "constructive" activity, for example, in regard to agrarian reform and civil rights. If they did this, they believed the government would find it impossible to dismiss the Duma. Perhaps the Kadets were overly optimistic and naive, some even believing that the government might ask the party to form a ministry more or less responsible to the Duma, and the majority welcoming the Duma "with clear hopes in our hearts, with a childish, unique faith in ourselves, in the future of Russia."[51]

The difficulty was that the tsar and his advisers were not really prepared to accept the outcome of the elections and its implications and did not intend to join in satisfying most of the people's demands as espoused by the Kadets. Moreover, whatever the attitude of the government and the good intentions of the Kadets, there was a psychological barrier which made cooperation between them all but impossible. Mistrust and intransigence, built up over decades, abounded on both sides, reinforced for the Kadets by their clear mandate from the people and for the government by its distaste for the election results and by the growing degree of its restored authority and confidence, now that the worst of the revolutionary storm had passed. Both parties wanted the same eventual goals—order, stability, legality, progress—but their means and routes were vastly different and opposed. Neither side wished to compromise, so "government and society continued to stand one against the other, as two hostile camps."[52] Thus, in many ways the fate of the First Duma was sealed before it ever opened.

However fruitless, it is fascinating to speculate on what might have happened *if* Witte had behaved differently and *if* he had not been dismissed. As noted earlier, Witte was largely disinterested in the elections for both pragmatic and philosophical reasons. If he had tried to turn the elections to his own advantage, to form a party or to back one of the existing center parties, to win at least some measure of popular support, it is still doubtful that the outcome of the elections would have been changed very much, given the mood of the country. But with some slender base of political support Witte might have been in a stronger position *vis-à-vis* the tsar and conservative circles generally. And if he had not been forced out of office, might he not have been better able to work with the Kadets, to hold the fragile constitutional structure together until it had become stronger, more widely accepted? The answer is probably "no," for in general Witte was not sympathetic to the Kadet approach nor to many points of their program, and he was as dismayed at their success as many at court. Nevertheless, Witte was above all a pragmatist and he might have been able to give just enough ground to the Kadets, while pursuing his own goals, to make the Duma work. Alas, we shall never know, and Witte spent his last weeks in office trying to shape the new order in accord with his own views, largely ignoring the elections, their results, and their meaning.

IX

THE FUNDAMENTAL LAWS OF APRIL
1906: A RUSSIAN CONSTITUTION

*All this time I have been tormented by doubts whether I have
the right before my ancestors to change the prerogatives of power I
received from them. . . . The Act of October 17 was given by me fully
consciously, and I have firmly decided to carry it to its conclusion.
But I am not convinced of the necessity under it to renounce my
autocratic rights. . . .*
— Tsar Nicholas II
April 9, 1906

*[The Fundamental Laws] established a constitution but a con-
servative constitution and one without parliamentarianism—this was
the hope of the regime of October 17, and it assured finally that there
would be no return to the old order.*
— Witte
Vospominaniia

THE OCTOBER 17 MANIFESTO was not a constitution. It was
merely a pledge of reforms to come, a signpost indicating the
direction that government and society were to travel. The Manifesto committed the government to the granting of civil freedom,
to the broadening of the voting franchise, and to establishing as
"an unbreakable rule" that no law would take effect without the
consent of the Duma (as well as of the tsar). (See Appendix A.)
But the Manifesto provided no guarantees; it was only a collection
of promises and platitudes. The logical fulfillment of the Manifesto
was a constitution that would establish the structure and machinery of the new legislative order and that would provide legal
safeguards for the rights of Russian citizens.

The Fundamental State Laws, sanctioned by the tsar on April

23 and published on April 24, 1906, were a constitution just as surely as were the constitutions of The Netherlands, Denmark, and Prussia in 1848, 1849, and 1850, respectively.[1] The fact that the Fundamental Laws of 1906 were not usually referred to as a constitution does not affect their nature. They were the supreme law of the land, the rules by which the state was to be governed and to which all future laws were to conform. Although it was a far less liberal document than the Kadets and other opposition groups desired and although it was a gift from the tsar rather than the product of a constituent assembly, measured against other monarchist constitutions of Western Europe, it was by no means a reactionary statement. It confirmed, if not established, that absolutism was finished in Russia. The tsar was obligated to obey the Laws as were his subjects. In a variety of ways tsarist privileges were protected, but by defining what he could do, the Laws made clear that he was no longer privileged to do whatever he chose.

To his regret, Witte was not assigned the task of drafting the Fundamental Laws, but he clearly left his stamp on them. He participated actively in the discussions of the laws extending from February through April. While many of Witte's positions and pronouncements were frankly conservative and while occasionally he was hesitant and inconsistent, he clearly made a persistent and concerted effort to establish a constitutional order for Russia. His illiberal positions and his ambivalence arose from his lack of confidence in the public, a distrust nurtured first by the experiences of his first months as chairman of the Council of Ministers and then by the results of the elections to the Duma. But by word and by deed he demonstrated that he was dedicated to the construction of a constitutional order, although he refused to refer to it as such. He insisted that Russia was not an absolutist country but that it was a country based on law; he argued that even the tsar must conform to the law and that if sometimes extraordinary conditions required extraordinary action, then provision must be made so that the tsar could act promptly but legally. He insisted that the rights and duties of citizens be specified so that they would be recognized and observed by law. Although the collection of the Fundamental Laws was no doubt a conservative constitution, Witte himself admitting this, it was no less a constitution, one which preserved autocracy while providing the opportunity for representative and perhaps progressive government.[2]

February Sessions of the Crown Council

ALTHOUGH VARIOUS INDIVIDUALS and groups both within and outside the government were given an opportunity to present ideas and proposals concerning the state system that Russia should have in the future, final decisions concerning the content of the Fundamental Laws were made in sessions of two special Crown Councils held in February and April 1906, both presided over by the tsar. The first Crown Council met on February 14 and 16. In attendance were members of the Council of Ministers, certain selected members of the State Council, several grand dukes, and a few others close to the court. The principal objective of the February meetings was to agree upon the structure of the revised State Council. Although the tsar warned against introducing "superfluous" issues into these sessions, discussion often ranged beyond the question under review.[3]

As we saw in chapter three, there was considerable discussion in 1904–05 of the importance of transforming the old State Council into an elective or partly elective body. Witte recommended such a change in his report to the tsar on October 9, and concurrently a similar proposal was submitted to Count Sol'sky, chairman of the State Council. Although there was general agreement and a draft ukase providing for transformation of the State Council into a body that would be partly elected and partly appointed was actually prepared, Nicholas finally decided to have the whole matter reviewed by a special commission under Sol'sky. In this commission Witte, changing his earlier opinion that the new State Council should have an advisory role only, supported the view that it should have virtually equal rights with the Duma, a position the Sol'sky commission finally adopted. The proposal of the commission discussed in the February Crown Council and ultimately incorporated in the Fundamental Laws provided for a State Council in which elected members and those appointed by the tsar were represented "in equal numbers." The ninety-eight elected members, who were expected to be a conservative group, were to be chosen as follows:

six from the Orthodox clergy (three from the black or monastic clergy, three from the white or married clergy; no other faiths were represented);

eighteen from the nobility;

fifty-six from gubernia zemstvos (or special congresses of landowners where no zemstvo existed);

six from Moscow and St. Petersburg Universities and the Academy of Sciences;

twelve representatives of industry and commerce (six each).

The State Council members were to serve for nine years, with one-third elected every three years.[4]

There was by no means complete agreement among the participants at the February meetings as to whether the State Council should be changed, and if it were, on what basis. At the session on February 14 Count Aleksei P. Ignatiev, a member of the existing State Council, spoke against its revision. He reminded the participants that while the October 17 Manifesto had promised a Duma, it had not indicated any change in the State Council.[5] Ignatiev warned that such a move might be but one more step on the road to a constitutional order and, therefore, a step that should not be taken. Aleksandr S. Stishinsky, also a member of the existing State Council, a former assistant minister of Interior, and a well-known conservative, opposed the equality of elected and appointed members proposed for the new State Council. He argued that he could foresee a time when the tsar would need to increase the proportion of appointed members in the State Council to insure its conservative disposition.[6]

Witte attacked both these positions. First of all, he stressed the importance of establishing the State Council on the new basis. He argued that an upper house was needed to protect the government from the "lack of restraint of the lower." He stated that the State Council was necessary to guarantee the conservative side of government and to avoid a direct collision between the tsar and the Duma. "In a word, the upper house must become a buffer," he exclaimed. Then Witte responded to Stishinsky's desire to add more appointed members, pointing out that those who would be elected to the State Council were certain to be essentially conservative. Therefore, there was no need to increase the proportion of those appointed to those elected as it was clear that the State Council would be conservative anyway. At this stage of the discussion Witte was arguing for a State Council that would resemble the Herrenhaus, the upper house of the Prussian parliament, which served as a bulwark against the popularly elected lower house.

Yet later, during the same session on February 14, Witte reacted vigorously to a discussion in which the participants were regularly referring to the Duma and State Council as a lower and upper house respectively. He exclaimed that there was altogether too much talk of upper and lower houses. The use of these terms implied a constitutional order. Russia did not have a constitution nor did the proposed law establish one. All that was involved, according to Witte, was that the tsar had chosen to establish a new state structure. This was not a constitution nor did it imply a commitment for a constitution. Therefore, it was quite unnecessary to use upper and lower house when referring to the State Council and Duma.

It is difficult to explain this outburst. Witte himself had used the terms upper and lower house earlier in the session and did so again both on February 14 and 16. Furthermore, all his efforts during the discussions concerning the Fundamental Laws were directed toward establishment of a constitutional order in Russia. His reluctance to use the word constitution, and he demonstrated this reluctance more than once in the sessions that followed, stemmed from the fact that "constitution" was a word particularly repellent to Nicholas II. Probably Witte hoped to lead the tsar to a constitutional order while not calling it by that name. Such a tactic seems incredibly devious, but Witte, who was well aware of his tenuous relationship to the tsar and of the tsar's own prejudices, was not above resorting to such a stratagem. He apparently used a similar approach during the negotiations on the election law of December 1905, although on that occasion it resulted in failure.

Witte also surprised the participants by opposing that portion of the proposal that stated that "no law" could take effect without approval of the Duma and State Council. Witte said he believed this provision to be "extremely ill-advised" if it was intended to limit the tsar's rights to issue not only laws but commands and decrees as well. Count Sol'sky reminded Witte that the Manifesto had stated as "an unbreakable rule" that no law would be valid without the consent of the Duma.[7] Witte explained later in his memoirs that he had sought to distinguish between law [*zakon*] and decree [*dekret*].[8] The former had to be approved by the Duma and the State Council, while the latter remained the prerogative of the tsar. Witte's reasons for insisting on this distinction are not entirely clear, either from his memoirs or from the contemporary documents available. From his comments from February to April it seems evident Witte was genuinely concerned that if every state, governmental, and administrative action was construed as a law—and therefore had to be approved by the Duma—the government would be paralyzed and administration would break down. On the other hand, as the Fundamental Laws took shape, Witte's opinions, especially in sessions of the April Crown Council, increasingly emphasized the importance of reserving to the tsar the right, without consent of the Duma, not only to issue orders and regulations which implemented laws but also to enact, in emergency situations or extraordinary circumstances, decrees and ukases with the force of law.[9]

Two members of the Council of Ministers, Prince A. D. Obolensky and N. N. Kutler, suggested a rather startling revision in the proposed law governing the Duma and State Council. The preliminary draft provided that a bill originating in either the Duma or the State Council had to be approved by the other legislative body before being forwarded to the tsar for his approval or disapproval. Prince Obolensky argued that there was a danger that the State Council would prevent any Duma-sponsored measure from reaching the tsar. Therefore, he, along with Kutler, proposed that if the Duma passed a measure which the State Council then rejected, the Duma could reconsider this measure. If the measure were passed once again in the Duma, this time by at least a two-thirds majority, it would be sent directly to the tsar, by-passing the State Council. Obolensky added that he did not oppose the State Council. However, as the Duma was expected by the public, while the new State Council would come as a surprise, guarantees should be offered to insure that the Duma would not be denied access to the tsar. Witte stated that while he saw psychological merit in the Obolensky-Kutler proposal, he sided with the majority view and in favor of the original provision in the draft. The tsar agreed with the majority, and it was decided that a measure passed in either the State Council or the Duma had to be approved in the other body before being sent to the tsar, whose signature was then required before the law took effect.[10]

Witte's dilemma, which led him into marked inconsistencies of position, was what attitude to take toward the public. He constantly vacillated between two widely divergent points of view:

one in which he expressed confidence in Russian citizens' loyalty, integrity, and good judgment, and another in which he revealed an almost paranoic suspicion and distrust of the public's behavior and intentions. He displayed the latter attitude on February 14, when he argued that sessions of the Duma and State Council should be closed to the public. Witte asserted that as a result of the public's savagery and lack of restraint, serious scandals were certain to occur during the first weeks of the Duma. He agreed that the diplomatic corps must be permitted to observe the sessions of the legislature but not those Russians who "hurl rotten apples." In other countries, Witte said, people were "more cultured." To the observation that the place for the public was in the balcony watching the Duma, Witte replied, "Lawyers, yes; but the public, never." Witte believed that the members of the Duma would devote most of their energies to playing to the galleries and that this would cause the general public to "persecute the ministers." In exceptional cases Witte thought the public could possibly be admitted but only by prior arrangement, as through agreement between the president of the Duma and the chairman of the Council of Ministers. Nevertheless, Witte was in the minority; and the tsar ruled that sessions of the Duma were to be public although he agreed that plans must be made to "guard" members of the Duma.[11]

Two days later, at the Crown Council session on February 16, Witte evinced a change of heart. Rather than distrusting the public, he adopted a position that seemed to reflect an almost naive faith in the good will and intentions of the citizenry. Witte startled the participants by reopening an issue that had been settled two days before—the Obolensky-Kutler proposal by which the Duma could by-pass the State Council—and by assuming a position on this issue exactly opposite to the one he had embraced on February 14.[12] Witte now said that he believed Obolensky had raised an important principle and that in general all legislative questions should be decided in the Duma. If the Duma did not endorse a proposal, it would go no further. If it did pass a measure, this would be sent to the State Council which would either accept or reject it. In the proposed draft if the State Council rejected the bill, it would not reach the tsar. The danger in this situation lay in the differing groups that would comprise the two legislative bodies—the State Council, aristocrats; the Duma, primarily peasants. "What is the psychology of peasants?" Witte asked. If the State Council were to reject the

Duma's measures time after time, the peasant Duma members would become convinced that bureaucrats stood between them and their tsar.[13]

Although Witte had stated the problem in a way very similar to that of Obolensky and Kutler, he suggested a different solution. He proposed that in those instances when the State Council refused to approve a measure originating in the Duma and, if that measure had enjoyed strong majority support in the Duma, then the tsar, if he found major points in the Duma bill to his liking, could order one of his ministers to write a new bill including the major points from the Duma measure and to submit it to the Duma for its approval. If passed in the Duma, the measure would be sent to the State Council; if it were refused in the State Council, the Duma could send it directly to the tsar for his action. Kokovtsov vigorously attacked Witte's suggestion by pointing out that it centered complete control in the Duma and that Witte's new position violated his official report published along with the October 17 Manifesto. Witte answered that he did not have, nor had he ever had, any intention of placing control in one chamber. "But," he said, "it is useless to copy a constitutional situation in which an upper chamber keeps the lower away from the monarch. Therefore, I suggest that if the State Council refuses a bill from the Duma, the Duma can take its views to the tsar."[14]

It was a remarkable about-face, even for such a chameleon as Witte. On February 14 he argued for a buffer between the radicals in the Duma and the tsar; two days later he wished to abolish the buffer and to provide direct access to the tsar for the elected representatives of the public. Furthermore, he now expressed his ideas not in terms of distrust or suspicion of the people but in phrases implying an almost mystical faith in the union between the tsar and the Russian people. A Slavophile could hardly have expressed it better.

Andrei A. Saburov, a member of the State Council, attacked Witte's proposal of February 16 using Witte's argument of February 14. Saburov said it was necessary to have two houses. As the Duma would consist of radicals, the State Council must be an intermediary to prevent a direct collision between the tsar and people. Saburov argued if the Duma could appeal directly to the tsar and he failed to adopt their proposals, a dangerous situation would result.[15] Count Konstantin I. Palen, former minister of Justice and member of the State Council, also opposed Witte's suggestion. He could not understand why Witte avoided the idea Russia was destined to have a constitutional regime. "What was the October 17 Manifesto if not a constitution?" Palen asked. "There is no doubt, of course, that Russia will be ruled in a constitutional manner."

Witte replied that the October 17 Manifesto was not a constitution because the tsar had adopted it on his own initiative. Witte said even the "extreme elements" in the country agreed to this. There was no constitution in Russia according to Witte. But, to him, this was beside the point.[16] What Witte was concerned about was that nothing should stand between the people and their tsar. The psychology of society—especially the peasant—was "God and Tsar." This must be preserved.[17] Obolensky added that the Manifesto had stated that no law would take effect without the approval of the Duma. Nothing must be done to destroy this principle. Others replied ideas growing out of the Duma would not be secrets kept from the tsar. If Nicholas believed the Duma's ideas to be good, the State Council would probably adopt a friendly attitude toward Duma proposals. Witte failed to win majority support, and the tsar ruled against his proposal.[18]

Despite this Slavophilic interlude, later in the very same session Witte returned to his earlier attitude of distrust of the elected representatives of the people when he suggested that there should be a provision to punish those members of the Duma who insulted the tsar. Such members should either be prevented from attending sessions of the Duma or punished in some other way. Witte asked, "What will happen to the government if members of the Duma allow themselves to insult monarchical authority?"[19]

Witte also wished to establish limits on the Duma's privilege to interpellate ministers. Although a minister could refuse to appear before the Duma, Witte believed it likely the Duma would "heap" interpellation requests on the ministers unless it was made clear ministerial appearances before the Duma would be made only when such appearances bore directly upon immediate problems under Duma consideration. Witte was fearful the ministers would be paraded before the Duma simply to serve as convenient targets for Duma attacks on the government and its policies.[20]

The decisions of the February 14 and 16 Crown Council sessions were the subject of an imperial manifesto dated February

20, 1906.[21] The provisions of this manifesto were later included in and superseded by the Fundamental Laws of April 23, 1906. The manifesto of February 20 specified there were to be two legislative bodies—the Duma and the State Council. Members of the State Council were to be equally appointed by the tsar and elected by certain privileged groups. An individual was not permitted to be a member of the State Council and the Duma simultaneously. It was stipulated no new law could become effective without the approval of the State Council, the Duma, and the tsar, although under certain conditions the tsar was permitted to take action without prior approval of the Duma and the State Council.[22] Members of the State Council and Duma were also given the right to interpellate ministers of the government, despite Witte's objections. Both the State Council and the Duma were permitted to initiate legislation if a bill on the given topic had not been introduced by a minister; they could also repeal and amend laws, but changes in the Fundamental State Laws could be proposed only by the tsar.

Review of the Draft Fundamental Laws

AT ABOUT THIS TIME the first draft of the Fundamental Laws as a whole began to be circulated within the government. It seems only logical that as the one person primarily responsible for the new political order in Russia, Witte would have been chosen by Nicholas to draft the Fundamental Laws. The fact that Nicholas did not select him for this all-important task reflected the tsar's growing lack of confidence in Witte.[23] The assignment was given instead to the imperial secretary of the State Council, Baron Iu. A. Ikskul'-Gildenbandt, and his assistant, P. A. Kharitonov. In drawing up a preliminary draft in December they noted and reviewed a liberal constitution composed by a group of future Kadets earlier in 1905, but naturally the draft they finally prepared was far more conservative.[24] In the third week of February their draft was sent to Witte, who wrote Nicholas almost immediately that it was deficient, particularly because it did not distinguish between laws and decrees. Witte concluded that "in my opinion it is necessary to introduce into the Fundamental Laws an article which defines the right of the Monarch to issue decrees; otherwise there will be a mass of difficulties."[25] He also urged that the Fundamental Laws be issued before the Duma convened.

At the same time Witte asked several specialists and advisers to review the draft for him. In sending it to Baron Nol'de, head of the secretariat of the old Committee of Ministers, on February 20, Witte wrote:

> I especially ask you to compare it with the conservative constitutions (Prussian, Austrian, Japanese, English) and to borrow from them useful conservative principles. The chief question is: what is a law and what is a decree? . . . It is necessary to define this in the fundamental laws, and to provide the Council of Ministers with broad authority in this area or to let imperial ukases have corresponding significance.[26]

Witte also asked Professor Martens for an opinion on the foreign policy provisions of the draft. Witte urged that the draft be changed in order to exclude the Duma completely from the formulation or discussion of foreign policy, but Martens replied that this was impossible since questions of foreign policy were so vital to the life of the people and the state that they were bound to be discussed in the Duma.[27] Witte also asked the advice of I. I. Tkhorzhenskii, formerly a specialist in state law at St. Petersburg University, who submitted thirteen pages of comments and amendments, a number of which Witte and the Council of Ministers adopted.[28]

On March 2 Nicholas finally asked the Council of Ministers to review the draft of the Fundamental Laws; he provided no guidelines, asking only that the Council's consideration take place "in complete secrecy."[29] Knowledge that the government was preparing a "constitution" before the opening of the Duma would, of course, have evoked a storm of protest from Kadet and other oppositionist ranks. On March 9 Witte submitted the draft, with his notes and suggestions, to the Council of Ministers. As one participant in the process of drawing up the Fundamental Laws comments, Witte's corrections and proposals tended "not to limit the prerogatives of authority and not to encourage groundless hopes on the part of the citizenry."[30] For example, Witte urged clarification of the exclusive authority of the tsar to conduct and control foreign policy, denying to the Duma and State Council any right to ratify treaties. He opposed the possibility that the Council of Ministers would be in any way responsible to the Duma. He proposed, on the advice of Nol'de and Tkhorzhenskii, that freedom of correspondence and letters not be included among the rights guaranteed citizens on the grounds it might be harmful to the security of the state. On the other hand Witte recommended that the word "unlimited" be dropped from the definition of the tsar's authority and, returning to his favorite theme, that laws be distinguished from decrees, resolutions, and ukases. According to Witte, the latter should serve primarily to effectuate laws and should not contradict any law.[31]

In the Council of Ministers, which met five times (March 10, 12, 14, 18, and 19) to review the Fundamental Laws, Durnovo took an extreme position, maintaining that the government should not only not issue but not even discuss the Fundamental Laws because news of such deliberations would inevitably leak out and would only serve to inflame the public and to stir up new disorders.[32] Nevertheless, on Witte's urging, the Council soon agreed that the Fundamental Laws should be issued before the Duma convened. It also accepted all the modifications suggested by Witte and his advisers. (See Appendix C.) In a few cases it even went beyond those amendments: The Council not only approved the tsar's exclusive control of foreign policy but also extended his authority over the armed forces (Article 13 in draft of the Council of Ministers—see Appendix C); it also cast Witte's distinction between laws and decrees in a new form, giving the tsar power to issue, without consent of the Duma, decrees designed to protect public order and to improve the people's welfare (Article 11).

In addition, the Council of Ministers proposed several further steps to strengthen the prerogatives of the tsar and to weaken the Duma. The monarch was given the exclusive right to mint money and to declare martial law or states of "extraordinary security" (Article 18). The Council also incorporated in the Fundamental Laws the provisions of its decree of March 8, which limited the budgetary rights of the Duma. Certain budgetary areas were entirely removed from the jurisdiction of the Duma (for example, financing the tsar's household and lands), and it was also established that if the Duma failed to approve a new budget, that of the preceding year would automatically go into effect (Article 60). In the same vein the Council recommended that if the Duma failed to approve new levies for the army by May 1 of the new year, those of the preceding year would be in force (Article 61). On one issue the Council of Ministers disagreed. Some members, led by Witte, urged that the tsar's privileges be broadened to include the right to remove all civil servants, including judges (Article 15), but a minority insisted that the judicial reform of 1864, which made judges immutable, provided a basic right that should be an integral part of the new state order. In the April Crown Council the minority position was upheld.

The Council of Ministers then made a few additional changes in the Fundamental Laws. In Part II on the rights of citizens (a sort of "Bill of Rights"), which were to be exercised within limits set by law and not in areas under martial law, it eliminated entirely *habeas corpus*-like provisions (Articles 24–27 in the original draft). At the same time the Council added an article reaffirming the decree of April 17, 1905, providing for freedom of religious belief (Article 34). Finally, and apparently on Witte's urging, an affirmation that private property was inviolable was amended by adding "except for state and public needs and then only with just compensation" (Article 30). As we shall see, this proviso was to cause lively debate in the April sessions of the Crown Council and may have contributed to Witte's dismissal.

On March 20 the Council of Ministers submitted a memoir to Nicholas explaining its recommendations for changes in the Fundamental Laws, together with drafts of a manifesto and an ukase which it urged be issued at the same time as the Fundamental Laws.[33] The introduction to the memoir made clear the Council's concern that the Fundamental Laws define precisely the rights of the people, of the Duma and State Council, and of the government and the tsar. It urged both that the limits of the authority of the people's representatives be clearly established and that "those areas in which the Supreme Power is realized personally" be plainly safeguarded. The Council therefore recommended that since the government was giving up some of its prerogatives, it would be useful to issue an ukase explaining this, "and at the same time to remind the people of the right of the tsar to issue ukases aimed at preserving state and public security and order and guaranteeing the people's well-being." Finally, the Council of Ministers stressed its belief that only the tsar should have the right to initiate any review or amendment of the Fundamental Laws themselves, and it urged that the Fundamental Laws be published before the

Duma opened, since otherwise there would be "dangerous and fruitless debate in the Duma concerning the extent of its own rights and the nature of its relationship to the Supreme Authority." In short, Witte and his ministers were afraid that the Duma would transform itself into a constituent assembly.[34]

Witte's concern about the relationship between the Duma and the government increased as the results of the Duma elections came in during March 1906. At first Witte was relieved by the election returns as he believed that the Duma would be friendly to the government. At a meeting of the Council of Ministers held shortly after the first election results were known, Witte exclaimed, "Thank heaven! The Duma will be predominantly peasant." Later election returns revealed, however, that the Kadets would be the single greatest influence in the Duma. Fully aware of the Kadet's hostility to the government, Witte became increasingly nervous about the future.[35] By early April he concluded that the Duma might possibly be an "insane asylum."

Yet Witte's growing alarm about the forthcoming Duma did not detract from his commitment to establish a constitutional order in Russia. It, however, strengthened his resolve to structure the constitution in such a way that it would not be at the mercy of the Duma. He continued to favor progressive government that involved the public in matters of legislation, but he was equally committed to keeping full control of the affairs of state out of the hands of the radicals. Throughout discussion of the Fundamental Laws in the April Crown Council, Witte argued for constitutional government but a government that would be securely established on a sound, conservative basis before the Duma had a chance to raise its voice.

April Sessions of the Crown Council

THOSE ATTENDING the April Crown Council meetings were largely the same individuals who had attended the February sessions. As the meeting opened on April 7, Witte addressed himself to the important question of when the Fundamental Laws should be published.[36] Witte reiterated his arguments before the Council of Ministers that the laws should be published before the Duma began its session in order to prevent the Duma from transforming itself into a constituent assembly. Not all the participants shared Witte's view. Saburov declared: "The act of October 17 proclaimed that not one law could be published without the Duma or State Council. Certainly if this is true of ordinary laws, it must be true of the Fundamental Laws." State Secretary Eduard V. Frish' agreed with Saburov, arguing that if there had been disorders after publication of the October 17 Manifesto, taking away a key right extended by the Manifesto would surely give rise to new unrest. Ivan Ia. Golubev, chairman of the Department of Civil and Spiritual Affairs of the State Council, added that the manifesto of February 20, 1906, had reaffirmed the general rule that no law could take effect without approval of the Duma. Therefore since the Fundamental Laws were only a collection of laws, they had to be submitted to the Duma. If they were published prior to the Duma, the Duma would quickly set out to amend them, Golubev concluded. Witte was not swayed by these statements of principle. He was concerned only about the practical implications. He knew that excluding the Duma from a discussion of the Fundamental Laws might cause trouble, but he insisted that it was "better to suffer dissatisfaction now and protect everything that should remain exclusively under the tsar than to risk future trouble in all the government."[37]

Witte further revealed his concern about the future Duma when the problem of Finland was being discussed. The question was how to define Finland's relationship to Russia and how much local autonomy to give Finland. Witte said that if the Duma were nationalistic, it would seek to extend greater control over Finland than the tsar himself would ask. But if the Duma were revolutionary—as he expected it would be—it would join with the revolutionaries in Finland in joint cause against the tsarist regime. Witte then observed: "If the Duma is peasant, without ideas, and falls under the control of revolutionaries and the so-called intelligentsia, then it will be an insane asylum."[38]

On April 9 Witte reiterated his distrust of the Duma. He stressed that since the Duma was potentially dangerous, the duties and responsibilities both of the Duma and of the monarch should be clearly defined in the Fundamental Laws; and certain areas—aspects of the budget, including concluding loans, foreign affairs, and control of the army and navy—should be closed to the Duma and reserved for the tsar. Nothing should be left undone or unexamined. In preparing the final draft of the Fundamental Laws, Witte said, it was necessary to cover each point, deciding what should be left to the Duma and what should be reserved to the tsar. Again, he asserted that the Laws should be published before the opening of the Duma.[39]

Discussion on April 9, however, centered on Article 4 of the Fundamental Laws, which Tsar Nicholas described as the most important of the entire code. Article 4 defined the nature of the tsar's autocratic power. The issue causing debate was whether the word "absolute" should be excluded from this definition of authority. The tsar indicated that he had received many petitions and telegrams requesting him to reassert his authority. Although he recognized certain elements would oppose this, he believed eighty percent of the Russian people would support him. Yet Nicholas was clearly torn, as we saw in chapter five, between what he believed to be his duty to his predecessors, to the God-given rights of the tsar, and the promises he had made on October 17 and the needs of the state in the current situation. In a moving and candid appeal Nicholas declared to the Crown Council:

> All this time I have been tormented by doubts whether I have the right before my ancestors to change the prerogatives of power which I received from them. Struggle still continues in me, and I still haven't reached a definite conclusion. It seemed to me easier to decide this question a month ago than now after long reflection, when circumstances insist it be decided. . . . Frankly speaking, I believe that if I were convinced that Russia wanted me to renounce my autocratic powers, I would do this gladly for the common good. The Act of 17 October was given by me fully consciously, and I have firmly decided to carry it to its conclusion. But I am not convinced of the necessity under it to renounce the autocratic rights and to change the definition of the Supreme Power which has existed for 109 years in Article 1 of the basic laws.[40]

In response Witte asserted that the entire future of Russia depended upon the answer given to the question of the tsar's prerogatives. Nevertheless Witte declared he did not agree with those who believed that while yielding some of his legislative functions by the October 17 Manifesto, the tsar had remained absolute. Witte used Turkey as an example of absolutism, adding that Russia was not absolutist as it had not been subject to a ruler's caprice since the reign of Alexander I. According to Witte, Russia was a country in which law rather than tsar was supreme. Witte wanted the new laws to be fully established before the opening of the Duma and to have Russians recognize that all were subject to these laws, including the tsar.[41]

Count Palen agreed that the tsar no longer had absolute power but asserted that the tsar had yielded this power himself by the October 17 Manifesto. As the tsar had ceased to be absolute since October 17, he no longer had the right to establish laws for others. The Fundamental Laws should be submitted to the Duma. Minister of Justice Akimov urged the tsar to exclude the word "absolute" from the Fundamental Laws. Surprisingly both the Grand Duke Nikolai Nikolaevich and the Grand Duke Vladimir Aleksandrovich supported him. Minister of Interior Durnovo argued that the word "absolute" was inconsistent with the October 17 Manifesto and the law of February 20, 1906, but the word should be retained anyway. Stishinsky, a conservative, reasoned that the tsar's privilege to pass on all legislation was in practice an "absolute" power, but there was no reason to state it as such. "It happens that only the word is excluded, but the authority is protected," Stishinsky said, trying to reassure himself.[42] This issue was then dropped and not finally resolved until the last session of the Crown Council on April 12. The tsar reported near the close of that session that he had given considerable thought to whether the word "absolute" should be included in the Fundamental Laws. He finally decided to exclude "absolute," thereby leaving Article 4 to define the nature of Russian autocratic power as follows: "The Emperor of all the Russias possesses Supreme and Autocratic power. To obey His authority not only from fear but also from conscience is ordered by God Himself."[43]

Although Witte was anxious to establish a constitutional order that required the tsar to operate within the limits of the law, just as was expected of other citizens, he also came to believe that there might be periods of crisis during which the tsar should be free to take any action he believed desirable to protect the safety of the nation, either internally or externally.[44] This view caused Witte to walk a very thin line between a truly constitutional order and absolutism, for if the tsar were free to act outside the law whenever he thought it necessary, what was there to prevent a return to absolute autocracy? Somehow, Witte believed, a method had to be devised by which the tsar could operate autocratically, but legally, when the times required such action. During the Crown Council session on April 11, techniques to insure tsarist control were discussed. Witte argued forcibly that foreign affairs—including the right to conduct negotiations, to formulate policy, to declare war, and to make peace—should be exclusively in the hands of the tsar and outside the purview of the Duma.[45] Witte also believed the tsar should have full control over the army and navy. In addition, Witte gained Nicholas' assent to include in the Fundamental Laws an article that granted the tsar the right to negotiate loans during times of war or other crises (Article 76—see Appendix C). This gave the tsar partial financial independence from the Duma.[46] Also adopted was the suggestion of the Council of Ministers that should the Duma and State Council fail to pass by May 1 of each year measures permitting more men to be drafted into the military services, the tsar could draft new recruits by ukase, provided that no more were taken than were provided for in the previous year's law.

As we saw earlier, Witte, who feared judges might succumb to revolutionary pressure, also favored giving the tsar the right to remove them at will. The majority of Crown Council members supported Witte, but Goremykin and Palen vigorously opposed him on this point. They argued for an independent judiciary with the right of tenure. Nicholas, who said he was not opposed to the idea of irremovability of judges, ruled against Witte and the majority.[47]

Not only did Witte seek to reserve important areas of government authority exclusively for the tsar, but he urged provision be made to handle unforeseen difficulties that might arise. Witte asserted it was important to frame the Fundamental Laws in such a way that when the situation required exceptional action, the tsar could assume extraordinary powers. Witte noted that in almost all states there came a time when the government was forced to undertake a *coup d'état*. He believed this was undesirable and the new Fundamental Laws should be written so as to make this unnecessary. Witte declared: "It is necessary for all Russia to know that the emperor can take extraordinary measures in required cases and that this will not be a *coup d'état*."[48] To some degree this was assured by retaining for the tsar the right to issue ukases and decrees. But a more important guarantee was that provided for in Article 45 (87), which the Crown Council approved as part of the Fundamental Laws.[49]

Witte also suggested that legislation initiated by the tsar

should be submitted to the Council of Ministers or to the appropriate minister before it was introduced in either legislative chamber. This would eliminate the possibility of a minister having to defend before the Duma a project which he opposed. Ministers would have to give full support to the tsar's proposals or resign when they were unable to do so.[50] The tsar reacted favorably to the idea, which, in a slightly altered form, was included in the published Fundamental Laws.

The last Crown Council session on the Fundamental Laws was held on April 12. A brief debate took place on whether Part II of the draft Fundamental Laws, which established the rights of individuals, should be included. Witte argued strongly that the rights of citizens should be spelled out just as clearly as the rights of the tsar.[51] This was consistent with his position that the Fundamental Laws should be as explicit as possible concerning the relationship of the people to the state. The Crown Council finally endorsed the inclusion of Part II.

While the Crown Council was discussing the provision of Part II relating to the sanctity of private property, Witte warned the participants that within two months the Duma would prepare measures of agrarian reform. Although Witte indicated he did not support the Kutler project, something similar to it involving confiscation of land would be offered by the Duma; and the government must be ready for it. Goremykin, the man who was to succeed Witte as chairman of the Council of Ministers in less than two weeks, said this was a closed issue to be touched only by the tsar. The radicals in the Duma must not be permitted to start dividing the land. If they tried to do so, the Duma should be dissolved at once. Witte charged that Goremykin's position on land reform and his attitude toward the Duma would result in revolution since the Kadets as well as other parties were already preparing land programs involving forced alienation of land, while proroguing the Duma could only lead to violence.[52] Most of those present, including the tsar, warmly welcomed Goremykin's stand, and Witte later speculated that this exchange between Goremykin and himself helped seal his own dismissal and may have influenced Nicholas to replace him with Goremykin.[53] Nevertheless, the tsar approved inclusion of the statement that forcible alienation of land could take place when it was deemed necessary for state or social needs provided just compensation was paid. Three months later, however, when the Duma proposed compulsory expropriation, Nicholas dismissed the Duma—without provoking revolution.

Confirmation of the Fundamental Laws

THE FUNDAMENTAL LAWS were confirmed on April 23 and published on April 24, 1906. In his memoirs Witte asserted that Nicholas delayed approving the Fundamental Laws for ten days after the last Crown Council session because of doubts raised in his mind by a liberal critique of the Laws which a group of Kadets submitted to Nicholas, through Trepov, after they heard the Laws had been formulated. Witte also claimed that the Fundamental Laws were issued only after he—as a private person since he had already resigned—had sent urgent messages to the tsar that they must be promulgated before the Duma opened April 27.[54] These assertions are dubious, however; other evidence suggests that the Kadets took no specific action against the Fundamental Laws except to criticize them in a series of articles in *Rech'* and to declare, after their publication, that "no barriers created by the government will restrain the people's elected representatives from fulfilling the tasks which the people have entrusted to them."[55] Moreover, Nicholas had all along agreed with the wisdom of publishing the Fundamental Laws before the Duma convened, and his slight delay in confirming them was apparently due to certain minor corrections he wished to see introduced in them.[56] Nevertheless, presenting the Duma deputies with a *fait accompli* by proclaiming the Fundamental Laws only a few days before the Duma met, when it might have had a chance to discuss and revise them, aroused enormous suspicion and distrust in the public and contributed to the hostility which existed between the First Duma and the tsar's government.[57]

The Fundamental Laws defined the rules which would order the future political life of Russia.[58] Although the tsar was no longer termed absolute, he was still the "supreme autocratic power" whose person was sacred and inviolable. He had the right to initiate legislation, and all laws required his signature in order to become effective. He alone had the right to initiate changes in the Fundamental Laws. According to the provisions of the new Laws, the tsar had total executive power. He was in complete charge of foreign affairs with the authority to formulate and to direct foreign policy, to declare war, and to make peace. He was the commander-in-chief of the army and navy. He administered the currency, appointed the Council of Ministers—who were responsible solely to him rather than to the Duma—and retained exclusive control of crown and appanage lands. Ukases and orders were to be countersigned by the chairman of the Council of Ministers or the appropriate minister in order to insure a unified, executive policy. Judicial power was also exercised in the tsar's name. While judges had tenure and were not removable by the tsar, he could grant pardons, commute sentences, and stop proceedings against any prisoner.

The Fundamental Laws guaranteed certain individual rights. Freedom of domicile, movement, and choice of occupation were secured. Freedom of assembly, speech, organization, and conscience were also provided within the "limits of the law." The fact that certain laws regulating these latter freedoms had been promulgated earlier made them somewhat less than complete, however. Property was inviolable and could be expropriated only for fair compensation. All citizens were liable for taxation and military service.

The Fundamental Laws, which incorporated the provisions of the law of February 20, 1906, provided for a two-house legislature. The members of the Duma were chosen according to the terms of the December 11, 1905, election law. The State Council was divided between appointed and elected members according to the terms of the February 20 manifesto. Both the Duma and the State Council met annually at the call of the tsar, who also determined the length of each session. The tsar also had the right to dissolve the Duma and the elective half of the State Council and to set within four months dates for new elections. The State Council and the Duma could amend or repeal legislation and could enact new bills into law. Bills passed in one chamber required the approval of the other before being transmitted to the tsar. Measures approved by both chambers and approved by the tsar became laws. If the tsar vetoed a bill, it could not be reintroduced until the next session. On the other hand, a bill passed by either the Duma or the State Council but rejected by the other body could be reintroduced during the same session if requested by the tsar.

The State Council and Duma were able to summon ministers to answer questions. They could also censure ministers but censure did not bring automatic dismissal, as each minister was responsible to the tsar rather than to the Duma. The chairman of the Council of Ministers was the chief executive of the government after the tsar, but ministers and heads of departments were individually responsible for their actions to the tsar.

Nearly one-third of the budget was withheld from the purview of the Duma and the State Council. The tsar alone controlled sums to cover existing loans and obligations, credits for the imperial family and household, and credits and loans for war purposes. All other items were contained in a budget that was submitted to the Duma and to the State Council for their action. If a budget was disapproved for any year, the previous year's budget took effect.

Perhaps the most controversial provision in the entire code of Fundamental Laws was Article 45 (87).[59] Although the precise origin of this article, which was included in the original draft of the Laws and which was based on Article 14 of the Austrian constitution, is unclear, it accomplished for the tsar the purpose Witte had intended—to make it possible to circumvent the Duma and State Council legally when extraordinary conditions required action. Article 45 (87) provided that if measures requiring legislative action were urgently needed at a time when the Duma and the State Council were not in sesssion, the Council of Ministers could recommend a law directly to the tsar, who could promulgate it in an imperial ukase. Measures adopted under these circumstances could not affect the Fundamental Laws, the regulations of the State Council or the Duma, or the electoral procedure of either chamber (though in 1907 Stolypin violated this provision when he restructured the electoral system after dismissal of the Second Duma). When the Duma and the State Council had reconvened, the emergency measure had to be submitted within two months from the opening of the new session or it was invalidated. If the Duma or State Council rejected the measure, it likewise became null and void. This article became a powerful weapon in the hands of the monarchy because it provided a way of by-passing the Duma, making it possible for the tsar, after adjourning or dissolving the Duma and the State Council, to rule as he pleased during the time between sessions. It provided the "legal *coup d'état*" that Witte had argued in the Crown Council sessions the government must have.

There can be no doubt that Witte played a significant role

in the final formulation of the new Fundamental Laws. The exact nature of that role is subject to interpretation. Gurko believed that Witte's efforts were directed toward establishing conditions whereby the tsar would be able to rule autocratically and to enact both administrative and legislative measures without participation of the Duma.

> In his heart Witte was a partisan of enlightened absolutism; he accepted the constitutional regime out of necessity, but the constitution he had in mind was a very limited one in which control would still reside in the Monarch and a government appointed by him. As for the people's representatives, Witte dreamed of winning their favor and then using it as a moral force which would be his chief support before the throne.[60]

It is tempting to agree with Gurko. Many of Witte's speeches in the February and April sessions of the Crown Council reflect an ultraconservative philosophy, a philosophy far removed from the spirit of the October 17 Manifesto. Yet Witte was neither so reactionary as many of his statements in the spring of 1906 suggest nor so liberal as the October 17 Manifesto seemed to imply. Witte had always preferred autocratic to democratic forms of government. He suggested a program of reform in October not to destroy the government but to save it, and he continued to favor reform in the spring of 1906 for the same reason. At the same time he opposed absolutism, argued forcibly for a government based on law, and insisted that the basic rights of Russian citizens be included as part of the Fundamental Laws.

His defense of tsarist prerogatives in areas of finance, foreign policy, and military affairs stemmed primarily from his concern for Russia's international position. In his opinion, such vital questions should not be the responsibility of amateurs elected to the Duma. But, for Witte, this did not mean that the Duma should not be intimately involved in other aspects of the legislative process. He assumed that members of the Duma would have both the experience and the competence to wrestle with many domestic issues, including the peasant question. Most of Witte's illiberal utterances in the Crown Council sessions reflected the frustration he had experienced as chairman of the Council of Ministers in trying to win public support for his government. He was not certain how far Russian citizens could be trusted. He was aware that the revolution had been brought to a halt more by the force of the tsarist police and army than by promises of reform. What could one reasonably expect from a Duma representing a mass of people so recently in revolt against tsarist power? The result was that Witte sometimes idealized the public and other times approached it as if it were an enemy.

The October 17 Manifesto was wildly acclaimed in Russia, while the Fundamental Laws were greeted with hostility. In part this arose from the essential differences between the two documents. The Manifesto promised much and guaranteed nothing; the Fundamental Laws established the limits to which the government was willing to go. The Manifesto was various things to different people; a person was able to make of it what he wished. The Fundamental Laws expressed in formal language the precise freedoms available to Russian citizens and the exact relationship between the people's representatives and the tsar. Although the Laws seemed to offer far less than the Manifesto had promised, they guaranteed far more. But, most important of all, with publication of the Fundamental Laws on April 24, 1906, constitutional government, regardless of how limited or conservative it might be, was created in Russia. As Witte himself put it, writing half a decade later: "In the last analysis I am convinced of the fact that Russia is a constitutional state *de facto,* and in it, as in other civilized states, the bases of civil freedom are firmly established."[61] But it was left to the government and to society to determine how effective the new order would be, a story of conflict, suspicion, and misunderstanding in which Witte, the chief architect of the reformed system, was destined to play almost no part.

X

CONCLUSION

He [Witte] will provide a glorious food for discussion for the future historian, and even at present the world would be a duller and grayer place without this enigmatical chameleon.

—MAURICE BARING
A Year in Russia

Witte's Last Act: A Government Program for the Duma

FOLLOWING FORMULATION of the Fundamental Laws and on the very eve of Witte's resignation as chairman of the Council of Ministers, he submitted to the tsar, as his last official act, a program of proposed legislation to be presented to the Duma on behalf of the government. The Council of Ministers, as we saw in chapter five, had first discussed this program on January 24, when Witte and the cabinet, in their report to Nicholas, had stressed the great importance of broad-scale and integrated legislation to give the peasants equal rights in all spheres and to end their special—and inferior—administrative, legal, and social status. The Council returned to this project on March 5, sending a memoir containing their conclusions to the tsar, who fully approved it on March 10. The ministers reported they had decided "to introduce before the elected representatives of the people a fully prepared and harmonious program on the most important issues so as not to be caught unawares by the opening of the first session of the Duma." Witte noted in the memoir that since the proposed program included the agrarian question, this issue, if not others, would undoubtedly evoke opposition in the Duma. Nevertheless, "he hoped that under the direction given by the government program there would be the least possible danger that the Duma would fruitlessly waste its strength in wrangling with representatives of the government in view of the path opened before it of useful and serious work."[1]

At this time, however, the proposal of the Council of Ministers was an idea only, as no complete and detailed program had yet been prepared. Two days later, on March 7, the Council discussed and approved the only draft program already formulated, that of the Ministry of Finance, which had been submitted to the Council as early as January 31, perhaps because Minister of Finance Shipov had been the first minister to urge, as early as in mid-January, the need for a government program for the Duma. On March 31 the Ministry of Justice submitted its proposal; on April 11 one arrived from the Ministry of Trade and Industry; those of the Ministry of Interior and of the Chief Administration for Land Organization and Agriculture may have been presented even later, as they are undated.[2] There is no record the other ministries ever submitted drafts. The summary program presented to the tsar is dated April 23, actually a week after Witte's formal resignation; presumably it was so late because of delays in organizing it into final form. There is a notation Nicholas read it on April 26, the day before the Duma opened, but no indication of his reaction. In any case, the tsar did not include the main points or even the general tenor of Witte's legislative program in his speech the next day, when the Duma convened.

Finally, two and one-half weeks later, on May 13, Witte's successor, I. L. Goremykin, presented to the Duma Witte's program, with minor changes and additions—but to little effect.[3] In the first place the Goremykin government failed to follow up the general guidelines of the program, and introduced only a few specific draft bills implementing it. Second, and more importantly, by then the government and the Duma were already hopelessly deadlocked over such issues as the formal relationship between them, a general amnesty, and agrarian reform involving compulsory alienation of land. Relations were so strained that no one, probably including the ministers themselves, took the government's program seriously, while many predicted, correctly at is turned out, that it was only a matter of time until the tsar dissolved the Duma. It is interesting to speculate as to what might have happened had the government, as Witte wished, taken the initiative and presented its program as soon as the Duma opened in an effort to guide it into "constructive" action. Or what the outcome might have been had Witte himself been permitted to remain in office and to attempt to steer his proposals through the Duma. In either case the results probably would have been little different—Witte's program was undoubtedly too moderate and cautious for the Kadets and leftists to endorse or work for—but certainly the outcome could hardly have been worse than what actually happened. At the very least a basis for discussion and a desire for earnest cooperation and serious purpose on the part of the government would have been established at the outset.

Witte's program was modest and incomplete, certainly offering far less than the majority of Duma members wanted; yet much of it was sensible and forward-looking. Most of it was later adopted and implemented by Stolypin. As in Witte's memoir to the tsar on January 24, the main emphasis was on the necessity of giving the peasantry equal rights and status, with all the social, economic, legal, and administrative changes this entailed.[4] The first and longest part of the program was devoted to the peasant question; many of the arguments and much of the comprehensive and almost sociological sweep of the memoir of January 24 were reaffirmed, but greater stress was placed on the benefits to the general welfare of the country that the proposed changes would bring and on their being the logical consequence of earlier actions and policies. For example, it was argued that since the Manifesto of October 17 had granted peasants, as all subjects of the tsar, equal political and civil rights, the peasants should now be made full citizens in every other sense, on a par with all other *sosloviia* or classes before the courts, in the legal and social order, and in the administrative system. Moreover, it was maintained, the November 3 decree ending redemption dues opened the way to abolition of all limitations on the right of private ownership of communal land since the main purpose of binding the peasant to the commune in 1861 had been to ensure collective responsibility for the redemption debt.

The program proposed the following land reforms for the peasants: a transition from communal to personal ownership of allotment lands; measures to facilitate voluntary withdrawal from the commune and establishment of private, consolidated plots; the institution of full legal and economic equality for peasants, particularly in buying and leasing land; and, finally, an extension of peasant land holdings in four ways—through improvement of land organization and utilization, through encouraging purchases via the Peasants' Bank, through the free gift to certain land-poor or landless peasants of some state lands, and through migration to Siberia and other underpopulated areas.[5] There followed detailed draft regulations governing not only withdrawal from the commune, establishment of personal property rights to land, expansion of the activity of the Peasants' Bank, and creation of the system of Land Organization Commissions (in accord with the ukase of March 4), but also the institution of equal rights for peasants before the law and in courts and the abolition of the special administrative system for peasants (census, land captains, village and volost administration and courts), which was to be replaced by integrating governance of the peasants into the regular administrative system of the state.

The Ministry of Justice, the Ministry of Interior, and the Chief Administration for Land Organization and Agriculture submitted less detailed but supportive and complementary draft proposals on the parts of these reforms that fell within their competence. The Ministry of Interior added recommendations to ease the internal passport system for all citizens. The Ministry of Justice proposed not only that local judicial power be taken away from volost courts and land captains and concentrated in the hands of elected justices of the peace, but that the latter be integrated into the regular judicial and appeals system, that justice throughout the empire be made uniform, and that the whole legal and judicial process be made simpler, closer to the people, cheaper, and more efficient and expeditious in its action. It also recommended revised regulations concerning the civil and criminal responsibility of officals and concerning acts against them.

The last set of draft proposals dealt with fiscal and economic questions. The Ministry of Finance recommended an income tax, the review of several indirect taxes, and a new law governing inheritance taxes. The Ministry of Trade and Industry proposed a system of elected institutions of representatives of trade and industry for exchange of views, collection of data, and promotion of their interests, as well as a series of technical bills dealing, for example, with the activities of bourse courts, the role of purchasing commissioners and agents, trade in flax and hemp, and the reestablishment of rapid sea transport in the Far East following the war. On the question of labor policy the Ministry presented no drafts, simply reporting it was working on such matters as accident and sickness insurance for workers, improvement of workers' living quarters, and regulation of working hours.[6] The Witte program as a whole had obvious gaps and inadequacies, yet the recommendations added up to a quite reasonable legislative beginning on the solution of some of Russia's more pressing problems. Like its sponsor, it was neither radical nor reactionary, and it certainly belied the charge that Witte, fearing the Duma, wanted to by-pass it or to turn over to it only inconsequential issues. It might, under other circumstances, have provided a point of departure for the government and the Duma to work together to build a reformed system and a more modern society.

Witte's Resignation

THE DAY AFTER WITTE submitted the program of his government to Nicholas, the Duma, a key promise of the October Manifesto and a vital part of Witte's whole conception for both restoring order and reforming Russian society, convened for its opening session in the splendor of the Winter Palace. A photograph of that moment shows Tsar Nicholas, looking uncannily like his cousin, George V of England, on a dais, surrounded by nobles, high Orthodox clergy, and court officials and ladies, reading the address from the throne to the Duma deputies standing before him, with the gentry and upper classes grouped to one side and the middle class, peasants, and workers to the other, in unconscious imitation of the Estates-General of 1789. Joyous hopes and high expectations filled the hearts and minds of the liberals, who saw the event as the crowning success of their long struggle for freedom, while conservatives and bureaucrats looked on with trepidation and scorn. The tsar spoke in a trembling voice, though clearly, but his words were received in a tomblike silence.[7] For his speech was general and vague, presenting no specific program, neither Witte's nor one suggested to him by the Kadets, nor anyone else's, and his remarks concerning the position and role of the Duma were entirely unsatisfactory to the bulk of the deputies. Thus, the new era opened on a sour note, which was, however, only a mild portent of the struggle and bitterness that were often to mar relations between the government and the Duma in the ensuing decade.

Yet Witte, the chief creator of the Duma system, played no part in the drama and pathos of that historic occasion, nor was he later to have a significant role in the stormy history of Duma Russia, for in an ukase of April 20, 1906, a week before the Duma opened, Nicholas had publicly announced Witte's resignation as chairman of the Council of Ministers, thus bringing to a close Witte's leadership of the government, exactly six months after it had officially begun. The tsar replaced Witte with Ivan L. Goremykin, a conservative bureaucrat who had impressed Nicholas during the April conferences on the Fundamental Laws by his uncompromising stand against letting the Duma propose forcible alienation of land. After two meetings with Goremykin, French Ambassador Bompard summed him up in what surely must be one of the most devastating thumbnail sketches in the annals of diplomatic reporting:

> Nourished in the offices, having served a great number of administrations, he [Goremykin] knows perfectly all the regulations and these provide him with a reply to everything. There is no difficulty, including mutinies and pillaging, that the rules do not cover. . . . All the problems which pose such a menacing threat today evoke in his memory some legal article where he finds a solution which satisfies him. Here is a receiver of registrations presiding at a revolution.[8]

Whatever one thinks of Witte and his program, Goremykin was hardly a worthy successor—which probably is exactly why Nicholas appointed him.

Witte's dismissal followed a letter he sent to the tsar on April 14, only two days after the foreign loan was issued, asking to be relieved of his post. In this letter Witte complained that the pressures of the office had shattered his nerves and that he found it impossible to continue working with Minister of Interior Durnovo, who regularly pursued policies that Witte opposed. Witte charged that there was no longer unity either in the Council of Ministers or in other spheres of government with regard to such critical concerns as religious, minority, and peasant problems. Witte noted that he had been under bitter and unceasing attack from all sides, including from certain individuals in and near the court. He argued that he had successfully completed the last major task before the government—the conclusion of the large international loan—and that he believed the tsar should choose a new minister to take charge of the government prior to the opening of the Duma. In view of these and other reasons he chose not to detail, Witte suggested that he deserved the release that he had been denied earlier in the year.[9]

Nicholas lost no time in accepting Witte's resignation. He approved Witte's dismissal on April 15, and sent Witte a letter of acceptance the next day.[10] In it the tsar congratulated Witte on the success of the loan and praised him for his "zeal" and "devotion," but then went on to criticize Witte indirectly by stating that the Duma representatives were so radical not because of the repressive policy of the government, as Witte had implied, but because of the excessive liberalism of the electoral law of December 11, the apathy of the conservative majority of the population, and the complete non-interference of the government in the elections.

As we saw in chapter five, Nicholas had been increasingly disillusioned with Witte at least since December, if not earlier, and Witte's influence at court and on policy had steadily declined throughout the winter. An oblique but nonetheless suggestive indicator of Witte's waning power is given in the tsar's diary: In January Nicholas received Trepov six times and Witte two; in February Trepov, eight and Witte, two; in March, Trepov, twelve and Witte, two.[11] Moreover the actions of Witte's government, and particularly those of Durnovo, had alienated whatever liberal support Witte had had after Portsmouth and the October Manifesto; the oppositionists came to consider him simply another bureaucrat, masking his determination to preserve the autocracy and the old order behind devious maneuvers, insincere pronouncements, and narcissistic ambitions. Yet the conservatives and court reactionaries liked him even less. Sullenly resenting the concessions made in the peace with Japan, secretly despising the October 17 program, and fearing both Witte's power in the government and his alleged weakness and vacillation before the revolutionary movement, they never trusted him and always suspected that he might work with and not against the Duma. Miliukov wrote graphically and accurately: "He [Witte] remained alone—cast off from one shore and not yet arrived at the other."[12] Aware of his fall from favor and embittered by the attacks on him from both right and left, Witte had tried, perhaps half-heartedly, to resign earlier, but he had not been permitted to do so while the loan was pending.

In contemporary opinion it was widely believed that Witte was being kept in office only until his financial prestige and skill had managed negotiation of the loan and that he would be expected to resign—or face being dismissed—as soon as that goal had been achieved.[13] In his memoirs Witte indicated that in 1906 he had been aware of his situation.[14] Nevertheless, it is barely possible, Gurko suggested in his memoirs, that Witte's conceit and ambition were so great that, as on earlier occasions, his April resignation was intended as a gesture, that it was in fact designed to strengthen his political position by extracting concessions from Nicholas as the price of Witte's remaining, and that Witte never expected that his resignation would be accepted.[15] But the overwhelming weight of other evidence indicates that Witte knew that unless he resigned, Nicholas would dismiss him.[16] To be sure, Witte was bitter, as the following incident shows, but this was undoubtedly because of his resentment at what he considered shabby treatment at the hands of the tsar and of public opinion. On April 19 Kokovtsov visited Witte and found him cleaning out his office. Witte told Kokovtsov: "You see before you the happiest of mortals. The tsar could not have shown me greater mercy than by dismissing me from this prison where I have been languishing. I am going abroad at once to take a cure; I do not want to hear about anything and shall merely imagine what is happening over here. All Russia is one vast madhouse."[17]

In any case Nicholas obviously had no regrets at his parting company with Witte. When Kokovtsov met the tsar immediately after Witte's dismissal, Nicholas indicated his relief by saying, "What is important to me is that Goremykin will not act behind my back, making agreements and concessions to damage my authority."[18] Immediately after his dismissal Witte went abroad for a prolonged rest, and in July Nicholas made it known through Baron Fredericks, his court aide, that Witte's "return to Russia at the present time would be very undesirable." Witte was properly outraged and offered to resign his position as an appointed member of the State Council at once.[19] Baron Fredericks apparently never transmitted this request to the tsar and the whole affair blew over, but in November 1906, when Witte finally did return to St. Petersburg, Nicholas confided to his mother: "As long as I live, I will never trust that man again with the smallest thing. I had quite enough of last year's experiment. It is still like a nightmare to me. Thank God I have not seen him yet!"[20] Nicholas' bitterness over the damage he came to believe Witte had done to his inherited authority and autocratic prestige did not disappear with the passage of time, either. In a remarkable statement from a man who was generally considered personally kind and humane, Nicholas wrote his wife on March 14, 1915:

> I have such a feeling of calmness in my soul that even I am surprised. Whether this is because I met yesterday evening with Our Friend [Rasputin], or because I saw in the newspapers, which Buchanan gave me, news of the death of Witte, or perhaps because of a feeling that the war is going somewhat better, I cannot say, but in my heart reigns a truly Easter-like peace.[21]

An Evaluation of Witte as Chairman of the Council of Ministers

WITTE MAY HAVE BEEN the most misunderstood Russian of his time. It was difficult to be neutral toward Witte; he stimulated strong reactions among those who supported him as well as those who opposed him. Yet to all he remained essentially an enigma. Nicholas II believed him to be a chameleon and a traitor to autocracy. To some, he was but a political opportunist, one who was willing to adopt any idea or to advance any program that furthered his own career. To others, he was a brilliant statesman, committed to introducing a reformed, though conservative, system in Russia and to advancing the economic strength and general welfare of the country. The fact that he represented a new type of Russian minister—businesslike and professional rather than aristocratic—contributed to the confusion about him. No label, conservative, liberal, reactionary, quite describes his elusive personality. In part Witte's enigmatic qualities arose from his skill as a tactician. A master at political intrigue, he revealed only that part of his motives and plans that furthered his goals.

Both historians and Witte's contemporaries have differed widely in their assessment of his qualities, motives, and achievements. Although there is almost unanimous agreement on Witte's brilliance, energy, and general ability, overall favorable judgments are in the minority, as might be expected in regard to a man who was so controversial, who lacked a warm and sympathetic personality, and who, by his own pragmatic standards at least, failed. Two of his confidants believed that he was not only talented and original, but also sincere and skillful in his effort to reform Russia and that but for the total lack of support and understanding for his policies he might have succeeded in saving the tsarist system while gradually limiting the tsar's power.[22] A leading right-wing liberal, V. A. Maklakov, maintained that Witte was one of the greatest figures of his time, "the last of the leaders of the 'liberal autocracy' as it had been known in the epoch of the 1860's." In Maklakov's view, the liberals should have supported Witte's effort, in the tradition of the great reforms, to build a new Russia based on capitalism and law.[23]

On the other hand, Witte's detractors have found much in him to criticize. Some historians, as well as contemporaries, viewed him as unscrupulous and opportunistic, a man without principle or ideology. One group attributed this to his vanity, ambition, and lust for power.[24] Others, including most Soviet historians, argued that Witte, insofar as he believed in anything, was basically a monarchist (though not necessarily an absolutist), who favored a kind of enlightened despotism and who cynically used the promise and illusion of reform and a sham constitutionalism to attempt to preserve the essentials of the autocracy and the old order.[25] However they viewed Witte's motives, a number of writers concluded that Witte failed because of defects of character, because his moral qualities were not equal to his talents and mental abilities. Thus, Witte has been accused of trying above all to curry favor with the tsar and court circles, of being unable to act decisively and consistently, of being weak and vacillating, of being too temperamental, and of lacking the courage to meet the challenges he faced.[26] Perhaps the most scathing indictment of Witte along these lines was set out by Bompard, who argued that Witte could have led Russia on a new path, could have saved Russia, but

> he was inferior to the task, I would say, even to his own capacity. . . . For two years [1903–05] he suffered because he was deprived of the great power he had exercised for ten. He tried to get back in the tsar's good graces, and thus in 1905 he refused to stand forth as the creator of a constitutional government and the leader of a constitutional party but instead defended the autocracy, thereby losing all chance for real power and finding himself in a position where he could later be cast aside.[27]

Not everyone has judged Witte's failure so harshly. Several authors have pointed out Witte faced enormous problems and he had to try to cope with them virtually alone, without significant support either from within the government or from the public. As the British journalist Dillon put it, Witte "was a solitary man fighting his enemies boldly and his 'friends' hesitatingly, the trustee of a State that distrusted him, the spokesman of a body that frequently disavowed and silenced him, the champion of a community that paralyzed him, a limb torn off from society."[28]

In two separate but remarkably similar incidents two years after his resignation, Witte evaluated his own efforts as chairman of the Council of Ministers. In June 1908, when asked about his attitude toward constitutionalism, Witte answered:

> There is really no love for constitutionalism in my heart or soul. But I urged it [the October 17 Manifesto] as a physician would urge a patient to take a laxative. The remedy was the product of my mind. I realized that this operation, if it may be called so, was absolutely essential. Without it the Russian Government was on the point of . . . crumbling away.[29]

In the same year Samuel Harper and Bernard Pares interviewed Witte and asked, "What do you think of a constitution now?" Witte replied, "I have a constitution in my head . . . but as to my heart . . ." and then Pares said that he spat before them on the ground.[30]

Although the two statements are similar, there is an important difference. The first implies that Witte cynically used the Manifesto as a weapon to save the autocracy and had no real interest in a constitutional order. The second quotation implies that there was a conflict raging within Witte, a conflict between his instincts that were autocratic and his reason that told him that constitutionalism must become a reality. It is primarily the difference reflected in these statements that has divided historians in their interpretations of Witte.

Von Laue, who has studied Witte's career more thoroughly than any other Western historian, concluded that Witte's motives were much more complex than simply an attempt to save the autocracy, and he has used the second of these quotations as the basis for an interpretation of Witte's career as chairman of the Council of Ministers. According to von Laue, in his heart Witte favored autocracy but in his mind he recognized the historical inevitability of constitutional government. The reason therefore that Witte failed to demonstrate his usual steadfastness during these six months "was the inner conflict between head and heart and the deeper contradictions it symbolized." Von Laue recognized the major paradoxes that ran through Witte's tenure as prime minister: his desire to restore order but the equally strong desire to initiate genuine reform; his desire to retain the sources of power for the monarch, but also his wish to involve the public in governmental affairs. Witte was trying to pursue conflicting goals. He maintained his loyalty to autocracy, yet he was willing to promote measures designed to limit the prerogatives of the autocrat. According to von Laue, Witte was never fully aware of the deep contradictions that distinguished his policies—contradictions that debilitated his leadership and that justified his dismissal.[31]

In the disillusionment and frustration that he experienced after his discharge in April 1906, and that are reflected both in these statements and in his memoirs, Witte failed to do justice to the complexity of his thinking as he sought to rescue Russia from revolution. It is true that by instinct Witte was a monarchist, but he had concluded by October 1905, that concessions were necessary to regain for the government the support of the majority of the public. Witte told the tsar on October 9, 1905, that the government always seemed to be trying to catch up with society; it must somehow recapture the leadership it had lost. According to Witte, the government was too frightened of words such as "constitution." It must provide a system that advanced the spiritual and material well-being of all its citizens and not worry about labels or about preserving one form of rule or another.

Unfortunately for Witte, he did not make his conception for resolving the crisis completely clear to the tsar. Witte wished only for the government to commit itself to a program of political and social reform; the exact measures to be enacted would require time and study before they could be established in any definite way. But the tsar, anxious to restore order immediately and suspicious that Witte sought power for himself, favored announcing specific reforms in the form of an imperial gift. The result was that Witte was forced to operate under the terms of a Manifesto whose publication he had sought to avoid.

The Manifesto served to bind Witte; he was believed responsible for its writing and its publication and was held accountable to its terms by all classes of Russian society. Any deviation or apparent retreat from its promises was sure to bring down on Witte the wrath of the opposition. How much better off Witte would have been if he could have operated under the far less restrictive terms of his own report. Moreover, the Manifesto was a psychological jolt to Russian society. After centuries of repression and decades of struggle, the bonds of tyranny seemed miraculously loosened. The "days of freedom" were intoxicating but contributed little to a sense of responsibility; instead they led to renewed conflict with the authorities and fed growing anarchic trends.

Thus the October Manifesto did not bring order, peace, and harmony. New violence occurred, and old disturbances continued. Faced with strikes at home and rebellion in the provinces, in late December and January Witte approved policies aimed at suppressing disorder, policies whose severity surprised even the tsar.

A public demand for wide-scale social reform matched with an almost equal demand for restoration of order; a need to win public confidence in the government while maintaining the support of the tsar: these were the salient, usually contradictory, demands Witte had to accommodate. Through it all, Witte, a professional bureaucrat who preferred to work under the shelter of a monarchy but who realized the former political system was no longer adequate for the task, tried to lay the foundation for a new order by preserving the advantages of the monarchy while meeting the demands of the public for political power. His solution was a legislature which would represent the public and engage its leaders in the legislative process and an executive branch firmly in the control of the tsar, whose ministers were responsible only to him for their actions. While Witte's conception of a constitutional regime may have been limited, it was one that was based upon law rather than tsarist caprice, that protected the rights of its citizens as well as its monarch and that involved the leaders of the public in governmental affairs: an imaginative conception for a *chinovnik*.

The Times and the Man

AT THE VERY BEGINNING of this study the words of Thomas Carlyle were quoted regarding the relationship between significant times and great men. There is no doubt that Witte's six-month tenure as chairman of the Council of Ministers was an important half-year in Russian history. Not only was this period a brief segment of a larger, crucial era during which Russia was in flux socially, politically, and economically, but this period was important in its own right. The government had been challenged by its own citizens in a way and to a degree it had never been before nor would be again until twelve years later, when it ultimately fell. The discontent which had been smoldering beneath erupted violently for all to see. Into this crisis Witte, undoubtedly the ablest and most resourceful leader in Russia, was thrust.

His record is a puzzling one. For here was a man who, in the midst of disorder and violence, succeeded almost single-handedly in instituting rudimentary civil liberties in Russia, in setting up modern Russia's first national representative assembly, in conducting free and orderly elections among some forty or fifty million largely illiterate and inexperienced voters, in helping shape and establish a state order based on law (through the Fundamental Laws), in working out a comprehensive and basic reform of all phases of peasant life—in scope, degree of radical change, and number of people affected, certainly one of the major social revolutions of modern times when it was finally implemented—and in concluding the largest international loan in history to that date, which had major implications for European international relations. And all this was accomplished in six months! Yet Witte as prime minister is generally considered a failure. How is this possible?

The answer lies in the character of the man himself, in the individuals, groups, and conditions with which he had to contend, and in the nature of the social and political crisis he faced. Despite his Herculean effort this combination of forces proved in the end too much for Witte, with tragic results. Though he saved the monarchy from disaster, this was only a reprieve. The basic ingredients necessary to make a reformed and modernized Russia work—trust and understanding between government and people and social responsibility among all classes—Witte could not create or develop, and ironically his tenure in office probably worsened the chances of such cooperation ever being realized in Russia. As we have seen, much of the explanation for this can be found in the conflict that raged within Witte himself. In addition, both instinct and reason convinced Witte that order must be restored and the government saved before reform could be effected. As Witte declared in July 1905, on the eve of the crisis:

> The world should be surprised that we have any government in Russia, not that we have an imperfect government. With many nationalities, many languages, and a nation largely illiterate, the marvel is that the country can be held together even by autocracy. Remember one thing: if the tsar's government falls, you will see absolute chaos in Russia, and it will be many a year before you see another government able to control the mixture that makes up the Russian nation.[32]

Moreover, his conception of what Russia needed, while not necessarily inherently faulty, had two politically fatal defects. Witte wanted a benevolent monarchy exercizing its rule through a rational and centralized bureaucracy, with the people's representatives having their say in, but not control of, domestic affairs. But this was too pragmatic and utilitarian to capture the popular imagination or even to be properly understood; it could not be articulated ideologically; and it of course failed entirely to meet the principled demands of the liberal leaders of "society." Second, this conception, coupled with his own inner contradictions and with his concern for order, made Witte's actions and policies seem inconsistent and vacillating. They were *ad hoc* responses to particular issues, in which neither the conservatives nor the liberals could find a satisfactory pattern. Thus, Witte was unable to establish any sort of a base of political power nor to reach an understanding or even accommodation with social and political forces to the left or to the right. The consequence was that early in his premiership he became widely distrusted, almost totally isolated, and increasingly impotent. He plunged ahead with his plans for "reform from above" but failed to please anyone. He was a moderate caught in the vise of a revolutionary crisis.

A second major factor contributing to the tragedy of Witte's attempt to "save" Russia was the forces with which he had to deal. Given the nature of the autocratic system, reform could come only through and with the support of the tsar, unless the whole structure were to be replaced.[33] Yet Nicholas was too limited to understand Witte's basic conception, too unimaginative to see the advantages of "reform from above," too jealous of his prerogatives to do what had to be done, except under duress, and too suspicious of Witte to give him the support he needed. After October Nicholas thought he had given all he could—and perhaps more than he should have, though he was determined not to go back on his word. Therefore, he was understandably puzzled when his gracious gift failed to restore order and to satisfy his subjects. Moreover, the autocracy as an institution was self-limiting in its ability to effect change, which if it were to go too far, would undermine the bases of the system itself. Thus there were severe personal and institutional limitations on what Witte could achieve—the wonder is not that he failed in the end but that he was able to accomplish as much as he did in the way of "within-system" changes.

In addition, Witte had to battle an entrenched and blind conservatism which exerted its influence on the court, throughout the government and administration, among the landed gentry, and even in certain industrial circles and among the masses (viz., the Union of Russian People). Though poorly organized and largely inarticulate, the hidden force and resistance to change of conservative opinion were immense and clearly played a significant role in defeating Witte. Finally, there were the liberals, hypnotized by their "mystique of revolution." Committed to principle, deeply scarred by the tradition of struggle and hatred against the government, distrustful of Witte, they understandably were unable to meet him half-way, to join in a common effort to reform the old order. They wanted a new order, a fresh basis for society, which were probably unrealistic goals at that time. Whether it would have made any difference if they had supported Witte remains a matter for speculation, yet it is tempting to believe that the tsar and the conservatives might have hesitated to act against the combined force of both Witte and the oppositionists.

Criticized by the liberals, undercut by the conservatives, Witte found himself struggling alone. Moreover, his adversaries were shadowy phantoms: the conservatives sniped at him from the labyrinth of the bureaucracy and through the intrigues of the court, while the opposition, fractured and splintered after the October Manifesto, never provided a cohesive force with which one could negotiate, deal—or even which one could effectively suppress. Worst of all, perhaps, Witte had to face elemental forces in Russian society which were basically emotional and irrational, as the reaction to the October Manifesto showed. The peasant revolt, the pogroms, the excesses of the revolutionary struggles in December all revealed deep-seated anarchic trends in Russian life that were hardly amenable to control through reason and gradual reform. Witte decided force had to be used, which succeeded in restoring a kind of sullen order but which served also to widen the gap between government and people, between "the two Russias."

Lastly, the crisis confronting Witte may have been insoluble, regardless of his defects or the forces opposing him. It is ironic that Witte was called upon to resolve a situation which his own earlier policies as minister of Finance had helped create. Russia was in the throes of profound social, economic, cultural, and political upheaval created by the undermining of old values and institutions in the process of modernization. The attempt rapidly to transform the whole society from traditional agrarianism to industrial capitalism within the framework of an antiquated government and social structure created stresses, the manfestations of which were readily apparent in the revolution of 1905. Thus, Witte, concerned with tradition but reform-minded, confronted social revolution and extremist plans and organizations fed by the growing needs and expectations of a dislocated populace. As in many emerging nations today, the dilemma of order and reform was sharply posed in 1905 in Russia, the first of the modern developing societies. It is hardly surprising that Witte was unable to find the answer to a puzzle which few since have been able to solve.

Appendix A

The Manifesto of October 17, 1905[*]

UNREST AND DISTURBANCES in the capitals and in many parts of Our Empire fill Our heart with great and heavy grief. The welfare of the Russian Sovereign is inseparable from the welfare of the people, and the people's sorrow is His sorrow. The unrest, which now has made its appearance, may give rise to profound disaffection among the people and become a menace to the integrity and unity of Our State.

The great vow of Tsarist service enjoins Us to strive with all the force of Our reason and authority for the quickest cessation of unrest so perilous to the State. Having ordered the proper authorities to take measures to suppress the direct manifestations of disorder, rioting, and violence, and to guard the safety of peaceful people who seek to fulfill in peace the duties incumbent upon them. We, in order to carry out more successfully the measures designed by Us for the pacification of the State, have recognized the necessity to coordinate the activities of the higher Government.

We impose upon the Government the obligation to carry out Our inflexible will:

1.) To grant the population the unshakable foundations of civic freedom based on the principles of real personal inviolability, freedom of conscience, speech, assembly, and union.

2.) Without halting the scheduled elections to the State Duma, to admit to participation in the Duma, as far as is possible in the short time remaining before its call, those classes of the population which at present are altogether deprived of the franchise, leaving the further

[*] *Polnoe sobranie zakonov'*, vol. XXV, Part II, no. 26803. (Our translation)

development of the principle of universal suffrage to the new legislative order, and

3.) To establish it as an unbreakable rule that no law can become effective without the approval of the State Duma and that the elected representatives of the people should be guaranteed an opportunity for actual participation in the supervision of the legality of the actions of authorities appointed by Us.

We call upon all the faithful sons of Russia to remember their duty to their Fatherland, to aid in putting an end to the unprecedented disturbances, and together with Us to make every effort to restore peace and quiet in our native land.

Issued at Peterhof on the seventeenth day of October in the year of Our Lord, nineteen hundred and five, and the eleventh year of Our reign. The original text signed in His Imperial Majesty's own hand.

NICHOLAS

Appendix B

OFFICIAL REPORT OF COUNT SERGEI WITTE
SANCTIONED BY TSAR NICHOLAS II ON OCTOBER 17, 1905[*]

THE UNREST which has seized the various classes of the Russian people cannot be looked upon as the consequence of the partial imperfections of the political and social order or as the result of the activities of organized extreme parties. The roots of that unrest lie deeper. They are in the disturbed equilibrium between the aspirations of the thinking elements and the external forms of their life. Russia has outgrown the existing régime and is striving for an order based on civic liberty. Consequently, the forms of Russia's political life must be raised to the level of the ideas which animate the moderate majority of the people.

The first task of the Government is immediately to establish the basic elements of the new order, notably personal inviolability and the freedom of the press, of conscience, of assemblage, and of association, without waiting for the legislative sanction of these measures by the Imperial Duma. The further strengthening of these foundations of the political life of the country must be effected in the regular legislative procedure, just as the work of equalizing all the Russian citizens, without distinction of religion and nationality, before the law. It goes without saying that the civic liberties granted to the people must be lawfully

[*] Witte, *Vospominaniia*, III, 4–7. The translation is by Abraham Yarmolinsky from *The Memoirs of Count Witte*, tr. and ed. by Abraham Yarmolinsky (London: 1921), 234–36. Those passages which are in italics were not included in the Yarmolinsky translation and have been translated and added by the authors from the text in *Vospominaniia*.

restricted, so as to safeguard the rights of the third persons and peace and the safety of the State.

The next task of the Government is to establish institutions and legislative principles which would harmonize with the political ideals of the majority of the Russian people and which would guarantee the inalienability of the previously granted blessings of civic liberty. *This task requires the construction of a legal order.* The economic policy of the Government must aim at the good of the broad masses, at the same time safeguarding those property and civil rights which are recognized in all the civilized countries.

The above-outlined foundations of the Government's activity will necessitate a great deal of legislative and administrative work. A period of time is bound to elapse between the enunciation of a principle and its embodiment in legislative norms or, furthermore, the introduction of these norms into the life of the people and the practice of the Governmental agents. No Government is able at once to force a new political régime upon a vast country with a heterogeneous population of 135 million, and an intricate administration brought up on other principles and traditions. It is not sufficient for the Government to adopt the motto of civic liberty to inaugurate the new order. Alone the untiring and concerted efforts of a homogeneous Government, animated by one aim and purpose, will bring it about. *But even the ministry composed insofar as possible of people of one political persuasion will have to be supplemented in its work by ideas arising from all levels of authority. The concern of the Government must be to promote civic freedom.*

The situation demands that the Government should only use methods testifying to the sincerity and frankness of its intentions. Consequently, the Government must scrupulously refrain from interfering with the elections to the Imperial Duma, and also sincerely strive to carry out the reforms outlined in the decree of December 12, 1904. The Government must uphold the prestige of the future Duma and have confidence in its work. So long as the Duma's decisions are not out of keeping with Russia's grandeur, the result of the age-long process of her history, the Government must not oppose them. In accordance with the letter and spirit of his Majesty's manifesto, the regulations relating to the Imperial Duma are subject to further development, in proportion as the imperfections of that institution come to light and as new demands arise. Guided by the ideas prevalent among the people, the Government must formulate these demands, constantly striving to satisfy the desires of the masses. It is very important to reconstruct the

Imperial Council on the basis of the principle of elected membership, for that alone will enable the Government to establish normal relations between that institution and the Imperial Duma.

Without enumerating the other measures to be taken by the Government, I wish to state the following principles which, I believe, must guide the authorities at all the stages of their activity:

1. Frankness and sincerity in the establishment of all the newly granted rights and privileges.
2. A firm tendency toward the elimination of extraordinary regulations.
3. Coördination of the activities of all the Governmental agents.
4. Avoidance of measures of repression directed against acts which do not threaten either Society or the State, and
5. Firm suppression of all actions menacing Society or the State, in strict accordance with the law and in spiritual union with the moderate majority of the people.

It goes without saying that the accomplishment of the outlined tasks will only be possible with the broad and active coöperation of the public and on the condition of peace, which alone will enable the Government to apply all its forces to fruitful work. We have faith in the political tact of the Russian people. It is unthinkable that the people should desire anarchy, which, in addition to all the horrors of civil war, holds the menace of the disintegration of the very State.

Appendix C

Fundamental Laws*

	Draft of Council of	
Original Draft	Ministers	Final Version
1. The Russian Empire consists of all lands in its sovereign possession and is a united and indivisible state.	1. The Russian State is united and indivisible.	1. (Same as Council of Ministers)

Part I: On the Nature of Supreme Autocratic Authority

5. The Tsar Emperor, the All-Russian Autocrat, possesses Supreme Power in the State.	4. The All-Russian Emperor possesses Supreme and Autocratic power. To obey His authority not only from fear but also from conscience is ordered by God Himself.	4. (Same as Council of Ministers)
Absent	Absent	8. (Last part) Only on the initiative of the Tsar can the Fundamental State Laws be submitted to review by the State Council and State Duma.

* This chart is based on comparisons found in a report in TsGIAL, Fund 1276, op. 2, d. 7, and on the official version of the Fundamental Laws (see Ch. 9, n. 58). See also *Krasnyi arkhiv*, XI–XII, 121–42.

Original Draft	*Draft of Council of Ministers*	*Final Version*
10. The Tsar Emperor confirms laws and issues ukases necessary for putting laws into effect.	11. The Tsar Emperor with respect to the supreme administration issues, in conformity with the laws, Ukases and orders necessary to fulfill laws, to organize parts of the state administration, to preserve state and public security and order, and also to guarantee the peoples' well-being. Ukases issued with respect to the supreme administration are promulgated by the Governing Senate.	11. The Tsar Emperor, with respect to the supreme administration, issues, in conformity with the laws, ukases to organize and to establish different parts of the state administration, as well as orders necessary to fulfill laws.
Absent	Absent	12. The Tsar Emperor is the supreme conductor of all foreign relations of the Russian State with foreign powers. He defines the direction of the international policies of the Russian State.
14. The Tsar Emperor is the Mighty Leader of the Russian army and fleet. He possesses supreme command over all military and naval forces of the Russian State.	13. (First two sentences identical with original draft.) He determines the organization of the army and navy, issues orders regarding the stationing of the army, its mobilization, its combat training, and the terms of service of members of the army and navy. He establishes the limits of the rights of habitation and property in localities which are fortified regions or defense points for the army and navy.	14. (Same as Council of Ministers, with addition of phrase at end of third sentence: "and in general everything relating to the maintenance of the armed forces and the defense of the Russian State.")

Original Draft	Draft of Council of Ministers	Final Version
Absent	18. The Tsar Emperor declares localities under martial law or under a state of extraordinary security.	15. (Same as Council of Ministers)
12. The Tsar Emperor appoints and dismisses the Chairman of the Council of Ministers, Ministers, and all other responsible officials, provided that for the last group no other procedure governing their appointment and dismissal has been established by law.	15. (Majority report) The Tsar Emperor appoints the Chairman of the Council of Ministers, Ministers, and Heads of separate departments, as well as other responsible officials, provided that for the last group no other procedure governing their appointment has been established by law. His Majesty has the right to dismiss from state service all, without exception, responsible officials. [i.e., including judges]	17. (Same as original)
15. Acts issued by the Tsar Emperor concerning the administration of the state will be countersigned by the Chairman of the Council of Ministers or a designated Minister.	Absent	26. Ukases and orders of the Tsar Emperor in furtherance of the supreme administration will be countersigned by the Chairman of the Council of Ministers or a designated Minister or Head of a department and will be promulgated by the Governing Senate.

Part II: Concerning the Rights and Duties of Russian Citizens

24. No one can be arrested otherwise than in instances defined by law, nor detained in places not established by law.	26. No one can be arrested otherwise than in instances defined by law.	31. (Same as Council of Ministers)

Original Draft	Draft of Council of Ministers	Final Version
25. Any person detained for 24 hours in a place where judicial authority exists, or in other places for 3 days from the time of his detention must be either released or presented to judicial authority, which after an immediate review of the circumstances of the detention must either release the detained individual or determine, with an explanation of the basis, the length of his further detention. For outlying rural areas, where adherence to these time limits is impossible, detention can be prolonged by a special law.	Absent	Absent
27. No punishment, exile, or limitation of rights can be imposed other than by judicial authority, except in instances specially defined by law.	Absent	Absent
29. Private correspondence is not subject to seizure and inspection except in instances defined by law.	Absent	Absent
31 Property is inviolable. Forcible alienation of property is permitted only in instances and under procedures defined by law.	30. Property is inviolable. Forcible alienation of property is permitted only in instances and under procedures defined by law, for state or public needs, and then only with just compensation.	35. Property is inviolable. Forcible alienation of immovable property, when this is necessary for some state or public purpose, is permitted only with just and proper compensation.

Original Draft	*Draft of Council of Ministers*	*Final Version*

32. All Russian citizens are free to meet for purposes not prohibited by law, both in closed places and under the open sky, peacefully and unarmed. The conditions under which meetings can proceed, the conditions of their obligatory closing, as well as any limitation of places for meetings and procedures for attendance at them by local authorities, will all be determined by law.

31. Russian citizens have the right to hold meetings for purposes not prohibited by law, peacefully and unarmed. The conditions under which meetings proceed, are obliged to close, as well as any limitation of places for meetings, will be determined by law.

36. (Same as Council of Ministers)

35. All Russian citizens are free to submit to government authorities petitions concerning public and state needs.

Absent

Absent

Absent

34. Russian citizens may exercise freedom of religion according to the dictates of their own consciences. The conditions of transfer from one faith to another or conversion to another faith will be determined by law.

39. Russian citizens may exercise freedom of belief. The conditions of the utilization of this freedom will be determined by law.

Part III: Concerning Laws

41. When the State Duma is not in session, if extraordinary circumstances require legislative action, the Council of Ministers may present a measure directly

40. (Same as original draft)

45. (Same as original draft—often referred to as Article 87; see 395, n. 59.)

Original Draft	*Draft of Council of Ministers*	*Final Version*
to the Emperor. This measure cannot, however, introduce changes either in the Fundamental State Laws, or in the institutions of the State Council and State Duma, or in regulations governing elections to the Council and Duma. Such a measure becomes void if a draft law corresponding to the measure is not submitted to the Duma by a Minister or responsible department head within the first two months after the Duma reconvenes, or if the draft law is not passed by the Duma and State Council.		

Part IV: Concerning the State Council and the State Duma and the Nature of their Activities

Absent	59. Commitments to pay state debts and other obligations incurred by the state cannot be curtailed.	72. In discussion of State Budgets commitments to pay state debts and other obligations incurred by the Russian State cannot be curtailed or abrogated.
Absent	60. If the state budget is not passed by the beginning of the fiscal period, then the last legally approved budget remains in effect, with only those changes stipulated by the fulfillment of subsequent le-	74. (Same as Council of Ministers)

Original Draft	*Draft of Council of Ministers*	*Final Version*
	gal amendments. Until publication of a new budget, by a declaration of the Council of Ministers funds can be gradually distributed to the Ministries and Chief Administrations for their actual needs, not exceeding in one month, however, one-twelfth of the total expenditures of the budget.	
Absent	62. Extraordinary extra-budget credits for needs in time of war or for special preparations for war can be distributed to all departments on bases determined by law.	75. (Same as Council of Ministers)
Absent	Absent	76. State loans to meet both budgetary and extra-budgetary expenses are made in a manner similar to that for approval of the State Budget. State loans to meet expenses in cases and within limits set forth in Article 74, and also loans to meet expenses arising from situations set forth in Article 75 are made by the Tsar Emperor through the supreme administration. The length and conditions of termination of state loans are determined by the supreme administration.

Original Draft	*Draft of Council of Ministers*	*Final Version*
Absent	61. If, after the timely introduction into the State Duma of a bill determining the number of men required to serve in the army and navy, it is not approved by May 1 of each year, then the number of men needed for military service, not to exceed the number called the preceding year, can be set by Imperial Ukase.	77. (Same as Council of Ministers)
56. Draft bills initiated and approved by the State Council or State Duma and not receiving Imperial approval cannot be reintroduced during that same session. Draft bills initiated and approved by the State Council or State Duma and rejected by the other body can be reintroduced during the same session at the request of the Tsar.	Absent	70. (Same as original draft)
57. Deputations and written or oral declarations and requests are prohibited from the State Council and State Duma.	Absent	Absent

Part V: Concerning the Council of Ministers

64. The Chairman of the Council of Ministers and the Ministers are jointly responsible for the overall conduct of	69. The Chairman of the Council of Ministers, the Ministers, and the Heads of departments are responsible,	81. (Same as Council of Ministers with omission of phrase "within limits of their authority.")

| | *Draft of Council of* | |
| *Original Draft* | *Ministers* | *Final Version* |

state affairs. Each of them is separately responsible for his personal activities and orders.

as a group, to His Imperial Majesty for the overall conduct of state affairs within the limits of their authority. Each of them is separately responsible for his personal activities and orders.

65. For violation of the principles of the Fundamental Laws or for similar damage to the interests of the state by excesses, inactivity, or abuse of authority, the Chairman of the Council of Ministers and the Ministers are to be held responsible in a manner determined by law. For, in the execution of their duties, infringement of laws or of the rights of private individuals the Chairman of the Council of Ministers and the Ministers can be held responsible in civil and criminal law.

70. For violation of their duty of service the Chairman of the Council of Ministers, Ministers, and Heads of departments are civilly and criminally responsible on bases determined by law.

82. For criminal acts while in office the Chairman of the Council of Ministers, Ministers, and Heads of departments are civilly and criminally responsible on bases determined by law.

Notes

PREFACE

1. Despite Witte's obvious importance to Russian history during the decade before and the one following the turn of the century, Witte's life and career have received inadequate attention. No biography of Witte exists. The fine monograph by Theodore H. von Laue, *Sergei Witte and the Industrialization of Russia* (New York: 1963), is by far the best study available on Witte, but it is limited to Witte's career as minister of Finance. Witte's memoirs are valuable but cannot be completely relied upon. The memoirs of his contemporaries—e.g., Gurko, Maklakov, Kokovtsov, Shipov, Miliukov, and Iswolsky—all yield interesting bits of information, but in general these men were unable to appraise Witte calmly and impartially.

CHAPTER I

1. *At the Court of the Last Tsar: Being the Memoirs of A. A. Mossolov*, ed. by A. A. Pilenco (London: 1935), 128. (Hereafter cited as *Mossolov Memoirs.*)

2. Unfortunately, no really satisfactory biography of Nicholas II exists. There is a popular account based on non-Russian sources, Robert K. Massie, *Nicholas and Alexandra* (New York: 1967), which is interesting and revealing on Nicholas' character, but historically often unsound. There are also two useful but inadequate histories: Sergei S. Ol'denburg, *Tsarstvovanie imperatora Nikolai II* [The reign of Emperor Nicholas II] (Belgrade-Munich: 1939) and Constantin de Grunwald, *Le Tsar Nicholas II* (Paris: 1955).

3. de Grunwald, chapter three.

4. *Recollections of a Foreign Minister: Memoirs of Alexander Iswolsky*, tr. by Charles Louis Seeger (Garden City, N.Y.: 1921), 291; (Hereafter cited as *Memoirs of Alexander Iswolsky*.); *Mossolov Memoirs*, 9.

5. Sergius Iu. Witte, *Vospominaniia* [Reminiscences], 3 vols., ed. by A. L. Sidorov (Reprinted, Moscow: 1960), II, 329. (Hereafter cited as *Vospominaniia*.)

6. Ibid., II, 540.

7. Nicholas II told Witte on December 11, 1904, "Certainly, I will never in any case consent to a representative government, because I believe it is dangerous to the people God entrusted to me. . . ." Nicholas II, *Das Tagebuch des letzten Zaren von 1890 bis zum Fall: Nach den unveröffentlichten russischen Handschriften herausgegeben* (Berlin: 1923), 214. (Hereafter cited as *Tagebuch.*)

8. Theodore H. von Laue, *Sergei Witte and the Industrialization of Russia*, 127.

9. Theodore H. von Laue, "Imperial Russia at the Turn of the Century: The Cultural Slope and the Revolution from Without," *Comparative Studies in Society and History*, vol. III (1960-1961): 365.

10. Donald W. Treadgold, *Lenin and His Rivals: The Struggle for Russia's Future, 1898–1906* (New York: 1955), 155.

11. Boris Savinkov, *Memoirs of a Terrorist* (New York: 1931), 316.

12. George Fischer, *Russian Liberalism from Gentry to Intelligentsia* (Cambridge, Mass.: 1958), 200.

13. No one saw this more clearly than Witte. In his book *Samoderzhavie i zemstvo* [Autocracy and the Zemstvo] (Stuttgart: 1901), Witte explained that autocracy and the zemstvos were incompatible for the zemstvos would inevitably press for national representative institutions, which would in turn undermine the basic principles of autocracy. This conflict between the zemstvoists and the bureaucrats was further demonstrated in two conferences that took place in 1901—one, between D. N. Shipov, a leader of the zemstvo movement, and V. K. von Plehve, minister of Interior, and the other between Shipov and Witte, at that time minister of Finance. These conversations are reported in D. N. Shipov, *Vospominaniia i dumy o perezhitom* [Reminiscences and thoughts about the past] (Moscow: 1918), 171–97.

14. P. N. Miliukov, *Russia and Its Crisis* (Reprinted, New York: 1962), 211.

15. See a translation of the "eleven theses" in Sidney Harcave, *First Blood* (New York: 1964), 279–82; see also Fischer, 181–82.

16. Fischer, 192. In Fischer's opinion, the First Zemstvo Congress and the November 1904 banquets were more important as factors bringing on the Russian revolution of 1905 than "Bloody Sunday" on January 9, 1905. Ibid., 160.

17. Vladimir Iosifovich Gurko, *Features and Figures of the Past: Government and Opinion in the Reign of Nicholas II* (Palto Alto, Calif.: 1939), 374.

18. Theodore H. von Laue, "Russian Peasants in the Factory, 1892–1904," *The Journal of Economic History*, vol. XXI (March 1961): 65–66.

19. Theodore H. von Laue, "Tsarist Labor Policy, 1895–1903," *Journal of Modern History*, vol. XXXIV, no. 2 (June 1962): 135–38.

20. Thomas G. Masaryk, *The Spirit of Russia*, 2 vols. (Reprinted, London: 1955), I, 175.

21. Alexis Antsiferov, Alexander D. Bilimovich, Michael O. Batshev, and Dimitry N. Ivantsov, *Rural Economy During the War: Russian Agriculture During the War* (New Haven: 1930), 45.

22. Geroid Tanquary Robinson, *Rural Russia Under the Old Regime* (New York: 1949), 94–96. Evidence of the growing distress is that by 1904 the arrears in redemption payments alone was 130,000,000 rubles.

23. Alexander D. Bilimovich, *The Land Settlement in Russia During the War: Russian Agriculture During the War* (New Haven: 1930), 311–16.

24. Robinson, 155–60, 173.

25. I. I. Petrunkevich, "Iz zapisok obshchestvennovo deiatelia" [From the notes of a public leader], *Arkhiv russkoi revoliutsii* [Archive of the Russian revolution], XXI (Berlin: 1934), Introd.

26. Nicholas II, *Tagebuch*, 214.

27. "Dnevnik Kn. Ekateriny Alekseevny Sviatopolk-Mirskoi za 1904–05 gg." [The diary of Princess Catherine Alekseevna Sviatopolk-Mirsky for 1904–05], *Istoricheskie zapiski* [Historical notes], No. 77, 1965, 264.

28. See text in Harcave, 282–85.

29. Ibid., 61–62; Treadgold, 135.

30. Harcave, 65–97. Gapon remains to this day a controversial figure. It is clear officials were aware of and condoned his activities; yet it is also evident Gapon had ingested certain socialist and liberationist concepts and genuinely believed in the necessity of reform. He apparently was convinced that Nicholas would receive his petition, a hodge-podge of nationalist, monarchist, liberal, and revolutionary ideas, and would act on it. After "Bloody Sunday," Gapon was for a time a hero to the revolutionaries while he lived in exile abroad. Later, he returned to Russia and once again offered his services to the police (see chapter three, 86–87). Shortly thereafter, in March 1906, Socialist-Revolutionary terrorists assassinated him.

31. Richard Charques, *The Twilight of Imperial Russia* (London: 1958), 114.

32. Bernard Pares, "The Reform Movement in Russia," chapter XIII of *The Cambridge Modern History*: vol. XII, *The Latest Age* (New York: 1910), 351.

33. See chapter four, 113–15, for a fuller discussion of the August 6 electoral law.

34. Witte, *Vospominaniia*, II, 485.

35. Ibid., I, 5, 13.

36. *Memoirs of Alexander Iswolsky*, 108; Evgenii Nikolaevich Schelking, *The Game of Diplomacy* (London: n.d.), 203; Vasilii Alekseevich Maklakov, *Vlast' i obshchestvennost' na zakate staroi Rossii: Vospominaniia sovremennika* [Government and society in the closing

years of the old Russia: reminiscences of a contemporary] (Paris: 1939), 258; Evgenii Viktorovich Tarle, *Graf S. Iu. Vitte: Opyt kharakteristiki vneshnei politiki* [Count S. Iu. Witte: an attempt to characterize his foreign policy] (Leningrad: 1927), 3.

37. Witte, *Vospominaniia*, I, 408.

38. *Memoirs of Alexander Iswolsky*, 108. According to one contemporary, "Upper court and bureaucratic circles never fully accepted Witte and considered him a *vyskochkoi* [upstart or *parvenu*]." Petrunkevich, 413.

39. von Laue, *Sergei Witte and the Industrialization of Russia*, 38.

40. The following discussion is based primarily on the excellent analysis of Witte's policies as minister of Finance contained in von Laue, *Sergei Witte and the Industrialization of Russia*.

41. Ibid., 59–61.

42. E. J. Dillon, *The Eclipse of Russia* (New York: 1918), 150–51.

43. von Laue, *Sergei Witte and the Industrialization of Russia*, 77.

44. Ibid., 95–96.

45. Alexander III first suggested the liquor monopoly as a way of reducing drunkenness. Witte was quick to see its economic advantages. Ibid., 102.

46. Ibid., 160.

47. *The Secret Letters of the Last Tsar: Being the Confidential Correspondence between Nicholas II and His Mother, Dowager Empress Maria Feodorovna*, ed. by Edward J. Bing (New York: 1938), 88.

48. Dillon, *The Eclipse of Russia*, 254–55; *Memoirs of Alexander Iswolsky*, 112, 120–21.

49. von Laue, *Sergei Witte and the Industrialization of Russia*, 171.

50. Robinson, 131.

51. Ibid., 172.

52. Witte, *Vospominaniia*, II, 522–35, and see chapter six, 184–86.

53. Theodore H. von Laue, "A Secret Memorandum of Sergei Witte on the Industrialization of Imperial Russia," *Journal of Modern History*, vol. XXVI, no. 1 (March 1954), 65–70.

54. Witte, *Vospominaniia*, I, 130–35.

55. von Laue, *Sergei Witte and the Industrialization of Russia*, 137.

56. Witte, *Vospominaniia*, II, 416–17.

57. von Laue, *Sergei Witte and the Industrialization of Russia*, 68.

58. Dillon, *The Eclipse of Russia*, 150–51.

59. Tarle, 7.

60. von Laue, *Sergei Witte and the Industrialization of Russia*, 163.

61. Theodore H. von Laue, "Count Witte and the Russian Revolution of 1905," *American Slavic and East European Review* (February 1958), 28.

62. Dillon, *The Eclipse of Russia*, 113; Ernst Seraphim, "Zar Nikolaus II und Graf Witte: Eine Historische-Psychologische Studie," *Historische Zeitschrift*, Bd. 161, Heft. 2, 284–85; 292.

63. Witte, *Vospominaniia*, III, 336.

64. Alexander Kerensky, *The Crucifixion of Liberty* (New York: 1934), 110.

65. See a student resolution of September 13 and a government report of September 24 on student activity in *Revoliutsiia 1905–1907 gg. v Rossii: Dokumenty i materialy: Vserossiiskaia politicheskaia stachka v oktiabre 1905 goda, chast' pervaia* [The revolution of 1905–1907 in Russia: documents and materials: The all-Russian political strike in October 1905, part I] (Moscow: 1955), 22–23, 25–27, (hereafter cited as *Vserossiiskaia politicheskaia stachka*, vol. I).

66. "Zapiska Departamenta politsii o skhodkakh i mitingakh v Moskovskom universitete 1–21 sentiabria," [Note of the Department of Police about gatherings and meetings in Moscow University September 1–21], *Vserossiiskaia politicheskaia stachka*, I, 40.

67. W. S. Woytinsky, *Stormy Passage: A Personal History through Two Russian Revolutions to Democracy and Freedom, 1905–1960* (New York: 1961), 18–29.

68. S. E. Sef, *Burzhuaziia v 1905 gody* [The bourgeoisie in 1905] (Moscow: 1926), 71 and 126–27, citing archives.

69. "Iz soobshcheniia Moskovskovo okhrannovo otdeleniia moskovskomu general-gubernatoru A. A. Kozlovu o prisoedinenii 24–25 sentiabria k bastuiushchim rabochim tipografi rabochikh moskovskikh khlebopekaren i bulochnykh" [From the report of the Moscow Secret Police to the Moscow Governor-General A. A. Kozlov about the Moscow bakers going out on strike to support the printers, September 24–25], *Vserossiiskaia politicheskaia stachka*, I, 71.

70. V. N. Pereverzev, "Pervyi vserossiiskii zheleznodorozhnyi soiuz 1905 goda" [First all-Russian railroad union in 1905], *Byloe*, no. 4 (32) (1925), 53; Woytinsky, 30.

71. "Spravka o zabastovkakh na zheleznykh dorogakh s 6 po 11 oktiabria, sostavlennaia v department politsii" [Report about the railroad strike from October 6 to 11, drawn up by the Police Department], *Vserossiiskaia politicheskaia stachka*, I, 210.

72. Ibid., I, 212; "25 let nazad: Iz dnevnika L. Tikhomirova" [Twenty-five years ago: from the diary of L. Tikhomirov], *Krasnyi arkhiv*, XL (1930): 74.

73. Woytinsky, 30–31. Woytinsky, one of the leaders in the Social-Democratic organization, opposed a general strike.

74. "Telegramma Nikolaia II na imia Trepova ot 12 oktiabria 1905 g." [Telegram from Nicholas II to Trepov on October 12, 1905], *Krasnyi arkhiv*, XI–XII (1925): 455. Observers abroad took a more serious view of the situation; Kaiser Wilhelm of Germany reportedly ordering warships to be ready to steam to St. Petersburg to evacuate Nicholas and the imperial family in the event of revolution. de Grunwald, 179.

75. Gurko, 394.

76. Quoted in I. V. Spiridonov, *Vserossiiskaia politicheskaia stachka*

v oktiabre 1905 g. [The All-Russian political strike in October 1905]
(Moscow: 1955), 95.

77. Woytinsky, 34–40.

CHAPTER II

1. See Appendices A and B for the complete texts of the October 17 Manifesto and Witte's report respectively.

2. *Secret Letters of the Last Tsar*, 184.

3. Witte, *Vospominaniia*, III, 52.

4. *Secret Letters of the Last Tsar*, 175.

5. Quoted from the archives in E. D. Chermenskii, "Russkaia burzhuaziia osen'iu 1905 goda" [The Russian bourgeoisie in the fall of 1905], *Voprosy istorii* [Questions of history], no. 6, (1966), 61. See also Wladimir Korostowetz, *Graf Witte, der Steuermann in der Not* (Berlin: 1929), 221.

6. Witte, *Vospominaniia*, II, 556.

7. Gurko, 396. Gurko was sometimes a sharp and at other times a friendly critic of Witte and his policies. Harcave, 192, accepts Gurko's assessment, but there is no documentary evidence to substantiate this view of Witte as scheming to be the savior of imperial Russia.

8. Witte, *Vospominaniia*, II, 557–59.

9. Ibid., III, 47.

10. The available evidence concerning who originated this idea is conflicting. Kryzhanovskii, a senior official in the Ministry of Interior, claims in his memoirs that he worked out such a plan in August and presented it to Bulygin, who deferred action on it (S. E. Kryzhanovskii, *Vospominaniia* [Memoirs], 50–51). It is attributed to Count Sol'sky in K. N. Mironenko, "Soviet ministrov po ukazu 19 oktiabria 1905 g." [The Council of Ministers according to the decree of October 19, 1905], *Uchennye zapiski 106*, seriia iuridicheskoi nauki, Leningradskii universitet [Learned papers, series of juridical science], vyp. 1, 1948. But Chermenskii, in his "Russkaia burzhuaziia osen'iu 1905 goda," p. 61, n. 33, cites the account of L. Kliachko, a liberal journalist (his memoir was not available to us), who asserts that the proposal was drafted by A. V. Krivoshein, a liberal bureaucrat.

11. Quoted from the archives in Chermenskii, 60–61.

12. Chermenskii, 61–62; *Out of My Past: The Memoirs of Count Kokovtsov* (Palo Alto, Calif.: 1935), 67; "Dnevnik A. A. Polovtseva," [Diary of A. A. Polovtsev], *Krasnyi arkhiv*, IV (1923): 65.

13. "Dnevnik A. A. Polovtseva," 71.

14. Witte, "Spravka o manifeste 17 oktiabria 1905 g." [Information on the Manifesto of October 17, 1905], *Vospominaniia*, III, 10–11. (Included in *Vospominaniia*, III, is a detailed memorandum which was written by Witte in early January 1907 to describe his role in the publication of the October 17 Manifesto and the report which accompanied

it. The memorandum may also be found in *Krasnyi arkhiv*, XI–XII (1925): 76–82, and in English translation in Sergius Iu. Witte, *The Memoirs of Count Witte*, tr. and ed. by Abraham Yarmolinsky (London: 1921), 237–44. Hereafter, the memorandum shall be noted as "Spravka.")

15. According to Chermenskii, the statement of Kuz'min-Karavaev in turn drew heavily for some of its ideas on the resolutions of the September Congress of Representatives of Zemstvos and City Dumas, but "in editing the note [of Kuz'min-Karavaev] Witte made several changes which limited the intended program of reform." Chermenskii, "Russkaia burzhuaziia osen'iu 1905 goda," 63, n. 39. The statement by Kuz'min-Karavaev was printed under the title, "Kanun 17-ovo oktiabria. Zadachi pravitel'stva" [On the eve of October 17. The tasks of the government] in his book, *Iz epokhi osvoboditel'novo dvizheniia*, Ch. 1: *Do 17 oktiabria 1905 goda* [From the epoch of the liberation movement, Part I: Before October 17, 1905] (Petrograd: 1918). A comparison of this statement with Witte's memorandum shows them to be almost identical, and thus Chermenskii's assertion is without foundation.

16. "Zapiska Vitte ot 9 oktiabria." [Witte's note of October 9], *Krasnyi arkhiv*, XI–XII (1925), 51–57.

17. Nicholas II, *Tagebuch*, 261.

18. *Tagebuch*, 261; Witte, "Spravka," *Vospominaniia*, III, 11.

19. Gurko, 396.

20. Witte, "Spravka," *Vospominaniia*, III, 11.

21. Ibid., 11. See also a letter from Nicholas to Maria Fedorovna, October 19, 1905, in *Krasnyi arkhiv*, XXII (1927), 168.

22. "Dnevnik A. A. Polovtseva," 75. This proposal became part of Witte's governmental program and was adopted in an imperial manifesto of February 20, 1906. It was later incorporated into the Fundamental Laws, sanctioned April 23, 1906. See chapter nine.

23. Sergei Iu. Witte, "Vsepoddanneishii doklad." [Official report], *Krasnyi arkhiv*, XI–XII (1925), 61.

24. Witte, "Spravka," *Vospominaniia*, III, 12; "Dnevnik A. A. Polovtseva," 76; Witte Collection, Archive of Russian and East European History, Columbia University, Box 8, Folder 50.

25. Witte, "Spravka," *Vospominaniia*, III, 12–13.

26. Sergei Iu. Witte, "Chernovnik vsepoddanneishevo doklada Vitte." [Rough draft of an official report by Witte], *Krasnyi arkhiv*, XI–XII (1925), 62–66. This undated report includes in an abbreviated way the ideas discussed in the longer memorandum of October 9. With minor editorial changes, this report is consistent with the one sanctioned by the tsar and published along with the October 17 Manifesto. This has led us to believe that this was the abstract ordered by the tsar on October 10, presented by Witte on October 14 and again on October 15, and finally approved by the tsar on October 17. See also Witte, "Spravka," *Vospominaniia*, III, 5, 13. This abstract of the October 9 memorandum is hereafter referred to as "Witte's report."

27. Chermenskii disputes the view of the Soviet historian I. V. Spiridonov (in *Vserossiiskaia politicheskaia stachka v oktiabria 1905 g.*, 132) that the content of Witte's report presented on October 14 was less liberal than that of the October 9 memorandum because the bourgeoisie had become frightened over the extent and nature of the growing revolutionary disorders and therefore put pressure on Witte to toughen his program. Chermenskii argues instead—it seems to us correctly—that the more moderate tone of the October 14 report reflected the different nature and purpose of the two documents: The report was specifically prepared to be published, and Witte did not want to commit the government in advance to too extreme and specific a program of reform (Chermenskii, "Russkaia burzhuasiia osen'ui 1905 goda," 64 n. 44).

28. Witte, "Spravka," *Vospominaniia*, III, 13.

29. Ibid., 35.

30. Ibid.; "Dnevnik A. A. Polovtseva," 77; Maurice Bompard, *Mon Ambassade en Russie, 1903–1908* (Paris: 1937), 174.

31. Witte, "Spravka," *Vospominaniia*, III, 13.

32. Ibid., 14.

33. Ibid., 14; "Zapiska kniazia A. D. Obolenskovo" [Note of A. D. Obolensky], Witte, *Vospominaniia*, III, 27. After Witte's resignation in April 1906, he was criticized by those near the court and by some public leaders for his role in the proclamation of the October 17 Manifesto. To protect himself, Witte asked Obolensky and N. I. Vuich—the two men who were of prime importance in the preparation of the Manifesto—to write brief statements describing the events leading up to its publication. Obolensky responded by drafting a note dated August–September 1906; Vuich's note is dated December 31, 1906. The notes are in fundamental agreement with each other and with Witte's own description referred to in this study as "Spravka." Each contributes certain details ignored by the others. These notes are printed in Witte's memoirs (III, 19–31), in *Krasnyi arkhiv*, XI–XII (1925), 66–76, and in *Arkhiv russkoi revoliutsii*, II, (1921). Hereafter, these notes will be cited as "Zapiska Vuicha" and "Zapiska Obolenskovo."

34. "Zapiska Vuicha," in Witte, *Vospominaniia*, III, 20.

35. Ibid., 21. The rough drafts and notes of the three participants during their discussion have been published in "Manifest 17 oktiabria." [Manifesto of October 17], *Krasnyi arkiv*, XI–XII (1925), 86–91. They tend to confirm Vuich's description.

36. Witte, "Spravka," *Vospominaniia*, III, 14.

37. "Zapiska Vuicha," ibid., 21.

38. Ibid., 21–22.

39. Witte, "Spravka," ibid., 15; "Zapiska Vuicha," ibid., 22. Polovtsev noted reports that Grand Duke Nikolai Nikolaevich gave strong support to Witte as the future prime minister. "Dnevnik A. A. Polovtseva," 77.

40. "Baron B. Fredericks D. F. Trepovu." [Baron B. Fredericks to D. F. Trepov], *Byloe*, 14 (1919), 109. Prince Orlov, a member of the

court, also wrote Trepov on October 15, urging him to scrutinize Witte's program carefully and arguing that reforms should come from the tsar, not a constitutional government headed by Witte, who would destroy the state as it had existed in the past. "Kniaz V. Orlov D. F. Trepovu," [Prince V. Orlov to D. F. Trepov], *Byloe,* 14 (1919), 110.

41. "Vsepoddanneishaia zapiska D. F. Trepova" [Official note of D. F. Trepov], *Byloe,* 14 (1919), 110–11.

42. Nicholas II, *Tagebuch,* 264.

43. "Okonchatel'nyi tekst proekta manifesta Goremykina-Budberga" [Final text of the draft of the Goremykin-Budberg Manifesto], *Krasnyi arkhiv,* XI–XII (1925), 96.

44. Witte, *Vospominanniia,* III, 39.

45. Witte, "Spravka," ibid., 15–17.

46. *Mossolov Memoirs,* 97.

47. This is based on a conversation between Witte and A. A. Mossolov, reported in Witte, *Vospominaniia,* III, 42.

48. Ibid., 41. This was reported to Witte by Baron Fredericks. See also "Zapiska A. F. Redigera o 1905 g." [Note of A. F. Rediger about 1905], *Krasnyi arkhiv,* XIV, (1931), 8.

49. M. A. Ushakov, "Vospominaniia o besede s velikim kniazem (15 oktiabria 1905 g.)" [Reminiscences of a conference with the grand duke (October 15, 1905)], *Krasnyi arkhiv,* IV (1923), 415. In a note on the copy of Ushakov's memorandum preserved in the Witte papers, Witte states that the date of Ushakov's meeting with the grand duke was probably October 14. Witte Collection, Columbia University, Box 8, Folder 14.

50. Gurko, 398; Ushakov, 416; Witte, *Vospominaniia,* III, 43, 45.

51. *Vospominaniia,* III, 51.

52. In "Zapiska Obolenskovo," Witte, *Vospominaniia,* III, 31, and in Witte, "Spravka," *Vospominaniia,* III, 17, the time is given as 6:00 P.M. Since these accounts were written more than a year after the event, the time stated by Nicholas II, *Tagebuch,* 264, seems more likely to have been accurate despite his headache and confusion. See Appendices A and B for texts of the Manifesto and of Witte's report respectively.

53. *Tagebuch,* 264.

54. *Secret Letters of the Last Tsar,* 180.

55. Cited from the archives in Chermenskii, "Russkaia burzhuaziia osen'iu 1905 g.," 65.

56. *Secret Letters of the Last Tsar,* 184–85.

CHAPTER III

1. *Secret Letters of the Last Tsar,* 188, 190.

2. Ibid., 192.

3. Bompard, 199.

4. Though touched on here, the problems raised by peasant riots,

rebellions in the border areas of Russia, and the fiscal crisis are more fully treated in later chapters.

5. "Zapiska Obolenskovo," Witte, *Vospominaniia*, III, 31.

6. "Dnevnik Kn. E. A. Sviatopolk-Mirskoi za 1904–1905 gg.," [Diary of Princess Sviatopolk-Mirsky for 1904–1905], *Istoricheskie zapiski*, no. 77, (1965), 288.

7. Bernard Pares, "The Reform Movement in Russia," *The Cambridge Modern History*, vol. XII, 359; D. N. Liubimov, "Russkaia smuta nachala deviatisotykh godov, 1902–1906" [The Russian time of troubles in the beginning of the twentieth century, 1902–1906] (Unpublished manuscript from the Archive of Russian and East European History and Culture, Columbia University), 327.

8. *Mossolov Memoirs*, 140.

9. Gurko, 438. The British journalist Maurice Baring said the first thing that made him fully aware Russia had been offered the promise of a constitutional order was when he went to a large Russian bath in Moscow shortly after the announcement of the Manifesto. Someone entered and asked for soap, whereupon the ten-year-old barber's assistant said "with the air of a Hampden, 'Give the citizen some soap.'" Maurice Baring, *A Year in Russia*, (London: 1907), 27.

10. Witte, *Vospominaniia*, III, 136. This order was not always respected. Particularly within the military ranks there was opposition to Witte's command to cease firing on the population and to "save the heads of the Russian people." One officer ignored the request and continued to shoot at the demonstrators because he believed they were not Russian people but rebels. "Raport SPB gradonachal'nika ot 24 oktiabria 1905 g. No. 98." [Report of the St. Petersburg Town Governor, October 24, 1905, No. 98], *Krasnyi arkhiv*, XI–XII, 1925, 462–63.

11. Gurko, 416; Woytinsky, 42; Platon Lebedev, "Krasnye dni v Nizhnem-Novgorode," [Red days in Nizhnii-Novgorod], *Byloe*, no. 5 (May 1907), 129; "Iz doneseniia moskovskovo gradonachal'nika G. P. Medema tovarishchu ministra vnutrennikh del D. F. Trepovu o demonstratsiiakh i stolknoveniiakh bastuiushchikh s voiskami i chernosotentsami 18–19 oktiabria." [From the report of the Moscow Town Governor G. P. Medem to the Assistant Minister of the Interior D. F. Trepov about demonstrations and fights between strikers and army and Black Hundreds, October 18–19], *Vserossiiskaia politicheskaia stachka*, I, 465.

12. V. A. Starosel'skii, "'Dni svobody' v Kutaiskoi gubernii." ['Days of freedom' in Kutaisky province], *Byloe*, no. 7 (July 1907), 178; "Raport i. d. ivanovo-voznesenskovo politseimeistere A. P. Saravenskovo vladimirskomu gubernatoru I. M. Leont'evu o mitingakh bastuiushchikh rabochikh 20–22 oktiabria i chernosotennikh pogromakh v g. Ivanovo-Voznesenske 23–24 oktiabria." [Report of the Ivanovo-Voznesensk Police Chief A. P. Saravensky to Vladimir Governor I. M. Leontev about meetings of striking workers on October 20–22 and about Black Hundred pogroms in Ivanovo-Voznesensk on October 23–24], *Vserossiiskaia politicheskaia stachka*, I, 514–17. The picture in Harcave, 199–204,

of widespread antigovernment demonstrations for three days followed by a reaction is not accurate. In many places the two kinds of demonstrations went on simultaneously.

13. "Iz doneseniia moskovskovo gradonachal'nika G. P. Medema tovarishchu ministra vnutrennikh del D. F. Trepovu o pokhoronakh N. E. Baumana demonstratsiiakh bastuiushchikh rabochikh i studentov i stolknoveniiakh ikh s politisiei i chernosotentsami 20 i 21 oktiabria." [From the report of the Moscow Town Governor G. P. Medem to the Assistant Minister of the Interior D. F. Trepov about the burial of N. E. Bauman, about demonstrations of students and strikers and their clashes with police and Black Hundreds on October 20 and 21], *Vserossiiskaia politicheskaia stachka*, I, 469–70.

14. Ibid.; Ol'denburg, 320; "25 let nazad," 84.

15. Cited in Treadgold, *Lenin and His Rivals*, 177.

16. Maurice Olgin, *The Soul of the Russian Revolution* (New York: 1917), 142. This is also referred to and quoted in Liubimov, 338–39.

17. Quoted in L. K. Erman, *Intelligentsia v pervoi russkoi revoliutsii* [The intelligentsia in the first Russian revolution] (Moscow: 1968), 167.

18. "Listovka tsentral'novo komiteta RSDRP 'K russkomu narodu' po povodu manifesta 17 oktiabria s prizyvom k prodolzheniiu bor'by." [Leaflet of the Central Committee of the RSDRP (Russian Social Democratic Workers' party) 'To the Russian people' on the occasion of the October 17 Manifesto with an appeal to continue the struggle], *Vserossiiskaia politicheskaia stachka*, I, 197. Within the ranks of the Social Democrats, however, the Bolshevik faction urged boycotting elections to the Duma, while Martov and others urged participation in an effort to turn electoral assemblies into embryonic units of an all-Russian constituent assembly.

19. Treadgold, 207–08.

20. Savinkov, 175.

21. Ibid., 176, 187; Treadgold, 208.

22. Quoted in S. L. Frank, *Biografiia P. B. Struve* (New York: 1956), 49.

23. Maklakov, *Vlast' i obshchestvennost'*, 405.

24. E. D. Chermenskii, *Burzhuaziia i tsarizm v revoliutsii 1905–07 gg.* [The bourgeoisie and tsarism in the revolution of 1905–07] (Moscow: 1939), 146–56; Sef, 75–78; Louis Menashe, "Alexander Guchkov and the Origins of the Octobrist Party: The Russian Bourgeoisie in Politics, 1905," Ph. D. dissertation, New York University, 1966, 125–30. All of these draw heavily on the pioneering and still useful article on the bourgeoisie by A. Ermanskii in L. Martov and others, eds., *Obshchestvennoe dvizhenie v Rossii v nachale XX veka* [The social movement in Russia at the beginning of the twentieth century], St. Petersburg: 1909–14), II, Part 2.

25. Quoted in Menashe, 125.

26. Quoted in Sef, 76.

27. These parties and their fate are discussed briefly in chapter eight.

28. See, for example, the situation in one city described in P. K., "Krasnoiarsk v kontse 1905 goda." [Krasnoiarsk at the end of 1905], *Byloe*, no. 6 (June 1907), 15; and see below, 68–69, for the collapse of the October general strike following publication of the Manifesto.

29. See chapter six for a fuller discussion of the agrarian problem.

30. See, for example, a report on October 20 of the commander of the St. Petersburg garrison concerning the appearance of soldiers, sailors, officers, and even clerks of the General Staff in street demonstrations in the capital. *Partiia bol'shevikov v revoliutsii 1905–07 godov: Dokumenty i materialy* [The Bolshevik party in the revolution of 1905–07; documents and materials] (Moscow: 1961), 507.

31. For a fuller description of unrest in the armed services, see 89–96 below. For evidence on the effect of the Manifesto on military personnel, see V. A. Petrov, *Ocherki po istorii revoliutsionnovo dvizheniia v russkoi armii v 1905 g.* [Outline of the history of the revolutionary movement in the Russian army in 1905] (Moscow-Leningrad: 1964), 250–51, 261–62, 264–65, 315–16.

32. See chapters four and five.

33. Though not included in the franchise for the Bulygin Duma, under the October Manifesto and the subsequent electoral law, Jews could vote and exercise civil rights. However, the Pale of Settlement and discrimination in education and the professions remained. For a detailed history of anti-Semitism in Russia, see S. W. Dubnow, *History of the Jews in Russia and in Poland From the Earliest Times Until the Present Day*, 3 vols. (Philadelphia: 1920).

34. Perhaps the most vivid description of the "Black Hundreds" is that of Betram Wolfe: "Under the banner of Holy Russia was gathered together a most unholy and variegated band: the backward, the degenerate, the brutalized, the bewildered, the enraged, the entrenched, the ruined: officers, landowners, and gilded youth, demobilized old soldiers and personal servingmen to whom loyalty to the master was the sum of all loyalties, criminals whose police record made them amenable to any instructions, ruined artisans and shopkeepers who were persuaded that the strikes and the eight-hour day were the cause of all their woes, hungry, degraded slum proletarians from the human scrapheap of the great cities, the more illiterate and credulous among the workingmen and peasantry." Bertram D. Wolfe, *Three Who Made a Revolution*, (Boston: 1962), 327.

35. Alfred Levin, "The Black Hundreds: The Reactionary Wing" (An unpublished manuscript), 6; Hans Rogger, "The Formation of the Russian Right, 1900 to 1906," in *California Slavic Studies*, III (1964), 82–94; Effie Ambler, "The Union of the Russian People" (An unpublished manuscript), 7–12.

36. Ambler, 19–20.

37. "Protokol pokazanii A. I. Prusakova ot 9, 12, i 15 iiunia 1917 g."

[Protocol of the testimony of A. I. Prusakov from the 9, 12, and 15 of June, 1917], *Soiuz russkovo naroda: Po materialam sledstvennoi komissii vremennovo pravitel'stva 1917 g.* [Union of the Russian people: according to the materials of the investigating commission of the Provisional Government] (Moscow: 1929), 46.

38. "Sovremennik," pseud., *Nikolai II, Razoblacheniia* [Nicholas II, the unmasking], (Berlin: n.d.), 318–21.

39. Ambler, 27–29.

40. Iu. Lavrinovich', "A Review of *Kievskii i odesskii pogromy v razsledovaniiakh senatorov Turau i Kuzminskovo*" [A review of the Kiev and Odessa pogroms in the investigations of Senators Turau and Kuzminsky. St. Petersburg, 1907], *Byloe*, No. 21 (September 1907), 309.

41. Figures compiled from press and official reports by a moderate publicist, V. P. Obninskii in *Polgoda russkoi revoliutsii* [A half-year of the Russian revolution] (Moscow: 1906), 42.

42. "Zapiska namestnika na Kavkaze I. I. Vorontsova-Dashkova na imia Nikolaia II o revoliutsionnom dvizhenii na Kavkaze 21–27 oktiabria." [Note of the Deputy to the Caucasus I. I. Vorontsov-Dashkov in the name of Nicholas II about the revolutionary movement in the Caucasus during October 21–27], *Revoliutsiia 1905–1907 gg. v. Rossii: Dokumenty i materialy: Vserossiiskaia politicheskaia stachka v oktiabre 1905 goda, chast' vtoraia.* [The revolution of 1905–1907 in Russia: documents and materials: the all-Russian political strike in October 1905, Part II] (Moscow: 1955), 272–76. (Hereafter cited as *Vserossiiskaia politicheskaia stachka*, II.)

43. Since many who were injured preferred to treat their own injuries rather than go to a hospital, many of the injured do not appear on the police records. It has also been estimated that 1,632 individual pieces of Jewish property were raided by the pogromists. This included stores, apartments, and homes, resulting in 3,668,824 rubles of damage. "Vsepoddanneishii otchet senatora Kuzminskovo: o prichinakh bezporiadkov proiskhodivshikh v gor. Odesse v oktiabre 1905 g., i o poriadke deistviia mestnykh vlastei." [Official report of Senator Kuzminsky: about the causes of the disorders which took place in the city of Odessa in October 1905, and about the procedures of local authorities], *Materialy k istorii russkoi kontr-revoliutsii.* [Materials toward the history of the Russian counterrevolution] (St. Petersburg: 1908), clxvi-clxvii. (Hereafter cited as "Kuzminsky Report.") The figure of 500 killed has been judged too low by some. Others have set the figure as high as 1,000 killed in the four-day pogrom. Witte, *Vospominaniia*, III, (ed. notes) 615.

44. "Odessa," *The Jewish Encyclopedia: A Descriptive Record of the History, Religion, Literature, and Customs of the Jewish People from the Earliest Times to the Present Day*, vol. IX (New York: 1905), 385.

45. "Kuzminsky Report," cciv; "Iz raporta komanduiushchevo voiskami Odesskovo voennovo okruga A. V. Kaul'barsa voennomu ministru

A. F. Redigeru o zabastovki i barrikadnykh boiakh v g. Odesse 13–20 oktiabria." [From the report of the Army Commander of the Odessa Military District A. V. Kaul'bars to Minister of War A. F. Rediger about the strike and fighting behind barricades in Odessa October 13–20], *Vserossiiskaa politicheskaia stachka,* II, 175–76. (Hereafter cited as "Kaul'bars' Report.") Kaul'bars claimed that half of those attending such meetings were Jews.

46. "Kaul'bars' Report," 175–79; "Kuzminsky Report," cciv–ccv, cxxxiv–cxxxv.

47. Louis Greenburg, *The Jews in Russia,* vol. II. *The Struggle for Emancipation, 1881–1917* (New Haven: 1951), 77.

48. "Ob'iasnenie Neidhardta, predstavlennoe senatoru Kuzminskomu." [Declaration of Neidhardt, presented to Senator Kuzminsky], *Materialy k istorii russkoi kontr-revoliutsii,* 19; "Kuzminsky Report," cxl. Harcave states, 204, that Neidhardt held back the police because he believed "the Jews had brought the trouble on themselves." This charge is not borne out in the testimony on which the account above is based.

49. "Kuzminsky Report," cxlvii.

50. Ibid., cxlviii; "Raport komanduiushchevo voiskami Odesskovo okruga voennomu ministru ot 12 noiabria 1905 g. za no. 23657." [Report of the commander of the Odessa military district to the minister of War, November 12, 1905, no. 23657], *Materialy k istorii kontr-revoliutsii,* 188–89. (Hereafter cited as "Report of Odessa Commander, no. 23657.")

51. "Kuzminsky Report," cli.

52. "Report of Odessa Commander, no. 23657."

53. "Kuzminsky Report," cliii.

54. "Ob'iavlenie evo zhe ot tovo zhe chiala (oktiabria 20, 1905 g.)." [Declaration from that same date (October 20, 1905)], *Materialy k istorii kontr-revoliutsii,* 173.

55. "Report of Odessa Commander, no. 23657."

56. "Ob'iasnenie Neidhardta," *Materialy k istorii kontr-revoliutsii,* 31.

57. Although Bezradetsky signed the order, it was issued by Kaul'bars' office. "Ob'iavleniia komanduiushchevo voiskami Odesskovo okruga ot 21 i 20 oktiabria 1905 g." [Declaration of the military commander of the Odessa district from October 21 and 20, 1905], *Materialy k istorii kontr-revoliutsii,* 175–76.

58. It is clear that the pogrom could have been controlled more quickly had the military acted decisively sooner. Neidhardt denied this to Senator Kuzminsky: ". . . they say that the pogroms stopped when the commander of the army appeared announcing that the military was ordered to destroy the robbers by arms. The text of this testimony of October 21 shows, of course, that the first demand was not to shoot at the robbers [see order of Lieutenant-General Bezradetsky, 62] but to stop the revolutionaries from firing from windows onto the army and police by threatening to destroy the houses. . . . The chief danger in all

of this [disorder], your excellency, was not in the pogrom but in the armed attacks on the authorities, army and police with the goal of carrying out revolution." "Ob'iasnenie Neidhardta," *Materialy k istorii kontr-revoliutsii*, 32.

59. "Kuzminsky Report," ccxiv.

60. Ibid., cxlviii, cliv, cxlix. After the pogrom the government removed Neidhardt. Harcave, 207.

61. S. W. Dubnow, 126.

62. *Secret Letters of the Last Tsar*, 187.

63. "Prince Urusov's Speech," in Baring, 252–55.

64. A. I. Gukovskii, *Pervaia russkaia burzhuazno-demokratiche-skaia revoliutsiia, 1905–07 gg.* [The first Russian bourgeois-democratic revolution, 1905–07] (Vologda: 1957), 227.

65. V. P. Semennikov, ed., *Revoliutsiia 1905 goda i samoderzhavie* [The revolution of 1905 and the autocracy] (Moscow-Leningrad: 1928), 58–61; Witte, *Vospominaniia*, III, 88, 111. According to Witte, Podgorichanii was neither dismissed nor prosecuted but appointed, later in 1906, as a police official in a small Black Sea town.

66. "Prince Urusov's Speech," in Baring, 255, and Bernard Pares, *Russia and Reform* (London: 1907), 537. In his memoirs Witte implied that he did not press the case since he was convinced that Minister of Interior Durnovo was unaware of Komissarov's activity. Though Witte suspected Court Commandant Trepov might have a link to Komissarov, it would obviously have endangered Witte's relations with the tsar to air a scandal that might involve one of Nicholas' most trusted advisors. Witte, *Vospominaniia*, III, 85–86.

67. Quoted from *Novoe vremia* of October 24 in de Grunwald, 183. On his later despair, see chapter five below.

68. Witte Collection, Columbia University, Box 8, Folder 50.

69. "Interv'iu S. Iu Witte s predstaviteliami pechati" [Interview of S. Iu. Witte with representatives of the press], *Krasnyi arkhiv*, XI–XII (1925), 99–105.

70. Soldiers were being used to protect the electric plants from sabotage by the workers.

71. "Manifest 17 oktiabria 1905 g.," 51.

72. K. N. Mironenko, "Manifest 17 oktiabria 1905 g." [Manifesto of October 17, 1905], *Uchenye zapiski Leningradskovo universiteta* [Scientific papers of Leningrad University], 1958, no. 225, Seriia iuridecheskoi nauki, vyp. 10 [Series of juridical science, issue 10], Voprosy gosudarstva i prava [Questions of state and law], 167–68.

73. Harcave, 214–15. In St. Petersburg the printers' union exerted a kind of anti-censorship, refusing to print material that had been submitted to the censors.

74. A. V. Piaskovskii, *Revoliutsiia 1905–1907 gg. v Rossii* [The revolution of 1905–1907 in Russia] (Moscow: 1966), 135. The decree entitled "About Lightening the Punishment of People Who, Before the Promulgation of the Imperial Manifesto of October 17, Engaged in

Criminal Activity Against the State" is in *Polnoe sobranie zakonov* [Complete collection of laws], (3rd ed.), XXV, no. 26,835. Trepov was also removed from the capital but became Nicholas' court commandant.

75. Piaskovskii, 135–36.

76. The telegrams dealing with the railroad strike are cited from the archives in Spiridonov, 138–39.

77. N. P. Eroshkin, *Ocherki istorii gosudarstvennykh uchrezhdenii dorevoliutsionnoi Rossii: posobie dlia uchitelia* [An outline of the history of state institutions in pre-revolutionary Russia: an aid for the teacher] (Moscow: 1960), 351. A decree of October 26 also established a new ministry, that of Trade and Industry.

78. Cited from the archives in A. D. Stepanskii, "Reform Gosudarstvennovo soveta v 1906 g." [The reform of the State Council in 1906], *Trudy Moskovskovo Gosudarstvennovo Istoriko-arkhivnovo Instituta* [Works of the Moscow State Historical-Archival Institute], vol. 20, 1965, 194.

79. Ibid., 195–201.

80. TsGIAL, fund 1544, op. 16 supplement, d. 19. Under pressure from the big landowners the commission agreed to twelve, then eighteen, special representatives from that class. When word leaked out that there were to be only twelve representatives of the bourgeoisie, there was a storm of protest from the industrialists—but to no avail.

81. Witte, *Vospominaniia*, III, 274.

82. Ibid., 241.

83. See telegrams of the Warsaw Governor-General G. A. Skalon to Trepov and Witte urging introduction of martial law, *Revoliutsiia 1905–1907 gg. v. Rossii: Dokumenty i materialy: Vysshii pod"em revoliutsii 1905–1907 gg.: Vooruzhennye vosstaniia noiabr'-dekabr' 1905 goda, chast' chetvertaia.* [The revolution of 1905–1907 in Russia: documents and materials: the highest point of the revolution of 1905–1907: the armed risings, November–December 1905, Part IV] (Moscow: 1957), 609, 610. (Hereafter cited as *Vysshii pod"em revoliutsii 1905–1907 gg.*, IV.)

84. "Tsirkuliarnoe pis'mo vp. general-gubernatora Varshavskoi gub. K. A. Veisa komandiram voiskikh chastei o taktike deistvii karatel'nykh otriadov." [Circular letter of the Governor-General of Warsaw Province K. A. Weis to the commanders of all troop sections about the tactics of punitive detachments], *Vysshii pod"em revoliutsii 1905–1907 gg.*, IV, 653–54.

85. Witte, *Vospominaniia*, III, 162.

86. Semennikov, 21, 22.

87. Witte, *Vospominaniia*, III, 276; *Polnoe sobranie zakonov* [Complete collection of the laws of the Russian Empire], vol. XXV, Part II, no. 26,847.

88. Reports of Witte to Nicholas, December 20, in Semennikov, 27–29.

89. Memorandum of Vuich, n.d. (but from internal evidence prob-

ably prepared in March or early April shortly before Witte's dismissal),
Witte Collection, Columbia University, Box 8, Folder 18.

90. Translated from the text in ibid.

91. Ibid.

92. Cited from the archives in Chermenskii, *Burzhuaziia i tsarizm
v revoliutsii 1905–07 gg.*, 151 n. 4.

93. Shipov, 334.

94. Maklakov, 431–32.

95. Shipov, 334–36.

96. Ibid. Although Shipov did not note this, Witte first considered
another zemstvoist for minister of Education. When his initial choice,
M. A. Stakhovich, refused, Witte then offered the post to Trubetskoi.
Witte, *Vospominaniia*, III, 68; Maxime Kovalevsky, *La crise russe: notes
et impressions d'un temoin* (Paris: 1906), 233.

97. P. N. Miliukov, *Tri popytki* [Three attempts] (Paris: 1921), 10.

98. Shipov, 338–39.

99. Although Miliukov was not an official member of the delegation, he was present at the confrontation with Witte and supported the
delegates by his presence. Maklakov, 435.

100. Shipov, 339–41.

101. Ibid., 342; Kovalevsky, 233.

102. Cited from the archives in Chermenskii, "Russkaia burzhuaziia osen'iu 1905 g.," 72.

103. Shipov, 343

104. Ibid., 344–45.

105. Witte, *Vospominaniia*, III, 107.

106. Later, in January 1906, without consulting Witte and much
to Witte's surprise and displeasure, Nicholas named Durnovo as full
minister of Interior. Ibid., 110–11. See 163 below on this incident.

107. Ibid., 109, 112.

108. Gurko, 404, 406. There were rumors at that time that Durnovo
exerted some sort of heavy pressure on Witte to force his own appointment. In his memoirs Witte refers at an earlier time—in 1904—to papers
collected by his bitter enemy, Plehve, which were apparently designed
to discredit Witte. This file was presumably known to Durnovo as head
of the police, but Witte does not indicate that Durnovo ever acted on
it, then or later. Witte, *Vospominaniia*, II, 221–22. After Witte's death
a friend, G. E. Afanas'iev, claimed in an article that in 1910 Witte had
shown him documents demonstrating that Witte opposed Durnovo's
nomination and after December wanted to get rid of Durnovo, but
Afanas'iev produced no evidence to substantiate this account. (Afanas'-
iev wrote in *Kievskaia mysl'*. The article was cited in *Rech'*, March 9,
1915, no. 66, and discussed in V. V. Vodovozov, *Graf Vitte i Imperator
Nikokai II* [Count Witte and Emperor Nicolas II] (Berlin: 1922), 88.
We found no such documents in the Witte Collection, nor have any
appeared in Soviet sources, so this allegation may never be cleared up.

109. Shipov, 346. This, by the way, indicated that Witte was not

above using "old regime" tactics while trying to advance the new political order. Durnovo had been fired in 1893 as head of the department of police because of a scandal in which he had used police agents to steal letters of one of his mistresses from the home of a foreign ambassador. Later he attempted to have his losses in the stock market covered from state funds. And on December 6, 1905, the newspaper *Molva* published a documented article alleging Durnovo had illegally been paid compensation for fraudulent claims of war losses to his property. This charge was never denied, but by this time Durnovo was already solidly ensconced in Nicholas' favor. Vodovozov, 72, 89.

110. Gurko, 410; Witte, *Vospominaniia*, III, 110-11.

111. *Vospominaniia*, III, 77, 112.

112. See, for example, the account of a liberal, N. S. Tagantsev, whom Witte approached as yet another candidate for minister of Education: Tagantsev claimed he finally refused because he did not trust Witte's whole program. N. S. Tagantsev, *Perezhitoe* [Experiences], (Petrograd: 1919), 97 ff.

113. Shipov, 334–36. In letters to Witte after the negotiations collapsed Stakhovich, Shipov, and Trubetskoi cited such reasons as those above for refusing to enter the cabinet; none of them mentioned the problem of Durnovo. Cited from the archives in Chermenskii, "Russkaia burzhuaziia osen'iu 1905 g.," 72.

114. P. N. Miliukov, *Vospominaniia* (1859–1917) [Reminiscences (1859–1917) volume I] (New York: 1955), 314–18, 328.

115. Kovalevsky tried to mediate the split between the liberals and Witte. He acknowledged that the liberals' ultimatums made it impossible for the two sides to resolve their differences. On the other hand, Kovalevsky believed that most of the liberals' demands were reasonable and within at least the spirit of the Manifesto. Kovalevsky, 234.

116. Maklakov, also a member of the Kadet party, was very critical of Miliukov's attitude toward Witte. He believed that the liberals deprived Witte of the only chance he had to resist reaction. Maklakov, 420–22.

117. See chapter seven n. 29.

118. Witte, *Vospominaniia*, III, 126; Gurko, 406.

119. "Dnevnik A. A. Polovtseva," 82.

120. While carrying a message from Nicholas II to Count Sol'sky on October 23, Baron Iu. A. Ikskul'-Gildenbrandt encountered Witte. Witte had just learned that Kokovtsov was to be appointed to head the Department of State Economy. Witte told Ikskul' that he would not serve as chairman of the Council of Ministers if Kokovtsov were permitted to retain his new position. Furthermore, Witte said he could not guarantee the continuation in office of the other ministers. Ikskul' reported this conversation to Nicholas. After reading of Witte's threat, Nicholas wrote at the bottom of Ikskul's memo, "I shall never forget such impudence." "Graf S. Iu. Vitte i Nikolai II v oktiabre 1905 g." [Count S. Iu. Witte and Nicholas II in October, 1905], *Byloe*, no. 4 (1925), 107.

121. Witte's reasons for choosing Tolstoi are interesting in view of the fact that the post was first offered to Stakhovich, then Trubetskoi—both liberal zemstvoists—and also to Tagantsev. Witte wrote that in a time of revolution it was important to select a man who would be sufficiently militant to restore order in the schools. He chose Tolstoi, former director of the Academy of Fine Arts, as a "man of conservative views who would be both respected and feared." This is quite a contrast from the reasons he gave for first attempting to attract liberals to the cabinet. Witte, *Vospominaniia*, III, 115–16.

122. Gurko, 407, 410.

123. See chapter six for a discussion of Kutler's plan for agrarian reform.

124. Witte, *Vospominaniia*, III, 214.

125. On the soviets, see 133 ff.

126. *Tysiacha deviat'sot piatyi god v Peterburge.* [The year 1905 in St. Petersburg] (Leningrad-Moscow: 1925), II, 38.

127. Witte, *Vospominaniia*, III, 139.

128. V. Kantorovich, "Khrustalev-Nosar'," *Byloe*, no. 4 (32) (1925), 141; Woytinsky, 56.

129. *Tysiacha deviat'sot piatyi god v Peterburge*, II, 39.

130. Memorandum on the revolutionary movement of 1905, from V. Litvinov-Falinskii to Witte, December 1908, Witte Collection, Columbia University, Box 7, Folder 19.

131. E. D. Chermenskii, *Istoriia SSSR: period imperializma (90-e gg. XIX v.–mart 1917 gg.): Posobie dlia uchitelia i studentov pedvuzov.* [The history of the U.S.S.R.: period of imperialism (the 90's of the nineteenth century to March 1917): an aid for students and teachers of higher teacher training institutions] izd. 2. (Moscow: 1965), 214–15.

132. N. Petrov, "Gapon i graf Vitte," [Gapon and Count Witte], *Byloe*, No. 1 (29) (1925), 26.

133. B. V. Anan'ich and R. Sh. Ganelin, "Opyt kritiki memuarov S. Iu. Vitte." [An effort at a criticism of the memoirs of S. Iu. Witte] in Akademiia nauk SSSR, *Voprosy istoriografii i istochnikovedeniia istorii SSSR: sbornik statei* [Questions of historiography and historical sources of the history of the U.S.S.R.: a collection of articles] (Moscow-Leningrad: 1963), 347–50; Vodovozov, 93–94; Witte, *Vospominaniia*, III, 193.

134. Launcelot Owen, *The Russian Peasant Movement 1906–1917* (London: 1937), 20; Robinson, 174.

135. "Ezhenedel'naia zapiska po departamentu politsii za period vremeni s 8 po 15 dekabria (1905)." [Weekly report by the Department of Police for the period of December 8 to 15 (1905)], *Krasnyi arkhiv*, XI–XII (1925), 170.

136. "Dokladnaia zapiska departamenta politsii predsedateliu soveta ministrov S. Iu. Vitte." [Report of the police department to the chairman of the Council of Ministers S. Iu. Witte], *Krasnyi arkhiv*, IX (1925), 93. For an analysis of peasant grievances, see chapter six.

137. S. M. Dubrovskii, *Krest'ianskoe dvizhenie v revoliutsii 1905–07 gg.* [The peasant movement in the revolution of 1905–07] (Moscow: 1956), 52–53.

138. Piaskovskii, 146; Harcave, 216–18.

139. Spassky, Witte's press secretary, believed that Witte had little to do with the punitive expeditions against the peasants, which were organized and sent by the tsar. Unpublished memoir of Spassky, Archive of Russian and East European History, Columbia University, 130.

140. A. K. Drezen, ed., *Tsarizm v bor'be s revoliutsiei 1905–07 gg.: sbornik dokumentov* [Tsarism in the struggle with the revolution of 1905–07: a collection of documents] (Moscow: 1936), 115.

141. Ibid., 9.

142. Ibid., 116.

143. Leningrad. Institut istorii partii, *Peterburgskie bol'sheviki v period pod"ema pervoi russkoi revoliutsii 1905–07 gg.: sbornik dokumentov i materialov* [The St. Petersburg Bolsheviks in the period of the upsurge of the first Russian revolution of 1905–07: a collection of documents and materials] (Leningrad: 1955), 516–17.

144. Semennikov, 25.

145. The figures are calculated from official reports of the Ministry of War in Petrov, 5.

146. Ibid., 160; army report in *Vysshii pod"em revoliutsii*, I, 106–10; John Maynard, *Russia in Flux* (Reprinted, New York: 1962), 84.

147. Petrov, 161, 195, 207–08. Petrov also cites Minister of War Rediger on the widespread discontent of the reservists and draftees and on the poor conditions of their service.

148. Ibid., 250–51.

149. Ibid., 251 n. 220.

150. Woytinsky, 53.

151. "Donesenie nachal'nika Kronshtadtskovo zhandarmskovo upravleniia polkovnika Kotliara direktoru Departamenta politsii A. A. Lopukhinu o vosstanii matrosov i soldat v Kronshtadte." [Report of the head of the Kronstadt police department Kotliar to the director of the Department of Police A. A. Lopukhin about the uprising of sailors and soldiers in Kronstadt], *Vysshii pod"em revoliutsii*, I, 197.

152. "Dokladnaia zapiska dvortsovovo komendanta D. F. Trepova Nikolaiu II o revoliutsionnykh sobytiiakh v strane v kontse oktiabria i pervoi polovine noiabria 1905 g." [Report of the Court Commandant D. F. Trepov to Nicholas II about revolutionary events in the country at the end of October and the first half of November 1905], ibid., 43.

153. The reaction of the St. Petersburg Soviet to the Kronstadt mutiny is discussed in chapter five. In fact none was shot; two were sentenced to hard labor, 123 were imprisoned, the rest freed.

154. A full description of the details of the Sevastopol mutiny is contained in "Raport glavnovo komandira chernomorskovo flota G. P. Chukhnina morskomu ministru A. A. Birilevu o khode vosstaniia 11–15

noiabria v Sevastopole." [Report of the Chief Commander of the Black Sea Fleet G. P. Chukhnin to the Minister of the Navy A. A. Birilev about the progress of the rebellion November 11–15 in Sevastopol], ibid., 248–301.

155. "Raport komandira 7-vo armeiskovo korpusa A. N. Meller-Zakomel'skovo Nikolaiu II o podavlenii vosstaniia v Sevastopole." [Report of the Commander of the Seventh Army Corps A. N. Meller-Zakomel'sky to Nicholas II about the suppression of the uprising in Sevastopol], ibid., 306.

156. Witte was asked to intercede on Shmidt's behalf on the ground that the lieutenant was mentally unbalanced. On February 21 Witte wrote to the tsar, reporting the views that Shmidt was insane, but adding: "I do not have nor am I able to have any opinion concerning this matter since I know nothing about it." On February 23 Nicholas replied: "I haven't the slightest doubt that if Shmidt is mentally ill, this will be established by a legal doctor." Shmidt was executed in mid-March. Semennikov, 58; Vitte, *Vospominaniia*, III, 143.

157. "Raport komandira 7-vo armeiskovo korpusa A. N. Meller-Zakomel'skovo Nikolaiu II o podavlenii vosstaniia v Sevastopole," *Vysshii pod"em revoliutsii*, I, 305; Ol'denburg, 328.

158. "Razlozhenie armii v 1905 g. na D. Vostoke." [Demoralization of the army in the Far East in 1905], ed. by N. Vishniakov, *Byloe*, no. 4 (32) (1925), ed. notes, 109.

159. "Glavnokomanduiushchii vsemi sukhoputnymi i morskimi vooruzhennymi silami, deistvuiushchimi protiv Iaponii. 12-vo dekabria 1905 goda No. 2136; Evo Prevoskhoditel'stvu A. F. Redigeru Voennomu ministru." [Commander in Chief of All Land and Sea Armed Forces in the Field against Japan, December 12, 1905, no. 2136; To His Excellency A. F. Rediger minister of War], *Byloe*, no. 4 (32) (1925), 110.

160. Ibid., 111.

161. "Pis'mo N. P. Linevicha A. N. Kuropatkiny 6 ianvaria 1906." [Letter of N. P. Linevich to A. N. Kuropatkin, January 6, 1906], *Krasnyi arkhiv*, XI–XII (1925), 327–28.

162. "Pis'mo A. N. Kuropatkina I. P. Nadarovy 28 noiabria 1905 g." [Letter of A. N. Kuropatkin to I. P. Nadarov, November 28, 1905], ibid., 319.

163. "Razlozhenie armii v 1905 g. na D. Vostoke," *Byloe*, ed. notes, 115.

164. Ferdinand Ossendowski, *From President to Prison* (New York: 1925), 137.

165. "Protokol zasedaniia stachechnovo komiteta sluzhashchikh i rabochikh Kitaisko-Vostochnoi zheleznoi dorogi 27 noiabria 1905 goda." [Protocol of the conference of the strike committee of employees and workers of the Chinese Eastern railway, November 27, 1905], *Krasnyi arkhiv*, XI–XII (1925), 303.

166. Ossendowski, 142.

167. Semennikov, 56–57. This note belies Ossendowski's claim in

his memoirs that friends appealed to Witte, who saw to it that Ossendowski, originally sentenced to be shot, was retried in a civil court, receiving eighteen months in prison.

168. See, for example, the analysis in Kh. I. Muratov, *Revoliutsionnoe dvizhenie v russkoi armii v 1905–07 gg.* [The revolutionary
movement in the Russian army in 1905–07] (Moscow: 1955), 336–37.

169. Memorandum of Vuich, Witte Collection, Columbia University.

170. Shipov, 408.

171. On the loan see chapter seven.

172. Semennikov, 25.

173. Quoted from the official government journal, *Pravitel'stvennyi
vestnik* in "Sovremennik," pseud., *Nikolai II, Razoblacheniia*, 315–18.

174. Harcave, 224–34; Lionel Kochan, *Russia in Revolution, 1890–
1918* (London: 1966), 94–100. Unconsciously, this view may have been
influenced by Lenin's well-known estimate at that time: "The autocracy
is *no longer* strong enough to come out against the revolution openly.
The revolution is *not yet* strong enough to deal the enemy a decisive
blow." V. I. Lenin, *Sochineniia* [Collected works] 5th ed. (1961),
XII, 28.

CHAPTER IV

1. G. Ul'ianov, "Soiuznitsa samoderzhaviia: ob uchastii pravoslavnoi tserkvi v podavlenii pervoi russkoi revoliutsii" [An ally of the
autocracy: concerning the participation of the Orthodox church in the
suppression of the first Russian revolution], *Nauka i religiia* [Science
and religion] no. 1 (1962), 40–41; M. M. Sheinman, "Revoliutsiia 1905–
07 gg. i pomoshch' Vatikana tsarizmu" [The revolution of 1905–07 and
the aid of the Vatican to tsarism], *Iz istorii rabochevo klassa i revoliutsionnovo dvizheniia: sbornik statei* [From the history of the working class
and the revolutionary movement] (Moscow: 1958), 399–based on
archival sources.

2. Drezen, 250 n. 38.

3. Cited in Gukovskii, 289.

4. TsGIAL, fund 1276, op. 1, d. 85.

5. Piaskovskii, 195–96; Erman, 234, 287.

6. In the literature this law is sometimes erroneously dated December 3. Memorandum of Vuich, Witte Collection, Columbia University; Chermenskii, *Burzhuaziia i tsarizm v revoliutsii 1905–07 gg.*,
157–58.

7. Cited from the archives in Erman, 288.

8. Akademiia nauk SSSR, Institut istorii, *Materialy po istorii SSSR:*
vol. IV, *Dokumenty po istorii revoliutsionnovo dvizheniia sel'skikh
rabochikh i krest'ian v pribaltike v period pervoi russkoi revoliutsii
1905–07 gg.* [Materials on the history of the U.S.S.R.: vol. IV, documents

on the history of the revolutionary movement of agricultural workers and peasants in the Baltic in the period of the first Russian revolution, 1905–07] (Moscow-Leningrad: 1957), 128, and documents *passim* (hereafter cited as *Masterialy po istorii SSSR*, IV); Anon, *The Revolution in the Baltic Provinces of Russia: A Brief Account of the Activity of the Lettish Social Democratic Workers Party by an Active Member* (London: Independent Labour Party, 1907?), 281.

9. Witte, *Vospominaniia*, III, 156–57, 160. *Materialy po istorii SSSR*, IV, 11; *Vysshii pod"em revoliutsii*, IV, 277–78. Witte claimed he suggested the appointment of Sollogub but that the soon-to-be infamous Orlov was named without Witte's knowledge.

10. *Vysshii pod"em revoliutsii*, IV, 327.

11. *Secret Letters of the Last Tsar*, 205–06.

12. Semennikov, 166, 43–44, 256 n. 50. In his memoirs Witte tried to leave the impression that he only acquiesced in the decision to use naval prisoners against the revolutionaries and that he ordered the recall of Captain Rikhter. The telegrams on this question, however, which are included in the above collection, do *not* bear this out.

13. *Revolution in the Baltic Provinces*, 66–69; *Materialy po istorii SSSR*, IV, 348–49; see also other documents on the repressive activity of the military expeditions.

14. *Materialy po istorii SSSR*, IV, 345–46.

15. *Krasnyi arkhiv*, XI–XII (1925), 151; Witte, *Vospominaniia*, III, 158.

16. Witte, *Vospominaniia*, III, 152–53; Semennikov, 30–31. A few days later Witte noted bitterly that although the idea was his, he first learned of the decision to send military expeditions along the railroad from the newspapers.

17. N. N. Polianskii, *Tsarskie voennye sudy v bor'be s revoliutsiei 1905–1907 godov* [Tsarist military courts in the struggle with the revolution of 1905–1907] (Moscow: 1958), 193; Drezen, 244 n. 6

18. Witte, *Vospominaniia*, III, 153; Semennikov, 165.

19. Cited from Meller-Zakomel'sky's report to the tsar in the archives, S. M. Sidel'nikov, *Obrazovanie i deiatel'nost' pervoi gosudarstvennoi dumy* [The formation and activity of the First State Duma] (Moscow: 1962), 84.

20. "Sibirskaia ekspeditsiia barona Mellera-Zakomel'skovo." [Siberian expedition of Baron Meller-Zakomel'sky], *Byloe*, No. 3 (25) (September 1917), 135–41.

21. "Iz pokazaniia na sledstvii byvsh. voennovo gubernatora Zabaikal'skoi obl. I. V. Kholshchevnikova o vooruzhennom zakhvate vosstavshimi oruzhiia i drugikh revoliutsionnykh sobytiiakh v Chite." [From the testimony in the investigation of the former Military Governor of the Zabaikal district I. V. Kholshchevnikov about the armed seizure of rifles and other revolutionary occurrences in Chita], *Vysshii pod"em revoliutsiia*, II, 979.

22 V. N. Pereverzev, "Karatel'naia ekspeditsiia general'-leitenanta

P. K. Rennenkampfa v Zabaikal'skom oblaste" [The punitive expedition of Lieutenant-General P. K. Rennenkampf to the Trans-baikal district], *Byloe,* no. 5–6 (27–28) (November–December 1917), 167.

23. "Donesenie P. K. Rennenkampfa Nikolaiu II o podavlenii vooruzhennovo vosstaniia v Chite." [Report of P. K. Rennenkampf to Nicholas II about the suppression of the armed rising in Chita], *Vysshii pod"em revoliutsiia,* II, 967.

24. Witte, *Vospominaniia,* III, 626 n. 43.

25. Ibid., III, 160. Commenting to the tsar on the capture of Chita, Witte declared on January 23 that it would now be necessary "quickly to judge by a military court those responsible." Semennikov, 56.

26. Kryzhanovskii, 53–55.

27. Ibid., 60–61.

28. The description of the Bulygin election plan which follows is based on that law found in *Polnoe sobranie zakonov,* vol. XXV, part II, nos. 26,661 and 26,662.

29. Witte, *Vospominaniia,* III, 127.

30. Though based on memory, this reconstruction of the tsar's reply undoubtedly captures the essence of his views. Kryzhanovskii, 66–67.

31. *Secret Letters of the Last Tsar,* 201; "Tsarskosel'skie soveshchaniia: Protokoly sekretnavo soveshchaniia pod predsedatel'stvom byvshavo imperatora po voprosy o rasshirenii izbiratel'navo prava," [Tsarskoe Selo Conferences: protocol of a secret conference under the chairmanship of the former emperor on the question of broadening the election law], *Byloe,* no. 3 (25) (September 1917), 158–59. (Hereafter cited as "December Crown Council.") Materials and the protocol for this conference are also in TsGIAL, fund 1544, suppl. to op. 16, d. 21.

32. "December Crown Council," 243. See also the quotation from the Octobrist newspaper, *Slovo,* of November 26—"Every step of delay [in calling the Duma] is a betrayal of Russia"—cited in Chermenskii, *Burzhuaziia i tsarizm v revoliutsii 1905–07 gg.,* 176. Durnovo was one of the few who expressed disbelief in this line of reasoning, Chermenskii, 175.

33. Copies are preserved in TsGIAL, fund 1276, op. 1, d. 39.

34. "December Crown Council," 244–45.

35. Materials for this conference are in TsGIAL, fund 1276, op. 1, d. 39 and in TsGAOR, fund 587, op. 1, d. 48–zh. See also Witte, *Vospominaniia,* III, 127; Shipov, 367; and Sidel'nikov, 64–67.

36. This represented a version, revised by Kryzhanovskii and Witte, of an earlier suggestion from Shipov and his colleagues that elections be direct in the cities and two-staged in the provinces and that voting for Duma deputies in the assemblies be by lists rather than general balloting. Witte apparently objected to these two provisions for fear of gentry opposition to direct elections in the cities and of the "politicization" of the election if Duma deputies were chosen by lists. Sidel'nikov, 64–65.

37. Shipov, 375. This meeting took place on December 3 and was arranged by M. A. Stakhovich at Witte's request.

38. "December Crown Council," 238–40.

39. Ibid., 241–42. After presenting their views, the four representatives of "society" withdrew. They later accepted the December 11 law on the grounds that rapid convocation of the Duma was the crucial issue.

40. Ibid., 243–46.

41. Tagantsev, 94.

42. "December Crown Council," 242, 248, 249.

43. Ibid., 252, 256.

44. Ibid., 258–59.

45. Shipov, 390; Kryzhanovskii, 68–69.

46. "December Crown Council," 264–65.

47. Witte, *Vospominaniia*, III, 130.

48. The discussion of the December election law which follows is based on that document found in *Polnoe sobranie zakonov*, vol. XXV, part II, no. 27,029. Its promulgation was accompanied by a lengthy and rather defensive justification printed in *Pravitel'stvennyi vestnik* for December 13.

49. Sidel'nikov, 73.

50. Ibid., 74–75.

51. Ibid., 74; J. H. L. Keep, "Russian Social Democracy and the First State Duma," *Slavonic and East European Review*, XXXIV (1955–56), 181.

52. Sidel'nikov, 76–77.

53. Ibid., 78; Memorandum of Vuich, Witte Collection, Columbia University.

54. Bernard Pares, *Russia and Reform*, (London: 1907), 539. In casting about for ways to end the Moscow uprising without admitting defeat, a Menshevik leader of the Moscow Soviet ingeniously suggested on December 14 that the workers claim victory over the government on the basis that their revolt had forced the tsar to grant the vote to workers, but his proposal was turned down. Robert M. Slusser, "The Moscow Soviet of Workers' Deputies of 1905; Origin, Structure, and Policies," Ph.D. dissertation, Columbia University, 1963.

55. Witte, *Vospominaniia*, III, 155, 160, 308–09.

56. Ibid., 308. Whether the imposition of martial law after the end of the war with Japan was legally justifiable in all cases is a moot point. At the same time beginning in 1881 the government had been given broad emergency powers, which were regularly renewed every three years. Polianskii, 19; Z. Brzezinski, "The Patterns of Autocracy," in C. E. Black, ed., *The Transformation of Russian Society* (Cambridge, Mass.: 1960), 99–100. By March 1, 1906, two-thirds of the provinces of the Russian Empire were, all or in part, being ruled under martial law.

57. The notation was apparently made by Vuich, Witte's cabinet secretary; it is not in Witte's hand. Witte's note and Manukhin's reply in TsGIAL, fund 1276, op. 1, d. 81.

58. Semennikov, 25–26; Drezen, 251 n. 43. Essentially the same draft law discussed by Witte and the Council of Ministers was finally enacted by Stolypin on August 18, 1906, after the dissolution of the First Duma, under the emergency powers of Article 45 (87) of the Fundamental Laws (see chapter nine). The law, entitled "About the Strengthening of Responsibility for Spreading Antigovernment Teachings and Views Among the Army and About the Transfer to the Jurisdiction of Military and Naval Courts of Judicial Actions Against Such Crimes," formed the basis for the infamous "Stolypin's neckties."

59. In 1904, 18 civilian cases were transferred to military courts; in 1905, 308; and in 1906, 4,698 (of which 254 resulted in death sentences). Under martial law and the state of "strengthened" or "extraordinary" security local authorities had other extensive powers: of administrative detention, imprisonment, and fining; of unlimited search; of prohibiting meetings, even private ones; of closing trade and industrial enterprises and educational institutions; of prohibiting publication of newspapers and journals; and of exiling individuals from the locality. Polianskii, 11–26, 33–34; Spiridonov, 141.

60. Witte, *Vospominaniia*, III, 309. In the scanty documentary evidence unearthed concerning this draft law there is no indication as to exactly when it was first proposed.

61. For a full discussion of the fate of this legislative proposal, see Wayne D. Santoni, "P. N. Durnovo as Minister of Internal Affairs in the Witte Cabinet," Ph.D. dissertation, University of Kansas, 1968, 443–57. See also the brief review of this proposal in a report from Witte to the tsar, Semennikov, ed., 38–39.

62. As we saw earlier, Witte claimed Timiriazev was fired for his role in the scandal connected with the effort to revive Gapon's organization in St. Petersburg. See chapter three, 86–87 and n. 132.

63. This brief review of the history of the project is based primarily on references to it contained in a report from Witte to the tsar, Semennikov, 38–39. No Soviet archival material on the law was found, and only fleeting references to it appear in Soviet secondary sources.

64. Witte, *Vospominaniia*, III, 309–10; Polianskii, 27–29; Memorandum of Vuich, Witte Collection, Columbia University.

65. Drezen, 77–78. For further details on efforts to speed up the trial of peasant rebels, see 195–96 in chapter six.

66. Drezen, 153–56.

67. Semennikov, 38–39. Note from Nicholas to Witte in Witte Collection, Columbia University, Box 8, Folder 50. Earlier, however, in an ukase of December 6 landowners had been given the right to form private guards units, paid out of their own pockets, to protect their estates; this was done primarily in the Baltic. Sidel'nikov, 63.

68. Memorandum of Vuich, Witte Collection, Columbia University.

69. Ibid.

70. See 173–74 in chapter five regarding this law.

71. TsGAOR, fund 102, op. 236 (II), d. 555. On January 18 all police chiefs received a similar injunction, with the warning that any carelessness or delay in executing orders would lead to dismissal.

72. *Vysshi pod"em revoliutsii*, I, 170. For the discussion in the Council of Ministers which prompted this circular, see 158–59.

CHAPTER V

1. Since the history of the soviets has been dealt with extensively in Soviet literature and in a number of works in English, they will be treated here primarily in their relationship to Witte and the government. One of the best brief secondary accounts in English is J. H. L. Keep, *The Rise of Social Democracy in Russia* (Oxford: 1963), 229–42; see also Kochan, 96–101.

2. George Khrustalyev-Nosar', "The Council of Workmen Deputies," *The Russian Review*, II (1913), 92–94; Oskar Anweiler, *Die Rätebewegung in Russland 1905–1921* (Leiden: 1958), 68; Keep, *The Rise of Social Democracy in Russia*, 230, 234.

3. Khrustalyev-Nosar', 95; Anweiler, 61–62.

4. Anweiler, 76.

5. Witte, *Vospominaniia*, III, 98; Khrustalyev-Nosar', 96.

6. Woytinsky, 36.

7. Ibid., 37; Khrustalyev-Nosar', 93–94.

8. Cited in Keep, *The Rise of Social Democracy in Russia*, 236. At the height of its strength the Executive Committee numbered thirty-one: twenty-two workers' deputies and three from each of the three revolutionary parties.

9. Ibid., 235–37.

10. Khrustalyev-Nosar', 94.

11. Ibid., 95.

12. Woytinsky, 44.

13. Ibid., 44; Anweiler, 71; "Otchet o zasedanii Soveta rabochikh deputatov 19 oktiabria." [Report of the meeting of the Council of Workers' Deputies on October 19] *Vserossiiskaia politicheskaia stachka*, I, 384.

14. "Dokladnaia zapiska dvortsovovo komendanta D. F. Trepova Nikolaiu II o revoliutsionnykh sobytiiakh v strane v kontse oktiabria i pervoi polovine noiabria 1905 g." [Report of Court Commandant D. F. Trepov to Nicholas II about revolutionary events in the country at the end of October and the first half of November 1905] *Vysshii pod"em revoliutsii 1905–1907 gg.*, I, 49.

15. Wolfe, 324.

16. "Otchet o zasedanii Soveta rabochikh deputatov 19 oktiabria," *Vserossiiskaia politicheskaia stachka*, I, 385.

17. Witte, *Vospominaniia*, III, 98.

18. Khrustalyev-Nosar', 95.

19. Witte, *Vospominaniia*, III, 139; Wolfe, 325.

20. Woytinsky, 51; Hugh Seton-Watson, *The Decline of Imperial Russia, 1855–1914* (New York: 1960), 228.

21. "Otchet o zasedanii Peterburgskovo soveta rabochikh deputatov 29 oktiabria," *Vserossiiskaia politicheskaia stachka*, I], 398.

22. "Soobshchenie gaz. *Novaia zhizn* o zasedanii Soveta rabochikh deputatov 12 i 13 noiabria po voprosu o vvedenii revoliutsionnym putem 8-chasovovo rabochevo dnia." [Report of the newspaper *New Life* about the meeting of the Council of Workers' Deputies on November 12 and 13 on the question of the introduction of the eight-hour workday by revolutionary means] *Vysshii pod"em revoliutsii 1905–1907 gg.*, I, 392.

23. Woytinsky, 55; "Resoliutsiia Peterburgskovo Soveta rabochikh deputatov ob ob'iavlenii vseobshchei politicheskoi zabastovki v znak protesta protiv voenno-polevovo suda nad matrosami uchastnikami kronshtadskovo vosstaniia i vvedeniia voennovo-polozheniia v Pol'she." [Resolution of the St. Petersburg Council of Workers' Deputies about the declaration of a general political strike as a sign of protest against field courts-martial for sailor-participants in the Kronstadt uprising and the introduction of martial law in Poland] *Vysshii pod"em revoliutsii 1905–1907 gg.*, I, 352.

24. "Dokladnaia zapiska dvortsovovo komendanta D. F. Trepova Nikolaiu II o revoliutsionnykh sobytiiakh v strane v kontse oktiabria i pervoi polovine noiabria 1905 g." *Vysshii pod'em revoliutsii 1905–1907 gg.*, I, 48; "Svedeniia peterburgskovo gradonachal'nika V. A. Dediulina, napravlennye v Departament politsii o bastuiushchikh predpriiatiakh Peterburga," [Information of the St. Petersburg Town Governor V. A. Dediulin, sent to the police department about strikes in businesses in St. Petersburg] ibid., I, 361.

25. Ibid., I, 363–64, 369.

26. Keep, *The Rise of Social Democracy in Russia*, 239–40.

27. Khrustalyev-Nosar', 97–98.

28. Ibid., 97–98.

29. Woytinsky, 86.

30. "Iz 'vsepoddanneishikh zapisok' upravliaiushchevo Ministerstvom vnutrennikh del P. N. Durnovo Nikolaiu II o revoliutsionnykh sobytiiakh v strane." [From the 'Official Reports' of the head of the Ministry of the Interior P. N. Durnovo to Nicholas II about revolutionary events in the country], *Vysshii pod"em revoliutsii 1905–1907 gg.*, I, 53; Anweiler, 73. Nosar' was exiled to Siberia, but this was mild treatment compared to that which he received from the Soviet government, which shot him in 1918.

31. Khrustalyev-Nosar', 98.

32. Witte, *Vospominaniia*, III, 140.

33. " 'Finansovyi manifest' Tsentral'novo Komiteta i Organizatsionnoi komissii RSDRP, Peterburgskovo Soveta rabochikh deputatov

i drugikh organizatsii," ['Financial Manifesto' of the Central Committee and Organization Commission of the RSDWP (Russian Social Democratic Workers' party), the St. Petersburg Council of Workers' Deputies and other organizations], *Vysshii pod"em revoliutsii 1905–1907 gg.*, I, 26.

34. "Dokladnaia zapiska nachal'nika Peterburgskovo okhrannovo otdeleniia A. V. Gerasimova upravliaiushchemu Ministerstvom vnutrennikh del P. N. Durnovo ob areste Peterburgskovo Soveta rabochikh deputatov." [Report of the head of the St. Petersburg Secret Police A. V. Gerasimov to the head of the Ministry of the Interior P. N. Durnovo about the arrest of the St. Petersburg Council of Workers' Deputies], *Vysshii pod"em revoliutsii 1905–1907 gg.*, I, 443. The police report does not indicate the arrest of non-Soviet observers who attended the meeting. One such person was Woytinsky, who, although not a member of the Soviet, attended the meeting, was arrested, and imprisoned. Perhaps the police treated all those at the meeting as members of the Soviet. Woytinsky, 88.

35. Witte, *Vospominaniia*, III, 140; *Secret Letters of the Last Tsar*, 195.

36. Gurko, 443.

37. Memorandum of Vuich, Witte Collection, Columbia University.

38. Khrustalyev-Nosar', 94. Trotsky, in almost identical language, referred to the Soviet as "true, unadulterated democracy." Leon Trotsky, *Our Revolution: Essays on Working-Class and International Revolution, 1904–1917*, trans. by Moissaye J. Olgin, (New York: 1918), 155.

39. Anweiler, 74.

40. Ibid., 69.

41. Keep, *The Rise of Social Democracy in Russia*, 243.

42. "Ezhenedel'naia zapiska po departamentu politsii za period vremeni s 8 po 15 dekabria." [Weekly report of the Department of Police for the period December 8–15], *Krasnyi arkhiv*, XI–XII (1925), 166–69. For a detailed but tendentious account of these risings, see N. N. Iakovlev, *Vooruzhennye vosstaniia v dekabre 1905 g.* [Armed uprisings in December 1905] (Moscow: 1957).

43. In fact, Moscow was traditionally more conservative than other major Russian cities but in 1905 its administration had been weakened and disorganized by frequent changes of personnel, from the governor-general down. Keep, *The Rise of Social Democracy in Russia*, 218–19.

44. Witte, *Vospominaniia*, III, 166, 173; *Vysshii pod"em revoliutsii 1905–1907 gg.*, I, 581. The tsar wished to appoint Bulygin, but he refused. Dubasov was reluctant to take the post, but Witte pressured him into accepting. Letter from Witte to Nicholas, January 8, 1906, Semennikov, 41–42.

45. Keep, *The Rise of Social Democracy in Russia*, 244–46; Slusser, 50–51.

46. *Vysshii pod"em revoliutsii 1905–07 gg.*, I, 644–45.

47. Slusser, 97–109.

48. "Reshenie Moskovskovo Soveta rabochikh deputatov ob ob'iav-lenie s 7 dekabria vseobshchei politicheskoi zabastovki." [Decision of the Moscow Council of Workers' Deputies about the declaration of a general political strike beginning December 7], *Vysshii pod"em revoliutsii 1905–07 gg.*, I, 647–48.

49. Ibid., 649–50.

50. Slusser, 3.

51. Witte, *Vospominaniia*, III, 174–76; *Vysshii pod"em revoliutsii* I, 616–17, 676–77. Witte claimed that when he telephoned Dubasov to tell him help was on the way, he finally located the governor-general at the home of the military commander of the region, who was so old and enfeebled that all staff meetings had to be held there and large numbers of troops placed on guard in that area.

According to Gukovskii (248), Minister of War Rediger was so fearful of releasing troops from St. Petersburg that he considered a proposal from Dubrovin, the head of the Union of Russian People, to muster 20,000 Old Believers from Vitebsk for guard duty in the capital.

52. Keep, *The Rise of Social Democracy in Russia*, 244, 246, 252; A. M. Pankratova, *Pervaia russkaia revoliutsiia 1905–1907 gg.* [The first Russian revolution, 1905–07] (Moscow: 1951), 176. Keep estimates the total government forces in Moscow at a little over eight thousand. Interestingly enough, the leaders of the railway workers' union, believing the army as a whole was revolutionary, acted to facilitate the return of troops from the Far East in the hope that these soldiers would add their rifles to the small cache of arms held by the Soviet. V. N. Pereverzev, "Pervyi vserossiiskii zheleznodorozhnyi soiuz 1905 goda," *Byloe*, 4 (32), 1925, 63.

53. *Vysshii pod"em revoliutsii*, I, 157; Letter from Minister of War Rediger to Witte, December 17, in Witte Collection, Columbia University, Box 10, Folder 2; Drezen, 18.

54. *Vysshii pod"em revoliutsii*, I, 692–95.

55. Chermenskii, *Burzhuaziia i tsarizm v revoliutsii 1905–07 gg.*, 224–26; N. N. Demochkin and others, *Revoliutsiia 1905–07 gg. v. Rossii: posobie dlia uchitelia* [The revolution of 1905–07 in Russia: an aid for the teacher] (Moscow: 1965), 159. Both references are based on archival sources.

56. Baring, 55–58.

57. "Zapiska upravliaiushchevo Ministerstvom vnutrnnikh del P. N. Durnovo predsedateliu Soveta ministrov S. Iu. Vitte o deistviiakh i metodakh bor'by boevykh druzhin." [Note from the head of the Ministry of the Interior P. N. Durnovo to the chairman of the Council of Ministers S. Iu. Witte about the activities and methods of struggle of the combat squads], *Vysshii pod"em revoliutsii*, I, 677–78.

58. Nicholas II, *Tagebuch*, 268–69; Sovremennik," *Nikolai II, razoblacheniia*, 321.

59. *Vysshii pod"em revoliutsii*, I, 713–15.

60. V. Shtriker, "Sudebnyie protsessy o dekabr'skom vooruzhennom vosstanii v Moskve," [Trials on the December uprising in Moscow], *Sovetskiia iustitsiia* [Soviet justice], no. 23 (1961), 22.

61. Semennikov, 34, 167, 168.

62. Ibid., 32–33.

63. Letter from Witte to Nicholas, January 8, enclosing letter of January 7 from Dubasov to Witte, ibid., 41–43; Witte, *Vospominaniia*, III, 177–78 and 627–28 n. 48.

64. Slusser, 4; report dated December 21 of the French Consul Engelhardt, who also noted that in the face of the turmoil in Moscow many workers simply returned to their native villages, cited in René Girault, "La révolution russe de 1905 d'après quelques témoinages françaises," *Revue historique*, CCXXX (July–Sept. 1963), 114–15; Pankratova, *Pervaia russkaia revoliutsiia 1905–07 gg.*, 197.

65. On the fiscal crisis, see chapter seven, 212–13.

66. Chermenskii, *Burzhuaziia i tsarizm v revoliutsii 1905–07 gg.*, 154–55.

67. Witte, *Vospominaniia*, III, 155–60.

68. "Dnevnik G. O. Raukha," [Diary of G. O. Raukh], *Krasnyi arkhiv*, XIX (1926), 90–91.

69. Semennikov, 27.

70. Ibid., 30–32.

71. The tsar, perhaps stung by Witte's remark, underlined the word "perhaps."

72. Ibid., 34–36; see also for Witte's reports of December 21 and 23, *Byloe*, no. 3 (1918), 4–7.

73. *Byloe*, no. 3 (1918), 4–7.

74. Note from Nicholas to Witte, December 24, Witte Collection, Columbia University, Box 8, Folder 50.

75. Protocols of the meetings of the commission are in *Krasnyi arkhiv*, XXXI (1928), 87–100; the tsar's order in *Revoliutsiia 1905–07 gg. v. Rossii: Dokumenty i materialy: Vtoroi period revoliutsii 1906–07 gody* [The revolution of 1905–07 in Russia: documents and materials: the second period of the revolution, 1906–07], Part II, Book I (Moscow: 1966), 588. (Hereafter cited as *Vtoroi period revoliutsii*.)

76. Only the security aspects of the Council's discussion are treated here; for the agrarian reform program the Council proposed, see chapter six, 198–200.

77. See letter from Witte to Durnovo and Rediger, January 28, reporting this decision and the subsequent action taken, TsGIAL, fund 1276, op. 1, d. 7.

78. See Semennikov, 54–55, for Witte's letters of January 11 and 14 to Nicholas on this subject; according to the editor, neither the memoir of the Council nor the draft ukase were found in the archives.

79. "Iz pisem gen. N. N. Levashova A. N. Kuropatkinu." [From the letters of General N. N. Levashov to A. N. Kuropatkin], ed. by M. Klevenskii, *Krasnyi arkhiv*, XV (1926,) 220.

80. *Secret Lettters of the Last Tsar*, 211.
81. "Dnevnik A. A. Polovtseva," 90. The same conclusion about Witte was recorded in Korostowetz, 245.
82. Nicholas II, *Tagebuch*, 273–74; "Sovremennik," *Nikolai II, razoblacheniia*, 318–20.
83. "Sovremennik," *Nikolai II razoblacheniia*, 324–25.
84. *The Memoirs of Count Kokovtsov*, 67.
85. *Agrarnyi vopros v sovete ministrov, 1906 g.* [The agrarian question in the Council of Ministers, 1906], ed. by B. Veselovskii and others (Moscow-Leningrad: 1924), 110–12. The manifesto Nicholas proposed was never issued; see chapter six, 197–98.
86. "Sovremennik," *Nikolai II, razoblacheniia*, 327.
87. Menashe, 143–45, 185–89; Chermenskii, *Burzhuaziia i tsarizm v revoliutsii 1905–07 gg.*, 235.
88. *Memoirs of Alexander Iswolsky*, 18–19.
89. TsGIAL, fund 1276, op. 2, d. 2.
90. "Petitsiia zemlevladel'tsev," [Petition of landowners], *Krasnyi arkhiv*, XI–XII (1925), 155–56; Semennikov, 57; Witte, *Vospominaniia*, III, 208–10.
91. Witte Collection, Columbia University, Box 7, Folder 19. In his memoirs Witte notes the tsar's statement but not the context in which it was made. Witte, *Vospominaniia*, III, 334.
92. On the dismissal of Timiriazev, see chapter three, 87; on that of Kutler, chapter six, 194.
93. Witte, *Vospominaniia*, III, 211–12.
94. This suggestion was made in connection with Witte's report of January 10 on the agrarian question, for which see chapter six, 195–96.
95. Witte, *Vospominaniia*, III, 160.
96. Witte Collection, Columbia University, Box 7, Folder 19.
97. *Polnoe sobranie zakonov*, 3rd ed., XXVI, Part 1, no. 27,371; Drezen, 244 n. 7.
98. This instruction of the Council of Ministers has not been published, as far as we know, and no copy of it was found in the archives, but it is summarized, with the tsar's notation, in a report from Witte to Nicholas on February 17 (TsGIAL, fund 1276, op. 1, d. 81), and it is referred to in several other documents of this period.
99. Witte's report of February 17 and the final reply of the Ministry of War of March 8 on this affair are in TsGIAL, fund 1276, op. 1, d. 81.
100. Vodovozov, 102, citing the newspaper *Molva* for January 7, 1906.
101. The reports of January 10 and 24 are discussed fully in chapter six; the former has been printed in a number of sources, the latter is in TsGIAL, fund 1276, op. 2, d. 4.
102. Witte, *Vospominaniia*, III, 316–17; TsGIAL, fund 1276, op. 2, d. 130. The government's lack of publications media was so great that it had to call on the editors of a minor journal, *Sel'skii vestnik*, in order

to have popular brochures on the October Manifesto, the decree of November 3, and the new electoral law prepared.

103. *Secret Letters of the Last Tsar*, 211

104. Witte, *Vospominaniia*, III, 334–36.

105. Bompard, 205.

106. An incident recounted by Woytinsky illustrates this attitude well. In early January, returning home from prison following his release, Woytinsky asked his cab driver, "How is business these days?" The driver replied, "Thank God, it is picking up. One should not complain; there is order. It was hard under freedom. . . . They [the revolutionaries] would not let one drive, would cut his harness. And in our business, whether or not one has a fare, one must pay three rubles a day to the boss for the droshky, horse, hay, and oats." Woytinsky, 91.

107. On the changed mood of the public, see Bernard Pares, *Russia and Reform*, 536; Chermenskii, *Burzhuaziia i tsarizm v revoliutsii 1905–07 gg.*, 220, 238.

108. Chermenski, 232–38.

109. Ibid., 174–75.

110. Durnovo's proposal to the Council of Ministers and the action on it are in TsGIAL, fund 1276, op. 2, d. 133; his circular of January 13 in TsGAOR, fund 102, op. 236 (II), d. 555.

111. See, for example, reports to the tsar by Durnovo on January 11 and by Trepov on January 26 and February 9, *Vtoroi period revoliutsii*, I, 83–86, 93–95, 99–103; also A. Morskoi, *Iskhod rossiiskoi revoliutsii 1905 g. i "pravitel'stvo" Nosaria* [The outcome of the Russian revolution of 1905 and the "government" of Nosar'] (Moscow: 1911), 109–10.

112. A. Ia. Grunt' and V. N. Firstova, *Rossiia v epokhu imperializma, 1890–1907 gg.* [Russia in the epoch of imperialism, 1890–1907] (Moscow: 1959), 151; Baring, 94; Olgin, 161–62; Obninskii, *Polgoda russkoi revoliutsii*, 69, which gives an estimate, based on press reports alone, of over fifty thousand, with the peak in January and February. In return, the revolutionaries assassinated 128 government officials, according to Obninskii, 152.

113. S. R. Mintslov, "14 mesiatsev svobody pechati: 17 oktiabria 1905 g.–1 ianvaria 1907 g." [Fourteen months of freedom of the press: October 17, 1905–January 1, 1907], *Byloe*, no. 15 (March 1907), 124.

114. Witte, *Vospominaniia*, III, 65.

115. It is difficult to be certain of the exact number of people and papers affected by the government clamp-down in this period. Liubimov wrote that from December 1905 through January 1906, sixty-three publications were closed by the government. Liubimov, 364. Spector claimed that from December 12, 1905, to January 12, 1906, the government closed seventy-eight periodicals in major cities. In addition, fifty-eight editors were arrested, most of whom were released on bail, however. Ivar Spector, *The First Russian Revolution: Its Impact on Asia* (Englewood Cliffs, N. J.: 1962), 20. The journal *Byloe*, nos. 2–4, in 1906 esti-

mated three hundred eighty legal and administrative measures against the press for the months January to March inclusive (cited in Vodovozov, 92). Obninskii claimed one hundred twenty-nine papers, fifty-five publishing houses, and three libraries were closed from December to March, Obninskii, *Polgoda russrkoi revoliutsii*, 131.

Mintslov, who surveyed a somewhat more extended period—October 17, 1905, to January 1, 1907—arrived at the following statistics for that period:

1. Confiscated books [individual titles]—361
2. Confiscated periodicals in St. Petersburg alone—433
3. Forcible closing of periodical publishing houses in Russia—371.
4. Numbers of editors and publishers imprisoned or otherwise punished—607
5. Closure of printing shops—97

Mintslov, 134.

116. Memorandum of Vuich, Witte Collection, Columbia University; Mironenko, "Manifest 17 oktiabria 1905 g.," 167–68, based on archival sources; and *Polnoe sobranie zakonov* (3rd ed.) XXVI, Part I, no. 27,574 and no. 27,815. Both decrees clarified and tightened the November 24 rules, while changing the censorship committees into Committees on Press Affairs.

117. Tagantsev, 49.

118. Witte, *Vospominaniia*, III, 321, 637–38 n. 68; Mironenko, 168–69.

119. Mironenko, 168–69; TsGAOR, fund 102, op. 236 (II), d. 555.

120. TsGAOR, fund 102, op. 236 (II), d. 133.

121. Memorandum of Vuich, Witte Collection, Columbia University; *Polnoe sobranie zakonov* (3rd ed.), XXVI, Part I, no. 27,395.

122. See, for example, a report of the chief of police in St. Petersburg on March 5, TsGIAL, fund 1276, op. 1, d. 81, and protests from the Kadets about the obstruction of meetings cited in Chermenskii, *Burzhuaziia i tsarizm v revoliutsii 1905 g.*, 220, 232, 239.

123. *Polnoe sobranie zakonov*, 3rd ed., XXVI, Part 1, no. 24,479 and no. 24,480; Piaskovskii, 179; Witte, *Vospominaniia*, III, 322. In practice, under the March 4 law no political parties to the left of the Octobrists were legally registered.

124. Chermenskii, *Burzhuaziia i tsarizm v revoliutsii 1905 g.*, 237–38; Sidel'nikov, 85–86.

125. Sidel'nikov, 87.

126. These two issues will be dealt with, respectively, in chapters nine and seven.

Chapter VI

1. See chapter three, 87–89, for a description of the peasant unrest.
2. Lenin was one of the first to face up to this fact, drawing appro-

priate lessons from it that proved useful in 1917. Only a few Soviet historians have acknowledged the fact.

3. Woytinsky, 67 ff.

4. Ibid., 61.

5. For accounts of peasant actions, see ibid., 60; *Vysshii pod"em revoliutsii 1905–07 gg.*, II, 212; and *Vtoroi period revoliutsii*, 1, II, 81–83.

6. "Dokladnaia zapiska po departamentu politsii predsedateliu soveta ministrov S. Iu. Vitte," *Krasnyi arkhiv*, IX, 74.

7. "Doklad ministra vnutrennikh del P. N. Durnovo Nikolaiu II ob otvetakh gubernatorov na zapros Ministerstva vnutrennikh del otnositel'no prichin krest'ianskikh volnenii." [Report of the Minister of the Interior P. N. Durnovo to Nicholas II about the answers of governors to the inquiry of the Ministry of the Interior concerning the reasons for peasant agitation] *Vtoroi period revoliutsii 1906–1907 gody*, I, 96–98.

8. Robinson, 152–53; Robinson wrote, "Economic hardship created a need for change; peasant tradition as well as revolutionary propaganda suggested the remedy; official preoccupation and indecisiveness invited the storm; and soon the greatest agrarian disturbance since the days of Pugachev was under way." Ibid., 155.

9. von Laue, *Sergei Witte and the Industrialization of Russia*, 115–16.

10. Witte, *Vospominaniia*, II, 522–28.

11. Cited in von Laue, *Sergei Witte and the Industrialization of Russia*, 176.

12. Ibid., 223–30; Witte, *Vospominaniia*, II, 532–37.

13. Cited in von Laue, *Sergei Witte and the Industrialization of Russia*, 229.

14. Cited from the protocols of the Commission in Soviet archives, in M. S. Simonova, "Agrarnaia politika samoderzhaviia v 1905 g." [Agrarian policy of the autocracy in 1905] *Istoricheskie zapiski* [Historical notes], No. 81 (1968), 199.

15. For a useful review of Russian and Soviet specialized literature on the evolution of tsarist agrarian policies in this period, see M. S. Simonova, "Politika tsarizma v krest'ianskom voprose nakanune revoliutsii 1905–07 gg." [Tsarist policy on the peasant question on the eve of the revolution of 1905–07], *Istoricheskie zapiski*, no. 75 (1965), 212–14.

16. Simonova, "Agrarnaia politika samoderzhaviia v 1905 g.," 201–07, based on archival records of the conference.

17. Witte, *Vospominaniia*, III, 197.

18. *Agrarnyi vopros v sovete ministrov (1906 g.)*, 8–9.

19. Witte Collection, Columbia University, Box 8, Folder 5.

20. Ibid.; Migulin's project was also printed in N. N. Kutler, *Agrarnyi vopros* [The agrarian question] (Kharkov: 1906), not available to us.

21. P. P. Migulin, "Russkaia agrarnaia problema i sel'skokhoziaistvennaia katastrofa v Sovetskoi Rossii." [Russian agrarian problem and

the agricultural catastrophe in Soviet Russia], 1931, 173–82. Unpublished manuscript from the Archive of Russian and European History, Columbia University.

22. Witte, *Vospominaniia*, III, 197–98.

23. Surprisingly, on October 30 Witte, who several years before had unsuccessfully urged the State Council to abolish redemption dues, told Polovtsev that he opposed their cancellation as it would upset the budget. Yet only a day or so later he supported the ending of redemption dues before the Council of Ministers. "Dnevnik A. A. Polovtseva," 82.

24. *The Memoirs of Count Kokovtsov,* 100.

25. Witte, *Vospominaniia*, III, 199–201.

26. Kutler's plan entitled "On Measures to Broaden and Improve Peasant Agriculture," and his "Explanatory Note," with charts, are in *Agrarnyi vopros v sovete ministrov (1906 g.),* 27–51.

27. This would have been even more favorable to landowners than Migulin's proposed 100 rubles per desiatin, according to Simonova, "Agrarnaia politika samoderzhaviia v 1905 g.," 211.

28. Witte, *Vospominaniia*, III, 201.

29. See chapter two, 35–36; also see Simonova, "Agrarnaia politika samoderzhaviia v 1905 g.," 209, where this reference is interpreted as a definite suggestion of expropriation.

30. *Agrarnyi vopros v sovete ministrov (1906 g.),* 63–70.

31. "Sovremennik," *Nikolai II, razoblacheniia,* 324–26.

32. Witte Collection, Columbia University, Box 8, Folder 50; Witte, *Vospominaniia*, III, 202–04. Nicholas refused to appoint Kutler to the Senate or State Council, normal practice for dismissed or retired ministers, but, at Witte's insistence, the tsar finally granted Kutler a meager pension of 7,000 rubles. Later, Kutler became an active member of the Kadet party.

33. Semennikov, 33.

34. See Trepov's note on Witte's letter, summarizing the tsar's reaction, Semennikov, 33, and letter from Nicholas to Witte, December 24, 1905, Witte Collection, Columbia University, Box 8, Folder 50. The special conference under Nicholas was never convened.

35. Semennikov, 45–51.

36. This report, Durnovo's endorsement of it dated January 7, and the memoir of the Council of Ministers on it dated January 10 are in TsGIAL, fund 1276, op. 1, d. 97.

37. On Witte's letter to Durnovo and Rediger, dated January 28, see chapter five, no. 77 and TsGIAL, fund 1276, op. 1, d. 97.

38. TsGIAL, fund 1276, op. 1, d. 97.

39. On the memorandum to the tsar, probably from A. V. Krivoshein, see below; on Nicholas' proposal, see his letter of February 10 to Witte, discussed and extensively quoted in chapter five, 161 and printed in *Agrarnyi vopros v sovete ministrov (1906 g.),* 110–12.

40. *Agrarnyi vopros v sovete ministrov (1906 g.),* 113.

41. Ibid., 123–25. Expropriation in such special circumstances had

been approved by a congress of marshals of nobility which met in Moscow in early January.

42. Ibid., 113–18; S. M. Dubrovskii, *Stolypinskaia zemel'naia reforma* [The Stolypin land reform] (Moscow: 1963), 96.

43. Drezen, 123–26.

44. TsGIAL, fund 1276, op. 2, d. 135.

45. Beside Witte's reference to Kutler's project, Nicholas noted, "I do not agree."

46. *Agrarnyi vopros v sovete ministrov (1906 g.)*, 111.

47. Ibid., 80–82.

48. Because of overlapping membership and common concerns these two commissions are often confused in the literature on tsarist agrarian policy. Our attempt at clarity is based primarily on the documents in ibid., 102–10, 118–23, and 126–31, and on Dubrovskii, *Stolypinskaia zemel'naia reforma*, 95–101, which draws on archival material. Members of the Nikol'skii commission were Prince V. Kochubei, head of the department of appanage lands, A. Putilov, head of the Peasants' Bank, A. V. Krivoshein, then head of the department of migration, shortly to be deputy minister of Agriculture, Gurko, head of the department of peasant affairs in the Ministry of Interior, and Nikol'skii, then head of the state savings banks, shortly to be minister of Agriculture.

Members of the Gurko commission were A. A. Rittikh from the Ministry of Agriculture, A. I. Lykoshin from the Ministry of Justice, a representative of the Ministry of Finance, and Gurko.

49. Memoir of the Council of Ministers, January 24, in TsGIAL, fund 1276, op. 2, d. 4. See chapter nine for other aspects of the government's program which were worked out later.

50. *Agrarnyi vopros v sovete ministrov (1906 g.)*, 105–10. Nicholas saw Witte's January 24 report on February 2, this memorandum on February 3, according to notations on the documents.

51. There is, however, some confusion concerning this document since it appears, in almost identical form, in the Soviet fiftieth-anniversary collection of documents as a formal report from Witte to Nicholas, dated February 3, *Vtoroi period revoliutsii 1906–07 gg.*, I, 144–47. It is of course possible either that Witte was simply transmitting Krivoshein's views to the tsar and failed to make this clear in his report, or that Witte appropriated Krivoshein's memorandum as his own. Neither, however, seems likely since Witte, as we saw in chapter five, was at this very time rejecting Krivoshein as a possible replacement for Kutler as minister of Agriculture on the ground that Krivoshein was too close a confidant of Trepov.

The editors of *Agrarnyi vopros* attribute the document to Krivoshein, apparently on the basis of his similar article in *Novoe vremia* and of a reference to a report by Krivoshein in a memoir of discussions in the Council of Ministers on February 10 and 17, *Agrarnyi vopros v sovete ministrov (1906 g.)*, 4 n. 2, and 118. We have concluded that Krivoshein probably did prepare the memorandum, and its attribution to Witte is an error. Though confusing, the question of the authorship of the memorandum is not of great importance since the ideas expressed in it in any case reflected the dominant trend of thinking within government circles at the time, and it contained little, if anything, to which Witte would have seriously objected.

52. Memoir of the Council of Ministers, February 10 and 17, ibid., 118–23.

53. TsGIAL, fund 1276, op. 2, d. 2.

54. *Agrarnyi vopros v sovete ministrov (1906 g.)*, 102–05.

55. Ibid., 126–31.

56. TsGIAL, fund 1276, op. 2, d. 135.

57. George L. Yaney, "The Concept of the Stolypin Land Reform," *The Slavic Review*, vol. XXVIII, no. 2 (June 1964), 277.

58. Simonova, "Agrarnaia politika samoderzhaviia v 1905 g.," 212–13.

59. Dubrovskii, *Stolypinskaia zemel'naia reforma*, 98–99.

60. Ibid., 100–02; "Dnevnik A. A. Polovtseva," 96–97. After this defeat Witte formed a new interdepartmental commission under Nikol'skii to prepare drafts of reform legislation on peasant problems. Following Witte's dismissal the commission presented these drafts to Stolypin in June, and they formed the basis for much of his subsequent action on land reform.

61. S. Prokopovich, "Formy i resul'taty agrarnavo dvizheniia v 1906 goda" [Forms and results of the agrarian movement in 1906], *Byloe*, no.1 (January 1907), 175.

Chapter VII

1. Witte, *Vospominaniia*, III, 249.

2. Olga Crisp, "The Russian Liberals and the 1906 Anglo-French Loan to Russia," *The Slavonic and East European Review*, XXXIX, no. 93 (June 1961), 500 n. 10, estimates total French loans to Russia between 1888 and 1904 at six billion francs.

3. James W. Long, "The Economics of the Franco-Russian Alliance, 1904–06," Ph.D. dissertation, University of Wisconsin, 1968, 83–94, 96–98.

4. Witte, *Vospominaniia*, III, 218–19; *The Memoirs of Count Kokovtsov*, 14–18.

5. *The Memoirs of Count Kokovtsov*, 83.

6. A. L. Sidorov, ed., "Denezhnoe obrashchenie i finansovoe polozhenie Rossii (1904–07 gg.)" [Monetary circulation and the financial position of Russia in 1904–07], *Istoricheskii arkhiv*, III (1956), 89. A law approved by the State Council in early 1906 provided up to two years in prison for undermining state credit by rumors or for inciting runs on banks. Long, 127.

7. Long, 130.

8. A. L. Sidorov, ed., "Finansovoe polozhenie tsarskovo samoderzhaviia v period russko-iaponskoi voiny i pervoi russkoi revoliutsii." [The financial position of the tsarist autocracy in the period of the Russo-Japanese war and the first Russian revolution], *Istoricheskii arkhiv*, II (1955), 140–41.

9. Ibid., 124.

10. Witte, *Memoirs*, 285.

11. Witte, *Vospominaniia*, II, 404–05. See also René Girault, "Sur quelques aspects financiers de l'alliance franco-russe," *Revue d'histoire moderne et contemporaine*, VIII (January–March 1961), vol. 8, 70–74.

12. Witte, *Vospominaniia*, II, 448; Crisp, 503.

13. Rouvier believed that British participation would be "a possible element of rapprochement between England and Russia and a first token of the well-meaning disposition of the British Government." Cited in Crisp, 500 n. 12.

14. Witte, *Vospominaniia*, II, 452.

15. Ibid., II, 463.

16. In his memoirs Witte often refers to his project for a European consort of nations; and he says that if he had remained in power, he would have bent all his energy to affect a rapprochement among Russia, France, and Germany. The inherent conflict between Witte's ambition to forge a continental alliance against English and American power in world affairs and his open attempts to secure support for Russia's international loan in London and New York either did not bother him—or perhaps he failed to see it. On several occasions he intimated that he could woo France to such a bloc if he were made ambassador to Paris. See Bompard, 151, and draft letter to Count Eulenberg, March 1906, Witte Collection, Columbia University, Box 7, Folder 17.

17. Letter from William II to Bülow on September 14, 1905. *Correspondance secrète de Bülow et de Guillaume II*, trans. by Gilbert Lenoir (Paris: 1931), 156. Hereafter cited as *Correspondance de Bülow*.

18. Witte's influence in urging a more tractable policy on William is confirmed by a letter of September 13 from the kaiser to Nicholas. Isaac Don Levine, ed., *Letters From the Kaiser to the Tsar* (New York: 1920), 193–98. See also Bompard, 150–51.

19. Letter from Bülow to the kaiser, September 12. *Correspondance de Bülow*, 151.

20. Witte, *Vospominaniia*, II, 463.

21. Witte later felt that German civility and flattery at Rominten "were only steps to fascinate me." The Germans knew that upon his return to St. Petersburg Witte could be influential in confirming the Björkö Treaty.

22. The existence of the Björkö Treaty was not made known to the world at large until the Soviet government published its text in 1917. The text is in *Krasnyi arkhiv*, IV (1924), 25–26.

23. Long, 110 n. 23.

24. The kaiser realized this, for he presented Witte with his portrait inscribed: "Portsmouth-Björkö-Rominten. Wilhelm rex." Witte, *Memoirs*, 422.

25. *The Memoirs of Count Kokovtsov*, 60, 71–73; Witte, *Vospominaniia*, III, 225. The British Foreign Office denied that the participation of British bankers had any political significance, but as the London *Times* correspondent in St. Petersburg pointed out at the time, English participation in a loan to Russia could not help influencing favorably Anglo-Russian relations in general. Long, 109.

26. Long, 111 and 117 n. 36.

27. Ibid., 113–14.

28. Ibid., 113–14.

29. Witte and Kokovtsov, who had been quite good friends, quarreled and fell out at about this time, and they remained enemies the rest of their political and personal lives. The cause of the quarrel is not entirely clear, either in their memoirs or from contemporary accounts. The likeliest supposition is that it stemmed from rivalry and jealousy between two ambitious and able men and was based primarily on their contention over two issues: the loan, who was to negotiate it and, above all, who was to get credit for it; and Witte's conception of the new premierlike role of the chairman of the Council of Ministers, an idea Kokovtsov opposed strongly in various meetings during September and October, much to Witte's displeasure. Subsequently, when Witte was made chairman of the revised Council, he refused to appoint Kokovtsov as minister of Finance, although Kokovtsov was obviously the ablest man for the post.

In his memoirs, which were written first, Witte lost no opportunity to denigrate Kokovtsov and to deride his role in Russian affairs. (For example, Witte, *Memoirs*, 306, 310.) Kokovtsov, writing over a decade after publication of Witte's reminiscences, defended himself vigorously and did not hesitate to vent his own spleen at the expense of Witte. (*The Memoirs of Count Kokovtsov*, 440–45.) The polemics of the two men are valuable for an understanding of the character of each, but their personal vindictiveness complicates the task of accurately assessing, from their memoirs, the role of each in negotiating the loan, or even of reconstructing the actual events. Witte, who believed he alone had the prestige in international financial circles necessary to negotiate such a large loan, consistently depicted Kokovtsov's part in the negotiations as that of a glorified errand boy, incapable of understanding the vast implications of the loan and acting only under Witte's specific instructions. In December 1913 Witte even circulated to the tsar and to members of the government a pamphlet in which he tried to show that Kokovtsov had done nothing. See *Spravka o tom, kak byl zakliuchen vneshnii zaem 1906 g., spasshii finansovoe polozhenie Rossii* [Information on how the foreign loan of 1906, which saved the financial position of Russia, was concluded], reproduced in part in E. A. Preobrazhenskii, ed., *Russkie finansy i evropeiskaia birzha v 1904–06 gg.* [Russian finances and the European bourse in 1904–06] (Moscow-Leningrad: 1926).

30. Kokovtsov was surprised at Witte's suggestion because hardly more than a month before Witte had driven him from the government. Just before Witte's proposal, Kokovtsov said Witte pushed a note across the table to him which read: "You see what horrors surround us; I am utterly exhausted and lonely, my nerves are in shreds, and my head refuses to work. You are rested, your head is clear; do help us, take the matter into your hands." *The Memoirs of Count Kokovtsov*, 85.

31. Ibid., 87.

32. Ibid., 88–89. It should be remembered that this was during the Moscow uprising, and just as Witte was making the painful decision to agree to the sending of punitive expeditions to Siberia and the Baltic; see chapter five.

33. Actually as early as November 22 instructions had already been given to the Russian representative to the Algeciras Conference, Count A. P. Cassini, that he was to give "neogranichennuiu podderzhku" [unlimited support] to the French. "Proekt sekretnoi instruktsii rossiis-komu pervomu upolnomochennomu na mezhdunarodnoi konferentsii po delam Marokko d. t. s. grafu Kassini." [The draft of secret instruc-tions to the chief Russian representative to the international conference on the Moroccan affair, Count Cassini], *Krasnyi arkhiv,* XLI–XLII (1930), 10.

34. Witte, *Vospominaniia*, III, 225.

35. "Telegramma Kokovtsova gr. Vitte: iz Parizha ot 21 dekabria 1905 g." [Telegram from Kokovtsov to Count Witte: From Paris on December 21, 1905], *Krasnyi arkhiv*, X (1925), 13–14.

36. "Telegramma stats-sekretaria V. N. Kokovtsova iz Parizha predsedateliu Soveta ministrov S. Iu. Vitte o khode peregovorov o zaime." [Telegram of State Secretary V. N. Kokovtsov to the chairman of the Council of Ministers S. Iu. Witte about the progress of conversa-tions concerning the loan], *Vysshii pod"em revoliutsii 1905–1907 gg.,* I 177.

37. "Telegramma gr. Vitte Kokovtsovu v Parizh ot 4 ianvaria 1906 g." (December 21, 1905 o.s.) [Telegram of Count Witte to Kokovtsov on January 4, 1906. (December 21, 1905 o.s.)], *Krasnyi arkhiv*, X (1925), 14; "Telegramma Kokovtsova Shipovu iz Parizha ot 29 dekabria 1905 g./ 11 ianvaria 1906 g." [Telegram from Kokovtsov to Shipov from Paris on December 29, 1905/January 11, 1906], ibid., 21.

38. Witte, *Vospominaniia*, III, 228.

39. These conditions are summarized from Kokovtsov's analysis of the situation, *The Memoirs of Count Kokovtsov*, 100–03. Nevertheless, at the turn of the year 1905–06 the Russian government had had to resort to issuing 150 million rubles in notes without the gold backing the law required, but it succeeded in concealing this fact at the time. Sidorov, ed., "Denezhnoe obrashchenie," 123.

40. Long, 151.

41. G. P. Gooch and Harold Temperley, eds., *British Documents on the Origins of the War, 1898–1914*, III (London: 1928), 178. Hereafter cited as *British Documents*.

42. An examination of the correspondence of the Russian ambassador in Paris, A. N. Nelidov makes this dependence on French whim very evident. See "Novye dokumenty ob Alzhezirasskoi konferentsii i zaime 1906 g." [New documents concerning the Algeciras Conference and the loan of 1906], *Krasnyi arkhiv*, XLIV (1931), 161–65. Hereafter cited as "Novye dokumenty."

43. For example, telegrams from Witte to Rafalovich on January 29, February 24, and March 4. Preobrazhenskii, 271, 276, 282.

44. "Novye dokumenty," 163.

45. Witte, *Vospominaniia*, III, 230–31.

46. Witte, *Memoirs*, 298–300.

47. Bompard, 192.

48. Letters and telegrams in Preobrazhenskii, 272–74, 281.

49. Witte, *Vospominaniia*, III, 235, and Witte Collection, Columbia University, Box 7, Folder 17. The full text of Witte's letter in the archive contains a diatribe against Jewish bankers, who, he alleged, opposed the loan.

50. In a letter to Bülow of November 12, 1905. *Correspondance de Bülow*, 169.

51. Witte, *Memoirs*, 296.

52. Ibid., 292.

53. Preobrazhenskii, 272–74.

54. Ibid., 290.

55. Ibid., 293.

56. Long, 173.

57. These two telegrams in Preobrazhenskii, 293 and 295.

58. Ibid., 315–16; Witte, *Vospominaniia*, III, 247.

59. G. P. Gooch, *Before the War: Studies in Diplomacy*, II (London: 1938), 4.

60. Ibid., 20.

61. *British Documents*, IV, 219.

62. See a dispatch from Spring-Rice, to whom Dillon reported Witte's proposal. Ibid., IV, 219–20.

63. Reported in a telegram from Ambassador Bompard to Paris, which is cited from the archives of the French Foreign Ministry in Girault, "Sur quelques aspects financiers de l'alliance franco-russe," 73.

64. Ibid., 75; Jacob Viner, "International Finance and Balance of Power Diplomacy, 1880–1914," *Southwestern Political and Social Science Quarterly*, vol. IX (March 1929), 417.

65. Witte, *Memoirs*, 170, 304, 431.

66. In a letter from Noetzlin to Witte on April 17 summarizing the whole affair. Preobrazhenskii, 320.

67. Ibid., 278–79.

68. In an article by Un Ami de l'Alliance (probably Lysis, a

pseudonymic writer who was the chief French propagandist against loans to Russia) entitled "Le gouvernement français et les finances russes," *La Revue*, vol. 67 (April 1, 1907), 291.

69. Witte, *Memoirs*, 293–94.

70. These talks are reported in Witte, *Vospominaniia*, III, 229–30; *The Memoirs of Count Kokovtsov*, 107–12.

71. Witte, *Vospominaniia*, III, 241.

72. For Poincaré's doubts, see correspondence of Russian representatives in Paris printed in *Krasnyi arkhiv*, XLI–XLII (1930), 54–55, and XLIV (1931), 163–65.

73. Long, 176–80.

74. *The Memoirs of Count Kokovtsov*, 115.

75. Long, 71–76.

76. Ibid., 200–06.

77. Maklakov's memorandum is reprinted in Crisp, 508–11.

78. Long, 206–14.

79. Preobrazhenskii, 317.

80. Long, 218–22.

81. P. Miliukov, *God bor'by* [Year of struggle] (St. Petersburg: 1907). In this collection of his writings from 1905 and 1906 the articles on the loan span pp. 292–303 and are from *Rech'* on March 30, 31, April 3, 5, and 11, 1906.

82. There was some truth in this contention. The repayment of the French and German short-term securities would take 190 million rubles, and the deficit for 1905 and 1906 totaled 660 million rubles while the sum realizable on the loan in 1906 would be only about 565 million rubles. However, in practice the whole sum of the loan would be credited to the State Treasury; this credit could be transferred to the State Bank, thereby permitting the emission of more currency. This whole situation is outlined in a telegram of Witte to Kokovtsov on April 3 and in Kokovtsov's reply. Preobrazhenskii, 309.

83. Miliukov, *God bor'by*, 302. From *Rech'* of April 11. Briefly, in the Vyborg Manifesto after the dissolution of the First Duma, the Kadets endorsed repudiation of tsarist loans, but they soon retreated from that position.

84. Chermenskii, *Burzhuaziia i tsarizm*, 258; B. V. Anan'ich, "Vneshnie zaimy tsarizma i dumskii vopros v 1906–07 gg." [The foreign loans of tsarism and the Duma question in 1906–07], *Istoricheskie zapiski*, no. 81 (1968), 173.

85. Preobrazhenskii, 13; Girault, "Sur quelques aspects financiers de l'alliance franco-russe," 71.

86. Long, 131.

87. Cited in Girault, "Sur quelques aspects financiers de l'alliance franco-russe," 76.

88. *The Memoirs of Count Kokovtsov*, 121–22; also a letter from Kokovtsov to Verneuil on September 29, Preobrazhenskii, 341.

89. Quoted in Preobrazhenskii, 17. An exception was the socialist

newspaper, *L'Humanité,* which consistently attacked the loan as financially risky and as an instrument for suppressing the freedom of the Russian people.

90. Preobrazhenskii, 279.

91. Ibid., 279.

92. Ibid., 286.

93. "Ponedel'nik 16 marta 1906 g." [Note of March 16, 1906], *Krasnyi arkhiv,* XLIV (1931), 163.

94. "Telegramma Kassini Lamsdorfu 18 marta 1906 g." [Telegram from Cassini to Lamsdorff, March 18, 1906], *Krasnyi arkhiv,* XLI–XLII, (1930), 54.

95. See Noetzlin's letter to Witte of February 27 for the clearest exposition of his argument, which he had first set forth in Russia earlier in February and which he iterated in Paris at the end of March. Preobrazhenskii, 277–79.

96. *The Memoirs of Count Kokovtsov,* 120.

97. Witte, *Vospominaniia,* III, 241–42, 246.

98. *The Memoirs of Count Kokovtsov,* 128.

99. Crisp, 497.

100. Preobrazhenskii, 378–80, 320; Long, 231–36. Other provisions of the 1906 loan were the right of conversion after ten years, the loan to run for fifty years, and the payments on it to start in 1917 [the poor French!]; the taking price was 83.5, and the offering price was 88.5; the expense of the stamp-duty was assumed by the Russian government while payments to the press were borne by the syndicate; by January 12, 1907, payments to the Russian government were to total 66 percent of the sum (about 565 million rubles), and the remainder was to be paid by June 6, 1907.

Although there were so many points of disagreement between the government and the leaders of the First Duma that the loan was never debated in that body, news of the political conflicts associated with the First and Second Dumas alarmed foreign financial circles and the price of the loan securities fell from their offering at 88 to a low of 68 by midsummer 1906. After some selective bolstering by the Russian government the slump was checked, and by 1908 the 1906 bonds had returned to 88. *The Memoirs of Count Kokovtsov,* 157.

101. Witte, *Vospominaniia,* III, 250.

102. Witte, *Memoirs,* 308, and see chapter five, 168–69.

103. Witte, *Vospominaniia,* III, 250, 335; Encarnacion Alzona, *Some French Contemporary Opinions of the Russian Revolution of 1905* (New York: 1921), 95.

104. Baring, 184–85.

105. Witte, *Memoirs,* 360.

106. Witte, *Vospominaniia,* III, 219.

107. It is significant that during a review of the military terms of the Franco-Russian alliance, held concurrently with the loan negotiations but apparently not directly related to them, the French succeeded

in eliminating a convention for joint action against England which had been adopted in 1901. Long, 192–97.

108. Sontag argues that both Western and Soviet historians have erred by emphasizing the influence that Russian debts to France and Great Britain played in Russian foreign policy to 1917. His reading of the pertinent diplomatic documents of Russia, France, Great Britain, and Germany has lead him to conclude that Russian diplomacy was relatively little influenced by the fact that Russia was dependent upon France and Britain for finance capital after 1906. Moreover, he concluded from an examination of Russian financial and commercial relations with Europe during this period that the Russian economy was quite healthy and "that foreign borrowing resulted from a growing capacity of the Russian economy to absorb outside investment, and not from a shortage of foreign exchange needed to repay foreign creditors." John P. Sontag, "Tsarist Debts and Foreign Policy," *Slavic Review*, vol. XXVII, no. 4 (December 1968), 529–41.

While we are not prepared to challenge Sontag's conclusions regarding the capacity of the Russian economy to sustain itself during the period between 1906–14, our reading of the documents for the period 1905–06 leads us to believe that Russian diplomacy and the question of a foreign loan were inextricably tied together and that the Russian government was willing to pay, and did pay, a high diplomatic price to gain the funds it needed to save its tottering economy.

Chapter VIII

1. The eligibility of voters in each curia is described in chapter four, 113–15.

2. *Polnoe sobranie zakonov*, vol. XXV, Part II, no. 26, 662, Arts. 24–29.

3. Ibid., Arts. 3, 14, 30–39.

4. Tagantsev, 49.

5. On these regulations, which were largely reaffirmed in the electoral law of December 11 and in an ukase of March 4, see chapter five, 173–74.

6. TsGIAL, fund 1327, op. 2, d. 8.

7. Ibid.; Memorandum of Vuich, Witte Collection, Columbia University.

8. TsGAOR, fund 102, op. 236 (II), d. 133.

9. TsGIAL, fund 1327, op. 2, d. 8. At all stages of the electoral process only representatives, delegates, and electors for that particular district and level were permitted to attend electoral assemblies and to be elected by the given assembly; there were no candidates from distant constituencies. Originally, moreover, only voters of a given district or unit could even attend campaign rallies, but this restriction was eliminated in the December 11 law.

10. Chermenskii, *Burzhuaziia i tsarizm*, 176; F. I. Kalinychev, *Gosudarstvennaia duma v Rossii: sbornik dokumentov i materialov* [The State Duma in Russia: a collection of documents and materials] (Moscow: 1957), 74–75, 136.

11. The only reference we found to officially sponsored interference by the central government in the freedom of the elections is a claim (without citation or source) in a Soviet text that in early January secret instructions were sent to all *zemskie nachal'niki* (land captains) to watch orators who promised free distribution of private lands and to prevent "unreliable" persons from voting in the villages. A. M. Pankratova and G. D. Kostomarov, eds., *Ocherki po istorii SSSR: Pervaia russkaia burzhazno-demokraticheskaia revoliutsiia 1905–1907 gg.* [An outline of the history of the U.S.S.R.: the first Russian bourgeois-democratic revolution, 1905–1907] (Moscow: 1955), 235. This alleged document was not discovered in the archives, nor has it been printed in the various documentary collections on 1905.

12. Kryzhanovskii, 52–53.

13. Hans Rogger, "Was There a Russian Fascism?" *Journal of Modern History* (December 1964), 401.

14. Reported in Kryzhanovskii, 76.

15. Bompard, 195–96. It is significant that Witte does not treat the elections at all in his memoirs.

16. Ambler, 3–9; A. Tyrkova-Vil'iams, *Na putiakh k svobode* [On the paths to freedom] (New York: 1952), 248–49; Rogger, "Was There a Russian Fascism?" 401.

17. Hans Rogger, "The Formation of the Russian Right, 1900–1906," 72.

18. Sidney Harcave, "The Jews and the First Russian National Election," *American Slavic and East European Review*, vol. IX, no. 1 (February 1950), 33–38. Twelve Jewish deputies were elected to the Duma, of whom nine were Kadets.

19. The discussion of these parties is based primarily on Chermenskii, *Burzhuaziia i tsarizm*, 178–90, and Piaskovskii, 168–69.

20. This discussion of the Octobrists is based primarily on Chermenskii, *Burzhuaziia i tsarizm*, 190–200, 239–43, and on Menashe, 136–84.

21. Chermenskii's analysis of seven Octobrist provincial committees showed the following composition: industrialists and merchants—forty percent; gentry—ten percent; government officials—twenty percent; professional classes—nineteen percent; traders and peasants—seven percent; and priests—three percent.

22. The following treatment of the Kadets is based on Sef, 111–14; Tyrkova-Vil'iams, 250–58; Chermenskii, *Burzhuaziia i tsarizm*, 201–28, 245–57; and Sidel'nikov, 115–24.

23. Quoted in Chermenskii, *Burzhuaziia i tsarizm*, 215.

24. Piaskovskii, 169.

25. See especially Keep, *The Rise of Russian Social Democracy*,

214–28 and Oliver Radkey, *The Agrarian Foes of Bolshevism* (New York: 1958), 24–46, 75–78.

26. Quoted in Piaskovskii, 169.

27. The description of the electoral campaign that follows is based primarily on a sampling of the over five hundred pages of reports on the elections in each gubernia submitted to or compiled by the secretariat of the Council of Ministers and preserved in TsGIAL, fund 1276, op. 2, d. 8, and on Sidel'nikov, who also used party records in Soviet archives.

28. Quoted in Chermenskii, *Burzhuaziia i tsarizm*, 243.

29. Tyrkova-Vil'iams, 248–49. The glaring political weakness of the Russian right from 1905–21 urgently needs study and explication, in the opinion of the authors of this work.

30. In this period Miliukov was followed from meeting to meeting by one persistent, very young socialist heckler, who turned out to be Krylenko, one of the leaders of the Bolshevik seizure of power in October 1917.

31. Both quotations from a report of the St. Petersburg mayor, March 2, 1906, in TsGIAL, fund 1276, op. 2, d. 138.

32. Letters and reports in ibid. See also police reports on meetings in TsGAOR, fund 102, Op. 00/1905, d. 2246. Durnovo, however, exacted revenge for this indirect rebuke to his position, when only a few days later Witte complained officially to the minister of Interior concerning allegedly defamatory remarks against Witte made at a public meeting of the Union of Russian People by its leader, Dr. Dubrovin. Durnovo replied that there was not enough evidence to take action against Dubrovin other than to warn him, which had already been done. He then added with what must have been ironic relish: "The authorities must be very careful not to violate the right of free speech, which is also permitted to those at the other extreme from Dubrovin."

33. Overall, instances of village elders or local officials directing the vote were remarkably few when compared with the first national elections in Indonesia in 1956, which one of the authors observed and in which cases of the village headman casting the vote for an entire village were frequent.

34. TsGIAL, fund 1276, op. 2, d. 8. This was balanced by an electoral assembly in Tauride which ran out of ballot balls, sent someone to buy several pounds of nuts, and finished the balloting with those.

35. Kryzhanovskii, 78–79.

36. Unfortunately, no figures exist on the total registered and the total voting. The impressions that follow are based upon partial and random figures given in gubernia reports on the elections in TsGIAL, fund 1276, op. 2, d. 8 and fund 1327, op. 2, d. 40.

37. Sidel'nikov, 151–54, for example.

38. Ibid., 134–36.

39. Because of loose and shifting party alignments and contradictory data, exact figures cannot be compiled. Those given, based on the sources indicated, have been adjusted slightly in accord with informa-

tion in Warren B. Walsh, "The Composition of the Dumas," *Russian Review*, vol. 8, no. 2 (1949), 111–12, and "Political Parties in the Russian Dumas," *Journal of Modern History*, vol. 22 (1950), 145–46.

40. Data on this subject are even more imprecise and conflicting than that on party affiliations and should be regarded with caution.

41. Age, education, and religion estimates are based on the analysis in the archives cited for the table on 280 and on Levin, *The Second Duma*, 67.

42. A. D. Stepanskii, "Politicheskie gruppirovki v Gosudarstvennom sovete v 1906–07 gg." [Political groupings in the State Council in 1906–07], *Istoriia SSSR*, 1965, no. 4, 49–50.

43. TsGIAL, fund 1327, op. 2, d. 40, plus a few replies in fund 1276, op. 2, d. 9a. The categories given by Durnovo in his query helped shape the replies, but most governors ranged widely in their discussion, and some of the analysis was quite incisive and thoughtful.

44. From a *nakaz* of the peasants of a village in Nizhnii Novgorod gubernia, Kalinychev, 163, and quoted in Chermenskii, *Burzhuaziia i tsarizm*, 253.

45. Baring, 197.

46. Miliukov, *God bor'by*, 109.

47. Chermenskii, *Burzhuaziia i tsarizm*, 244–45; see also Sidel'-nikov, 197–98.

48. Rogger, "Formation of the Russian Right," 91.

49. Witte, *Vospominaniia*, 342.

50. Quotations from a letter of a noble, K. F. Golovin, to the tsar, April 15, cited in Sidel'-nikov, 183–84.

51. Tyrkova-Vil'iams, 258.

52. Ibid., 247.

Chapter IX

1. *Polnoe sobranie zakonov*, vol. XXVI, Part II, no. 27,805.

2. In his memoirs Witte wrote that in a sense "they [the Fundamental Laws] established a constitution but a conservative constitution and one without parliamentarianism—this was the hope of the regime of October 17, and it assured finally that there would be no return to the old order." Witte, *Vospominaniia*, III, 306.

3. "Tsarskosel'skie soveshchaniia: Protokoly sekretnavo soveshchaniia v fevrale 1906 goda pod predsedatel'stvom byvshavo imperatora po vyrabotke Uchrezhdenii Gosudarstvennoi Dumy i Gosudarstvennavo Soveta." [Tsarskoe Selo conferences: protocol of a secret conference in February 1906, under the chairmanship of the former emperor for the working out of the institutions of the State Duma and the State Council], *Byloe*, No. 5–6 (November–December 1917), 292. [Hereafter cited as "February Crown Council."]

4. Tagantsev, 113–16.

5. Technically, of course, Ignatiev was correct; but as was indicated earlier, Witte's report published simultaneously with the Manifesto had expressed a desire to revise the State Council. This incident demonstrates, to a degree at least, the confusion which resulted when the Manifesto and Witte's report, which were not in perfect agreement, were both approved by the tsar and published simultaneously.

6. "February Crown Council," 293.

7. Ibid., 294.

8. Witte, *Vospominaniia*, III, 295. For a discussion of the confusing and complex terminology and legal definitions involved, see Marc Szeftel, "The Form of Government of the Russian Empire Prior to the Constitutional Reforms of 1905–06" in J. S. Curtiss, ed., *Essays in Russian and Soviet History*, (New York: 1963), 107–09.

9. See 306–07 below.

10. "February Crown Council," 301–02.

11. Ibid., 303–04.

12. Kokovtsov described this incident in his memoirs but not with perfect accuracy. He reported that Witte had introduced the idea of circumventing the State Council on February 14, when, according to the Crown Council minutes, the idea was proposed by Obolensky, supported by Kutler, and rejected by Witte. Kokovtsov wrote that when Witte returned to this idea on February 16, he "annoyed" everyone present. *The Memoirs of Count Kokovtsov*, 105–06.

13. "February Crown Council," 305–06.

14. Ibid., 306–07.

15. Ibid., 309.

16. Witte's argument is also beside the point. Constitutions are not necessarily the result of mass action or constitutional conventions. They can be, and often have been, the result of monarchical initiative.

17. "February Crown Council," 307–09.

18. Ibid., 311.

19. Ibid., 315.

20. Ibid., 318.

21. This manifesto has been published in B. Glinskii, "K voprosu o titule 'samoderzhets.'" [Toward the question about the title 'autocrat.'] *Istoricheskii vestnik*, 131 (February 1913), 574–76.

22. This provision was later expanded into Article 45 (87) in the Fundamental Laws published on April 23, 1906, and is discussed below.

23. In his memoirs Witte accused the tsar, instigated by Trepov, of deliberately trying to exclude him from any say in the drafting of the Fundamental Laws, but Witte claimed that he was successful in his insistence the Council of Ministers review the draft Laws. Witte, *Vospominaniia*, III, 294–96.

24. Mironenko, "Sovet ministrov po ukazu 19 oktiabria 1905 g.," 366 n. 2.

25. Witte Collection, Archive of Russian and East European History, Columbia University, Box 7, Folder 28. See also "Doklad S. Iu.

Vitte ob osnovnykh zakonakh" [Report of S. Iu. Witte about the Fundamental Laws], *Krasnyi arkhiv*, XI–XII (1925), 115–16, and Witte, *Vospominaniia*, III, 295–96, where the last two paragraphs of his letter are, however, omitted.

26. Quoted in Tagantsev, 157.

27. Cited from the archives in Sidel'nikov, 97. See also Tagantsev, 168.

28. Tagantsev, 157–58. Witte also submitted the draft to Tagantsev for special advice on the question of Finland.

29. Sidel'nikov, 98, and Witte, *Vospominaniia*, III, 296.

30. Tagantsev, 168. See Appendix C for an outline of major changes in the draft Fundamental Laws proposed by Witte and by the Council of Ministers. This shows also whether these changes were incorporated in the final version of the Fundamental Laws.

31. Tagantsev, 162–67.

32. This summary of the consideration of the Fundamental Laws by the Council of Ministers is based on drafts, notes, and comparisons in TsGIAL, fund 1276, op. 2, d. 7, and on Tagantsev, 171–82. See also Sidel'nikov, 98; Witte, *Vospominaniia*, III, 296–301.

33. TsGIAL, fund 1276, op. 2, d. 7. See also Witte Collection, Columbia University, Box 7, Folder 38, for a copy of the memoir alone and Tagantsev, 182–84, for extracts from it.

34. In his memoirs Witte argued that he feared such an outcome would lead to dissolution of the Duma, violence, and the resulting destruction of all the gains of the new October 17 order. Witte, *Vospominaniia*, III, 196–97.

35. Gurko, 454–55.

36. "Tsarskosel'skie soveshchaniia: Protokoly sekretnavo soveshchaniia v aprele 1906 goda pod predsedatel'stvom byvshavo imperatora po peresmotru osnovykh zakonov." [Tsarskoe Selo conferences: protocol of a secret conference in April 1906, under the chairmanship of the former emperor to review the Fundamental Laws] ed. by V. Vodovozov, *Byloe*, No. 4 (October 1917), 192–93. [Hereafter cited as "April Crown Council."]

37. Ibid., 193–95.

38. Ibid., 199. The Crown Council finally adopted quite ambiguous and innocuous wording concerning Finland's status, as recommended by the Council of Ministers.

39. Ibid., 202.

40. Ibid., 204–05. Durnovo, indignant at what he considered the ease with which Nicholas surrendered his basic rights in the Fundamental Laws, remarked privately: "This is the kind of man who when asked for his last shirt takes it off and gives it to you." Kryzhanovskii, 75.

41. "April Crown Council," 205–06. Witte's views on absolutism were not the result of momentary inspiration. Before these sessions of the Crown Council Witte delegated an unidentified St. Petersburg professor to prepare a memo for him on the historical bases of autocracy

and absolutism in Russia. Witte's arguments were influenced by this rather long memo, which can be found in B. Glinskii, "K voprosu o titule 'samoderzhets'," *Istoricheskii vestnik*, 131 (February 1913), 577–601.

42. "April Crown Council," 206–08.

43. Ibid., 245; *Polnoe sobranie zakonov*, vol. XXVI, Part II, no. 27,805.

44. "April Crown Council," 211.

45. Ibid., 216–17. In his memoirs Witte wrote that he believed that permitting the Duma to meddle in foreign affairs would have undermined Russia's position among the great powers. Witte, *Vospominaniia*, III, 298.

46. "April Crown Council," 218.

47. Ibid., 219–23.

48. Ibid., 227.

49. See 310 below.

50. "April Crown Council," 228.

51. Ibid., 231.

52. Ibid., 234–35.

53. Witte, *Vospominaniia*, III, 303.

54. Ibid., III, 304–05.

55. Quoted in Sidel'nikov, 198. See also Vodovozov, 15.

56. See a draft ukase of April 23, with a note at the top, "Compiled and presented to the tsar by General Trepov on April 22, when His Majesty did not accept the Fundamental Laws on preliminary consideration." The changes proposed in the ukase were insignificant. Witte Collection, Columbia University, Box 7, Folder 38.

57. Shipov, 430; Bompard, 197.

58. The following description of the Fundamental Laws is based on *Polnoe sobranie zakonov*, vol. XXVI, Part II, no. 27,805.

59. Some confusion has arisen over the numbering of this article because it bore different numbers in different publications of the Fundamental Laws. Levin in *The Second Duma*, 17 n. 22, cites *Polnoe sobranie zakonov*, vol. XXVI, Part II no. 27,805, but inaccurately refers to the article in question as Article 87. The last article of the Fundamental State Laws in this citation is Article 82. The article to which Levin refers should be cited as Article 45. Other authors relying on secondary accounts rather than referring back to the original source have repeated this error. A possible explanation of the error is contained in Pierre Chasles, *Le Parlement russe—son organisation—ses rapports avec l'empereur* (Paris: 1910), p. 211, in which in a footnote he indicated that when a new series of laws was issued in Russia they were eventually incorporated into the Code of Laws. According to Chasles, Article 87 refers to its number in the Code rather than in the original Fundamental Laws of April 23, 1906. The scholar who wishes to check Article 45 of the Fundamental Laws against Article 87 will find the latter reprinted in D. K. Lavrent'ev, *Khrestomatiia po zakonovedeniiu* [an anthology on legislation] (St. Petersburg: 1912), 299.

60. Gurko, 451.
61. Witte, *Vospominaniia*, III, 323.

CHAPTER X

1. Quoted from the memoir of the Council of Ministers, March 5, 1906, in Soviet archives, by Dubrovskii, *Stolypinskaia zemel'naia reforma*, 100.
2. The draft programs of the Ministries of Finance, Justice, and Trade and Industry are in TsGIAL, fund 1276, op. 2, d. 4, as is the final summary program Witte submitted to Nicholas. The final program is also given as an appendix in the Memorandum of Vuich, Witte Collection, Columbia University, and it is summarized in Sidel'nikov, 235–36.
3. Sidel'nikov, 235–36.
4. See n. 2 for places the program may be found.
5. As is evident, this program was largely a combination, with some refinements, of the measures enunciated in the ukase of the Council of Ministers of March 4 and of the proposals of the Gurko Commission for abolition of the commune, which Witte supported but which the State Council rejected by a narrow vote at the end of March. See chapter six, 205–07.
6. The proposals of the Ministry of Trade and Industry were not included in the government program presented by Goremykin on May 13. He added, however, recommendations in education—to establish general elementary education, to reform the middle schools, and to re-establish self-government for higher schools—that were not part of the Witte program.
7. Tagantsev, 35–36.
8. Bompard, 206.
9. Witte, *Vospominaniia*, III, 337–41.
10. Nicholas II, *Tagebuch*, 287; Witte, *Vospominaniia*, III, 341–42.
11. *Journal intime de Nicolas II*, trans. by A. Pierre (Paris: 1925), 253.
12. From *Rech'* of March 17 and quoted in Miliukov, *God bor'by*, 194. Shipov expressed the same thought in Shipov, 432.
13. See chapter five, 168–69.
14. Witte, *Memoirs*, 308 and 315.
15. Gurko, *Features and Figures of the Past*, 452, 457. Gurko's only really telling support for this contention is his report that only three days before his dismissal Witte told the Council of Ministers of the tactics he planned to use to reach an understanding with the Duma.
16. See, for example, the testimony of Dillon, a friend and confidant of Witte. E. J. Dillon, *The Eclipse of Russia*, 7.
17. *The Memoirs of Count Kokovtsov*, 124.
18. Ibid., 127.
19. Letters exchanged between Witte and Baron Fredericks, July–

September 1906, in the Witte Collection, Columbia University, Box 8, Folder 50. See also Witte, *Vospominaniia*, III, 377–78.

20. *The Secret Letters of the Last Tsar*, 220.

21. Quoted in Anan'ich and Ganelin, "Opyt kritiki memuarov Vitte," 299.

22. Baron P. P. Rosen, *Forty Years of Diplomacy*, 2 vols., (New York: 1922), I, 290; E. J. Dillon, "Two Russian Statesmen," *The Quarterly Review*, vol. CCXXXVI (October 1921), 413; Dillon, *The Eclipse of Russia*, 112–13, 379.

23. V. A. Maklakov, "Iz proshlavo" [Out of the past], *Sovremennye zapiski*, vol. 47 (1931), 325 and 327.

24. E. V. Tarle, *Graf S. Iu. Vitte; Opyt kharakteristiki vneshnei politiki* [Count S. Iu. Witte: An attempt to characterize his foreign policy], 3, 91; *Memoirs of Alexander Iswolsky*, 110–11, 127; Gurko, 451.

25. Vodovozov, 103–20; Petrunkevich, 417; R. Charques, *The Twilight of Imperial Russia*, (London: 1958), 59–60, 127; Pankratova, *Pervaia russkaia revoliutsiia, 1905–07 gg.*, 150.

26. *Memoirs of Alexander Iswolsky*, 133–34; obituaries by Gessen and the liberal historian A. A. Kornilov in *Rech'*, nos. 58 and 97, 1915, and by Struve in *Russkaia mysl'*, no. 3, 1915, all cited in Vodovozov, 5 n. 1.

27. Bompard, 203–04. Bompard was, of course, using Western standards of political behavior and conduct to judge Witte, but such standards hardly applied in Russia of that time.

28. Dillon, "Two Russian Statesmen," 413. In the same vein see Korostowetz, 251–52.

29. Herman Bernstein, *With Master Minds* (New York: 1913), 29–30.

30. Bernard Pares, *My Russian Memoirs* (London: 1931), 184.

31. Theodore H. von Laue, "Count Witte and the Russian Revolution of 1905," *American Slavic and East European Review* (February 1958), 24–46.

32. To an Associated Press correspondent, quoted in Rosen, 240.

33. Z. Brzezinski, "The Patterns of Autocracy," in *The Transformation of Russian Society*, 96.

Bibliography

Full references not found in the Notes as well as an expanded number of references will be found in the Bibliography.

Bibliography and Historiography

Borodin, N. A. "Literatura o pervoi Gos. dume (knigi i broshiury)." [Literature about the first State Duma (Books and Brochures)]. *K 10-letiiu 1-oi gosudarstvennoi dumy: Sbornik* [On the tenth anniversary of the First State Duma: A Collection]. (Petrograd, 1916).

Cherniak, E. B. "Angliiskaia i amerikanskaia istoriografiia revoliutsii 1905–07 godov." [English and American historiography of the revolution of 1905–07]. *Voprosy istorii* [Questions of history], 12 (1955): 126–38.

Chernysheva, N. F. "Politicheskaia literatura perioda revoliutsii 1905–07 gg." [Political literature of the period of the revolution of 1905–07]. *Zapiski Gosudarstvennoi Publichnoi Istoricheskoi Biblioteki* [Notes of the State Public Historical Library], II (1955): 38–57 (Rotaprint).

Derenkovskii, G. M., ed. *Pervaia russkaia revoliutsiia, 1905–1907 gg.: Annotirovannyi ukazatel' literatury* [The first Russian revolution of 1905–07: an annotated guide to the literature]. M.: 1965.

———. and Vartan'ian, A. D. "Dokumental'nye izdaniia po istorii pervoi russkoi revoliutsii" [Documentary publications on the history of the first Russian revolution]. *Istoricheskii arkhiv* [Historical Archive], 6, (1956): 185–97.

Derman, G. K., ed. *Pervaia russkaia revoliutsiia: Ukazatel' literatury* [The first Russian revolution: a guide to the literature]. M.: 1930.

Golikov, K. I., comp. *Pervaia russkaia revoliutsiia 1905–07 gg.: Ukazatel' literatuary vyshedshei v 1954–57 gg. v sviazi s 50–letiem revoliutsii* [The first Russian revolution of 1905–07: a guide to the literature issued in 1954–57 in connection with the fiftieth anniversary of the revolution]. (M.: 1957).

Golikov, K. I., and others, comps. *Pervaia russkaia revoliutsiia 1905–07* gg.: *Kratkii ukazatel' literatury* [The first Russian revolution of 1905–07: a short guide to the literature]. M.: 1955.

Grigor'ev, A. L. *Pervaia russkai revoliutsiia 1905–07 gg. i zarubezhnaia literatura* [The first Russian revolution of 1905–07 and foreign literature]. L.: 1956.

Istoriia SSSR: Ukazatel' sovetskoi literatury za 1917–52 gg. [The history of the U.S.S.R.: a guide to Soviet literature for 1917–52]. vol. II, *Istoriia SSSR v period kapitalizma, 1861–1917* [The history of the U.S.S.R. in the period of capitalism, 1861–1917]. M.: 1958.

"Materialy rasshirennovo zasedaniia uchenovo soveta Instituta Istorii AN SSSR, posviashchennovo 50-letiiu pervoi russkoi revoliutsii (Oct. 26–27, 1955)" [Materials of an enlarged meeting of the Scientific Council of the Institute of History of the U.S.S.R. Academy of Sciences dedicated to the fiftieth anniversary of the first Russian revolution]. *Doklady i soobshcheniia Instituta Istorii* [Reports and communications of the Institute of History], 9 (1956): 3–144.

Melamedova, V. I., and Pliukhina, M. A. "Obzor dokumental'nykh materialov TsGIAL SSSR o rabochem dvizhenie v revoliutsii 1905–07 gg." [A review of documentary materials in the Central State Historical Archive, Leningrad, on the workers' movement in the revolution of 1905–07]. *Istoricheskii arkhiv*, 3 (1956): 194–210.

Ocherki istorii istoricheskoi nauki v SSSR. vol. IV (M.: 1956): 411–27. (By I. F. Ugarov and N. N. Iakovlev, on Soviet historiography concerning the Revolution of 1905 from 1917 to mid-1930's.)

Primak, N. I. "Sovetskaia istoriografiia pervoi russkoi revoliutsii 1905–07 gg. (seredina 30-kh—60-e gody)" [Soviet historiography of the first Russian revolution of 1905–07 (from the mid-'30's to the '60's)]. *Sovetskaia istoriografiia klassovoi bor'by i revoliutsionnovo dvizheniia v Rossii* [Soviet historiography of the class struggle and the revolutionary movement in Russia], ed. by V. A. Ovsiankin. Part II (L.: 1967), 31–52.

"Spisok zashchishchennykh v 1948–54 gg. dissertatsii o pervoi russkoi revoliutsii 1905–07 gg." [List of dissertations on the first Russian revolution of 1905–07 defended in 1948–54]. *Istoricheskie zapiski*, 49 (1954): 427–31.

Tysiacha deviat'sot piatyi god: Katalog knig [1905: A catalogue of books]. M.-L.: 1927.

"Ukazatel' literatury po 1905 gody" [A guide to the literature on 1905], *Proletarskaia revoliutsiia* [Proletarian revolution], 10 (45) (1925), 258–76 and 22 (46) (1925): 312–32.

Vol'tsenburg, O. E. *Bibliograficheskii putevoditel' po revoliutsii 1905 g.: Sistematicheskii obzor knig i zhurnal'nykh statei* [A bibliographic guide to the revolution of 1905: a systematic review of books and journal articles]. L.: 1925.

Zverev, comp. *Krasnyi arkhiv, istoricheskii zhurnal, 1922–41: Annotirovannyi ukazatel' soderzhaniia* [The red archive, an historical journal, 1922–41: an annotated guide to its contents]. M.: 1960.

Collected Works

Lenin, V. I. *Sochineniia* (4th ed., M.: 1946–58; 5th ed., M.: 1961–).
Pokrovskii, M. N. *Izbrannye proizvedeniia* [Selected works]. vols. III and IV. M.: 1967.
Trotsky, Leon. *Our Revolution: Essays on Working-Class and International Revolution, 1904–1917,* trans. by Moissaye J. Olgin. New York: 1918.

Documentary Sources

Articles

Several short articles from Byloe *and from* Krasnyi arkhiv *are not listed below but are fully cited in the footnotes.*

"Agrarnoe dvizhenie v Chernigovskoi gub. v 1905–1906 gg." [The agrarian movement in Chernigov province in 1905–1906.], ed. by I. Kuznetsov. *Krasnyi arkhiv* [The Red Archive], LXXVIII (1936): 98–127.
"Agrarnoe dvizhenie v 1905 g. po otchetam Dubasova i Panteleeva." [The Agrarian Movement in 1905 according to the Reports of Dubasov and Panteleev.] *Krasnyi arkhiv,* XI–XII (1925): 182–92.
Bakst, E. and Leskova, L. "Khronika revoliutsionnoi bor'by. (O novykh dokumentakh, otrazhaiushchikh revoliutsionnye sobytiia v Moskve v sent. 1905– ianv. 1906 g.)" [A Chronicle of revolutionary struggle (concerning new documents reflecting revolutionary events in Moscow, Sept. 1905–Jan. 1906]. *Nauka i zhizn'* [Science and life], 12 (1965): 2–3.
"Bor'ba S. Iu. Vitte s agrarnoi revoliutsiei." [The struggle of S. Iu. Witte with the agrarian revolution.], ed. by I. Tamarova. *Krasnyi arkhiv,* XXXI (1928): 81–102.
"Baron B. Frederiks D. F. Trepovu (15 oktiabria 1905 goda)." [Baron B. Fredericks to D. F. Trepov (October 15, 1905).], *Byloe,* 14 (1919): 109.
Budberg, R. "S'ezd zemskikh deiatelei 6–9 noiabria 1904 goda v Peterburge" [The Zemstvo Congress of November 6–9, 1904, in St. Petersburg.]. *Byloe,* 15 (March 1907): 70–88.
"Dekabr'skie dni v Donbasse v 1905 g." [December days, 1905, in the Donets Basin.], ed. by A. Pankratova. *Krasnyi arkhiv,* LXXIII (1935): 91–125.
Demochkin, N. N., ed. "Partiia i Sovety v 1905 g." [The party and the Soviets in 1905.]. *Voprosy istorii KPSS,* [Questions of the history of the C.P.S.U.], 1 (1965): 70–85.
"Dnevnik A. A. Polovtseva" [The diary of A. A. Polovtsev]. *Krasnyi arkhiv,* IV (1923): 63–128.

Bibliography

"Dnevnik G. O. Raukha" [The diary of G. O. Raukh]. *Krasnyi arkhiv,* XIX (1926): 83–109.

"Doklad S. Iu. Vitte (20 dekabria 1905 g.)" [S. Iu. Witte's report (December 20, 1905.)]. *Krasnyi arkhiv,* XI–XII (1925): 146–147.

"Doklad S. Iu. Vitte" [S. Iu. Witte's report]. *Krasnyi arkhiv,* XI–XII (1925): 148.

"Doklad S. Iu. Vitte (8 ianvaria 1906 g.)" [S. Iu. Witte's report (January 8, 1906.)]. *Krasnyi arkhiv,* XI–XII (1925): 152.

"Dokladnaia zapiska departamenta politsii predsedateliu soveta ministrov S. Iu. Vitte." [Report of the police department to the chairman of the Council of Ministers S. Iu. Witte.]. *Krasnyi arkhiv,* IX (1925): 68–93.

"Dvizhenie v voiskakh na Dal'nem Vostoke." [Unrest in the armies in the Far East.]. *Krasnyi arkhiv,* XI–XII (1925): 289–386.

Girault, René, "La révolution russe de 1905 d'après quelques témoinages françaises." *Revue historique,* CCXXX (July–Sept. 1963): 97–120.

"Graf S. Iu. Vitte i Nikolai II v oktiabre 1905 g." [Count S. Iu. Witte and Nicholas II in October 1905.]. *Byloe,* 4 (32) (1925): 107.

"Graf Vitte v bor'be s revoliutsiei: Doklad gr. Vitte Nikolaiu II v dekabre 1905–ianvare 1906 g." [Count Witte in the struggle with the revolution: reports of Count Witte to Nicholas II, December, 1905–January, 1906.]. *Byloe,* 3 (31) (March 1918): 1–10.

"Iz arkhiva S. Iu. Vitte." [From the archive of S. Iu. Witte.]. *Krasnyi arkhiv,* XI–XII (1925): 107–43.

"Iz bumag D. F. Trepova." [From the papers of D. F. Trepov.]. *Krasnyi arkhiv,* XI–XII (1925): 448–66.

"Iz dnevnika A. N. Kuropatkina." [From the diary of A. N. Kuropatkin.]. *Krasnyi arkhiv,* VII (1924): 55–69.

"Iz dnevnika A. N. Kuropatkina (s 23 dekabria 1905 g. po 12 marta 1906 g.)." [From the diary of A. N. Kuropatkin (From December 23, 1905 to March 12, 1906.]. *Krasnyi arkhiv,* VIII (1925): 70–100.

"Iz dnevnika Konstantina Romanova" [From the diary of Konstantin Romanov.]. *Krasnyi arkhiv,* LXIV (1931): 126–51.

"Iz istorii bor'by s revoliutsiei v 1905 g." [From the history of the struggle with the revolution in 1905.], ed. by G. Vereshchagin. *Krasnyi arkhiv,* XXXII (1929): 216–32.

"Iz pisem gen. N. N. Levashova A. N. Kuropatkinu." [From the letters of Gen. N. N. Levashov to A. N. Kuropatkin.], ed. by M. Klevenskii. *Krasnyi arkhiv,* XV (1926): 216–22.

"K istorii bor'by samoderzhavia s agrarnym dvizheniem v 1905–1907 gg." [Toward a history of the autocracy's struggle with the agrarian movement in 1905–1907.], ed. by M. Lurie. *Krasnyi arkhiv,* LXXVIII (1936): 128–60.

"K istorii karatel'nikh ekspeditsii v Sibiri." [Toward a history of the punitive expeditions to Siberia.]. *Krasnyi arkhiv.* I (1922): 329–43.

"K istorii manfesta 17 oktiabria 1905 goda." [Toward the history of the Manifesto of October 17, 1905.]. *Byloe,* 14 (1919): 108–11.

"K istorii manifesta 17-vo oktiabria: Zapiski N. I. Vuicha i N. [A.] D. Obolenskovo." [Toward the history of the Manifesto of October 17: notes of N. I. Vuich and N. [A.] D. Obolensky.]. *Arkhiv russkoi revoliutsii.* [Archive of the Russian revolution], II (1921): 5–13.

"K peregovoram Kokovtsova o zaime v 1905–1906 gg." [Toward the negotiations of Kokovtsov on the loan in 1905–1906.]. *Krasnyi arkhiv,* X (1925): 3–37.

"Karatel'naia ekspeditsiia polk. Rimana." [The punitive expedition of Colonel Rieman.]. *Krasnyi arkhiv,* XI–XII (1925): 398–420.

"Khronika vooruzhennoi bor'by." [A chronicle of the armed struggle.]. *Krasnyi arkhiv,* XI–XII (1925): 159–81.

"Kniaz V. Orlov D. F. Trepovu." [Prince V. Orlov to D. F. Trepov.]. *Byloe,* 14 (1919): 110.

"Krest'ianskoe dvizhenie v tsentral'noi polose v 1905 g." [The peasant movement in the central part (of Russia) in 1905.]. *Krasnyi arkhiv,* LXXIII (1935): 126–69.

"Manifest 17 oktiabria." [The Manifesto of October 17.]. *Krasnyi arkhiv,* XI–XII (1925): 39–106.

"Novye dokumenty ob Alzhezirasskoi konferentsii i zaime 1906 g." [New documents concerning the Algeciras Conference and the loan of 1906.]. *Krasnyi arkhiv,* XLIV (1931): 161–65.

"O formirovanii druzhin i opolcheniia: Doklad S. Iu. Vitte." [About the formation of armed workers' and people's militia: a report of S. Iu. Witte.]. *Krasnyi arkhiv,* XI–XII (1925): 149–50.

"O karatel'noi ekspeditsii v Pribaltiiskom krae: Doklad S. Iu. Vitte (25 dekabria 1905 g.)." [About the punitive expedition to the Baltic: report of S. Iu. Witte (December 25, 1905).]. *Krasnyi arkhiv,* XI–XII (1925): 150.

"O leitenante Shmidte: Doklad S. Iu. Vitte (21 fevrale 1906 g.)." [About Lieutenant Schmidt: report of S. Iu. Witte (February 21, 1906.)]. *Krasnyi arkhiv,* XI–XII (1925): 158.

"Perepiska graf S. Iu. Vitte k P. A. Stolypinu." [Letter from Count S. Iu. Witte to P. A. Stolypin.], ed. by L. L'vov. *Russkaia mysl'* [Russian thought], 1 (March 1915): 134–52.

"Petitsiia zemlevladel'tsev (23 ianvare 1906 g.)." [Petition of Landowners (January 23, 1906).]. *Krasnyi arkhiv,* XI–XII (1925): 154–57.

Petrov, N. "Gapon i graf Vitte." [Gapon and Count Witte]. *Byloe,* 1 (29) (1925): 15–27.

"Pis'mo N. N. Gerard (20 dekabria 1905 g.)." [Letter from N. N. Gerard (December 20, 1905).]. *Krasnyi arkhiv,* XI–XII (1925): 148.

Popov, A. "Zaem 1906 g. v doneseniiakh russkovo posla v Parizhe." [The loan of 1906 in the reports of the Russian ambassador in Paris.]. *Krasnyi arkhiv,* XI–XII (1925): 421–32.

"Presnia v dekabre 1905 g." [Presnia in December 1905.], ed. by M. Syromiatnikova. *Krasnyi arkhiv,* LXXIII (1935): 204–09.

"Pribaltiiskii krai v 1905 godu." [The Baltic in 1905.]. *Krasnyi arkhiv,* XI–XII (1925): 263–88.

Bibliography

"Razlozhenie armii v 1905 g. na D. Vostoke." [The demoralization of the army in the Far East in 1905.], ed. by Vishniakov. *Byloe*, 4 (32) (1925): 108–16."

"Rossiia i Alzhezirasskaia konferentsiia." [Russia and the Algeciras Conference.], ed. by A. Erusalimskii. *Krasnyi arkhiv*. XLI–XLII (1930): 3–61.

"Russko-Germanskii dogovor 1905 goda." [Russian-German Treaty of 1905.], *Krasnyi arkhiv*. V (1924): 1–49.

"Sevastopol'skoe vosstanie (1905 g.)." [Sevastopol uprising (1905).], *Byloe*, 5–6 (27–28) (November–December, 1917): 25–31.

Sheinman, M. M. "Revoliutsiia 1905–07 gg. i pomoshch' Vatikana tsarismu." [The revolution of 1905–07 and the aid of the Vatican to tsarism.]. *Iz istorii rabochevo klassa i revoliutsionnovo dvizheniia. Sbornik statei.* Pamiat akad. A. M. Pankratovoi, [From the history of the working class and the revolutionary movement. A collection of articles in memory of academician A. M. Pankratova.]. (M.: 1958): 398–404.

Shtriker, V. "Sudebnye protsessy o dekabr'skom vooruzhennom vosstanii v Moskve." [Trials on the December armed uprising in Moscow.]. *Sovetskaia iustitsiia.* [Soviet justice], 23 (1961): 22–23.

"Shturm Presni." [The assault on Presnia.]. *Krasnyi arkhiv*, XI–XII (1925): 387–97.

"Sibirskaia ekspeditsiia barona Mellera-Zakomel'skovo." [The Siberian expedition of Baron Meller-Zakomel'sky.]. *Byloe*, 3 (25) (September 1917): 134–53.

Sidorov, A. L., ed. "Finansovoe polozhenie tsarskovo samoderzhaviia v period russko-iaponskoi voiny i pervoi russkoi revoliutsii." [The financial position of the tsarist autocracy in the period of the Russo-Japanese war and the first Russian revolution.]. *Istoricheskii arkhiv.* [Historical archive], II (1955): 121–49.

———, ed. "Denezhnoe obrashchenie i finansovoe polozhenie Rossii (1904–07 gg.)." [Monetary circulation and the financial position of Russia in 1904–07.]. *Istoricheskii arkhiv.* III (1956): 88–123.

Sviatopolk-Mirskaia, E. A. "Dnevnik kn. Ekateriny Alekseevny Sviatopolk-Mirskoi za 1904–1905 gg." [The diary of Princess Catherine Alekseevna Sviatopolk-Mirsky.]. *Istoricheskie zapiski* [Historical notes], 77 (1965): 236–93.

"Telegramma generala-leitenanta Sologuba." [Telegram from Lieutenant-General Sollogub.]. *Krasnyi arkhiv*, XI–XII (1925): 151.

"Tsarskosel'skie soveshchaniia: Protokoly sekretnavo soveshchaniia pod predsedatel'stvom byvshavo imperatora po voprosy o rasshirenii izbiratel'navo prava." [Tsarskoe Selo Conferences: protocol of a secret conference under the chairmanship of the former emperor on the question of broadening the election law.], ed. by V. V. Vodovozov. *Byloe*, 3 (25) (September 1917): 117–65.

"Tsarskosel'skie soveshchaniia: Protokoly sekretnavo soveshchaniia v fevrale 1906 goda pod predsedatel'stvom byvshavo imperatora po vyrabotke Uchrezhdenii Gosudarstvennoi Dumy i Gosudarstvennavo

Soveta." [Tsarskoe Selo Conferences; protocol of a secret conference in February 1906, under the chairmanship of the former emperor on the working out of the institutions of the State Duma and the State Council.]. *Byloe*, 5–6 (27–28) (November–December 1917): 289–318.

"Tsarskosel'skie soveshchaniia: Protokoly sekretnavo soveshchaniia v aprele 1906 goda pod predsedatel'stvom byvshavo imperatora po peresmotru osnovnykh zakonov." [Tsarskoe Selo Conferences; protocol of a secret conference in April 1906, under the chairmanship of the former emperor on the revision of the Fundamental Laws.], ed. by V. Vodovozov. *Byloe*, 4 (26) (October 1917): 183–245.

"25 let nazad: Iz dnevnika L. Tikhomirova." [Twenty-five years ago: from the diary of L. Tikhomirov.]. *Krasnyi arkhiv*, XL (1930): 59–96; XLI–XLII (1930): 103–47.

Ul'ianov, G. "Soiuznitsa samoderzhaviia: ob uchastii pravoslavnoi tserkvi v podavlenii pervoi russkoi revoliutsii." [Ally of the autocracy: concerning the participation of the Orthodox church in the suppression of the first Russian revolution.]. *Nauka i religiia*. [Science and religion],1 (1962): 39–41.

von Laue, Theodore H. "A Secret Memorandum of Sergei Witte on the Industrialization of Imperial Russia." *Journal of Modern History*. XXVI, 1 (March 1954): 60–74.

"Vsepoddanneishaia zapiska D. F. Trepova (16 oktiabria 1905)." [Official note of D. F. Trepov (October 16, 1905).]. *Byloe*, 14 (1919): 110–11.

"Zapiska Peterburgskovo okhrannavo otdeleniia na imia direktora departamenta politsii ot 8 oktiabria 1913 goda No. 20172." [Note from the St. Petersburg okhrana to the director of the department of police on the lessons of 1905, dated October 8, 1913, No. 20172.]. *Krasnyi arkhiv*. XVIII (1926): 225.

Books

Agrarnyi vopros v sovete ministrov (1906 g.) [The agrarian question in the Council of Ministers, 1906.], ed. by B. Veselovskii and others. M.-L.: 1924.

Alekseev, S. A., ed. *Samoderzhavie i liberaly v revoliutsii 1905–07 gg.* [The autocracy and the liberals in the revolution of 1905–07.]. M.-L.: 1925.

Correspondance secrète de Bülow et de Guillaume II, trans. by Gilbert Lenoir. Paris: 1931.

Drezen, A. K. ed. *Tsarizm v bor'be s revoliutsiei 1905–1907 gg.: sbornik dokumentov* [Tsarism in the struggle with the revolution of 1905–1907: a collection of documents.]. M.: 1936.

Gooch, G. P. and Temperley, Harold, eds. *British Documents on the Origins of the War, 1898–1914*. 11 vols. London: 1926–38.

Journal intime de Nicholas II, trans. by A. Pierre. Paris: 1925.

Bibliography

Kalinychev, F. I. *Gosudarstvennaia duma v Rossii: sbornik dokumentov i materialov* [The State Duma in Russia: a collection of documents and materials.]. M.: 1957.

Leningrad, Institut istorii partii, *Peterburgskie bol'sheviki v period pod"ema pervoi russkoi revoliutsii 1905–1907 gg.: sbornik dokumentov i materialov.* [Petersburg Bolsheviks in the period of the upsurge of the first Russian revolution, 1905–1907: a collection of documents and materials.], ed. by A. P. Konstantino. L.: 1955.

Levine, Isaac Don, ed. *Letters from the Kaiser to the Tsar.* (New York: 1920).

Materialy k istorii russkoi kontr-revoliutsii; Tom I: Pogromy po offitsial'nym dokumentam [Material on the history of the Russian counter-revolution; volume I; pogroms according to the official documents.]. St. Petersburg: 1908.

Materialy po istorii SSSR, IV: Dokumenty po istorii revoliutsionnovo dvizheniia sel'skikh rabochikh i krest'ian v pribaltike v period pervoi russkoi revoliutsii, 1905–1907 gg. [Materials on the history of the U.S.S.R.; vol. IV: Documents on the history of the revolutionary movement of agricultural workers and peasants in the Baltic in the period of the first Russian revolution, 1905–1907.], ed. by Ia. P. Krastyn. M.-L.: 1957.

Nicholas II. *Das Tagebuch des letzten Zaren von 1890 bis zum Fall: Nach den unveröffentlichten russischen Handschriften herausgegeben.* Berlin: 1923.

Obninskii, V. P. *Letopis' russkoi revoliutsii.* [A chronicle of the Russian revolution.]. M.: 1907.

———. *Polgoda russkoi revoliutsii* [A half-year of the Russian revolution.]. M.: 1906.

Partiia bol'shevikov v revoliutsii 1905–1907 godov: Dokumenty i materialy [The Bolshevik party in the revolution of 1905–1907: documents and materials.]. M.: 1961.

Polnoe sobranie zakonov rossiiskoi imperii. Sobranie tretie, tom XXV, 1905, otdelenie II; tom XXVI, 1906, otdelenie II [Complete collection of the laws of the Russian Empire. Third collection, volume XXV, 1905, Part II; volume XXVI, 1906, Part II.]. St. Petersburg: 1908, 1909.

Preobrazhenskii, E. A., ed. *Russkie finansy i evropeiskaia birzha v 1904–1906 gg.* [Russian finances and the European bourse in 1904–1906.]. M.-L.: 1926.

Revoliutsii 1905–1907 gg. na Ukraine: Sbornik dokumentoc i materialov v dvukh tomakh: Revoliutsionnaia bor'ba na Ukraine v period pervoi russkoi revoliutsii (1905 g.) tom 2, chast' pervaia [The revolution of 1905–1907 in the Ukraine: a collection of documents and materials in two volumes: the revolutionary struggle in the Ukraine in the period of the first Russian revolution (1905), vol. 2, Part 1.]. Kiev: 1955.

Revoliutsiia 1905–1907 gg. v Rossii: Dokumenty i materialy [The revolution of 1905–1907 in Russia: documents and materials]. This multivolume collection of documents was published in Moscow by the Institute of History of the Academy of Sciences of the U.S.S.R., beginning in 1955. Volumes used in this study are:

1) *Vserossiiskaia politicheskaia stachka v oktiabre 1905 goda.* [The all-Russian political strike in October 1905.]. Parts I and II.

2) *Vysshii pod"em revoliutsii 1905–1907 gg.: Vooruzhennye vosstaniia noiabr'–dekabr' 1905 goda.* [The highest point of the revolution of 1905–1907: the armed risings in November–December, 1905.]. Parts I, II, III (two books), and IV.

3) *Vtoroi period revoliutsii 1906–1907 gody:* [The second period of the revolution, 1906–1907.]. Parts I (two books) and II (one book).

Revolution from 1789–1906: Documents Selected and Edited with Notes and Introductions, ed. by R. W. Postgate. New York: 1962.

Semennikov, V. P., ed. *Revoliutsiia 1905 goda i samoderzhavie* [The revolution of 1905 and the autocracy.]. M.-L.: 1928.

Soiuz russkovo naroda: Po materialam sledstvennoi komissii vremennovo pravitel'stva 1917 g. [The Union of Russian People: according to the materials of the investigating commission of the Provisional Government.]. M.: 1929.

"Sovremennik," pseud., *Nikolai II, Razoblacheniia* [Nicholas II, the unmasking.]. Berlin: n.d.

The Secret Letters of the Last Tsar: Being the Confidential Correspondence between Nicholas II and His Mother, Dowager Empress Maria Feodorovna, ed. by Edward J. Bing. New York: 1938.

The Willy-Nicky Correspondence: Being the Secret and Intimate Telegrams Exchanged between the Kaiser and the Tsar, ed. by Herman Bernstein. New York: 1918.

Tysiacha deviat'sot piatyi god v Peterburge [The year 1905 in St. Petersburg.]. vols. I and II. M.-L.: 1925.

Memoirs and Autobiographies

Articles

Fotieva, L. A. "Pamiatnye dni. (Iz vospominanii uchastnitsy revoliutsionnykh sobytii 1905 g.)." [Memorable days (from the memoirs of a participant in the revolutionary events of 1905).] *Oktiabr'* [October], 11 (1965): 121–33.

Gessen, I. V. "V dvukh vekakh. Zhiznennyi otchet." [In two centuries: a living report.] *Arkhiv Russkoi Revoliutsii* [Archive of the Russian revolution], XXII (Berlin: 1937).

Khrustalyev-Nosar', George. "The Council of Workmen Deputies." *The Russian Review (A Quarterly Review of Russian History, Politics, Economics, and Literature),* 2 (1913): 89–100.

Bibliography

Lebedev, Platon. "Krasnye dni v Nizhnem-Novgorode." [Red days in Nizhnii-Novgorod.] *Byloe*, 5 (May 1907): 124–48.

Levitskii, V. "Oktiabr'skie dni 1905 goda v Sevastopole." [October days, 1905, in Sevastopol.] *Byloe*, 4 (32), (1925): 93–106.

Maklakov, Vasilii Alekseevich. "Iz proshlavo." [Out of the past.] *Sovremennye zapiski* [Contemporary notes], 47 (1931); 56 (1934); 58 (1935).

P. K. "Krasnoiarsk v kontse 1905 goda." [Krasnoiarsk at the end of 1905.] *Byloe*, 6 (June 1907): 11–40.

Pereverzev, V. N. "Pervyi vserossiiskii zheleznodorozhnyi soiuz 1905 goda." [The first all-Russian railroad union in 1905.] *Byloe*, 4 (32), (1925): 36–69.

Petrunkevich, I. I. "Iz zapisok obshchestvennovo deiatelia." [From the notes of a public leader.] *Arkhiv russkoi revoliutsii*, XXI (Berlin: 1934): 5–467.

Rabotnii, N. G. "1905 god v Iaroslav': Vospominaniia." [The year 1905 in Yarsoslavl: reminiscences.] *Byloe*, 4 (32), (1925): 70–92.

Somov', S. "Iz istorii sotsialdemokraticheskavo dvizheniia v Peterburge v 1905 godu: Lichnyia vospominaniia." [From the history of the social-democratic movement in St. Petersburg in 1905: personal reminiscences.] *Byloe*, 4 (April 1907): 22–55.

Starosel'skii, V. A. " 'Dni svobody' v Kutaisskoi gubernii." ['Days of freedom' in Kutaisky province.] *Byloe*, 7 (July 1907): 278–306.

Ushakov, M. A. "Vospominaniia o besede s velikim kniazem (15 oktiabria 1905 g.)." [Reminiscences of a meeting with the grand duke (October 15, 1905).] *Krasnyi arkhiv*, IV (1923): 413–17.

Books

Alexander, Grand Duke of Russia. *Once a Grand Duke*. New York: 1932.

Anon. *The Revolution in the Baltic Provinces of Russia: A Brief Account of the Activity of the Lettish Social Democratic Workers' Party by an Active Member*. London: n.d., probably 1907.

At the Court of the Last Tsar: Being the Memoirs of A. A. Mossolov, ed. by A. A. Pilenco. London: 1935.

Baring, Maurice. *A Year in Russia*. London: 1907.

Bompard, Maurice. *Mon Ambassade en Russie, 1903–1908*. Paris: 1937.

Chernov, Victor Mikhailovich. *Pered burei: Vospominaniia*. [Before the storm: reminiscences.] New York: 1953.

Gurko, Vladimir Iosifovich. *Features and Figures of the Past: Government and Opinion in the Reign of Nicholas II*. Palo Alto, California: 1939.

Hidden Springs of the Russian Revolution: Personal Memoirs of Katerina Breshkovskaia, ed. by Lincoln Hutchinson. Palo Alto, California: 1931.

Koni, A. F. *Sergei Iul'evich Vitte: Otryvochnye Vospominaniia*. [S. Iu. Witte: fragments of a memoir.] M.: 1925.

Kryzhanovskii, S. E. *Vospominaniia.* [Memoirs.] Berlin: n.d.

Kuz'min-Karavaev, V. D. *Iz epokhi osvoboditel'novo dvizheniia.* [From the epoch of the liberation movement.] Petrograd, 1918.

Maklakov, Vasilii Alekseevich. *The First State Duma,* trans. by Mary Belkin. Bloomington, Indiana: 1964.

————. *Vlast' i obshchestvennost' na zakate staroi Rossii: Vospominaniia sovremennika.* [Government and society in the closing years of old Russia: reminiscences of a contemporary.] Paris: 1939.

Miliukov, P. N. *Political Memoirs 1905–1917,* ed. by A. P. Mendel and trans. by Carl Goldberg. Ann Arbor, Michigan: 1967.

————. *Vospominaniia (1859–1917).* [Reminiscenes (1859–1917).] 2 vols. New York: 1955.

Olgin, Maurice J. *The Soul of the Russian Revolution.* New York: 1917.

Ossendowski, Ferdinand. *From President to Prison.* New York: 1925.

Out of My Past: The Memoirs of Count Kokovtsov. Palo Alto, California: 1935.

Pares, Bernard. *A Wandering Student: The Story of a Purpose.* Syracuse: 1948.

————. *My Russian Memoirs.* London: 1931.

————. *Russia and Reform.* London: 1907.

Recollections of a Foreign Minister: Memoirs of Alexander Iswolsky, trans. by Charles Louis Seeger. Garden City, New York: 1921.

Rosen, Baron P. P. *Forty Years of Diplomacy,* 2 vols. New York: 1922.

Savinkov, Boris. *Memoirs of a Terrorist.* New York: 1931.

Savinsky, A. *Recollections of a Russian Diplomat.* London: n.d.

Schwarz, Solomon M. *The Russian Revolution of 1905: The Workers' Movement and the Formation of Bolshevism and Menshevism,* trans. by Gertrude Vakar. Chicago: 1967.

Shipov, Dmitrii Nikolaevich. *Vospominaniia i dumy o perezhitom.* [Remembrances and thoughts about the past.] M.: 1918.

Tagantsev, N. S. *Perezhitoe.* [Experiences.] St. Petersburg: 1919.

The Russia I Believe In: The Memoirs of Samuel N. Harper, 1902–1941, ed. by Paul V. Harper. Chicago: 1945.

Trubetskoi, Prince Michael. *Out of Chaos: A Personal Story of the Revolution in Russia.* London: 1907.

Tyrkova-Vil'iams, A. *Na putiakh k svobode.* [On the paths to freedom.] New York: 1952.

Urusov, Prince Sergei Dmitriyevich. *Memoirs of a Russian Governor.* New York: 1952.

Witte, Sergei Iu. *The Memoirs of Count Witte,* trans. and ed. by Abraham Yarmolinsky. London: 1921. This English translation of Witte's memoirs is an edited and greatly abridged version of his three-volume memoirs.

————. *Vospominaniia.* [Reminiscences.] 3 vols., ed. by A. L. Sidorov. M.: 1960. The three volumes of Witte's memoirs are divided as follows: volume I covers Witte's life and career from 1849–1894; volume II covers his career under Nicholas II from 1894–October, 1905; volume III covers the period October 17, 1905 to 1911.

Woytinsky, W. S. *Stormy Passage: A Personal History through Two Russian Revolutions to Democracy and Freedom, 1905–1960.* New York: 1961.

Secondary Works

Articles

Anan'ich, B. V. "Finansovyi krizis tsarizma v 1905–06 gg." [The financial crisis of tsarism in 1905–06.] *Vnutrenniaia politika tsarizma (seredina XVI–nachalo XX v.)* [The internal policy of tsarism (from the middle of the 16th to the beginning of the 20th centuries)], Trudy, vyp. 8, Leningradskoe otdelenie instituta istorii [Works, no. 8, of the Leningrad section of the Institute of History] (L.: 1967): 281–320.

———. "Vneshnie zaimy tsarizma i dumskii vopros v 1906–07 gg." [The foreign loans of tsarism and the Duma question in 1906–07.] *Istoricheskie zapiski,* 81 (1968): 172–98.

———, and Ganelin, R. Sh. "Opyt kritiki memuarov S. Iu. Vitte." [An effort at a criticism of the memoirs of S. Iu. Witte.] *Voprosy istoriografii i istochnikovedeniia istorii SSSR: Sbornik statei.* [Questions of the historiography and historical sources of the history of the U.S.S.R.: a collection of articles.] (M.-L.: 1963): 298–374.

Chermenskii, E. D. "Russkaia burzhuaziia osen'in 1905 goda." [The Russian bourgeoisie in the fall of 1905.] *Voprosy istorii.* [Questions of history.] 6 (1966): 56–72.

———. "Zemsko-liberal'noe dvizhenie nakanune revoliutsii 1905–1907 gg." [The zemstvo-liberal movement on the eve of the revolution of 1905–1907.] *Istoriia SSSR.* [History of the U.S.S.R.], 5 (1965): 41–60.

Crisp, Olga. "The Russian Liberals and the 1906 Anglo-French Loan to Russia." *The Slavonic and East European Review,* XXXIX, 93 (June 1961): 497–511.

Deborin, G. and Manusevich, A. "Istoricheskii opyt pervoi russkoi revoliutsii." [The historical experience of the first Russian revolution.] *Kommunist,* 3 (1965): 29–37.

Dillon, E. J. "Two Russian Statesmen." *The Quarterly Review,* CCXXXVI (October 1921): 402–17.

Girault, René. "Sur quelques aspects financiers de l'alliance franco-russe." *Revue d'histoire moderne et contemporaine,* 8 (January–March 1961): 67–76.

Glinskii, B. "Graf Sergei Iulevich Vitte: Materialy dlia biografii." [Count Sergei Iulevich Witte: material for a biography.] *Istoricheskii vestnik.* [Historical herald], 140 (April 1915): 232–79; 140 (May 15, 1915): 573–89; 141 (August 1915): 520–55; 141 (September 1915): 893–906; 142 (December 1915): 893–907.

————. "K istorii sostavleniia osnovykh zakonov v 1906 godu." [Toward the history of the composing of the Fundamental Laws in 1906.], *Istoricheskii vestnik*, 131:3 (March 1913); 977–87.

————. "K voprosu o titule 'Samoderzhets.'" [On the question about the title 'autocrat.'], *Istoricheskii vestnik*, 131 (February 1913): 567–603.

————. "Razvenchannye geroi revoliutsii 1905 g." [The debunking of the hero of the revolution of 1905.], *Istoricheskii vestnik*, 133 (July 1913): 233–65; 133 (August 1913): 598–629.

Harcave, Sidney. "The Jews and the First Russian National Election," *American Slavic and East European Review*, vol. IX, no. 1 (February 1950), 33–41.

Izgoev, A. S. "Na pereval: S. Iu. Vitte." [In passing: S. Iu. Vitte.] *Russkaia mysl'* [Russian thought], 1 (March 1915): 153–58.

Kalinychev, F. I. "Politicheskie i pravovye idei pervoi russkoi revo-liutsii." [Political and legal ideas of the first Russian revolution.] *Sovetskoe gosudarstvo i pravo.* [Soviet state and law.], 9 (1965): 33–39.

Kantorovich, V. "Khrustalev-Nosar.'" [Khrustalev-Nosar.] *Byloe*, no. 4 (32), (125): 117–53.

Karpovich, Michael. "Two Types of Russian Liberalism: Maklakov and Miliukov" in *Continuity and Change in Russian and Soviet Thought*, ed. by Ernest J. Simmons. (Cambridge: 1955.) 129–43; Reprinted in *Readings in Russian History*, ed. by Sidney Harcave. (New York: 1962), 91–104.

Kaufman, A. E. "Cherty iz zhizni gr. S. Iu. Vitte." [Features from the life of Count S. Iu. Vitte.] *Istoricheskii vestnik*, 140 (April 1915): 220–31.

Keep, J. H. L. "Russian Social Democracy and the First State Duma." *Slavonic and East European Review*, XXXIV (1955–1956): 180–99.

Kir'ianov, Ia. I.; Lebedev N. M.; and Simonova, M. S., "Problemy istorii revoliutsii 1905–1907 gg. v Rossii." [Problems of the history of the revolution of 1905–1907 in Russia.] *Istoriia SSSR*, 3 (1966): 213–17.

Kuzin, V. V. "Pervaia russkaia revoliutsiia i voennyi apparat samoder-zhaviia." [The first Russian revolution and the military apparatus of the autocracy.] *Vestnik Moskovskovo universiteta.* [Herald of Mos-cow University], 7, (1952).

Lavarychev, V. Ia. "Moskovskie promyshlenniki v gody pervoi russkoi revoliutsii." [Moscow industrialists in the years of the first Russian revolution.] *Vestnik Moskovskovo universiteta; Istoriia*, 3 (1964): 37–53.

Lavrinovich, Iu. Review of *Kievskii i odesskii pogromy v razsledo-vaniiakh senatorov Turau i Kuz'minskovo.* [Kiev and Odessa pogroms in the investigations of Senators Turau and Kuzminsky.] *Byloe*, 9 (September 1907): 309–13.

Makarov, N. I. "Mezhdunarodnoe znachenie revoliutsii 1905–1907 gg." [The international significance of the revolution of 1905–1907.] *Vop-rosy istorii KPSS*, 11 (1965): 3–13.

Mintslov, S. R. "14 mesiatsev svobody pechati: 17 oktiabria 1905 g.–

ianvaria 1907 g." [Fourteen months of freedom of the press: October 17, 1905–January 1, 1907.]. *Byloe*, 15 (March 1907): 23–48.

Mironenko, K. N. "Manifest 17 oktiabria 1905 g." [The Manifesto of October 17, 1905.] *Uchenye zapiski 255, Leningradskii universitet*, Seriia iuridicheskikh nauk, vyp. 10. Voprosy gosudarstvo i prava, [Scientific notes, 255, Leningrad University, series of juridical sciences.], (1958): 158–79.

———. "Sovet ministrov po ukazu 19 oktiabria 1905 g." [The Council of Ministers according to the decree of October 19, 1905.] *Uchenye zapiski 106, Leningradskii universitet*, Seriia iuridicheskikh nauk, [Scientific notes, 106, Leningrad University, series of juridical sciences.], I (1948): 348–70.

Parchevskii, N. L. "Rol' kazachestva v epokhu revoliutsii 1905 g." [The role of the Cossacks in the epoch of the revolution of 1905.] *Istoricheskii vestnik*, 133 (September 1913): 936–64.

Pares, Bernard. Chapter XII: "Reaction and Revolution in Russia" and Chapter XIII: "The Reform Movement in Russia" in *The Cambridge Modern History*, XII, *The Latest Age*. New York: 1910.

Pereverzev, V. N. "Karatel'naia ekspeditsiia general-leitenanta P. K. Rennenkampfa v Zabaikalskom oblastie." [The punitive expedition of Lieutenant-General P. K. Rennenkamf to the Trans-Baikal district.] *Byloe*, 4 (April 1907): 132–63.

———. "Karatel'naia ekspeditsiia general-leitenanta P. K. Rennenkampfa v Zabaikal'skom oblaste." [The punitive expedition of Lieutenant-General P. K. Rennenkampf to the Trans-Baikal district.] *Byloe*, 5–6 (27–28) (November–December 1917): 133–211. The first half of this article was reprinted from the article immediately preceding this one. The second half was not printed in 1907 as a result of censorship.

Plavnik, L. B. "Vitte i revoliutsiia 1905–1907 gg." [Witte and the revolution of 1905–1907.] in Gosudarstvennyi muzei revoliutsii SSSR, *Sbornik*, I (M.: 1947): 150–84.

Presniakova, A. E. "1905-yi god." [The year 1905.] *Byloe*, 4 (32) (1925): 3–35.

Prokopovich, S. "Formy i resul'taty agrarnovo dvizheniia v 1906 godu." [Forms and results of the agrarian movement in 1906.] *Byloe*, 1 (January 1907): 155–77.

Rogger, Hans. "Reflections on Russian Conservatism: 1861–1905." *Jahrbücher für Geschichte Osteuropas*, (June 1966): 195–212.

———. "The Formation of the Russian Right, 1900 to 1906." *California Slavic Studies*, III (1964): 66–94.

———. "Was There a Russian Fascism?" *Journal of Modern History*, (December 1964): 398–415.

Schapiro, Leonard. "The *Vekhi* Group and the Mystique of Revolution." *The Slavonic and East European Review*, XXXIV (1955): 56–76.

Seraphim, Ernst. "Zar Nikolaus II und Graf Witte: Eine Historische-

Psychologische Studie." *Historische Zeitschrift,* 161, (2): 277–308.

Simonova, M. S. "Agrarnaia politika samoderzhaviia v 1905 g." [The agrarian policy of the autocracy in 1905.] *Istoricheskie zapiski,* 81 (1968): 199–215.

———. "Politika tsarizma v krest'ianskom voprose nakanune revoliutsii 1905–1907 gg." [The policy of tsarism on the peasant question on the eve of the revolution of 1905–1907.] *Istoricheskie zapiski,* 75 (1965): 217–42.

Sobolev', A. "Iz smutnovo vremeni v pribaltiiskom krae." [From the troubled times in the Baltic territory.] *Istoricheskii vestnik,* 133 (July 1913): 198–206.

Sontag, J. P. "Tsarist Debts and Tsarist Foreign Policy." *Slavic Review,* XXVII, 4 (December 1968): 529–41.

Stepanskii, A. D. "Politicheskie gruppirovki v Gosudarstvennom sovete v 1906–1907 gg." [Political groupings in the State Council in 1906–1907.] *Istoriia SSSR,* 4 (1965): 49–64.

———. "Reforma Gosudarstvennovo soveta v 1906 g." [The reform of the State Council in 1906.] *Trudy Moskovskovo Gosudarstvennovo Istoriko-arkhivnovo Instituta.* [Works of the Moscow State Historical-Archival Institute.], 20, (1965): 179–211.

Struve, Petr. "Graf S. Iu. Vitte: Opyt kharakteristiki." [Count S. Iu. Witte: an attempt at a characterization.] *Russkaia mysl',* 1 (March 1915): 129–33.

Szeftel, Marc, "The Form of Government of the Russian Empire Prior to the Constitutional Reforms of 1905–06" in John S. Curtiss, ed. *Essays in Russian and Soviet History.* New York: 1963.

Tompkins, Stuart. "Why Witte Failed to Solve the Peasant Problem." *Journal of Modern History,* IV, 2 (June 1932): 235–39.

———. "Witte as Minister of Finance, 1892–1903." *Slavonic Review,* II, 33 (April 1933): 590–606.

Treadgold, Donald W. "The Constitutional Democrats and the Russian Liberal Tradition." *The American Slavic and East European Review,* X, 2 (April 1951): 85–94.

Tuck, Robert L. "Paul Miliukov and Negotiations for a Duma Ministry, 1906." *The American Slavic and East European Review,* X, 2 (April 1951): 117–29.

Viner, Jacob. "International Finance and Balance of Power Diplomacy, 1880–1914." *Southwestern Political and Social Science Quarterly,* IX (March 1929): 398–427.

von Laue, Theodore H. "Count Witte and the Russian Revolution of 1905." *American Slavic and East European Review* (February 1958): 25–46.

———. "Imperial Russia at the Turn of the Century: The Cultural Slope and the Revolution from Without." *Comparative Studies in Society and History,* III (1960–1961): 353–67.

———. "Russian Peasants in the Factory 1892–1904." *The Journal of Economic History,* XXI (March 1961): 61–80.

Bibliography

————. "The 'Vitte System' in Mid Passage, 1896–1899." *Jahrbücher für Geschichte Osteuropas*, S, 2 (1960): 195–229.

————. "Tsarist Labor Policy, 1895–1903." *Journal of Modern History*, XXXIV, 2 (June 1962): 135–45.

Walsh, Warren B. "The Composition of the Dumas." *Russian Review*, VIII, 2 (1949): 111–16.

————. "Political Parties in the Russian Dumas." *Journal of Modern History*, 22 (1950): 144–50.

Yaney, George L. "The Concept of the Stolypin Land Reform." *The Slavic Review*, XXVIII, 2 (June 1964): 275–93.

Books

Almedingen, E. M. *The Empress Alexandra 1872–1918: A Study*. London: 1961.

Alzona, Encarnacion. *Some French Contemporary Opinions of the Russian Revolution of 1905*. New York: 1921.

Antsiferov, Alexis; Bilimovich, Alexander D.; Batshev, Michael O.; and Ivantsov, Dimitry N. *Rural Economy during the War*; Bilimovich, Alexander D. *The Land Settlement in Russia during the War*. These two monographs comprise *Russian Agriculture During the War*. New Haven: 1930.

Anweiler, Oskar. *Die Rätebewegung in Russland 1905–1921*. Leiden: 1958.

Bernstein, Herman. *With Master Minds*. New York: 1913.

Billington, James H. *Mikhailovsky and Russian Populism*. London: 1958.

Black, C. E., ed. *The Transformation of Russian Society*. Cambridge, Massachusetts: 1960.

Charques, Richard. *The Twilight of Imperial Russia*. London: 1958.

Chasles, Pierre. *Le Parlement russe—son organisation—ses rapports avec l'empereur*. Paris: 1910.

Chermenskii, E. D. *Burzhuaziia i tsarizm v revoliutsii 1905–1907 gg.* [The bourgeoisie and tsarism in the revolution of 1905–1907.] M.: 1939.

————. *Istorii SSSR: Period imperializma* (90-e gg. XIX v.-mart 1917 g.): *Posobie dlia uchitelei i studentov pedvuzov*. [The history of the U.S.S.R.: period of imperialism (the 90's of the 19th c. to March 1917): an aid for teachers and students of higher teacher training institutions.], izd. 2. M.: 1965.

Demochkin, N. N. *Sovety 1905 goda—organy revoliutsionnoi vlasti*. [The soviets of 1905—organs of revolutionary power.] M.: 1963.

————, Erman, L. K., and Chermenskii, E. D., *Revoliutsiia 1905–1907 gg. v Rossii. Posobie dlia uchitelei*. [The revolution of 1905–1907 in Russia: an aid for teachers.] M.: 1965.

Dillon, E. J. *Russia Today and Yesterday*. London: 1928.

————. *The Eclipse of Russia*. New York: 1918.

Dubnow, S. W. *History of the Jews in Russia and in Poland from the Earliest Times until the Present Day.* vols. II and III. Philadelphia: 1920.

Dubrovskii, S. M. *Krest'ianskoe dvizhenie v revoliutsii 1905–1907 gg.* [The peasant movement in the revolution of 1905–1907.] M.: 1956.

———. *Stolypinskaia zemel'naia reforma.* [The Stolypin land reform.] M.: 1963.

Emeliakh, L. I. *Antiklerikal'noe dvizhenie krest'ian v period pervoi russkoi revoliutsii.* [The anti-clerical movement of the peasantry in the period of the first Russian revolution.] M.-L.: 1965.

Erman, L. K. *Intelligentsiia v pervoi russkoi revoliutsii.* [The intelligentsia in the first Russian revolution.] M.: 1966.

Eroshkin, N. P. *Ocherki istorii gosudarstvennykh uchrezhdenii dorevoliutsionnoi Rossii: posobie dlia uchitelia.* [Outlines of the history of state institutions of pre-revolutionary Russia: an aid for the teacher.] M.: 1960.

Fischer, George. *Russian Liberalism from Gentry to Intelligentsia.* Cambridge, Massachusetts: 1958.

Frank, S. L. *Biografiia P. B. Struve.* [Biography of P. B. Struve.] New York: 1956.

Frankland, Noble. *Imperial Tragedy: Nicholas II, Last of the Tsars.* New York: 1961.

Gooch, G. P. *Before the War: Studies in Diplomacy.* 2 vols. London: 1938.

Greenburg, Louis. *The Jews in Russia:* vol. I, *The Struggle for Emancipation.* New Haven: 1944. vol. II, *The Struggle for Emancipation, 1881–1917.* New Haven: 1951.

Grunt, A. Ia. and Firstova, V. N. *Rossiia v epokhu imperializma (1890–1907 gg.).* [Russia in the epoch of imperialism (1890–1907).] M.: 1959.

Grunwald, Constantin de. *Le Tsar Nicolas II.* Paris: 1965.

Gukovskii, A. I. *Pervaia russkaia burzhuazno-demokraticheskaia revoliutsiia, 1905–1907 gg.* [The first Russian bourgeois-democratic revolution, 1905–1907.] Vologda: 1957.

Harcave, Sidney. *First Blood.* New York: 1964.

Hare, Richard. *Portraits of Russian Personalities between Reform and Revolution.* London: 1959.

Hough, Richard. *The Potemkin Mutiny.* New York: 1960.

Iakovlev, N. N. *Vooruzhennye vosstaniia v dekabre 1905 g.* [Armed uprisings in December 1905.] M.: 1957.

Iakushkin, V. E. *Gosudarstvennaia vlast' i proekty gosudarstvennoi reformy v Rossii.* [Government authority and a proposal for government reform in Russia.] St. Petersburg: 1906.

Jewish Encyclopedia. *A Descriptive Record of the History, Religion, Literature, and Customs of the Jewish People from the Earliest Times to the Present Day.* vol. IX. New York: 1905.

Keep, J. H. L. *The Rise of Social Democracy in Russia.* Oxford: 1963.

Kerensky, Alexander. *The Crucifixion of Liberty.* New York: 1934.

Klein, Alfred. *Der Einfluss des Grafen Witte auf die deutsch-russischen Beziehungen.* Munster: 1932.

Kochan, Lionel. *Russia in Revolution, 1890–1918.* London: 1966.

Korostowetz, Wladimir. *Graf Witte, der Steuermann in der Not.* Berlin: 1929.

Kovalevsky, Maxime. *La crise russe: notes et impressions d'un témoin.* Paris: 1906.

Laverychev, V. Ia. *Po tu storonu barrikad; iz istorii bor'by moskovskoi burzhuazii s revoliutsiei.* [On the other side of the barricades; from the history of the struggle of the Moscow bourgeoisie with the revolution.] M.: 1967.

Levin, Alfred. *The Second Duma: A Study of the Social Democratic Party and the Russian Constitutional Experiment.* New Haven: 1940; 2nd ed., Hamden, Connecticut: 1966.

Martov, L., and others, eds., *Obshchestvennoe dvizhenie v Rossii v nachale XX veka.* [The social movement in Russia at the beginning of the twentieth century]. 4 vols. St. Petersburg: 1909–14.

Masaryk, Thomas G. *The Spirit of Russia.* 2 vols. Reprinted London: 1955.

Massie, Robert K. *Nicholas and Alexandra.* New York: 1967.

Maynard, Sir John. *Russia in Flux.* Reprinted New York: 1962.

———. *The Russian Peasant and Other Studies.* New York: 1962.

Mazour, Anatole. *Russia Past and Present.* Princeton: 1951.

Mel'gunov, S. *Sud'ba imperatora Nikolaia II posle otrecheniia.* [The fate of Emperor Nicholas II after his abdication.] Paris: 1951.

Mendeleev, D. *K poznaniiu Rossii.* [Getting to know Russia.] St. Petersburg: 1907.

Miliukov, P. N. *God bor'by.* [Year of struggle.] St. Petersburg: 1907.

———. *Russia and Its Crisis.* Reprinted New York: 1962.

———. *Tri popytki.* [Three attempts.] Paris: 1921.

Morskoi, A. (pseud. of V. I. von Shtein.). *Iskhod rossiiskoi revoliutsii 1905 g. i "pravitel'stvo" Nosaria.* [The outcome of the Russian revolution of 1905 and the "government" of Nosar.] M.: 1911.

Muratov, Kh. I., *Revoliutsionnoe dvizhenie v russkoi armii v 1905–1907 gg.* [The revolutionary movement in the Russian army in 1905–1907.] M.: 1955.

Nicolaevsky, Boris. *Aseff: The Russian Judas.* London: 1934.

Ol'denburg, Sergei S. *Tsarstvovanie imperatora Nikolaia II: Chast' vtoraia: perelomnye gody 1904–1907.* [The reign of Emperor Nicholas II: part two: the turning-point years of 1904–1907.] Belgrade-Munich: 1939.

Owen, Launcelot. *The Russian Peasant Movement, 1906–1917.* London: 1937.

Pankratova, Anna Mikhailovna. *Pervaia russkaia revoliutsiia 1905–1907 gg.* [The first Russian revolution, 1905–1907.] M.: 1951.

———, and Kostomarov, G. D., eds. *Ocherki istorii SSSR: Pervaia russkaia burzhuazno-demokraticheskaia revoliutsiia 1905–1907 gg.* [An outline of the history of the U.S.S.R.: the first Russian bourgeois-democratic revolution, 1905–1907.] M.: 1955.

Pares, Bernard. *The Fall of the Russian Monarchy: A Study of the Evidence.* London: 1939.

Petrov, V. A. *Ocherki po istorii revoliutsionnovo dvizheniia v russkoi armii v 1905 g.* [An outline of the history of the revolutionary movement in the Russian army in 1905.] M.-L.: 1964.

Piaskovskii, A. V. *Revoliutsiia 1905–1907 gg. v Rossii.* [The revolution of 1905–1907 in Russia.] M.: 1966.

Piat'desiat let pervoi russkoi revoliutsii. Materialy nauchnoi sessii instituta marksizma-leninizma pri TSK KPSS. [Fifty years of the first Russian revolution. Materials of a scientific session of the institute of Marxism-Leninism under the C.C. of the C.P.S.U.] M.: 1956.

Pipes, Richard, ed. *The Russian Intelligentsia.* New York: 1961.

Polianskii, N. N. *Tsarskie voennye sudy v bor'be s revoliutsiei 1905–1907 godov.* [Tsarist military courts in the struggle with the revolution of 1905–1907.] M.: 1958.

Radkey, Oliver. *The Agrarian Foes of Bolshevism.* New York: 1958.

Riha, Thomas. *A Russian European: Paul Miliukov in Russian Politics.* Notre Dame, Indiana: 1969.

Robinson, Geroid Tanquary. *Rural Russia Under the Old Regime: A History of the Landlord-Peasant World and a Prologue to the Peasant Revolution of 1917.* New York: 1949.

Schapiro, Leonard. *The Communist Party of the Soviet Union.* New York: 1959.

Schelking, Evgenii Nikolaevich. *The Game of Diplomacy.* London: n.d.

Sef, S. E. *Burzhuaziia v 1905 gody.* [The bourgeoisie in 1905.] M.: 1926.

Seton-Watson, Hugh. *The Decline of Imperial Russia, 1855–1914.* New York: 1960.

Sidel'nikov, S. M. *Obrazovanie i deiatel'nost' pervoi Gosudarstvennoi dumy.* [The formation and activity of the first State Duma.] M.: 1962.

Spector, Ivar. *The First Russian Revolution: Its Impact on Asia.* Englewood Cliffs, New Jersey: 1962.

Spiridonov, I. V. *Vserossiiskaia politicheskaia stachka v oktiabre 1905 g.* [The all-Russian political strike in October 1905.] M.: 1955.

Stogov, Mikhael. *Komu nuzhny pogromy?* [Who needs pogroms?] Petrograd: 1919.

Tarle, Evgenii Viktorovich. *Graf S. Iu. Vitte: Opyt kharakteristiki vneshnei politiki.* [Count S. Iu. Witte: an attempt to characterize his foreign policy.] L.: 1927.

Treadgold, Donald W. *Lenin and His Rivals: The Struggle for Russia's Future, 1898–1906.* New York: 1955.

Troyat, Henri. *Daily Life in Russia under the Last Tsar,* trans. by Malcolm Barnes. London: 1961.

Vasilevskii, E. G. *Ideinaia bor'ba vokrug stolypinskoi agrarnoi reformy.*

Bibliography

[The ideological struggle surrounding the Stolypin agrarian reform.]
M.: 1960.
Vasilevskii, Ilia. *Graf Vitte i evo memuari.* [Count Witte and his memoirs.] Berlin: 1922.
Vassili, Count Paul (pseud.). *Behind the Veil at the Russian Court.* New York: 1914.
Vinogradoff, Paul. *Self-Government in Russia.* London: 1915.
Vodovozov, V. V. *Graf Vitte i Imperator Nikolai II.* [Count Witte and Emperor Nicholas II.] Berlin: 1922.
von Laue, Theodore H. *Sergei Witte and the Industrialization of Russia.* New York: 1963.
Vovchik, A. F. *Politika tsarizma po rabochemu voprosy predrevoliutsionnyi period, 1895–1904.* [The policy of tsarism on the worker's question in the prerevolutionary period, 1895–1904.] L'vov: 1964.
Walkin, Jacob. *The Rise of Democracy in Pre-Revolutionary Russia: Political and Social Institutions under the Last Three Czars.* New York: 1962.
Witte, Sergei Iu. *Samoderzhavie i zemstvo.* [Autocracy and the zemstvo.] Stuttgart: 1901.
———. *Zapiska po krest'ianskomu delu.* [A note on the peasant issue.] St. Petersburg: 1904.
Wolfe, Bertram D. *Three Who Made a Revolution.* Boston: 1962.

Unpublished Papers and Manuscripts

Ambler, Effie. "The Union of the Russian People." Unpublished seminar paper, Indiana University, 1961.
Central State Historical Archive, Leningrad (TsGIAL). Funds 1276, 1544, 1327, 1622.
Central State Historical Archive of the October Revolution and Socialist Construction, Moscow (TsGAOR). Funds 102, 431.
Hosking, Geoffrey. "Government and Duma in Russia, 1907–1914." Ph.D. dissertation, Cambridge University, 1969.
Levin, Alfred. "The Black Hundreds: The Reactionary Wing." Unpublished manuscript.
Liubimov, D. N. "Russkaia smuta nachala deviatisotykh' godov 1902–1906." [The Russian time of troubles in the beginning of the twentieth century 1902–1906.]. Unpublished manuscript in the Archive of Russian and East European History and Culture, Columbia University.
Long, James W. "The Economics of the Franco-Russian Alliance, 1904–06." Ph.D. dissertation, University of Wisconsin, 1968.
Menashe, Louis. "Alexander Guchkov and the Origins of the Octobrist Party: The Russian Bourgeoisie in Politics, 1905." Ph.D. dissertation, New York University, 1966.
Migulin, P. P. "Russkaia agrarnaia problema i sel'sko-khoziaistvennaia

katastrofa v Sovetskoi Rossii." [The Russian agrarian problem and agricultural catastrophe in Soviet Russia.], 1931. Unpublished manuscript in the Archive of Russian and East European History and Culture, Columbia University.

Papers of S. Iu. Witte. Archive of Russian and East European History and Culture, Columbia University.

Rooa, Ruth A. "The Association of Industry and Trade, 1906–1914: An Examination of the Economic Views of Organized Industrialists in Prerevolutionary Russia." Ph.D. dissertation, Columbia University, 1967.

Santoni, Wayne D. "P. N. Durnovo as Minister of Internal Affairs in the Witte Cabinet." Ph.D. dissertation, University of Kansas, 1968.

Slusser, Robert M. "The Moscow Soviet of Workers' Deputies of 1905: Origin, Structure, and Policies." Ph.D. dissertation, Columbia University, 1963.

"Vospominaniia kniazia A. D. Golitsyna." [Reminiscences of Prince A. D. Golitsyn.] Unpublished manuscript in the Archive of Russian and East European History and Culture, Columbia University.

August 6 Manifesto: reaction to, 31; and consultative Duma, 31; implementation of, 32; Witte on, 35, 115–16, 120–21; and franchise, 35, 45, 113, 114–15; changes in, 112–13; provisions of, 113–15; and social classes, 114, 115; and land value, 114; and cities, 115; and "four-tailed" formula, 115–16; and liberals, 115–16; weights representation, 115; Kryzhanovskii's role in, 116; and law of Dec. 11, 122, 246; Shipov's proposal on, 124

Austria, 223, 227

Autocracy, Russian: before 1900, 3; nature of, 3–4, 6; tsar on, 6, 15, 160, 161; and zemstvos, 9, 346 n.13; and gov't, 14; needs order, 16; Witte on, 20–21, 23–24, 34, 238, 311, 394 n.41; and nobility, 22; and financial policies, 23–24; and Oct. 17 Manifesto, 29; and peasants, 180, 187; and Fundamental Laws, 305; and change, 327–28

Autocrat, 24

Autonomy, 72–73, 261

Bakers, 26

Baltic fleet, 14

Baltic provinces: nationalism in, 13, 154; peasant uprisings in, 13, 107; discontent in, 72, 107; German landlords in, 72, 107; and Russification, 72, 107; socialists in, 107; strikes in, 107; and Oct. 17 Manifesto, 107; repression in, 107, 108–09, 157; Sollogub in, 107–09; and army, 108; Nicholas on, 108–09; Bekman in, 166

Banks: English, 21, 236; German, 21, 236; French, 219, 220, 236; Russian, 226, 236; Austrian, 236; Dutch, 236

Bankers: French, 221, 225; Jewish, 222; German, 223; American, 224; English, 224; Italian, 226–27

"Banquet Campaign," 10

Bauman, N. E., 51–52

Björkö Treaty: and Russo-German alliance, 214; and Witte, 214, 215, 383 n.21; and tsar, 215; terms of, 215; and Rouvier, 216; and German participation in loan, 216; Lamsdorff opposes, 217; abrogation of, 217; publication of, 383 n.22

"Black Hundreds," 57, 60–61, 63, 137, 356 n.34

"Bloody Sunday," 16–17, 25, 229

Boevaia organizatsiia. See Combat brigade

Bolsheviks: and Lenin, 7–8; and Mensheviks, 7–8; strength of, 8; and Oct. 17 Manifesto, 52; in St. Petersburg Soviet, 136; and Dec. uprisings, 144; on Kadets, 264; tactics of, 264; and Duma, 264, 280; boycott elections, 264, 355 n.18

Bourgeoisie, 55, 123, 149, 243

Bribery, 229, 231–33

British power, 383 n.16

Budberg, Baron A. A., 42

Budget, Russian, 212, 236, 300–01

Bulletin of the Soviet of Workers' Deputies, 52

Bulygin, A. G., 17, 249

Bulygin Duma. *See* Duma, Bulygin

Bulygin Manifesto of August 6. *See* August 6 Manifesto

Bureaucracy, 201

Bureaucrats; and Slavophiles, 4; in autocracy, 4; and August 6 Manifesto, 31; and gov't, 32; support Witte, 66; in Council of Ministers, 80, 82–83; activity restricted, 129

Burghers, Russian, 3, 114, 122, 123

Byelorussian Socialistic Gramad, 254

Cabinet. *See* Council of Ministers

Cabinet system, 4

Campaign rallies, 389 n.9

Cantons. *See* Volosts

Cassini, Count, 221, 222, 234, 385 n.33

Caucasus, 13, 72, 111, 154, 263–64

Censorship: and Oct. 17 Manifesto, 66, 67; and press, 66–67, 171–72; and gov't, 67; and St. Petersburg Soviet, 137; and Printers' Union, 359 n.73; extent of, 377 n.115

Chief Administration of Land Organization and Agriculture, 187, 203–06, 314, 316

Chinese Eastern RR, 95

Chinovnik. *See* Bureaucrat

Church and state, 266

Cities, 154–55

City dumas: role of, 5; activities limited, 16; Durnovo on, 170–71; and elections, 245–47; and Kadets, 259

City dwellers, 18, 245

Civil rights: and Fundamental Laws, 301, 307, 309; Witte on, 35, 311–12; and Oct. 17 Manifesto, 40, 41, 45; Trepov on, 42; Octobrists on, 162; and loan, 239; and elections, 247; and "bourgeois" parties, 255; socialists on, 264; of peasants, 315–16; of Jews, 356 n.33. *See also* Freedom of Assembly; . . . of Association; . . . of Religion

Civil servants, 105–06, 129, 159–60

INDEX

Classes: professional, 9, 10, 18; lower-middle, 122; social, 183–84
Class structure, 6–7, 9, 26
Clergy, 114
Combat brigade, 8–9
Committee of Ministers, 4, 31
Committee on Finances, 218
Commune: and Socialist Revolutionaries, 8; and workers, 10–11; and gov't, 11, 185, 205; and land distribution, 12; and technology, 12; and efficiency, 12; and Emancipation Act of 1861, 12; abolition of, 12, 200, 202; and conservatives, 13; and Slavophiles, 13; and Special Conference . . . Agricultural Industry, 23, 185, 186, 202; and unrest, 87–88; Witte on, 167, 182, 183, 184, 185–86, 199, 200, 201–02, 315; tsar on, 184; and taxes, 185; and Ukase of Feb. 3, 1903, 185; other views on, 186, 188–89; Conference . . . Peasant Landholding on, 186–87; Krivoshein on, 203; Marshals of Nobility on, 204; Gurko commission on, 206; and redemption dues, 208; and Peasants' Bank, 208; Octobrists on, 258
Compensation, 189, 191, 198, 208
Conference to Strengthen Peasant Landholding, 185–87
Congress of Marshals of Nobility, 204
Congress of Zemstvo and City Leaders, 74–75
Conservatism, 7, 328
Conservatives: on commune, 13; and Witte, 50, 75, 319; and constitutionalism, 57; and elections, 174–75; and Duma, 174–75, 317; on peasants, 286
Constituent assembly, 77, 260
Constitution: and tsar, 15, 47, 81; and workers, 44; and Oct. 17 Manifesto, 46, 297; Witte on, 81, 293, 297; Fundamental Laws as, 289–90, 392 n.2
Constitutional - Democratic party. See Party of the People's Freedom
Constitutionalism: and autocracy, 4; and Bulygin Duma, 18; and Oct. 17 Manifesto, 29, 289; and Witte, 31, 290, 302, 305–06, 323–25, 392 n.2; support for, 35; Trepov on, 42; tsar on, 45; and conservatives, 57; Kadets on, 82, 262; and soviets, 143; and State Council, 292; and Duma, 302
Constitutional monarchy, 257, 260
Constitution, Austrian, 310
Constitutions, conservative, 299
Consultative assembly. See Duma, consultative

Continental alliance, 213–16, 239, 383 n.16
Cossacks, 114, 122, 188, 245, 277
Council of Ministers: and tsar, 4, 32, 69–70, 83, 88, 163–64, 300–01, 309; role of, 4, 33, 75, 117, 249; ministers in, 32; chairman in, 32, 33, 69; reorganization of, 33, 69, 75; and Fundamental Laws, 33, 299–300, 301–02, 309; and pogroms, 63–64; and press, 67, 172; by-passed, 69; appointments to, 69, 80, 83, 163–64; and report of Oct. 9, 75; membership of, 75, 80–83; and Duma, 75, 175, 299–301, 314; zemstvoists on, 77; and bureaucrats, 80, 82–83, 129; Kadets in, 81; Shipov on, 81; Stakhovich on, 81; opposition to Witte in, 83; on repression, 86, 104, 105–06, 148, 156, 159, 196–98; and Crown Councils, 118, 291; on field military courts, 126–28, 156; on civil servants, 129; on armed forces, 129, 300; control of, 164; and civil rights, 173, 174, 301; on criminal penalties, 174; and peasant question, 189, 194–98, 199–200, 201–02, 205; reviews legislative program, 189, 313–14, 396 n.5; on alienation of land, 190, 192, 197–98, 203; on laws and decrees, 197–98, 300, 307; and Ukase of April 15, 1905, 198; on Krivoshein's memorandum, 204; on Nikol'skii commission, 205; and elections, 249, 271–72
Coup d'état, 306, 310
Courland. See Estonia
Court circles, 155
Courts: civil, 165, 195–96
— military: Witte on, 125–27; Pavlov on, 126; and antigovernment activity in army, 126; cabinet on, 126–28, 156; and death penalty, 127; extension of, 127, 128; tsar on, 128; State Council on, 128; and Kronstadt mutineers, 140; and revolutionaries, 165, 195–96; and Stolypin, 370 n.58
Crédit Lyonnais, 21
Credit, Russian, 212
Cri de Paris, 233
Criminals, 174, 270
Crown Council. See April . . . ; December . . . ; and February Crown Council
Curias, 117, 242, 243–45

Death penalty, 125–26, 127
December Crown Council, 118, 119, 120–21
Dec. 12 ukase. See Imperial Ukase of Dec. 12

INDEX

INDEX